Before
the Face
of God

Before the Face of God

BOOK 3

A Daily Guide for Living from the Old Testament

R. C. Sproul

Ligonier Ministries

Baker Books

A Division of Baker Book House Co
Grand Rapids, Michigan 49516

© 1994 by R. C. Sproul

Published by Baker Books
a division of Baker Book House Company
P.O. Box 6287, Grand Rapids, Michigan 49516-6287

Printed in the United States of America

Library of Congress Cataloging-in-Publication Data

Sproul, R. C. (Robert Charles), 1939–
    Before the face of God : a daily guide for living from the Old
Testament / R. C. Sproul.
      p.   cm.
    ISBN 0-8010-8340-0 (v. 1)
    ISBN 0-8010-8358-3 (v. 2)
    ISBN 0-8010-8378-8 (v. 3)
    1. Bible. Meditations. 2. Devotional calendars. I. Title.
BS2665.4.S67   1993
242'.2—dc20   92-31634

Studies for this book were adapted from meditations appearing in *Tabletalk*,
a publication of Ligonier Ministries, Orlando, Florida, the teaching fellowship
of R. C. Sproul. Adapting editor Robert F. Ingram, senior vice-president of Ligonier Ministries. Contributing material for studies on Ruth, Chronicles, Proverbs,
and portions of the Minor Prophets were Robert F. Ingram, Michael S. Beates,
Frederic C. Putnam, and James B. Jordan, respectively.

For Mike, Maureen, and Melissa,
without whose help this project
would not have been possible.

Contents

Preface

Coram Deo means "in the presence of God" or "before the face of God." It refers to living life in a sense of acute God-consciousness. It's the "Big Idea," in management jargon, of the Christian life.

We do not behold the face of God; he is invisible to us. But God's invisibility does not negate his presence. While the prodigal son left his father and ventured to a far country where he could live a riotous life in anonymity, there is no far country to which we can flee from the presence of God. His presence permeates every corner of our world. There is no refuge from his eye. His sight is not restricted to the interior chambers of a church building. His sovereignty extends to every arena of life.

The Christian life is God-centered. God is neither peripheral nor eccentric to human life. He must be at the core, the very center of our existence.

To live life Coram Deo *is to live all of life in the presence of God, under the authority of God, and to the glory of God.*

You will notice that each reading concludes with a section entitled *Coram Deo.* Our intention is to cause you to think of the life application that will remind you of God's sovereign authority over all of life. Each *Coram Deo* is but a suggested application; the reader will need to prayerfully consider how each lesson can be applied most effectively to life.

The intended result will be a growing ability to practice the presence of God in the whole of life.

PART 1

The Old Testament.

It stands as a giant, mysterious body of literature into which many Christians rarely venture. We are caught in a vicious circle: As believers we don't read the Old Testament because we don't understand it; we don't understand it because we don't read it. However, the Old Testament is the foundation and context out of which the New Testament grew. In order to fully appreciate the inheritance given us by Christ, we must grasp the significance of the ages prior to the Messiah's coming.

This volume will study the broad message and content of the Old Testament. A good place to begin this survey is with some preliminary reasons why studying the Old Testament is such a great need. It is one thing for the apostle Paul to remind Timothy that God breathed out the law on the holy mountain and the prophetic utterances of warning to his unfaithful people. It is quite another thing to see in the law and those ancient calls to repentance relevant messages for twenty-first-century men and women. Yet 2 Timothy 3:16 informs us both that those mes-

Foundations for God's Revelation

sages of the Old Testament were God-breathed and that they are useful.

As we begin our actual study of the text we will look carefully at Genesis 1 and 2. Because of the importance of these chapters, and the controversies that continually veil them from today's Christian, several meditations will linger over the same passages as we consider the overall issues of creation. Equally important, of course, is that we understand who we are as creatures resulting from that creation. Who are we in that we were made in the image of God? What does the fall into sin imply for that image? Part 1 will look at just a few of the interpersonal dimensions of our lives as fellow human beings, male and female, parents and children, and husbands and wives, in the light of creation and the darkness of sin.

Be faithful and ask God to bring new understanding as you study *coram Deo,* wholly before the face of God, in his presence, and unto his glory.

R.C. Sproul

11

1 The Old Testament Today

The Old Testament is greatly neglected. Its use has nearly disappeared from the Christian community and from the consciousness of Americans. People today are more familiar with the twelve signs of the zodiac than with the twelve tribes of Israel.

Evangelical Christians devote some attention to the Old Testament, primarily because of the attack on the inerrancy of the Bible by liberal theologians. Scholars defend the truthfulness and inspiration of the Old Testament, for instance, Mosaic authorship of the Pentateuch or the unity of Isaiah. The prophetic parts of the Old Testament receive careful inspection from evangelicals and fundamentalists searching for prophetic clues regarding the nation of Israel or the second coming of Jesus Christ. Such attention to words and phrases tends to obscure the larger Old Testament message.

The general teaching of the Old Testament, however, is not given much attention in evangelical churches. Many people have very limited knowledge of Mosaic law. Few know the history of Israel, even in broad outline. The prophetic books like Isaiah and Jeremiah, are complete

> Open my eyes that I may see wonderful things in your law.
> [Ps. 119:18]

mysteries. And singing the Psalms is no longer a regular part of worship.

One of the most important events in my Christian life occurred shortly after my conversion: I read the entire Bible in two weeks. Such rapid reading does not allow for careful meditation, study, and comparison of passages, but it did do one thing for me. When I was finished with the Old Testament, I knew that the God who had called me to himself was a God who plays for keeps.

Coram Deo

How well do you know the Old Testament? As we begin this new year, ask God to give you a real hunger for his Word so that you may be transformed by it. Commit yourself to learn more about the God who reveals himself in the pages of the Old Testament by reading through the entire Bible this year. If you do not know of a systematic Bible reading program, ask your pastor to suggest one.

For further study: Deuteronomy 18:14–22; Isaiah 7:10–16; 55:1–11

2 The Value of the Old Testament

hen Paul wrote to Timothy about the Scriptures he meant the Old Testament. Possibly, he also had in mind those New Testament books that had been written, but the "Bible" for the early church was the Old Testament. Thus, while 2 Timothy 3:16 applies to the whole Bible, its first application was to the Old Testament.

The Greek word translated "God-breathed" is *theopneustos*. The great nineteenth-century theologian B. B. Warfield showed persuasively that *theopneustos* does not mean merely "inspired," that God breathed something *into* the authors of the Bible—although this indeed is true. Neither does it mean that God dictated every character they wrote. Obviously God mediated his message through the writers' personalities, experiences, and knowledge. Rather, *theopneustos* means that God "breathed out" the Bible. Thus, Paul told Timothy: "All of the Old Testament is *breathed out* by God—all of it." What would be our attitude if we really believed that?

What does Paul go on to say about the Old Testament? To begin with, he said it is to be used. God intended it to be useful in four ways: First, it is to teach us about God—

14

> All Scripture is God-breathed and is useful for teaching, rebuking, correcting and training in righteousness. [2 Tim. 3:16]

his nature, character, standards of righteousness, promises of redemption, plan of salvation—everything we need to know.

Second, Paul said the Old Testament is to be used to confront and rebuke sin.

Third, it is to be used to correct and point the way of righteousness.

Fourth, the Old Testament is to be used to train people in righteousness—to realign their lives according to the will of God.

Coram Deo

When people first learn that Scripture provides the basis for confronting and rebuking sin, their first thought is how to apply this helpful reforming power on others, who surely do need it. Knowing our tendency toward self-deception, however, Jesus taught us to remove the log from our own eye first. Ask the Holy Spirit to reveal sin in your own life that needs to be confronted and rebuked.

For further study: Exodus 34:1–35; 2 Peter 1:12–21

15

3 The Covenant Pattern

I

f the Bible for the early church was the Old Testament, because the New Testament was only then being written, then the early church teaching and study related the Old Testament to its fulfillment in Christ. Early Christians studied law and gospel, shadows of expected deliverance and the substance now experienced. They related the Old Testament revelation of God with the new covenant. That comparative content is taught infrequently today.

One great unifying structure of the old and new covenants is the covenant structure itself. By coming to grips with that covenant pattern we can see one of the most important ways of relating the Old and New Testaments. Recent studies of ancient Near Eastern documents show that covenants between a lord and a vassal followed a certain format and contained certain elements. The covenant pattern began with a *preamble* identifying the parties involved, and particularly the superior party initiating the covenant. In Exodus 20 the preamble says that the Lord, *Yahweh,* is sovereign, and is "your" God. It identifies both parties.

The second element, the *historical prologue*, told what the master previously had done for his vassal, establish-

16

"I am the LORD your God, who brought you out of Egypt, out of the land of slavery." [Exod. 20:2].

ing why the vassal should serve the master. In the Biblical covenants the historical prologues state what God has done to redeem his people, the history of their being brought out of a life of slavery in Egypt. In theological terms we call this "grace." God graciously delivered his people, and on the basis of that grace he then gives them his law by which to live.

The third element in the covenant was a set of non-negotiable *stipulations* telling this vassal what was expected. In the Bible these laws morally bound an entire covenant community.

Coram Deo

The Old Testament covenants were never negotiated. God himself drew up all the stipulations. Despite the bounty of the new covenant, we still tend to seek to negotiate with God. Search for instances in your life where you have tried to add your own terms to the covenant of grace. Seek to live by and thank God for the riches of his covenant.

For further study: Genesis 15; Isaiah 43:14–28

4 Laws and Promises

In the Mosaic covenant's preamble, the master was *Yahweh* and Israel was the vassal. In the new covenant, Jesus is lord and the church is the vassal. The old covenant historical Prologue described the Exodus from Egypt; the new covenant looks to the exodus accomplished in the death and resurrection of Jesus, deliverance from sin and death.

Only after salvation and deliverance are we guaranteed that God will give his law. The vassal expresses gratitude in faithful obedience. We must remember two things about this. First, law in the Bible always comes in the context of a covenant God has sovereignly established by grace, never as a series of works *we* need to do to enter into covenant with God.

Second, there cannot be a covenant without law. The new covenant has Stipulations just as did the old covenant. Because God's character does not change, the fundamental ethical content of the Law does not change. Jesus said, "If you love me, you will obey what I command" (John 14:15).

Scholars have identified other elements of the covenant structure, such as representatives of the master who remind the vassal of duties (Old Testament: priests, New Testament: elders), and songs that encapsulate the covenant as reminders for the people.

> If you fully obey the Lord your God and carefully follow all his commands I give you today, the Lord your God will set you high above all the nations on earth. [Deut. 28:1]

We have listed the elements of preamble, prologue, and stipulations. A fourth is an enumeration of *sanctions*. The lord promises blessings to the vassal for obedience and threatens punishments for disobedience. In the Ten Commandments we find sanctions in Exodus 20:5–6, 12. All of Deuteronomy follows the covenant structure and sets out striking examples of blessings and curses. By ritual the people affirm God's sanctions in Deuteronomy 27:11–26. Deuteronomy 28 spells out these sanctions in detail.

Coram Deo

Evangelicals debate the relationship of grace to law and whether the law still applies for believers. Does God desire a lesser or a higher standard of obedience today than in the Old Testament? Have the sanctions changed through the atoning blood of Jesus Christ? As you consider your own life take care not to presume on the grace of God by looking past the implications of such passages as Deuteronomy 28:1 and John 14:15, 24.

For further study: Numbers 24:1–9; Deuteronomy 15: 4–6; 28:1; John 14:15, 24

5 An Old Heresy Revisited

T here has been an explosion of technical studies and new information about the Old Testament, but the average church-goer remains amazingly ignorant of it. Some church observers believe the church is afflicted with "neo-Marcionism."

Marcion was one of the first heretics of the Christian church. He and his followers rejected the Old Testament and excised portions of the New Testament that seemed, to them, to be overly influenced by the Old Testament. They rejected all the Gospels except Luke and yet still cut out large portions of Luke. Marcion tried to eliminate all reference to the Old Testament God, who he saw as an evil God of wrath, while Jesus was a God of love.

While few today go to this extreme, quite a number of people think the Old Testament focuses on God's justice and wrath, while the New Testament focuses on God's love; therefore the New Testament supersedes the Old. Nothing could be further from the truth.

If anyone reveals God's justice, severity, and wrath it is Jesus of Nazareth. Jesus pronounced repeated woes on the scribes and Pharisees, threatened and predicted wrath upon Jerusalem, and revealed the eternal torments of hell,

> "Brothers and fathers, listen to me! The God of glory appeared to our father Abraham while he was still in Mesopotamia, before he lived in Haran." [Acts 7:2]

which are not directly mentioned anywhere in the Old Testament. By statistical occurrence, Jesus talked more often about hell than about heaven. And look again at the God introduced in the Old Testament, a God who is consistently loving, long-suffering, patient, and merciful. In spite of their sin, God delivered Israel from Egypt. When they repeatedly rebelled, he chastised them but never cast them off. Israel's deliverance from sin and bondage was in each instance accomplished by a God who pursued lost people in love.

Coram Deo

There are undoubtedly portions of Scripture that each of us would prefer had never been included in the Bible. Often these are the "hard sayings" of Jesus— hard because they highlight our moral failures. What do you do about Scriptures that become uncomfortably personal? Reconsider your attitude about one troubling passage today, asking God to change you, rather than change his Word.

For further study: Matthew 5:17–20; Acts 22:1–21

6 Liberal Marcionism

editation 5 recalled Marcion, an early Christian heretic who wanted nothing to do with the "Old Testament God." One form of neo-Marcionism exists now in some British and American scholarly circles, and it dominates German New Testament scholarship.

Rudolph Bultmann and his followers maintain that the gospel comes shrouded in *myth* and needs to be *demythologized*. In particular, say these men, we need to rid ourselves of the idea that salvation results from the verifiable actions of God in history. The essential characteristic of a myth is that it is a "religious truth" not grounded in real history. Therefore, salvation is *punctiliar*—it happens in a moment of personal existential encounter with God. Salvation, for Bultmann, has no connection to the Old Testament kingdom of God that reaches its climax in the revelation and work of Jesus Christ. All this Old Testament background is "myth." The core of gospel must be stripped from its Old Testament context and worldview.

Orthodox Christian scholars maintain against Bultmann that God prepared the history of the world by his sovereign providence. The Old Testament events brought the world to the point of historical maturation for the events of the

And he began by saying to them, "Today this scripture is fulfilled in your hearing." [Luke 4:21]

gospel. Old Testament events also foreshadowed the events of the gospel and shed light on their meaning. The Old Testament worldview establishes the true picture of the world against all pagan worldviews. Only in that true world-picture do events of the gospel make sense.

The irony is that by demythologizing the gospel, Bultmann actually has substituted myth for truth, because if anything is a myth it is the "Jesus" of Bultmann. The Jesus of Christianity is a person of real history, not Bultmann's fabricated "religious truth." The real Jesus is not myth, but fact.

Coram Deo

While we heartily accept the miracles of Christ, too often we try to strip away his teachings that are uncomfortable, such as his hard teachings on eternal punishment. In your study of the Old Testament, commit to see and worship Christ as he is, rather than as we would like him to be. What have you, like Bultmann, been quick to add or delete to the biblically revealed portrait of Christ?

For further study: Isaiah 61:1–9; Colossians 1:15–17

7 Jesus in the Old Testament

An understanding of the Old Testament is absolutely necessary to a full understanding of the person of Jesus Christ. American church culture breeds spurious "Christian" conversions because of its impoverished understanding of Scripture and its incessant appeal to emotions.

You may have had a conversion experience, but be careful: You might know very little about the real Jesus and his saving love. What you consider a conversion experience may not be centered in the Christ of the Bible. Some are converted into a group with a particular lifestyle, a dynamic spirit, or an acceptance they feel lacking from others. Some are converted to friends, not Jesus.

If you have read the entire New Testament but have never read the Old Testament, chances are that you know precious little of Jesus Christ. No matter how many times you approach the text asking the Holy Spirit to illumine your mind and heart—without studying the Old Testament, you cannot possibly understand the New Testament Jesus.

Jesus' comes to us against the backdrop of the redemptive history of the Old Testament. Those events foreshadow the meaning of the events of Jesus' life. God used the lives and roles of kings, prophets, judges, priests, and patriarchs

24

What you worship as something unknown I am going to proclaim
to you. [Acts 17:23b]

to teach about the coming Christ. Their sinful efforts looked
forward to the perfect that was displayed in the person of
Jesus.

The Old Testament shows how God cultivated the world,
making it ripe for Jesus to confront the mightiest humanistic empire the world had ever seen, showing himself to be not only the true Patriarch, Judge, and King, but
also the true World Emperor. All the New Testament imagery used to describe Jesus is taken directly from the Old
Testament.

Coram Deo

No wonder the first converts from Judaism found
delight in Christ's fulfillment of all that had been spoken of him in the Old Testament Scriptures. Because
they were thoroughly immersed in the Scriptures,
their capacity to love and delight in him was enlarged.
Ask God to produce a similar delight in you. How is
Jesus like an Old Testament king? A priest? A patriarch? Record your answer where you can review it
after you finish this book to see if your delight has
been intensified.

For further study: Psalm 110; Matthew 22:41–46

8 Word and Deed Revelation

adical liberal theologians such as Rudolph Bultmann maintain that Scripture is not revelation—that neither words nor nature reveal God.
We must look to wordless "encounters" or mystical
experiences.

This is far removed from the multifaceted biblical concept of revelation. God reveals himself in many ways. First,
let us focus on the necessary relationship between God's
acts and God's words. Perhaps the best illustration of this
relationship is the crucifixion of Christ, which surely is
the central event of history. But what do we know about
this event? What does it mean? Here is a Jew being crucified outside Jerusalem. How would you interpret this
event? How does the Man on the center cross differ from
those crucified on either side of him? Does his death differ from theirs?

The Roman interpretation is that this man has been
charged, probably falsely, with insurrection. To prevent
trouble, however, they will play along with the Jewish leaders. The Jewish Sanhedrin is partly concerned that this
Man's teaching will bring down Roman wrath upon Israel.
They also are infuriated by his *claims* to be God in flesh.
One thief ridicules him as deluded; the other grasps at the

It was the third hour when they crucified him. [Mark 15:25]

chance to enter into God's kingdom. All of these perspectives interpret the event. Not all can be correct.

New Testament writings provide the true interpretation of this event. The New Testament says this Man was God incarnate, the promised Messiah. His death effected cosmic redemption. The New Testament writers and their believing readers based this interpretation on writings in the Old Testament that predicted and explained these events. Into the second century of the church, the primary defense of the faith was made by appealing to predictive Old Testament prophecy. Events without interpretive words are meaningless.

Coram Deo

The primary defense of the faith continues to be based upon Scripture. If the Bible's authority is undermined and inspiration denied, then all certainty is destroyed. Without a *sure* word from God, our hope of salvation is merely wish projection. Settle the question of scriptural authority or you will never have the assurance of salvation.

For further study: Psalm 119:49–64; Revelation 22:12–19

27

9 Varieties of Revelation

God revealed himself to the Old Testament prophets in a myriad of ways. We can learn something about God by reviewing some of them. One of the most important ways God revealed himself was through *theophanies*. In a theophany God shows himself in and through some created thing. In one of the most famous examples of a theophany, the burning bush, God revealed himself to Moses as the bush burned with his divine glory.

God also revealed himself through dreams. Famous dreams of Scripture include those of Jacob, Joseph, Nebuchadnezzar (in Daniel), and the night visions of Zechariah 1–6. God spoke in dreams to Joseph, the husband of Mary, and to Pilate's wife. Visions differ from dreams in that they happen while people are awake. Ezekiel experienced numerous visions. The vision of Isaiah 6 surely changed Isaiah's life and message. God spoke to Peter in a vision of the clean and unclean animals in Acts 10.

In yet another kind of revelation, God "opened the eyes" of people so that they might see things present in another dimension. In 2 Kings 6:17 the eyes of Elisha's servant were opened to see God's angelic army.

On occasion God spoke directly to men and indirectly

In the past God spoke to our forefathers through the prophets at many times and in various ways. [Heb. 1:1]

through prophets. God revealed himself through events, both providential and miraculous. Additionally, the whole of God's creation reveals him, just as a piece of art reveals its maker. The cosmos is the theater of God's revelation.

Finally, and most important, Jesus Christ is the ultimate revelation of God. Modernist theologian Karl Barth denies all other forms of revelation and says that Jesus Christ is the exclusive revelation of God. Historically orthodox Christianity says that Christ is not the *exclusive* revelation of God, but he is the *conclusive* revelation of God.

Coram Deo

Think of the symphonic nature of revelation. Even though God used many people and three languages over centuries to write the Scripture, its "song" expresses unity and harmony. Do you appreciate how each passage of the Bible offers God's inerrant communication to you through people and events of long ago? Thank God for the awesome character of his revelation.

For further study: Acts 7:30–38; Hebrews 4:12–13

10 The Old Testament Canon

he books written by Moses comprised the first *canon* or list of authoritative and God-breathed writings. Ancient Israel placed the five scrolls in the most holy place of the tabernacle, next to the ark of the covenant, as a memorial before God. They were to live by these books; God would call the people to account for what these five books recorded of the covenant between God and his people.

Other books were written later. Over time, through common use, study, and the guidance of the Holy Spirit, certain books gained authority as inspired. We do not know at what time the complete list of Old Testament books came into being, but by the New Testament era three different Old Testaments circulated. At one extreme, the Samaritan version accepted only the five books of Moses. Jesus did not take this view, for when he said the Samaritans did not understand God's revelation (John 4:22) he quoted other books as God's Word. At the other extreme, the *Alexandrian Canon* based on the *Septuagint* (the Greek translation of the Old Testament) seems to have included the Apocrypha.

By Jesus' time the orthodox Hebrew canon was almost certainly the *Palestinian Canon*—identical to the Protestant Old Testament in that it does not contain the Apocrypha. It looks different, since the books are divided and organized differently, so that the Hebrew Bible contains twenty-four books, corresponding to thirty-nine in the Christian Old Testament. They did not divide Samuel, Kings, and Chronicles and counted Ezra-Nehemiah as one book and all twelve Minor Prophets as one. Much of the reason for this is due to the length of the scrolls upon which the books were written.

The Jewish Bible is organized into three parts: (1) the *Law* (the five books of Moses); (2) the *Prophets* (Joshua, Judges, Samuel, Kings, Isaiah, Jeremiah, Ezekiel, and "The Twelve," what we call the Minor Prophets), and (3) the Writings (Psalms, Proverbs, Job, Song of Solomon, Ruth, Lamentations, Ecclesiastes, Esther, Daniel, Ezra-Nehemiah, and Chronicles).

Coram Deo

Most Christians readily agree with the traditional canon of Scripture. In practice, though, we often set up our personal "canon within the canon" of certain favorite books we read. We avoid others we dislike or do not understand. This week challenge yourself to read a book of the Bible you usually ignore.

For further study: Deuteronomy 31:24–27; Psalm 1

11 What About the Apocrypha?

We do not have the "annals of the kings of Judah," but we do have ancient Hebrew writings that are not part of what the Protestant church regards as the Bible. These writings are the Apocrypha and come down to us from the ancient Hebrews. Jewish writers since the first century, notably the historian Josephus, made it clear that these books were not authoritative, nor deemed inspired.

As noted (p. 30), the Greek Alexandrian Canon seems to include the Apocrypha. Ancient copies of the Greek Old Testament found in Alexandria, Egypt, include the apocryphal books. This does not mean Alexandrian Jews believed these books inspired. Our Bibles contain introductory articles, notes, and guides that we do not consider to be part of the Word of God. We cannot be sure how the Alexandrian Jews regarded the apocryphal books, but we know for certain that Palestinian Jews regarded them simply as edifying literature.

The Roman Catholic Church declared eleven of the fourteen apocryphal books to be canonical. This was stated at the Council of Trent in the 1500s and again at the First Vatican Council in the nineteenth century. While

> As for the other events of the reign of Ahaz, and what he did, are they not written in the book of the annals of the kings of Judah?
>
> [2 Kings 16:19]

these decisions are in error, it is unfortunate that Protestants have totally disregarded the Apocrypha. The Protestant Reformers, while declaring that the apocryphal books were not inspired as God's revelation, still maintained their value as literature. They provide the closest view we have of the period between Malachi and John the Baptist. Many Reformers believed that, apart from the Scripture, the Apocrypha contains our most important body of literature.

Nowhere does the New Testament quote the Apocrypha. Some of its teachings and miracle stories are questionable. The Apocrypha clearly is uninspired literature, but Christians should be familiar with it.

Coram Deo

Your Christian education is not complete if you have never read the Apocrypha. You will find some marvelous stories and some interesting wisdom, as well as some things to reject. Consider taking a semester in Sunday school to survey it.

For further study: 2 Chronicles 9:29; Proverbs 30:5–6

12 The Structure of Genesis 1

H istorically the church has generally interpreted the six days of Genesis 1 to refer to twenty-four-hour days. After the rise of modern science, however, that interpretation came into question, even among those believing in creation. Most scientists say the universe came into being over eons, so some Christians have looked for alternative explanations.

The Hebrew word for *day (yom)* can also mean "lifetime or age," so another position sets forth that the days of Genesis 1 were ages. The *day-age theory*, however, would mean that vegetation grew for an "age" before the sun and moon were created. Also, the order of events still would not correspond to the order set by science.

Some place a "gap" between the first two verses of Genesis 1. This *gap theory* says God created the universe in the distant past and it *became* void as a result of the fall of the angels. Genesis 1:3–31 describes the *re-creation*, not the *creation*. This allows for eons of time and can accommodate modern science. However, the gap theory puts a strain on the grammar of verse 2 to translate *was* as *became*, making it unlikely from a grammatical point of view.

A fourth approach notices the literary structure of Genesis 1, saying that *day* is simply a structuring device. The

> God saw all that he had made, and it was very good. And there was evening, and there was morning—the sixth day [Gen. 1:31].

first three days create realms, while the last three establish rulers. The first three days show acts of *forming*, while the last three show acts of *filling*.

Advocates of the literal-day position point out that the structure of Genesis 1 is more complex than the framework hypothesis allows. They also say that, just because God acted in a structural manner, does not mean he did not use six twenty-four-hour days.

God reveals himself in Scripture and in nature; the contribution of science to understanding natural revelation should be sought, not feared. Neither the scientists nor the commentator is yet finished.

Coram Deo

Without minimizing the importance of which interpretation is most accurate, don't be so concerned about *how* God created that you miss the wonder, glory, and majesty of *what* he created. Take a moment to contemplate the intricate beauty of one of your favorite objects in nature. Mentally note or write down what this object reveals about God, and how he should be praised as its Creator.

For further study: Psalm 90:1–6; 2 Peter 3:8–10

13 The King of Creation

enesis 1:1 says God created the heavens and the earth. This does not mean "sky and ground," but is a Hebrew way of saying God created *all things*. The statement that God created all things is not merely a philosophical idea, though it does tell us by whom the universe exists and so gives a foundation for philosophy. The immediate implication is that, since God created all things, God owns all things. He is the sovereign Lord of all the universe, and the sphere of authority covers the entire realm of created order.

This might seem obvious, but we live in a day when people confine God's authority to a special compartment of our existence that we call "religion," as if he is not considered relevant to government, art, cinema, agriculture, and economics. We have so separated *church and state* that we have separated *God from the state*.

God is the Creator King whose kingdom extends to every sphere. Genesis 1:1 introduces the theme of the kingdom of God that pervades Scripture. In one sense the kingdom of God is where his authority is gratefully acknowledged. In another sense it is everywhere, regardless of who acknowledges it or to what extent it is respected.

36

In the beginning, God created the heavens and the earth.
[Gen. 1:1]

Also implied in Genesis 1:1 is that God and nature are not "one." Throughout the Old Testament, especially in the Psalms, nature shows forth God's glory to his praise; but never is nature being worshiped. This is one of the most important contrasts between the religion of Israel and that of her neighbors. All of them had shrines and rituals dedicated to aspects of nature. God transcends his creation and is never to be confused with it.

However, the glory of God is mirrored in the creation, and the world reveals the Artist who made it.

Coram Deo

The resurgence of paganism as described in the above paragraph is the basis of the new age movement. God and nature become "one"; nature is worshiped and man ultimately becomes a god. If you are unfamiliar with new age beliefs, ask your pastor for resources that will help you understand how it attempts to dethrone the King of creation.

For further study: Psalms 50; 89:5–18

14 Creation or Chaos?

The creation myths of the pagan nations encircling Israel held that the world emerged from the power struggle among "gods" of the eternal forces of chaos and order. These were seen as equal beings, involved in an eternal power struggle. In some of those myths, we see the battle between the forces of light and darkness. For that reason some have said Genesis 1:2 reflects the same idea—this battle between the forces of light and darkness, between the deity and the sea monster who lurks in the depths.

However, unlike the pagan myths, Genesis says one God *created* these waters, this void, this darkness. The point of verse 2 is not to say that God prevailed over the "agents of chaos." Rather, it describes the stages of creation. God's plan triumphs over any possibility of chaos. Verse 2 shows us that God created raw material. As Artist he set his clay before him and went to work. The world had been created but not completed as a work of divine architecture.

It is tragic that in our own century, with the rise of existential philosophy, we hear voices say that creation never got beyond that stage. What was true at creation is still valid, particularly with respect to the meaning of existence. They tell us that life is ultimately chaotic and there is no purpose to the universe.

Now the earth was formless and empty, darkness was over the surface of the deep, and the Spirit of God was hovering over the waters. [Gen. 1:2]

Genesis 1:2 does not stop with formlessness. The sentence goes on with the word *and*. This last clause separates the Christian from the existentialist. It says the Spirit of God was also hovering over the surface of the waters. God immediately began to work with his raw material by means of his Spirit.

Some translations say that the Spirit was "brooding" over the deep, others that he was "sweeping across the waters." The Hebrew word denotes the mother eagle hovering over her nest, feeding and protecting her young. Likewise, God through the Spirit cared for his creation and brought harmony and purpose to the world.

Coram Deo

The news of wars and rumors of wars, of tragedies everywhere, certainly give the impression of a world out of control. Fortunately that is not the case in the least. As we see a "world in chaos" today, what comfort can we derive from the work of the Holy Spirit in Genesis 1:2 and the work of that same Holy Spirit today? Make specific applications of this comfort to your own life and the distresses you are going through.

For further study: Nehemiah 9:5–6; Job 38:28–41

15 "Let There Be Light"

As God works with the raw material of creation, he first separates darkness from light. Notice that the Bible does not give us a mechanical description of how this light was produced. Rather, the focus is on the "divine fiat" that called it into being by the power of God's word. The word *fiat* comes from the Latin phrase meaning "Let there be." God speaks and things happen.

Verse 3 clearly affirms the authority of God. The word *authority* is built on the word *author*. God, as Author of all things, has authority over all things. Only God has the power of *being* within himself. Only God can declare anything into existence. The great "I Am" is the Author who speaks.

Here we begin to understand God's power in creating all things. Theologians say the world was created *ex nihilo*, "out of nothing." They also say *ex nihilo, nihil fit*: "out of nothing, nothing comes." The modern secular view of the origin of the universe holds that the universe arose out of nothing "by chance." This expression is ultimately meaningless. *Chance* here can only refer to a mathematical concept, and a concept has within it no power of being. "By chance" means we don't know how it happened, but God didn't do it." Against such an absurd and self-contradictory philosophy, Christianity main-

> And God said, "Let there be light," and there was light. [Gen. 1:3]

tains that *ex nihilo, nihil fit:* out of nothing, nothing arises by itself.

The universe was not created *by* nothing. It was created *out of* nothing *by* God. It came from the creative act and word of God. It was spoken into existence.

Ancient philosophy, however, said that the universe was made out of the substance of God, as an outflow of his being. Against this notion, Christianity maintains that creation was *ex nihilo.* God made the universe neither out of himself nor out of any pre-existent eternal substance. Rather, he caused it to come into being out of nothing by power expressed in his creative act.

Coram Deo

As believers it is encouraging to remember that the same power displayed in creation raised our Savior from the dead. Further, this power is brought to bear by the Spirit of God in our personal redemption. Remember, if you have experienced this power, it will sustain you through any difficulty. If you have not experienced this power, turn to Christ in repentance and belief.

For further study: Luke 5:17–26; 2 Corinthians 3:7–4:7

16 Why Did God Create?

hy did God create the world? One of the most foolish answers advanced is that God was lonely and needed someone with whom to have fellowship. The doctrine of the tri-unity of God utterly opposes any such idea. God has eternal fellowship within himself, and has no need to create anything. Creation results completely from his sovereign will.

Others said the purpose of creation was to prepare the way for redemption: God created it and predestined the fall of humanity so Jesus could redeem the world. This notion looks pious, since it focuses on Jesus and his work, but it is inadequate to explain God's purpose as the Bible sets it out.

Looking at Genesis 1, some have said that the purpose of creation was to provide a world for human glory and happiness—that humanity is the crown of creation so that the world was made just for people. This distorts the truth that humanity was created as the *chief of creation* and in Jesus Christ is restored to that authority. Even in Genesis 1–2, the sixth day, on which man was made, was not the last day. The seventh and last day shows the goal and purpose of creation.

On the seventh day God rested from his work and sanctified the time of his rest. God is glorified in holiness on

> For from him and through him and to him are all things. To him be the glory forever! Amen. [Rom. 11:36]

the seventh day. We were created to glorify God, and can only find fulfilment in serving the Creator-king. God is glorified by his creation when we live in holiness and righteousness before him. This, after all, is the response to the question, "What is the chief end of man?" in the *Westminster Confession of Faith*.

How can a fallen world please and glorify God? God is glorified through his just punishment of the wicked and his merciful act of redemption at Calvary. Jesus fulfilled the purpose of creation and is enthroned in glory. As the redeemed people of God we seek to obey him that we might manifest his glory and holiness in the world. Only by Christ and in Christ is it possible for the creation to shine with the full majesty of God.

Coram Deo

Genesis 2:15 says that humanity was commissioned to "dress" (improve, glorify) the world, and to "keep" (guard) it. How does this relate to the reasons God created all things? In your own calling in life, think of ways you can make God's glory manifest in the world in these two respects.

For further study: Exodus 14:1–18; Romans 9:16–24

17 Who Created the World?

The word for *God* in Genesis 1:1 and the Old Testament is *elohim,* the plural of the Hebrew *el.* The verb *create* is singular, however, so we cannot translate the verse, "the gods created." Rather, the plural *elohim* refers to a singular Being. Because *elohim* is used, however, many expositors have believed this a cloaked reference to the Trinity. The Bible makes it clear that all three Persons of the Godhead were involved in creation, so it is felt that the use of a plural word here and elsewhere in the Old Testament hints at the tri-unity of God. We cannot be dogmatic about this, however, since in Hebrew the plural form is often a plural of majesty, as when a king uses *we* to refer to himself.

Christians often believe that creation was the work exclusively of the Father, that redemption was accomplished only through the activities of the Son Jesus Christ, and sanctification is the work of the Spirit alone. Actually, all three Persons are involved in each. We saw (p. 39) that the Holy Spirit hovered over the waters. Let us consider Jesus' place in the creation process.

The Gospel of John begins:

> In the beginning was the Word, and the Word was with God, and the Word was God. He was with God in the be-

For by him all things were created. [Col. 1:16a]

ginning. Through him all things were made; without him nothing was made that has been made. [John 1:1–3]

It is no accident that John commences his Gospel with the same words that open the book of Genesis. John is saying that the Word created all things with the Father and the Spirit. In his letter to the Colossians, Paul makes the same point. Speaking of the Son, he writes: "For by him all things were created: things in heaven and on earth, visible and invisible; . . . all things were created by him and for him" (1:16).

He made all things, and all things are for him. Therefore, in Christ, creation finds its origin, its destiny, and its meaning.

Coram Deo

Just as God reveals himself through creation, so he revealed himself through the Word incarnate. As you observe God's creation, look for what he has chosen to reveal through it. Did God further reveal some of these things in the life of Christ? Praise God for his creation and incarnation, thanking him for revealing himself clearly and abundantly.

For further study: Psalm 102:18–28; Revelation 1:4–8

18 The Creation of Man

The Bible tells us that humanity is a creation. How ironic, then, that we humans so fervently deny and resist the idea of being creatures. Satan tempted Adam and Eve in the garden by deceiving them into rejecting the limitations of creaturehood. They thought they could be gods. The atheistic German philosopher Friedrich Nietzsche said that lust for power differentiates humans from all other creatures. People cannot stand the fact that they are creatures.

Do you have trouble with authority? With humility? We have these problems because we want to be gods. We do not want to concede our dependence on anything or anyone else, and we do not want to be subordinate. Jesus Christ saves us from sin and makes us new creations, but he does not make us gods; even if he did make us gods we would be *created* gods, thus still creatures.

There is a massive qualitative difference between the creature and the Creator. Confusing the two is the sin of idolatry, for it involves worshiping creation. In the early church, various heretics tried to maintain that Jesus was a man who became God. The church replied the opposite, that Jesus was God who became man. This distinction is

46

> But who are you, O man, to talk back to God? "Shall what is formed say to him who formed it, 'Why did you make me like this?' " [Rom. 9:20]

maintained in the Nicene Creed, which states that Jesus is very God of very God, who through his incarnation, was made man. Creator and creature are *joined* in Christ, but not *merged*.

As a creature, human beings have a relationship with the Creator. No one can escape being dependent on God, because God sustains life. The relationship is inescapable; resisting and disclaiming this relationship cannot change it. All inescapably exist in relationship with God and give account to him as creatures.

Coram Deo

How easy it is for us to live as though we are self-sufficient. The wise Christian knows that his heart is "prone to wander" from submission to God and seeks to humble himself to God in prayer. Prayer expresses your dependence on God. Make this concern the theme of your prayer today. Through this day remind yourself of ways in which you are utterly dependent upon God.

For further study: Job 38:1–11; Psalm 8

19 The Image of God

What does it mean to be made in the image of God? Mormonism maintains that human beings are literal offspring of "God" and that "God" exists in a body. Because Christianity believes in creation *ex nihilo,* such unsubstantiated beliefs have no place in our faith. God created the physical universe and cannot himself be physical.

The traditional Christian view of the image of God distinguishes between his image in two senses. In a broad sense, human beings are spiritual image-bearers of God in all that they are, with the result that they govern creation. In a narrower sense, each person is to live in God's image in holiness and righteousness. Thus, when Adam sinned he lost the image in the narrow sense but retained it in the broad sense. This conception emphasizes the spiritual and moral core of humanity. However, we must be careful not to go too far to separate the spiritual from the physical qualities of human life.

Perhaps a variation on this idea might help us keep a balanced understanding. The Hebrew term for *image* means "reflection." Every individual has the *capacity* to mirror God as a spiritual being and the *responsibility* to reflect God in

So God created man in his own image, in the image of God he created him; male and female he created them. [Gen. 1:27]

thought and action. Jesus Christ, as the second Adam, was in his essential being the utter reflection of God. And Jesus utterly reflected God in the obedience and justice he demonstrated before the world. As that perfect image-bearer Jesus received dominion over all creation (Heb. 1:3). In the same way, as we are renewed to conform to the image of God, we are called to faithfully reflect God in all that we do.

Adam did not want to reflect God through *submitting* to him. Rather, he wanted to be like God in the sense of being the *same as* God. Thus, Adam distorted what it meant to be the image of God in the narrow sense, and that distortion corrupted all of God's image in the broader sense.

Coram Deo

In your prayers today, ask God to show you more fully what it means to reflect him in your home, your school, or in your work. Think about what you have to do today and lay those responsibilities before him in submission. Ask him to make you a better mirror of his holiness and glory.

For further study: Genesis 9:1–7; Exodus 4:1–12; 1 Corinthians 3:17–18

20 The Birth of Science

I n Genesis 2:19–20 we find the birth of science. One of the tasks of science is to harness the forces of the natural world, making them work for us rather than against us. We improve our agricultural skills; we discover fire and atomic energy; we devise ships for the sea and planes for the air. In this way we exercise dominion over the human environment, as God commanded in Genesis 1:28. Since the fall and the entrance of sin into the world, the ability to enjoy dominion has been greatly frustrated.

The enterprises of science begins with taxonomy—the separating of things into categories. In taxonomy, we see the process of *individuation*. What is the difference between (or what "individuates") a man and an ape?

To carry out individuation we must carefully note similarities and difference. For instance, medical science progresses through ever-more-precise differentiation. In the case of a new disease we must categorize whether it is caused by a bacteria or a virus or by something else. Researchers then distinguish among the different kinds of treatments to match a prescription to a disease. Each new distinction adds to the body of knowledge that comprises science.

> Now the L ORD God had formed out of the ground all the beasts of the field and all the birds of the air. He brought them to the man to see what he would name them; and whatever the man called each living creature, that was its name. [Gen. 2:19]

Thus, dominion over creation begins with taxonomy. When Adam named the animals, he noticed specific characteristics of how animals were similar and how they were different. He learned to distinguish "the livestock, the birds of the air, and all the beasts of the field" (v. 20).

The most important thing Adam had to notice was that there were two different kinds, or genders, to each animal. One was male, like himself, and the other was female. Adam sensed this parallel between himself and the animals, and became aware that he too should have a female counterpart. He came to echo God's conclusion that it was not good to be alone.

Coram Deo

Science in recent years has come to be viewed as the enemy rather than the child of Christianity. This attitude stems both from misguided efforts of science and the church. Seek to develop a more biblical understanding of the role of science, perhaps by reading a book about the life of Isaac Newton, scientist and theologian.

For further study: Job 41; Psalm 115:12–18

21 The Creation of Woman

hroughout Genesis 1 God pronounces his creation to be good. Then in Genesis 2 God says that something is not good: loneliness. Even though Adam had the fellowship of God, he also needed the fellowship of other human beings. Loneliness is a serious problem, especially as complicated by sin. Many technological advances only increase personal loneliness and alienation.

God made the woman from the flesh of the man and brought her to be his helper. It is difficult to discuss the role of the wife as helper to her husband, because in our society men have so grossly perverted this function of the woman. The feminist movement largely arose because of the abuse and degradation of women in pornography, the increasing phenomenon of abusive behavior, incest, and the failure of men to lovingly provide for their wives and families.

Sadly, some within the church have contributed to a distorted view of womankind by assuming that, if the woman is to be subordinate, this must mean she is inferior—foolish, lightheaded, helpless, and overly emotional.

The wise Christian knows that this is not the case. In

> The LORD God said, "It is not good for the man to be alone. I will make a helper suitable for him." [Gen. 2:18]

the Trinity the Son is subordinate to the Father with respect to vocation or calling, but is equal to him. The Spirit is subordinate to the Father and the Son, but the Spirit is in no way inferior to the Father and the Son. Yet, when God acts, the Father sends the Son, not the other way around. The Father and the Son send the Spirit.

The Trinity is God's model for marriage and the family. The Father never treats the Son abusively or condescendingly. In the same way, Paul commands husbands to love their wives as Christ loved the church and gave himself for her. Jesus suffered and died for his bride. He calls men to do no less for theirs.

Coram Deo

In our fallen state, we are characterized by an unwillingness to submit to properly established authority. No matter what form it takes we tend toward rebellion. Whatever your present life situation, consider to whom you should be in submission. Ask God for grace to submit out of reverence to him.

For further study: Proverbs 12:1–4; 31:10–31

22 Leaving and Cleaving

When two people marry it is important for them to leave their parents. It is sometimes difficult for parents to let their children leave, and it is sometimes just as hard for the children, but it is necessary. Leaving does not mean cutting off one's parents, but it does mean geographical separation. Leaving the boundaries of another couple's authority, the husband and wife establish a new home with their own authority and identity.

What happens when a couple wants to get married but they move in with his mom and dad? The young wife is soon thoroughly intimidated by the way his mother does things. Or in her parents' home the new husband is subordinate to his father-in-law, and his wife is subordinate to both her husband and father. She is caught in a terrible crunch. Such problems happen even if the newlyweds do leave, but they are multiplied if they do not. God commands us to leave for very good reasons.

The beauty of God's way is that when a young couple begins a new home, they have the opportunity to establish an adult relationship with their parents. This can be one of the most fulfilling and rewarding personal relationships a human being can have. Parents cannot help

> For this reason a man will leave his father and mother and be
> united to his wife, and they will become one flesh. [Gen. 2:24]

but think of their children as young and immature. But after the new couple has been away for a while and has acquired the maturity that comes with living together and having children, a new, mature relationship with the parents can blossom.

Leaving permits cleaving. Such unity results in a stronger marriage bond. For those who do not marry, a time comes to leave home for work or school. Notice that this principle of leaving and cleaving is a creation ordinance, given before sin's corruption. Even apart from sin, God intended for new families to come out from the authority of old at the point of marriage.

Coram Deo

If you have not already done so, seek to develop a more adult relationship with your parents or grown children. If you are younger, be sure your leaving was more than just physical. As the parents of grown children, show the strength to allow your children to leave when the time comes.

For further study: Matthew 19:3–9; Ephesians 5:22–33

23 God and Nakedness

It may seem strange that Adam and Eve were not ashamed of their nakedness before they fell into sin. Yet afterward their first thought seems to have been the shame of their uncovering. This needs to be understood in the context of Genesis 3, where, after they sinned against God, "the eyes of both of them were opened, and they realized they were naked" (3:7). This verse does not say they realized they had sinned. Rather, the first change in their psychology was the overwhelming realization of their nakedness, and their first impulse was to cover themselves.

When God asked Adam why he was hiding Adam said it was because he was naked (v. 10). He had been naked when God spoke with him before. What was different now? Adam was no longer comfortable being naked in God's presence. A deep psychological connection exists between nakedness and shame.

Two things stand out in this passage. The first is that each of us has a deep need to find a place of security where we can be naked without shame. We long for a place where we can bare our souls to someone. We need to have a close relationship with a spouse with whom we can be naked in more than one sense of the term. Marriage is intended to be such a place of security. The good news of the gospel is that in Jesus Christ we are able to draw near to God as we

> The man and his wife were both naked, and they felt no shame.
> [Gen. 2:25]

cannot even with a spouse, opening our hearts to him without fear and shame.

Second, God permits us to cover ourselves. He made clothes for Adam and Eve because he recognized that we do not want to expose ourselves. Sin's continuing reign on earth requires that we cover ourselves physically, spiritually, and psychologically. The "let it all hang out" attitude popular in the 1960s and 1970s has no foundation in biblical Christianity. Other people are untrustworthy. If you bare your soul to another sinner, be prepared to pay the consequences. With only a few people do we dare become intimate enough to bare our souls. The Bible forbids us to join in one flesh with anyone except our spouses. But we are invited to stand before our Lord unashamed and unafraid.

Coram Deo

Since the 1970s it seems that "serious" motion pictures must have at least token nudity. Other avenues of artistic expression brazenly flaunt nudity. Is such "artistic" nudity actually a form of active rebellion against God—an attempt to lose shame and guilt by searing the conscience? Evaluate your own exposure to such expression and ask God to help you deal responsibly with any struggle you may have with it.

For further study: Psalm 91:1–8; Lamentations 1:8–12

PART 2

In our survey of the Old Testament we began with several foundational concepts:

- The value of the Old Testament lies in more than its historical elements. In it God reveals his nature, character, standards, promises, and plan.
- Further, it is useful to confront and rebuke sin, to correct and point the way of righteousness, and to realign our lives according to God's will.
- In it God reveals his law and covenant as particular themes that point to Christ.
- In it God shows us that we must see him as both a God of wrath and judgment and a God of love. He is not one thing in the Old Testament and another in the New Testament.
- The Old Testament prepares us to hear Jesus' words and to see his actions as those of God. It shows us Christ.
- The Old Testament was set apart from other writings and passed down to us.

We then looked carefully at the Creation account in Genesis 1–2 and some related issues.

The Fall and
the Expansion of Sin

We now turn our attention to an event with devastating implications for our own lives—the fall of humanity and the resulting expansion of sin as seen in Genesis 3–5. Because of his particular insights into this material, some of these meditations are adapted from *The Three Faces of Adam,* a Ligonier Ministries series by John H. Gerstner. These studies take up the area of theological anthropology. They study who a human being is (anthropology) from God's (theological) perspective. This will help us consider more deeply what it meant for Adam to be created in God's image, to rebel against God, and what God has done to redeem his people from rebellion.

Regarding the expansion of that sinful rebellion we mean the aftermath of Adam's sin as Cain murders Abel and the human society begins its descent into an anarchy of wickedness. In order to understand how we are to live fully *Coram Deo,* we must understand where we are as his creatures.

Ask God to give you new awareness of self and him as you study his Word. Then, commit yourself to living righteously before the face of God.

R.C. Sproul

24 Making Fun of Satan

hen we move from Genesis 2:25 to Genesis 3:1 we note a change in textual tone. The statement that the serpent was the craftiest of the animals strikes a discordant note in the harmony that had prevailed to this point. In Genesis 3:1 we immediately read that this clever beast challenged God's commands to Adam and Eve.

The serpent personifies Satan throughout the Bible. We often envision the stereotypical little man in a red suit, horns and cloven hooves, carrying a pitchfork. This description is not found anywhere in the Bible, but was born in the minds of some medieval church scholars. These theologians were conscious of spiritual warfare, so they sought techniques to fight Satan and overcome his temptations. Peter tells us that Satan prowls around like a roaring lion seeking someone to devour (1 Peter 5:8), but James promises that if we resist him this lion will flee (James 4:7).

Such encouragement caused the godly men of the Middle Ages to resist Satan. They determined that Lucifer's greatest weakness is pride. Since a proud person cannot stand ridicule, these theologians used ridicule as a weapon against him. They wrote songs to mock him and drew cartoons poking fun at him. One of the most enduring and popular of these images was the silly creature in a red suit with a tail and horns.

Now the serpent was more crafty than any of the wild animals the LORD God had made. [Gen. 3:1]

In the Bible Satan is exposed as a counterfeit angel of light. He deceives the world by advocating and offering that which often sounds good but is not godly. He hisses subtle questions in our minds about the authority and inerrancy of God's Word, planting seeds of doubt. His most cherished territory for stalking his prey is among God's people of the church itself, the sacred garden where God meets men.

Satan is ultimately powerless against almighty God. However, we mere mortals should view him as a staunch enemy of our souls. His objective is to use every ounce of power to entice us away from a life committed to serving Jesus Christ.

Coram Deo

Many only laugh at the idea of Satan, oblivious to his staunch, powerful enmity. Do not permit his silly image to deceive you. You are unable on your own to stand. Read Ephesians 6, counting how many times we are told simply to "stand" against our enemy. Are you taking advantage of the protections Paul there tells us we must use?

For further study: Ephesians 6; James 4:4–12; 1 Peter 5:5–11; Revelation 20:2

25 The Root of the First Sin

There are a number of cultural myths about the sin of Adam and Eve in the garden. Probably the one most often encountered is that Adam and Eve sinned by having sexual intercourse. However, since God blessed their union and gave the gift of their sexuality and its expression in marriage, this could not have been a sin. *The precise nature of Adam's sin was his rejection of the Word of God.* The infallibility and authority of God's Word was at issue in the garden, just as it is in the church today.

The first attack was indirect. Satan asked Eve, probably with an incredulous tone of voice, "Did I hear God say you can't eat from any of these trees?" This question caused Eve to focus on the fact that God had indeed prohibited one tree. It steered her thoughts away from the fact that God had encouraged them to eat of all the rest of the trees. Eve told the serpent that God had only restricted the one tree, on pain of death.

Satan now attacked God's Word directly: "You most certainly shall not die." Here was a frontal assault on the veracity of God's Word. Eve deemed that Satan was correct and ate of the forbidden fruit. Then she offered a piece to Adam, who had been with her all along and had not moved to protect her. He also ate (Gen. 3:6). Thus, Adam allowed Eve to take all the risks and seeing that she did not die, joined her in the sin.

"You will not surely die," the serpent said to the woman. [Gen. 3:4]

The most controversial issue of twentieth-century Christianity is the trustworthiness of the Word of God. Satan's continuing ploy has been to cast doubt with subtlety and sophistry. His refrain remains, "Hath God said . . . ?" The church has been exposed to more than two centuries of criticism leveled against the veracity of the Bible. Even committed Christians divide over this issue. Thus, the test for us remains the same as it was for Adam and Eve: Will we live by trust in what God has said or negotiate the Bible with unbelief?

We need to follow the example of our Lord who, when tempted in the wilderness, replied, "It is written . . ." (Matt. 4:4, 7, 10).

Coram Deo

Adam's temptation to sin took place in paradise. He enjoyed the best of everything. Jesus, the Second Adam, was in the desert, having fasted for forty days when he encountered Satan's temptation to sin. Yet he prevailed. When you face temptation, pray for his strength that you might not fall. Even pride in your own spiritual strength can lead to sin.

For further study: Matthew 4:1–11; 2 Timothy 3:10–17; Hebrews 4:12–16

26 Death: The Price for Sin

God promised Adam that the day he ate of the forbidden tree, he would most certainly die (Gen. 2:17). Yet, when God came to judge Adam and Eve he did not put them to death immediately. He postponed carrying out the fulness of their sentence, giving them time to repent before they died physically.

In a sense Adam and Eve did die the day they sinned. First, *they died spiritually* in that they were cut off from fellowship with God and came under his judgment. Spiritual death is separation from God, and Adam and Eve experienced it as they were cast out of the Garden of Eden.

Second, *they died experientially* in that they lost the full measure of life they had enjoyed. They began to experience humiliation and pain, the preliminary forms of death that climax in the expiration of the physical body. The woman would undergo pain in the natural act of delivering children, one of the greatest moments of self-fulfillment a human being can experience. The man would experience fear and frustration in his work. Studies show that husbands have five times as many nightmares as their wives, and the recurring theme of these nightmares is fear of being unable to provide for one's family. Deep down inside, mar-

> "By the sweat of your brow you will eat your food until you return to the ground, since from it you were taken; for dust you are and to dust you will return." [Gen. 3:19]

ried men fear that the thorns and thistles will win out, and they will fail.

Finally, Adam and Eve received God's promise that *they would come to physical death* eventually. They would return to the dust from which they were made.

In this way God's death penalty was carried out in a merciful way. It would have been perfectly just for God to have slain Adam and Eve on the day they sinned, but instead he stretched out their experience of death. As a result, Adam and Eve would have many opportunities to think about death before they died, and through those very thoughts of their own mortality they would be encouraged to repent and return to God.

Coram Deo

Jesus' tears at the tomb of his friend remind us that we were not made to return to dust. Yet God still uses human mortality and its accompanying pain and frustration to turn us more and more from sin. What "friendly scourges" has God used to remind you of the inevitability of death? How do you respond to these foretastes?

For further study: 1 Corinthians 15:12–23; Hebrews 9:23–28

27 God's Death Sentence

e distinguish in theology between the *first sin* committed by Adam and Eve, and *original sin*, which is the state of corruption passed on to all people as a result of that first sin. Original sin is the *sin nature*, whereby I am wholly inclined to rebellion against God.

Reformation theology calls the state of original sin "total depravity," or more accurately, "radical depravity." It does not mean that people are as totally bad as they could possibly be. We could always get worse. Rather, our wickedness goes to the root *(radix)* and heart of our being (see Book 1, pp. 110–21).

Because we are radically depraved, we are comprehensively depraved. Wickedness infects every aspect of life. So we are also progressively depraved, becoming worse over time as we become more self-conscious and mature in hating God. Apart from the grace of God, humanity individually and collectively grows toward total and absolute depravity, a situation in which no evidence of goodness remains.

Paul writes in Ephesians 2:1 that original sin is an estate of death. This explains the relationship between Adam's first sin and our sin nature. The punishment for Adam's sin was death, and death passed to all people because we

> We know that the law is spiritual; but I am unspiritual, sold as a slave to sin. [Rom. 7:14]

were counted guilty in Adam. This death works death in us and is the wellspring of our depravity. Our sin nature is, in this sense, a *death nature*. God is the source of life, and our death nature moves us to hate God and reject his life in every sense.

Adam was our representative. His sin (apart from us) brought God's death sentence upon all humanity, one aspect of which is the death-and-sin nature we all inherit. Similarly, the obedience of Jesus our representative brought about God's justification of the new humanity and God's gift of resurrection life. That new life in Christ works in us a desire to obey and overcomes our death-and-sin nature.

Coram Deo

We speak of the Christian growing in godliness through sanctification. In radical depravity we see that the process also works the other way. What evidence do you see of our culture's growing maturity in its hatred of God? Consider today if your life shows the opposite signs of growing devotional love for the Lord. If it does not, what steps in the right direction should you begin to take?

For further study: Romans 3:9–23; 5:12–21

28 God's Holy War

G od meant what he said in pronouncing the death penalty on Adam and Eve. From time to time God has shown that people had better take his utter purity and holiness seriously. On one such occasion David and the Levites were transporting the ark of the covenant by oxcart to Jerusalem—disobedient to the clear command of Numbers 4:15 and 7:9 that the priests were to carry it on their shoulders. When the oxen stumbled and the ark started to fall toward the ground, the Levite Uzzah reached out to steady it.

As Numbers 4:15 warned would happen, Uzzah died the moment he touched it. Had it toppled, the mud would not have defiled the ark; it was the morally corrupt touch of man that was forbidden (see Book 1, pp. 62–63). David was angry at God for spoiling his festive day (2 Sam. 6:8), but soon he realized that God was not to be trifled with (v. 9). God is merciful and he withholds judgment for a time, but when he draws near and show us even a little of the judgment we deserve, we get angry.

People love to pretend to be holier than God. At the flood God stated that because of the depth of human wickedness he would destroy the whole human race. So he is blamed for excessive harshness. Then God had the audacity to wipe out the Canaanites, and he gave his own

people the privilege of prosecuting his holy war against
these degenerate people. Today people criticize God for
this, as if these Canaanites did not deserve death.

People often ask, "How can God allow all this suffering
in the world?" When Jesus was asked such a question, referring to the people Pilate had killed as they sacrificed to
God (Luke 13:1–5, see Book 2, pp. 340–41). What did Jesus
say? He said those who were killed deserved to die because
all deserve to die. He went on to say, "Unless you repent
you will all likewise perish."

The question should not have been, "Why did they die?"
but, "Why am I still alive?"

Coram Deo

Are there stories in the Bible that you regard as
harsh, savage, or barbaric because they show the reality of judgment? Jesus would answer that if you
think so you never have adequately understood God's
awesome right to be offended by human sin. What
does today's lesson teach you about passages like
Judges 1:4–7, Judges 5, 1 Samuel 15, and Psalm 58?
Read these passages seeking God's perspective.

For further study: Romans 1:16–32; 2 Corinthians 5:11–21

29 Humans Are Creatures

We now begin a study on the nature of humanity. The first thing we find in Genesis is that human beings are created by God. We have our origin, not in the flux of blind forces of an impersonal cosmos, but rather in the personal decision of a personal God.

Second, we were created body and soul and still exist as body and soul. A continuing problem in philosophy is the question of how to make mind-body or soul-body distinctions. Obviously a consciousness exists apart from the body, and people instinctively know that after death they will still exist. At the same time, the soul governs the body, and the body influences the mind or soul.

Third, human beings were created male and female and still exist as male and female. There is no third sex. Genesis 1:27 relates that humankind as a whole is made in the image of God, and that image is expressed through each male and female person. Genesis 2 teaches that, though there is but one image of God, there are two kinds of persons within this one image. Male and female are equal in essence but different in function.

Fourth, we were created with dominion over the crea-

> The LORD God formed the man from the dust of the ground and breathed into his nostrils the breath of life, and the man became a living being. [Gen. 2:7]

tures. Dominion is a function of imaging God, so that we reflect God's attribute of rulership by ruling over the rest of the cosmos. Because of sin, humans tend to dominate the creation in a perverse manner, wrecking instead of cultivating it. Or they endow nature with divine imaginings, bowing down and subjecting themselves to creation, permitting creation to have dominion over him.

Fifth, we were created holy and righteous—but we no longer have these qualities. And because of this all of the other four aspects of humanity we have noted have become warped and distorted.

Coram Deo

The solution to the identity crises which so plagues us and our children is found in a proper understanding of who we are as created by God. If you are a parent you will find this study of human nature especially valuable for the insights you can use in teaching your children. Use these studies to discuss the real crisis precipitated by sin and its consequences.

For further study: Psalms 8, 139

30 How Could They Fall?

esus said that good trees are not able to bear bad fruit. If that is so, and Adam and Eve were created righteous, how could they fall into sin? Ultimately the answer is a mystery. St. Augustine, however, provides some insights into the matter in his valuable little treatise on basic Christian doctrine, *The Enchiridion*.

Augustine argues that Adam's sin does not violate Christ's principle that a good tree cannot bring forth evil fruit. He points out that the context of Jesus' aphorism is his preceding statement that people cannot gather grapes from the thorn bushes or figs from thistles because grapes and figs do not grow on such plants (Matt. 7:16).

This parable presupposes that all four plants (grapes, figs, thorns, and thistles) grow in soil. For these plants to grow the soil must be good, because nothing grows in a pure desert.

Here is how the analogy works out, according to Augustine. The good tree is a good will, and out of a good will only good actions can proceed. Similarly, the bad tree is an evil will, out of which only evil actions proceed. Both the good and the evil wills, however, are attributes of human nature, and human nature, being created by God and in his image, is good. Human nature, as created by God, is

"A good tree cannot bear bad fruit, and a bad tree cannot bear good fruit." [Matt. 7:18]

good, but as willful sin distorts it, the human will and actions become ethically evil—bad fruit.

Human beings, thus, are like the soil. They have the potential to produce good or bad trees, with good or bad fruit. Adam was a good soil (Genesis 2:7), but he chose to turn his will into a bad tree and his fruit into bad fruit. As a result, all of his posterity came under the judgment of sin and are born with evil wills that produce corrupt fruit.

The raw material of humanity, however, is still good. Sin, tragically, takes something good—the image of God—and perverts it into something evil. People take his good gifts, by which they image God, and through an evil will transform them into evil actions, just as a bad tree transforms minerals and water into bad fruit.

Coram Deo

Augustine's good tree represents our *commitment* to take the raw materials God has given us in our soil and to transform them into good fruit. What raw materials has God given you? What kinds of fruit should you be looking for?

For further study: Mark 4:1–20; 7:14–23; Galatians 5:22–23

31 Humanity Hates God

Adam's sin in the garden was far more than disobedience to some abstract moral principle. Adam personally rebelled against a personal God, whose Word had been delivered to him "face to face." Adam knew exactly what God wanted and rejected the notion that God could tell him what to do. From that time on, humanity has been conceived in a condition of hatred toward God. We inescapably know God, because he is omnipresent to all human beings, and all (apart from Christ) hate him.

Because we hate God we would kill him if we could. Jesus said that those who hate in their heart are guilty of murder, and we are guilty of murdering God because we hate him. The fact that we cannot possibly murder God does not change the fact that we would if we could.

Ironically, the more we hate God, the more we claim to love him. Our world is very religious, filled with people who say they love God. In fact, what they love is their own false notions regarding the deity, and their religion cloaks intense hatred of the true God. The Bible says none seek God (Rom. 3:11). Every non-Christian, and therefore false, religion was created to help people flee from God.

The lost world, however, is not satisfied with mere mental murder. Since they cannot lay their hands on God, they

"When the tenants saw the son, they said to each other, 'This is the heir. Come, let's kill him and take his inheritance'."
[Matt. 21:38]

murder those closest to him, those who remind them of the hated presence and person of God. In the Parable of the Tenants Jesus explained that they murdered the prophets sent to warn them and finally murdered the Son. The Son became human and so put himself within the reach of evil men to die at their hands in order to save the world. Those who follow the Son also will suffer at the hands of those who hate God, as Jesus promised when he told us to rejoice when we are persecuted for the sake of righteousness and that our reward would be great when people falsely speak all kinds of evil against us (Matt. 5:10–12; 1 Peter 2:20b–25).

Coram Deo

Was it ordinary sinners or religious leaders who hated Jesus the most and sought his death? A person's faithfulness is often revealed by those who hate him or her. Are you opposed for righteousness sake, for your faith or ethics? If your life is devoid of Christian persecution, maybe you have not displayed Christ openly enough.

For further study: Psalms 2; 51; Isaiah 53:4–7

32 Humans Hate Each Other

ne would think that, since humanity hates God, all humankind would stand shoulder to shoulder, united in opposition to him. United against God, one might expect to find people loving each other, strengthening one another's hands against the common Foe. This is not the case.

The first great commandment is to love God; the second is to love our neighbors as ourselves. The reason we need these commandments is that by nature we hate God, our neighbors, and (as we shall see) ourselves. Humans hate God, so they hate the images of God they see in other people. This hatred erupts as wars and conflicts, as well as in more subtle envy, backbiting, gossip, and manipulation.

Doing false good is one of the most subtle ways we show hatred for our neighbor. We live and move and have our being in God (Acts 17:28). How can you possibly do me any good without any concern for the Being in whom I have my being? If you hate God, the context of my life, then you hate me as well. The apparent good you do is not really good at all, because it is divorced from God. Think of what we saw about false religions (see p. 68). That also applies to false good. The good deed that is not connected

> "I tell you that anyone who is angry with his brother will be subject to judgment. Again, anyone who says to his brother, 'Raca,' is answerable to the Sanhedrin. But anyone who says, 'You fool!' will be in danger of the fire of hell." [Matt. 5:22]

to God pretends that God is unnecessary. How can you promote my well-being if you are helping me to ignore God?

The appalling aspect of this is that we tend to hate most those closest to us. Consider two fathers. The first is a mean, sadistic bully. His terrorized children feel his hatred. It is easy to see that this man hates his children. The second is kind, provides well for his children, and is never mean to them—but is an atheist. This man also hates his children because he is sealing them against God. They will grow up feeling no need for him. No worse gift can be given from a father and mother to their children.

Coram Deo

The essential characteristic of a truly good work and of all real love is the motivation behind it. Only Christians can live and act in a manner that is truly pleasing to God. Concentrate on why you do and say as you do, striving to achieve that purity of heart commended in the Beatitudes.

For further study: Leviticus 19:9–18; Matthew 5:38–6:4

33 Humanity Hates Itself

he Bible commands us to love ourselves when it says, "Love your neighbor as yourself" (Lev. 19:18; Matt. 19:19). The command says as much about self-love as it says about loving others. We might assume that all people love themselves, but the Bible implies that we do not love ourselves at all.

What does it mean to love yourself? As the image of God, true self-love grows from God-love. Those who hate God hate themselves for the same reason: Self-hate grows from God-hate. Because other people are made in God's image, to love yourself is to love them—especially those God has put close to us. Paul writes: "He who loves his wife loves himself. After all, no one ever hated his own body, but he feeds and cares for it, just as Christ does the church" (Eph. 5:28b–29). Those we call "masochists" do hate their own bodies, but in some sense, everyone outside of Christ hates himself.

The Bible appeals to self-love. Jesus asked, "What good will it be for a man if he gains the whole world, yet forfeits his soul? Or what can a man give in exchange for his soul?" (Matt. 16:26). This exhortation to repent is grounded in enlightened self-interest. If we really loved ourselves, we would repent, put our trust in Christ and save ourselves; that we don't shows that we really hate ourselves. Apart

> Whoever fails to find me harms himself; all who hate me love death. [Prov. 8:36]

from God's intervening grace, people do not act out of enlightened self-interest.

Love of death (Prov. 8:36) and hatred of itself is concealed in what is perversely called "self-love." Christians call this counterfeit self-love "selfish love." Selfish love is self-centered, quick to resent, and grounded in rebellion. True self-love is grounded in love for God and embraces sacrificial love for other people. God is the Maker of the self, and the obligation to nurture and protect ourselves is a divine mandate. Apart from God, however, people work to destroy themselves, because they hate and seek to deface the image of God .

Coram Deo

Valentine's Day memorializes sentiment. True love of one's self and others, however, flows not from fleeting emotions but from the love of God. Seek to cultivate that understanding by celebrating that love given and received by the source of all love, God. Take inventory whether your self-love has grown from love for God and enhances your love for others.

For further study: Deuteronomy 6:3–5; 1 Corinthians 13:4–7

34 A Radical Experience

When Jesus told Nicodemus that he had to be born again to see the kingdom, Nicodemus realized that Jesus was saying something radical and asked for an explanation: "Since it is not possible to go back into our mother's womb to get a new start, just what kind of 'new birth' are You talking about, Jesus?" To understand what Jesus meant and what Nicodemus came to comprehend, we need to bear in mind what happened at the fall. Life in sin became distorted, and while the image of God in humanity was not utterly effaced, it was defaced. Our bodies died, our minds lost full use of their faculties, and our holy relationship with God was destroyed.

A corresponding part of what Jesus meant by rebirth is that the whole person who is born again is healthier than the person who remains in sin. The person may not be as healthy as an unbelieving Olympic athlete, but he or she will be healthier than would have been the case apart from Christ. The person has a more positive outlook, healthier habits, and the ability to better respond to crises.

A person who is born again also is smarter than would have been so in sin. The person may not be as smart as Albert Einstein, but because of the quickening work of the Spirit, he or she will be more interested in learning the Bible and discovering the world God made. The life-giving Spirit quickens intellectual and artistic abilities that would otherwise have been dormant. Most important, holiness lost by Adam in the fall is regained. The person passes from darkness to light, once again has God as Father, and has the church as mother, brothers, and sisters. The individual is adopted and placed into a new family, which was the old family Adam lost.

Going back into the womb and being reborn would be a radical experience, but it is nothing compared to the miraculous character of what Jesus was talking about: The new birth is nothing less than a new creation of God, on the level with his first creation of the first man.

Coram Deo

The effects of salvation are holistic—they imply change and new well-being throughout body and soul. Has your experience of salvation been this radical? Identify an area where you desire God to bring his Spirit more fully to bear in your life.

For further study: John 5:19–27; Titus 3:3–8

35 An Overview of Doctrine

The doctrine of justification by faith was restated in its original form during the Protestant Reformation. To understand the timing of this doctrine we must briefly review the overall history of Christian doctrines.

After the close of the canon of Scripture and the passing away of the apostolic generation, the church focused in on the most fundamental of all truths—*the person of Jesus Christ*. Thus, the opening centuries of Christian history saw debate after debate until the church came to a magnificent consensus that Jesus Christ is "very God of very God" and at the same time fully human. The two natures of Christ—one uncreated and the other created—are perfectly joined but not merged. This doctrine is based on the fact that, according to Genesis 1, the creation did not emerge from God as part of his being but was created by his free action outside of himself.

Once the difference between the Creator and the creature had been firmly fixed in the doctrine of the dual natures of Christ, it was no longer possible to believe that salvation was by a mystical re-merging with God, as early heretics purported. Rather, salvation restored a personal relationship between God and humanity. Accordingly, the next issue taken up concerned the work of Christ.

> "How then can a man be justified before God? How can one born of woman be pure?" [Job 25:4]

Since the creation is distinct from God, humans cannot merge into the being of God. The problem of reaching God is not one of distance, but of rebellion. Thus, with Augustine the doctrine of man's depraved hatred of God came into focus; and after him, with Anselm, the doctrine of the *substitutionary atonement* of Jesus Christ, which repaired this ruptured relationship.

Once the objective nature of the work of salvation had been laid out in the doctrine of the atonement, the next question was how we receive the benefits of the atonement. Do we earn the right to receive its benefits, or do we receive it simply by faith? Before the Reformation the church had not always been clear on this point, but the Reformers saw clearly that salvation was by faith alone.

Coram Deo

Luther said justification by faith alone is the article upon which the church stands or falls. It is also the article upon which you stand or fall. Why is this so? Think how this doctrine separates faith in Christ from every other religion's proposition. Read Romans 4 to reaffirm the biblical basis of this precious doctrine.

For further study: John 1:10–13; Romans 10:5–13

36 Justification by Faith

I
s our justification due exclusively to the work of
Christ or to his work together with our individual efforts? If we claim to contribute anything
to our own salvation, we inflate the importance of the sinner and deflate the work of Jesus Christ. To say that the
sinner partakes in his or her salvation inflates the sinner
by attributing to him or her a righteous capacity. The Bible
says that the thoughts of the wicked are evil continually
and that no one does any good. Because of this the sinner
never assists in his own salvation but, by sovereign grace
alone, is brought into the kingdom.

What is at issue is not how much assistance a person
can add, but whether it is possible to add *any*. To say
that the sinner assists in his salvation deflates the Savior because it removes from him some of the credit. The
old hymn says, "Jesus paid it all; all to him I owe." We
make no contribution to our salvation, which is why the
only way we can be saved is to receive it by faith as a
gift.

The Roman Catholic Council of Trent (1545–63), in rejecting the historic Christian faith that was being preserved by the Protestant Reformers, came up with some
complex and sophisticated ways to say that we contribute
slightly to our own salvation. Ultimately, however, it all

He was delivered over to death for our sins and was raised to life
for our justification. [Rom. 4:25]

boils down to this: Either I am saved by Christ or by Christ
plus myself.

Justification before God's law court involves two things.
First, Jesus Christ removed the guilt for our sins by enduring the wrath of God for us. Yet, there is something
even more wonderful in that we are clothed in Christ's righteousness. The filth of our sin is washed from our naked
bodies, and we are clothed in the robes of sonship.

We are not just made neutral and guiltless in God's sight;
we are adopted as holy and beloved members of his royal
family. From that point on the Spirit's work brings sanctification. The fruit that evidences change is our conformity to the image of Jesus Christ.

Coram Deo

Read Romans 8:30, noticing that the last verb in
this verse is past tense—yet it refers to something that
happens in heaven. How does this meditation explain
that the Christian's glorification already is an accomplished fact? Read on through the end of Romans
8 as a meditation on what it means to be justified in
the full sense.

For further study: Romans 3:21–26; 5:1–11; 8:30; Ephesians 2:1–10

37 The Biblical Yardstick

We are justified by faith alone, but not by faith that *is* alone. Good works are absolutely necessary to the Christian life, not as a means of salvation, but as proof of it. A man who claims to be saved by faith but who lives an immoral life is a counterfeit believer whose future is revealed in Matthew 7:21–23.

The scribes (teachers of the Law) and the Pharisees sought to justify themselves before God through the law. Jesus said that our behavior must be more righteous than the behavior of people who have made a religion out of behavior.

If we measure the behavior of Christians against that of moralistic "Pharisees," it sometimes appears that Christians do not measure up. This may indicate that some who claim to be Christians are not. However, it may indicate that we are using the wrong yardstick to measure righteousness. Some things that our society frowns upon (like corporal punishment for children or capital punishment for murder), the Bible says are righteous. Christians are sometimes intimidated by a *false morality* of the secular world.

The biblical yardstick of righteous behavior looks beyond actions at our motivations and heart attitude. True

> "For I tell you that unless your righteousness surpasses that of the Pharisees and the teachers of the law you will certainly not enter the kingdom of heaven." [Matt. 5:20]

good works spring from a heart of faith and love—something no "Pharisee" had. Thus, even the most feeble good work of the true believer is worth more than the heroic good works of an unbeliever. When we see some of the heroic deeds done by unbelievers, we need to ask why they do these deeds.

If they are not acting in faith, then they are simply acting out of ego, making their own statements as heroic mini-gods. Such heroic good deeds may in the providence of God be useful to society, but they have to be regarded as evil in that they reinforce man in his sinful self-sufficiency.

Coram Deo

Has a moralistic unbeliever or a member of some cult like the Mormons ever caused you to reconsider your lack of zeal for good works? Are you measuring yourself by their yardstick rather than by the yardstick of the Bible? Strive to deliver yourself from the bondage of false moral standards to the freedom of biblical obedience.

For further study: 1 Peter 3:13–19; 2 Peter 1:3–11

38 Assurance of Salvation

I f some who claim to be Christians are really hypocrites, either consciously deceiving others or else pitifully self-deceived, how can we be sure that *we* are true believers? There are two ways. The first is to examine ourselves inwardly, and the second is to examine ourselves outwardly.

We can ask ourselves: Am I trusting in Christ? Do I understand who he is? Is my heart warmed at the thought of him? Have I come to him? Have I committed my life to him? Do I say, "Speak, Lord, for your servant is listening"? Do I endeavor to do what he commands and to shun what he forbids because I love him? The fact that you are doing this daily devotion may be an indication that you love Jesus and want to serve him.

We need, however, to balance this internal look with an external one. Jesus warned in the Sermon on the Mount that on the Day of Judgment *many* will affectionately call him "Lord, Lord," and expect to enter heaven but will be cast out. Though they had done mighty works of preaching and miracles, they will be rejected because they practiced lawlessness (Matt. 7:21–23).

One who is truly saved "does the will of my Father who is in heaven" (v. 21). As Jesus put it on another occasion, "If you love me, keep my commandments" (John 14:15). The believer not only loves the *idea* of God, he loves *God* and does what he commands. The believer not only admires the *wisdom* of God's law as it is revealed throughout the Bible; he obeys it. Love translates into conscious conformity to the revealed will of God in the Bible.

We show evidence of love for God when we do what we otherwise would never be inclined to do because he has given the command. He has told us to love our enemies and to bless those who hate us, lie, spread gossip, slander, and tear us down. This is not something we feel like doing, but is a response to his love (Matt. 5:43–48). Consistency in obedience over long periods can be helpful in arriving at the assurance of salvation.

Coram Deo

Assurance of salvation is something every Christian can and should enjoy. It comes through obedience and trust. Use this lesson as a focus for self-examining meditation and prayer. Let the questions asked and the points raised be a stimulus for opening up yourself to God. Take the opportunity this week to speak with your pastor and other mature Christians about your assurance of salvation.

For further study: John 6:35–40; Romans 4:18–25; 1 John 5:6–13

39 The Final Estate of Man

As we end our study in the doctrine of humanity, we review four estates of humanity: First, Adam was created with the possibility of sinning. Second, after the fall, people have become so radically depraved that it is impossible not to sin. In the third estate, it is possible for the redeemed not to sin. Fourth, in the heavenly estate, it is impossible to sin. You may remember these four conditions by learning a bit of theological Latin, using the two words *posse* (able) and *peccare* (to sin):

1. *Posse peccare:* possible to sin (Adam's first estate)
2. *Non posse non peccare:* not possible not to sin (fallen man).
3. *Posse non peccare:* possible not to sin (redeemed man).
4. *Non posse peccare:* not possible to sin (glorified man).

In a sense, the fourth estate completes the work begun in the third. In heaven we shall remember our best works and see how impoverished they were. We shall look back on our most blissful times of fellowship with God and see that they were meager indeed. We shall never desire to abandon him again but shall enjoy the fullness of his love in greater measure as our capacity grows for all eternity.

"For the Lamb at the center of the throne will be their shepherd; he will lead them to springs of living water. And God will wipe away every tear from their eyes." [Rev. 7:17]

The sinner who has refused God's grace is not annihilated but continues to live a self-conscious existence forever under the wrath of God. The sinner will look back on the most miserable suffering he endured on earth and will view it as the greatest bliss imaginable compared with what he is undergoing. Contrary to some theologians, the sinner does not spend eternity unaware of God but rather in his presence. The sinner hates God worst of all and his punishment is to endure God's wrathful presence forever. This fearful future is revealed by a loving God in order to cause men to repent before it is too late.

Coram Deo

God gives each of us what he or she wants. How is this true both in heaven and in hell? Can you see this principle worked out in history as well? Consult Judges 3:7–8, 12; 4:1–2. God gave the Israelites what they wanted by putting them into the cultures formed by the false gods they chose to worship. Can you see how God is still granting people's desires today, which when granted, add to their punishment and condemnation?

For further study: 1 Corinthians 13:8–12; 15:50–57

40 The Acceleration of Sin

After Adam and Eve were banished from the Garden of Eden, they lived in the land of Eden and began to have children, first Cain and then Abel. Abel kept flocks while Cain tilled the soil. We are told that there came a time when both offered sacrifices to God: Cain brought the produce of the ground, while Abel offered "fat portions" (the best parts) of some of the first-born of the flock. God somehow indicated his approval of Abel and his offering, and showed displeasure of Cain and his offering.

The text does not tell us what was wrong with Cain's offering. It has been supposed that Cain should have known that only a blood sacrifice was acceptable and should have exchanged his produce for one of Abel's lambs. The account is clear that Cain's anger was unacceptable. Did Cain say, "I'm sorry I've done wrong in your eyes. Please tell me what to do, and I'll do it. I only want to please You?"

No, Cain was furious. God took the initiative and encouraged him to do right, warning that sin was like a wild beast crouching at the door of his heart.

Cain, however, would not offer an animal sacrifice. Instead he brought a human one. He slew Abel in the field, away from sight, thinking no would see—but God saw.

> On Cain and his offering he did not look with favor. So Cain was very angry, and his face was downcast. [Gen. 4:5).

Just as God came to Adam in the garden, now God came to Cain in the field. "Where is Abel?" God asked. "How should I know?" replied Cain. "Am I my brother's guardian?" The implied answer in the Bible to that question is that, yes, the older brother guards the younger. As Adam was to guard Eve in the garden, so Cain was to guard Abel in the field. In both cases the responsible man failed to guard. Adam blamed Eve, but Cain killed Abel.

Sin was maturing in the world, each generation becoming worse. As Adam was cast from the Garden of Eden, now Cain was cast from the land of Eden and lived out his days in the land of wandering.

Coram Deo

As sin tends to accelerate in the lives of nonbelievers, so it should decelerate in believers. Unfortunately, even for believers, the maturity of sin in our lives makes us uncomfortable about dying more and more to sin and living to righteousness. Ask the Spirit to increase awareness of your own sin and to give you a holy resolve to repent of it.

For further study: Mark 12:28–34; 1 John 2:15–27

41   A Brother's Blood

T he Romans believed that their city was founded by Romulus. The story is told that Romulus and his twin Remus were orphaned at birth and were found and raised by a she-wolf. When they were grown, Romulus plowed a circle in the ground. "Inside this circle is my city, and I am its god and king," said Romulus. Remus tested him by stepping into the circle, and instantly Romulus slew him. Thus Rome was built on the human sacrifice of a brother's blood.

Whether a Romulus and Remus ever lived, the first city on earth truly was built on the human sacrifice of a brother's blood, for it was after killing Abel that Cain built the city of Enoch. This city was a counterfeit Garden of Eden where the son of Cain, Enoch, could be god and reign supreme.

In this city a material culture first developed. Jubal perfected musical instruments; Jabal perfected agricultural techniques; and Tubal-Cain perfected metallurgy. But Jubal's music was used for false worship; Jabal's animal husbandry raised sacrifices for false gods; and Tubal-Cain's metallurgy developed weapons of violence and the architecture of false temples.

Not only were culture and worship perverted; so were

94

> Cain lay with his wife, and she became pregnant and gave birth to
> Enoch. Cain was then building a city, and he named it after his son
> Enoch. [Gen. 4:17]

the institutions of marriage and the family. The seventh from Cain—and remember from Genesis 2:1–3 that seven is the number of completion—was Lamech. Lamech took two wives, perverting marriage, and then murdered a young boy, possibly his own son. Then he produced the savage song of triumph recorded in Genesis 4:23–24—the first song in the Bible—to celebrate it.

The first city is a picture of the essence of humanistic civilization raised in defiance of God. We can praise God that his people are citizens of another city, the New Jerusalem in heaven.

Coram Deo

Augustine described two cities in conflict: the City of Man and the City of God. The Christian's city also is founded on a brother's blood. Abraham saw this city on the distant horizon (Hebrews 11:10). Contrast our city with Cain's: Whose sin put our Brother to death? Who builds that city? How do we enter it? Is it Cain's son or someone else's who rules?

For further study: Hebrews 11:10; Revelation 22:1–2, 17

42 The Society of the Future

From the unholy line of Cain we turn to the righteous line of Seth. Seth was born to Adam and Eve after Abel died. He was a replacement son, and about the time his son Enosh was born we read that "men began to call on the name of the LORD." This probably means true worship was instituted, a striking contrast to Cain's family.

While the Bible traces Cain's line only seven generations to the maturation of evil in Lamech, Seth's line is traced ten generations in Genesis 5 and in Luke 3 all the way to Jesus Christ. The City of Man sprang up like a mushroom, but it does not have staying power. The society of the future, the society destined to rule the cosmos for all eternity, is built on the worship of the true God. That society grows more slowly, but it grows to a mighty tree.

The strong, humanistic culture of Cain claims to speak for humanity, but Genesis 5:1–3 returns us, not to Seth, but to Adam and Eve. It reminds us that they were made in the "likeness" of God, just as their children were in their "likeness." True humanity follows the godly line of Seth, the true representatives of what Adam and Eve were supposed to be—the true children of God. As we shall see, they

Seth also had a son, and he named him Enosh. At that time men began to call on the name of the LORD. [Gen. 4:26]

are called "sons of God." True humanity exists in covenant with God.

True history is linked, not with the *City of Man*, but with the *City of God*. The chronology of life follows the line of Seth, not the line of Cain. Not the ungodly but the godly influence history through their preaching and prayers. The godly father of Noah prayed that God would deliver the world from the wicked and prophesied that in Noah's time it would come to pass (5:29). The godly Enoch, who like Lamech was seventh from Adam, preached righteousness to an ungodly generation and was rewarded by escaping death.

Coram Deo

Cain's physical line suddenly was overtaken by the judgment of God, but the culture of Cain survived the flood and burdens us still. What encouragement do you find as you face the culture of Cain today? Read Jude 14–15 to find a capsule of Enoch's preaching. Where do we find preaching like this today?

For further study: 1 Corinthians 1:18–2:5

43 The Sin of Intermarriage

enesis 6:1–4 is an enigmatic passage. Bizarre interpretations have been offered for its references to intermarriage of the "sons of God" with the "daughters of men," and their connection to the Nephilim, the "heroes of old." Some have suggested that *sons of God* refers to angels in Job 1 and 2, so this passage records that fallen angels intermarried with or raped human women and gave birth to giants.

There are two basic problems with this. First, Jesus said that angels do not marry, certainly implying that they do not cohabit with human beings (Matt. 22:30). Second, this interpretation has nothing to do with the context of this event. A similar interpretation says that the sons of God were demon-possessed men. A third view notes that *sons of God* is sometimes used of human rulers and says that powerful tyrants seized helpless women for harems. These interpretations also fail to take the context into account.

Genesis 4 and 5 prepare us for the tragedy described in Genesis 6. Genesis 4 presents the genealogy of the ungodly line of Cain, while Genesis 5 records the godly line of Seth. We are about to see that the whole earth has become corrupt and God is going to wash it clean with a universal flood. But whatever happened to the godly line of Seth?

The answer is in Genesis 6:1–4. The Sethites fell into the

The sons of God saw that the daughters of men were beautiful, and they married any of them they chose. [Gen. 6:2]

grave sin of intermarriage. These "sons of God," who had inherited all the privileges and ethical strengths of a righteous heritage, gave away that strength. As Eve saw that the fruit was fair and seized it unlawfully, so the Sethites took forbidden fruit on the basis of external beauty. The children who resulted from these forbidden marriages assumed the sinful dispositions, actions, and goals of Cain and Lamech, and they plunged the world into moral chaos and destruction. Such is normally the end result of such marriages.

Coram Deo

Being unequally yoked has primary implication for marriage, although it is not surprising to see similar problems result in business and other partnerships. With marriage the Scriptures clearly prohibit marriage to a non-Christian. However, if you find yourself in such a union, take heart. God's grace extends to those in mixed marriages and partnerships. Unbelieving mates do occasionally come to Christ, but God doesn't promise to take away the heartache or eliminate the consequences. If you are in that situation, live the faith.

For further study: Judges 16; 1 Kings 11; Ezra 9–10; Nehemiah 13:23–28

We have carefully studied the Creation accounts and the fall of humanity as they are found in Genesis 1–5. This was, of course, necessary in order to lay a proper theological foundation for the remainder of our study. What two themes could be of greater importance than the doctrines of God and of humanity? Part 3 will cover Genesis chapters 6–50. Obviously, at such a pace most of our studies will be broad brush overviews of this action and implication filled narrative.

As we survey the chronicle of Noah and the flood, followed by the patriarchal narratives, we can look beyond the familiar events to their larger significance. Following the flood sin once again expanded through the human race with devastating effects. Grace also expanded right along side it. Observe how God faithfully continued to affirm his covenant with Abraham and his descendants.

Finally, take note of the humanness of the subjects. Far from being a sanctified lot, in Genesis we are confronted by earthy people living in the real world. It becomes easy to see that God did not pick out a sophisticated or superior family in Abraham, Isaac, and Jacob. Quite the oppo-

Noah, the Flood, and the Patriarchs

site. They are set apart more by their perverseness and violence. Paul in 1 Corinthians sets all Christians in our proper place of humility and awe at God's love: "But God chose the foolish things of the world to shame the wise; God chose the weak things of the world to shame the strong. He chose the lowly things of this world and the despised things—and the things that are not— to nullify the things that are, so that no one may boast before him" (1:27–29). The people in Genesis certainly prove the truth of what Paul said. So do the lives of Christians now.

As you study, ask God to open the eyes of your heart to bring new understanding of his Word and his plan. You will be reminded of how the providential love and power of God works even in the rebellion of God's enemies to do exactly what he wants. Strive to go beyond simply acquiring such new knowledge. The implications of the Scriptures we will look at are immense, both to make us far more aware of our failings and of God's ability. Seek to apply what you learn to more faithful, confident life, to live *coram Deo*, before God and for his glory.

R. C. Sproul

44 A Local or Universal Flood?

as Noah's flood local or universal? Those who maintain that the flood was a local event do so from their interpretation of geology. There is insufficient evidence, they maintain, to support the idea that the entire globe was washed with water only a few thousand years ago, so we should read the biblical story of the flood carefully to see whether it really teaches a worldwide flood.

The Bible sometimes uses universal terms that are not necessarily all-inclusive. Words such as *all, every,* and *world* do not mean in Hebrew and Greek exactly what they mean in English. When Acts 2:5 says Jews from every nation under heaven were in Jerusalem, we need not understand this to mean that Jews from North and South America and from every nation and tribe of people living in Australia. Perhaps the universal language used in connection with the flood simply means that all the *known* world was flooded.

The Bible makes it clear that all of humanity died, so a flood would mean humanity had not spread very far since the time of Adam—and this is exactly what some advocates of the local flood theory propose.

Nevertheless, if we did not bring geological evidence

> They rose greatly on the earth, and all the high mountains under the entire heavens were covered. The waters rose and covered the mountains to a depth of more than twenty feet. [Gen. 7:19–20]

into the question, there would be little reason to interpret the text as meaning anything other than a universal flood. In Genesis 7:17–8:5, reference to a local flood is unlikely. Forty days of rain is more than a local flood. Covering the mountains requires more than a local flood. Waters covering the earth 150 days requires more than a local flood. The ark resting on a very high mountain (Ararat) requires more than a local flood. The universal language piles up in these verses.

Some scientists argue that the geological evidence, properly understood, supports a universal flood. This is doubtless a matter that will be much debated for many years to come.

Coram Deo

The debate over creation science should concern every believer. God is not only the inerrant author of Scripture; he is also the founder of true science. If you have not done so, begin a study of these important issues so that you may give an answer for the faith and hope that you have.

For further study: Matthew 24:36–44; 2 Peter 3:1–18

45 The Significance of Water

God told Noah to build an ark, a box-like boat that would float through the earth's floodwaters, to preserve two of every species of land animal and bird, as well as Noah and his family. Reports have surfaced for centuries of such an object high on Mount Ararat in Armenia. In recent years expeditions have tried to reach it. Political instability in the region and an unfriendly climate have stymied such efforts, and evidence so far collected is inconclusive. Whether remains of the ark survive, the record of the Bible is trustworthy. Noah and his descendants may even have dismantled the ark for other building projects.

The flood was an *ordeal* or test by water. In the Bible, passing through water is often a trial of a person's standing with God. The floodwaters killed almost all people, but buoyed up the ark and saved Noah and his family. Similarly, the waters of the Red Sea divided to allow Moses and the Israelites to pass through, but drowned Pharaoh's army.

It is interesting to notice that the Israelites were sprinkled by rain from God as they walked dry-shod through the Red Sea (Ps. 77:16–20). It seems there was a choice: be drowned by too much water, or receive a token drowning by being sprinkled with water from heaven.

The waters flooded the earth for a hundred and fifty days.
[Gen. 7:24]

God said the flood would "wipe" the earth (Gen. 6:7; 7:4, 23)—It would be cleansed and given a new start by water. Similarly, in the Levitical system ceremonial uncleanness—symbolic death—was cleansed by the sprinkling of water, an act that symbolized resurrection and the opening of a new life (Lev. 11:40; 15:5–12; John 3:5). Jews who were guilty of serious defilements were cleansed by sprinkling with water that had the ashes of a sacrificial heifer mixed in it (Num. 19:11–22; see Lev. 14:7). This water applied the death of a substitute, cleansing the sinner. These water ordeals relate to the meaning of baptism, the rite by which we pass into the kingdom.

Coram Deo

Water as a symbol conveys the meaning of God's cleansing and salvation. Be careful that your faith is not wrapped up in the externals of the faith, but rather in the God who is signified by the water. Think through the realities behind the symbols of baptism. How do each of the persons of the Godhead contribute to the cleansing of the soul from sin?

For further study: 1 Peter 3:13–22

46 The Noahic Covenant

After the flood, Noah brought a sacrifice of every clean animal to God. On the basis of that sacrifice, pointing to the future death of the Son of God for our sins, God reestablished his covenant with Noah, promising never again to destroy the world by water, even though humankind would continue to be sinful (Gen. 8:20–22).

God reiterated the original Adamic covenant to Noah, but made some additional responsibilities and privileges. First, God gave Noah permission to eat meat, just as he had given Adam permission to eat vegetation. Second, just as God had forbidden Adam to eat of one tree, so God forbade Noah to drink blood, a prohibition reiterated in the new covenant (Gen. 9:3–6; Acts 15:29).

People were permitted to shed the blood of animals, but not of other people. God told Noah that, from this time forth, those who shed the blood of another were to be put to death. In Hebrew, "shedding blood" should not be taken in the literal sense, in which a cut finger would be a form of shedding blood. The term is an idiom for killing, just as the "blood of Jesus Christ" refers to his death, not to his literal blood. Jesus actually did not bleed very much on the cross, and he did not die by bleeding to death but by giving up his own spirit.

"Whoever sheds the blood of man, by man shall his blood be shed; for in the image of God has God made man." [Gen. 9:6]

The Noahic covenant also shows the biblical basis for civil government. The magistrate has the authority and the duty to exercise capital punishment against murderers. Capital punishment is controversial with some Christians, because God places such a great premium on human life. The Bible makes it clear, however, that it is precisely because human life is so valuable that killing a human being can only be punished by death. Man is the image of God, and murder is an attempt to kill God by killing his image. God takes such action seriously and requires that we do as well.

Coram Deo

More than a dozen capital crimes were in the Law given at Mount Sinai. Capital punishment continues to be a matter of great debate in the United States. Watch for news reports covering this issue. Seek to discern the reasoning behind the arguments in comparison to what God says on the issue. Which reasoning guides your thinking?

For further study: Exodus 21:12–19; Numbers 35:16–32; Romans 13:1–7

47　Noah's Nakedness

After the flood the world started up anew. Just as we find God planting a garden after the creation of the world, so Noah, the image of God, planted a vineyard after the flood. Just as God's first created son, Adam, rebelled against him in the garden, so Noah's son Ham rebelled against him in the vineyard. Even as God passed judgment on Adam, so Noah passed judgment on Ham. This elevation of humanity to new authority is a result, as we have seen, of the Noahic covenant (Gen. 9:1–17).

There is one crucial difference between the two stories, however: God gave Adam no occasion to sin, while Noah got drunk. How drunk he was and whether this was an accident, we do not know. We do know that he uncovered himself in his inebriation in the privacy of his tent. His son Ham came into the tent and, instead of concealing his father's condition, he gleefully reported it to his two brothers, exposing his father to shame. Shem and Japheth put a cloak on their shoulders and walked backward into the tent, covering their father without looking at him.

Some have felt that Ham's sin must have been more than merely looking at his father and ridiculing him. There is nothing in the text to support this speculation. Whatever Ham did was countered by the actions of Shem and Japheth, and all they did was cover their father back up.

108

> Noah, a man of the soil, proceeded to plant a vineyard. When he drank some of its wine, he became drunk and lay uncovered inside his tent. [Gen. 9:20–21]

Adam and Eve had been created naked and not ashamed, but because of sin, their sense of shame and guilt had caused them to be uncomfortable with nakedness. We call the place on the body where shame is most concentrated our "private parts," and at this place male circumcision was performed, indicating the judgment of sin. God had given Adam and Eve clothing as a sign of his gospel, a promise that he would clothe them in righteousness through the work of his coming Messiah. To strip such clothing off a man or woman in ridicule brings shame on the image of God and receives severe condemnation in the Bible, as Ham discovered.

Coram Deo

When two believers are married they, because of the forgiveness of their sins, are blessed with the opportunity of experiencing a deeper intimacy with one another. Then nakedness and sexuality do not bring the guilt and shame that nonbelievers experience. If you know the liberating joys of a truly Christian marriage, thank God for the beauty of your sexual relationship.

For further study: Genesis 19:30–38; 2 Corinthians 5:1–10

109

48 The Tower of Babel

Adam fell in the garden, and his son Cain went out and built the City of Man in defiance of God (Gen. 4:17). Similarly, Ham fell in Noah's vineyard, and Ham's descendent Nimrod built two great cities in defiance of God, Babylon (Babel) and Nineveh (Gen. 10:8–12). God permitted Cain's sin to permeate the earth until the flood; but God promised never again to curse the creation in future judgments against humankind because of the evil intents of their hearts (Gen. 8:21). When next he acted in judgment God broke up the ungodly civilization of Nimrod after the flood.

In Genesis 11 the people were united in language and belief. They set about to build a city for themselves, with a tower in the middle that would "reach to heaven": a religious center for their anti-God faith. They hardly reached heaven; rather, God had to "come down" to see their puny tower. God declared that a unified humanity would have such great power that "nothing they plan to do will be impossible for them." To prevent evil from developing to its pre-flood strength, God rent their work simply by confounding their speech. Finding they could not understand one another, they had to abort the tower project.

Babel teaches several lessons: First, attempts to create

> That is why it was called Babel—because there the Lord confused the language of the whole world. From there the Lord scattered them over the face of the whole earth. [Gen. 11:9]

a one-world language are doomed to failure, as are attempts to found a one-world humanist state. Second, God intends humanity to exist in nations and have languages and cultures, each uniquely and beautifully reflecting his image and glory.

Third, while God frustrates the attempts of the wicked to achieve unity, he desires that Christians act in unity. Jesus prays for the unity of believers, and when we act as one, nothing we legitimately desire will be withheld (John 17:22–23). Finally, as a sign of the unity of God's kingdom, God transformed the Babelic judgment into a blessing on Pentecost by enabling people to understand one another's languages (Acts 2:5–12).

Coram Deo

Although the confusing of languages at Babel was a judgment of sorts, God used that judgment for his own glory, for humankind now praise God with a thousand tongues. Think today about what it will be like in the kingdom to praise God with all the tongues of the world. Strive to praise God as artfully and gloriously as possible.

For further study: Psalm 55:9–11; Acts 2:1–13

111

49 Historical Narratives

M uch of the Old Testament consists of historical narratives, so before we plunge into the lives of the Hebrew patriarchs, let us consider three rules to bear in mind. The first rule is that *one portion of Scripture is not to be set against another.* Its corollary holds that historical narratives must be interpreted by didactic (teaching) portions of Scripture. If we look merely at Jesus' crucifixion as recorded in the Gospels, we see a man dying on a cross. Other passages, especially in the Epistles, explain the *meaning* of this event.

The second rule is that *we are not to draw conclusions from historical narratives in isolation from the rest of Scripture.* If we consider Genesis 22:1–19 by itself we might conclude that God was up in heaven waiting to see whether Abraham would obey him or not. The rest of the Bible, however, makes it clear that God is omniscient. He had no need to check out whether Abraham feared him or not. The purpose of the events in Genesis 22 was to teach Abraham (and us) the nature of true faith.

The third rule is that *we should not imitate Bible heroes in all things.* Frequently the Bible tells us what happened without stopping to tell us whether it was right. Sarah of-

112

> "Do not lay a hand on the boy," he said. "Do not do anything to him. Now I know that you fear God, because you have not withheld from me your son, your only son." [Gen. 22:12]

fered her maid Hagar to Abraham as a surrogate mother, and Abraham slept with Hagar. The Genesis 16 record does not tell us whether these acts were right or wrong. Biblical silence on this issue is not an endorsement, for other places make it clear that monogamy is God's rule (Prov. 5:18–19; Mal. 2:14–15). Later events in the lives of Abraham and Sarah show that they should have trusted God and waited for him to provide them a child.

Imitating biblical heroes is good when we follow their praiseworthy acts, but we must avoid those things that God calls sinful in other passages of Scripture.

Coram Deo

Often we divorce the narratives of the Old and New Testaments from Scripture that clearly teaches. As we study the familiar stories of the Israelites, strive to keep these rules in mind. See the narratives as exemplars (positive and negative). Challenge yourself to mentally cross-reference teaching passages with the narratives you read.

For further study: Romans 4:18–25; James 2:18–24

113

50 Abram: Pro and Con

Genesis 12–13 records Abram's entry into the land of promise and his first years there. It is often remarked that Abram's willingness to leave his life as a nobleman in Ur and Haran indicates great faith. We can see from how Pharaoh and others treated Abram that he was powerful and impressive on the international scene. But he willingly obeyed God and moved to a place where he would dwell in tents and never be able to settle down permanently.

The first thing Abram did in the land was to build altars (12:7–8; 13:18). Abram began the conquest of Canaan by establishing true worship. These three key sites later became important in Joshua's military conquest.

Now we read several questionable actions of Abram. They illustrate the point that the Bible narrative does not always clearly relate how to evaluate the actions of biblical heroes. Should Abram have gone to Egypt (12:10)? Some say, "No, Abram should have trusted God in the famine, and to look to Egypt was faithless." Others say, "But remember, Egypt had not yet been defined as a bad place to go, and God told Jacob to go there in the face of famine" (46:3).

Did Abram sinfully deceive Pharaoh (12:11–20)? Some say, "Yes, he did not tell the whole truth, and was rebuked for it." Others say, "But Sarah really was Abraham's sister (20:12), and the brother is the sister's protector." Whatever culpability Abraham may have in this incident, Pharaoh

> Now there was a famine in the land, and Abram went down to Egypt to live there for a while because the famine was severe. [Gen. 12:10]

should have negotiated with Abraham for Sarah. When Pharaoh simply took her it was attempted rape. This seems to be how God viewed the matter, for it was Pharaoh, not Abram, who was plagued by God. Abram was blessed with spoil.

Should Lot have picked the best land (13:8–12)? Again, some say, "No, Lot should have allowed Abram as leader to do the picking, or picked second best." Others say, "But the best way for Lot to honor Abram was to obey him and to honor Abram's generosity by picking what he really wanted." Whether these were wise choices, God continued to lead Abram in such a manner as to fulfil all promises made to the patriarch.

Coram Deo

We must continually remember that the Bible records God's sovereignty in action. The focus in these stories is not on personal morality, but on the acts of God to bring in his kingdom. Can we really know the hearts of Abram and Lot? Can we truly even know our own (Jer. 17:9)? The admitted difficulty of reading their hearts should force us to grapple with our own motivations and actions.

For further study: Psalm 105; Jeremiah 17:9; Romans 8:27

51 Abram's Worthy Allies

Genesis 14 tells the story of the war of the four kings against the five kings. For twelve years the kings of the five cities in the Jordan Circle (now under the Dead Sea) were vassals of Kedorlaomer, an Elamite descendent of Shem (Gen. 10:22). From the Genesis 10–11 backgrounds of Kedorlaomer and his associates we see the beginning of the fulfillment of Noah's curse that the Canaanites would serve the Shemites, the Japhethites, and the other Hamites.

In the thirteenth year the kings of Sodom, Gomorrah, Admah, Zeboiim, and Bela rebelled, and Kedorlaomer moved in to stop the revolt. Evidently the five kings of the Jordan Circle dominated all of Canaan, because Kedorlaomer thoroughly trounced the various tribes in the whole land. These battles (Gen. 14:5–11) do not seem relevant until we realize that Israel would encounter the same locations centuries later. Israel would be afraid of these people, forgetting that Shemites had always been victorious over Canaanites.

Kedorlaomer made a strategic error: He took Lot prisoner. Abram, the true possessor of the land, gathered a small army and pursued Kedorlaomer. He defeated Kedorlaomer and brought Lot back home. Abram met two kings upon his return. The wicked king of Sodom was

The king of Sodom said to Abram, "Give me the people and keep the goods for yourself." [Gen. 14:21]

grateful to Abram and wanted to buy his favor by offering the spoils of the war. He wanted powerful Abram on his side, but Abram refused to make an alliance with him and took nothing except a tithe for the other king.

The other king was Melchizedek. This man also offered a covenant with Abram, bringing him bread and wine as signs and seals. He was a faithful Gentile (Noahic) believer and blessed the God of Abram using the Gentile name: *God Most High*, Creator of heaven and earth. Abram gladly allied with this great man, and paid him tithes of all the spoil. It was in his priestly lineage that Jesus is portrayed in the Book of Hebrews.

Coram Deo

If Abram only allied with fellow believers, does that challenge you in your allegiances: personal, business, or recreational? Just how closely should we be tied to non-believers? Consider your associations and speak with other believers about this important subject. Strive to deepen those relationships with others in the body of Christ.

For further study: Ecclesiastes 4:7–12; 2 Corinthians 6:14–18

52 Who Was Melchizedek?

The book of Genesis is full of genealogies. Therefore, it is unusual that Melchizedek appears on the scene with no genealogy or background. Some have thought that this mysterious man was Shem, the son of Noah, who was still alive if we take the chronology of Genesis 11:11–32 strictly. Some have thought him an angel, or an appearance of the Second Person of the Trinity—though he served a city as a king year after year, so this particular identification is unlikely.

The author of Hebrews observes that, since this man has no official genealogy, he must have received his priesthood directly from God and not by inheritance. This, says the author of Hebrews, makes him a *type* or *foreshadowing* of Jesus Christ (Heb. 7:1–3).

Hebrews also spotlights the fact that Melchizedek's city was Salem, later the site of Jerusalem. This must have been how David knew that Jerusalem was to be the capital. The word *Salem* means "peace," so this man was "King of Peace." Similarly, *Melchizedek* means "King of Righteousness." In these two respects Melchizedek is also a type of Christ. Establishing peace with God was his priestly work and promoting righteous government his kingly duty.

> This Melchizedek was king of Salem and priest of God Most High. He met Abraham returning from the defeat of the kings and blessed him. [Heb. 7:1]

Hebrews then speaks of how Abraham, the father of the faithful and the model of believers, related to Melchizedek (Heb. 7:4–10). Abraham allowed Melchizedek to bless him, submitting to his priestly authority. The sign of this blessing was the bread and wine that Melchizedek bestowed on Abraham. Abraham also paid Melchizedek a tithe, indicating his submission.

The point Hebrews makes to the Jews is this: The Mosaic priesthood and the Davidic kingship descended from Abraham, and thus were inferior to that of Melchizedek. Now that the greater Melchizedek had come, the lesser Aaronic and Davidic forms could pass away.

Coram Deo

Abraham immediately paid a tithe to Melchizedek, a mere shadow of the true king of righteousness, Jesus Christ. Yet only about 4 percent of professing Christians tithe. The greater Melchizedek has come. Be certain that you are found faithful, both in submitting to his priestly authority and in giving a tithe to the King.

For further study: Psalm 110; 2 Corinthians 9:6–9; Hebrews 7:1–28

53 Covenant with Abraham

God's initial proclamation of the Abrahamic Covenant promise to Abram is found in Genesis 12:1–3. God reiterated that promise after Abram's exodus from Egypt in Genesis 13:14–17. After Abram's defeat of Kedorlaomer, God appeared to him and actually "cut the covenant" with him in a vision (Gen. 15). Later God told Abram to use the rite of circumcision as a permanent memorial to the covenant and as a way of reiterating it generation after generation. He also changed Abram's name to *Abraham* (Gen. 17:5). God reiterated the covenant one last time to Abraham in Genesis 22:15–18, after Abraham had offered Isaac to God.

The two key passages are Genesis 15 and 17. In both we see that covenants are "cut" and involved death. The amazing story found in Genesis 15 shows that God's promise to Abraham is so secure that only if God himself can be killed and torn in half will it be broken. God's glory passed between the halved carcasses of sacrificial animals. By doing this God said, "May I be ripped in half like these animals if I break this covenant with Abraham."

What if Abraham broke the covenant? Then Abraham would deserve to be torn in half. He would deserve to be sacrificed, undergoing the curse of the covenant. God made

> "This is my covenant with you and your descendants after you, the covenant you are to keep: Every male among you shall be circumcised." [Gen. 17:10]

this clear in Genesis 17 with the rite of circumcision. Circumcision cuts a man in half symbolically, separating him from his foreskin. Circumcision has two sides. It promises that man will only suffer a little because someone else will take the greater punishment. Yet it forewarns that a covenant breaker will suffer the total punishment of the curse.

The blessing of circumcision is implied in the fact that the foreskin, rather than a finger or a toe, is cut off. This points to procreation and generation, to the Seed, the Son who is to come. It is he who will be "fully circumcised" in death for our sins. That is why, as a last sign of the nature of the covenant, God told Abraham to sacrifice his son Isaac and thus foreshadow the cross of Christ.

Coram Deo

Moral, civil, and ceremonial law results from God's cutting of covenants with humankind. As you continue to read through the Scriptures, recognize that the Deuteronomy laws were enacted by God in his covenant with Moses and Israel. Which in this reading are still operative in the new covenant? Why?

For further study: Deuteronomy 30:1–10; Romans 2:17–29

54 Living by Covenant

S

ince God's relationship with humanity is by covenant, deep human relationships may also be covenantal. In Malachi 2:14 marriage is called a covenant. When I worked more frequently with college students, I often was asked why marriage is necessary. "Why can't we just agree to be faithful to each other and live together? Why do we have to be licensed and go through some ceremony before a judge or preacher?" This question arises because people are no longer familiar with the nature of covenants.

Covenants establish relationships publicly and create accountability. If two people are simply living together, either partner may abandon the other without accountability. The covenant involves a promise to obey God and to be faithful—and also involves a curse: May God judge me if I break this pledge. People avoid the covenant of marriage because they want to have irresponsible relationships, but such relationships are hazardous to human life. God has created us so that we blossom as human beings when we conform to God's covenantal structures. When we live irresponsibly, we destroy ourselves and others.

Joining a local church is also a form of covenant-making. We stand before the congregation and pledge in the

> "The Lord is acting as the witness between you and the wife of your youth, because you have broken faith with her, though she is your partner, the wife of your marriage covenant." [Mal. 2:14]

sight of God to work for the peace and the purity of his church. The congregation pledges to assist us and to receive us as members. This kind of covenanting makes specific the covenant God made with us at baptism. It makes us accountable to leaders in a particular local church, something God requires (Heb. 13:17). That many Christians refuse to join the church shows irresponsibility and immaturity.

At the same time, all human covenants are subordinate to God's covenant. A sad factor due to sin is that a church or a marriage may become so corrupt that the relationship has to be resolved. But even in these circumstances biblical guidelines give direction as to why and how this should be done.

Coram Deo

Living by covenants is God's method to anchor our lives and provide security against the prevailing cultural disintegration. Ask your pastor to consider teaching on the rewarding difference covenant faithfulness brings to all of life.

For further study: Deuteronomy 28:1–29:1

55 Sodom and Gomorrah

enesis 18–19 contains one story with two halves. Abraham looked up one day and saw three "men" walking toward him. We are told that one was the Lord himself, and we see later that the other two were angels. The Lord told Abraham that in a year he would have a son by his wife Sarah. Sarah laughed, saying to herself that she was too old to have a child. God heard it and told her to name her son Isaac, which means in Hebrew "he laughs."

On this same occasion God also announced that he was about to destroy Sodom and Gomorrah. Here we see again the two-edged nature of God's dealings with humanity. He saves some, granting them joy, but he pours out his wrath on the impenitent. Abraham knew that Lot was living in Sodom and humbly asked God to spare the city for the sake of the righteous within it. God promised not to destroy the city if there were even ten faithful inhabitants.

The two angels that accompanied God walked off to Sodom. As they entered the city, they were approached by Lot, who was sitting in the gate, acting as a judge, because the gate was where the elders sat. Lot knew that the city was full of homosexual rapists and invited them to stay the night in the security of his home. Sure enough, a gang

> [Abraham] looked down toward Sodom and Gomorrah, toward all the land of the plain, and he saw dense smoke rising from the land, like smoke from a furnace. [Gen. 19:28; compare Gen. 15:17 and Exod. 19:18]

of sodomites tried to attack the men that very evening, but the angels blinded them and went away.

The angels ordered Lot and his family to escape the impending judgment. Even though he believed them, Lot was so indecisive that the angels had to grab him by the hand and pull him and his family from the city. Lot's wife disobeyed the command not to look back and became a pillar of salt. The angels encouraged Lot to go to Abraham's mountain, but he instead lived out his life in a cave (compare Gen. 3:19), drinking away his sorrows and was seduced by his own daughters. His descendants were the Ammonites and Moabites, enemies of God who perpetuated the ways and culture of Sodom.

Coram Deo

Lot made a series of compromises. He moved near Sodom and finally moved into the city and became a dignitary there. What good did it do him? Today in your prayers ask God to show you any places where you may be moving toward Sodom. If you are moving in such a direction ask God to reorient you toward Christ and his righteousness.

For further study: Ezekiel 16:44–63; Matthew 11:20–24

56 Abraham and Isaac

braham's sacrifice of Isaac reaches out to us on several levels. Most Christians rightly see in the account the primary point that all men and women, and their sons and daughters, are under God's death penalty for sin. God, however, makes a way to avoid his sentence of death by providing a substitute, a ram in the place of Isaac. By implication, Christians see that God sent his beloved only Son in the place of Abraham's beloved only son (Gen. 22:2).

Now let us focus attention on the human dynamics of this story. The Danish philosopher Søren Kierkegaard in his book *Fear and Trembling* asks why Abraham arose early in the morning to carry out this task. Surely any normal human being would be reluctant to kill his beloved child, and it is hardly realistic to say that Abraham burst from his bed full of joy at the thought of his privilege to obey God on this occasion. Kierkegaard concludes that Abraham got up early because in his anxiety he could not sleep.

Abraham chopped the wood himself instead of having a servant do it. He was working off steam and tension, every violent stroke of the ax squeezing out tears from his eyes. Finally Abraham got into a frame of mind in which he could carry out God's awful order. On the way up the mountain, Isaac said, "We have wood and fire and knife,

> "Early the next morning Abraham got up and saddled his donkey. He took with him two of his servants and his son Isaac. When he had cut enough wood for the burnt offering, he set out for the place God had told him about." [Gen. 22:3]

but where's the lamb?" At that moment the knife was in Abraham's heart.

Isaac was a young man old enough to carry the wood on his shoulders up the mountain. This is no small boy that could be bound and placed upon the altar against his will by an old man. He soon figured out what was going on, yet instead of fighting off his father and running away, he allowed himself to be tied to the altar. What was going on in his heart as his father raised the knife to kill him?

The Son of Man also could have bypassed his death. He was bound, tied to a tree and saw his Father in heaven raise his knife at Calvary. In that instance, no angel commanded God to stop. That sacrifice was finished; the Lord had provided for his people.

Coram Deo

Abraham demonstrated true courage, acting in the face of real fear. Without fear there is no courage. The true Christian is called not to have no fears, but to be faithful in the face of those fears. What are the fears in your life? Do they keep you from placing yourself on the altar of sacrifice (Rom. 12:1)? Do not hide your fear; rather, be encouraged by the Spirit.

For further study: Romans 4:1–25; Hebrews 11:11–19

57 Water: A Symbol of Grace

Genesis 2 calls attention to the well of water that sprang up in Eden and became four rivers that went, figuratively speaking, to the four corners of the earth. Throughout the Bible water is frequently a symbol of God's grace and provision. In the last chapter of the Bible, the water of life is seen flowing from the throne of the Lamb to provide life to all nations (Rev. 22:1–2).

We saw (p. 114) that Abraham built altars everywhere he went as a sign of his ministry to the unconverted. The image of Isaac's ministry is the well. At the beginning of Genesis 26 we read of another famine in the land. Under God's guidance (v. 3) Isaac took his family to Gerar for safety. The people there were undisciplined, and Isaac feared them. As had Abraham, Isaac told that Rebekah was his sister, but the truth soon emerged that she was his wife (though his sister by adoption, Gen. 24:59–60).

God blessed Isaac in Gerar, and soon those who lived there ordered him to move on. "You are too powerful for us," they said (vv. 12–16). So Isaac moved to the Valley of Gerar and dug a well, but the inhabitants took it away from him (vv. 17–20). He moved on and dug another well, but they quarreled over it too (v. 21). Finally he moved to Rehoboth and dug a well, and they left him alone (v. 22).

> Then they dug another well, but they quarreled over that one also; so he named it Sitnah. [Gen. 26:21]

At this well God appeared to Isaac. God reiterated the patriarchal covenant, and Isaac built an altar and established public worship (vv. 23–25). A little "garden of Eden" was restored. Then the king of Gerar, who had driven Isaac out, asked to make a covenant with him. Why? "We saw clearly that the LORD was with you." So Isaac made a covenant with them, including them in the extended family of the LORD, and feasted together. Then Isaac's servants reported that they had found yet another well. When persecuted, Isaac did not hit back. Instead he continued about this business of providing water. Eventually God changed the hearts of his adversaries, and many souls were saved.

Coram Deo

How do you plan to change the hearts of adversaries to the faith? Only God by his Spirit changes hearts, but he most often uses human means. Isaac's ministry was the well; by what means will you reach out to the lost? Ask God to give you the opportunity, love, and courage to "give away a well" and see lost souls come to him.

For further study: John 4:1–26; 7:38

58 Climbing Jacob's Ladder

J acob left the land of promise to spend time with his relatives in Mesopotamia. Isaac had sent him back there to get a wife. Esau had committed the sins of intermarriage and polygamy, and his wives made life miserable for Isaac and Rebekah (Gen. 26:34–35). Like the sons of God before the flood, Esau was unwilling to wait and married on the basis of his lusts.

On his way out of the land Jacob had a dream from God to assure that God would be with him, though he was leaving the land of promise. In his dream Jacob saw a stairway stretching from heaven to earth, with angels ascending and descending. He heard God promise that he would go with Jacob, and the vision of angels assured Jacob of angelic protection. When Jacob awoke, he said to himself, "God is here, too, not just at home. This place also is a house of God." The word in Hebrew for "house of God" is *Beth-El,* and as Jacob started on his journey, he stood outside the nearby city of Luz and renamed it Bethel, claiming it for God. Jacob also said, "This is the gate of heaven."

The first tower "to heaven" was the tower of Babel described in Genesis 11. *Babel* means "gate of heaven," and the tower was clearly to be a house of gods, a religious center. God struck down this counterfeit stairway to heaven.

God's own stairway is built from heaven down to earth.
Where we meet to worship God, there is the house of God,
and there is the gate of heaven, the place where the stairway touches the earth.

In John 1:51, Jesus told Nathaniel that he would see
heaven opened and angels ascending and descending on
the Son of Man. Here Jesus claimed to be the true tower
of Babel, the true gate of heaven. Jesus stated that he was
the point of mediation between earth and heaven, and
those who would come in contact with heaven would have
to ascend through him. Just as God promised to be with
Jacob in the strange land, so the true staircase to heaven
is with us always (Matt. 28:20–22).

Coram Deo

Jacob felt fear and awe when he realized that God
was with him. Can you identify with those feelings
from your times of worship? There is too much superficial lightness in the church today and too little
awe in the experience of worship. In your prayers ask
God to make you more aware of, and reverent toward,
his awesome presence.

For further study: Psalm 68; John 14:6; 1 Timothy 2:1–6

131

59 Joseph the Model Servant

J oseph is exhibited before us in Genesis as a model man. Though we can be sure Joseph sinned many times, as we all do, none of his sins are recorded for our instruction. We shall look at two aspects of Joseph's story: his model servanthood, and his suffering servanthood. Joseph is introduced as a model of faithfulness to his father. When he saw his older brothers abusing their responsibilities, he told his father. This faithfulness was rewarded, for Jacob came to favor Joseph and robed him with a special cloak that signified his special position in the family as his father's confidant (Gen. 37:2–3, 14).

His brothers hated him for this, and one day they seized him. They tore the robe that had so infuriated them and that symbolized his position over them. Then they sold him into slavery. In bondage, however, Joseph proved to be a valuable servant. So careful and hardworking was he that this master, Potiphar, put him in charge of his entire household.

Potiphar's wife tried to seduce Joseph, but he told her that it would be a sin against God, and also that her husband had entrusted the household to him and he was not going to abuse that trust. She falsely accused him of rape, but apparently Potiphar did not really believe her, because instead of putting Joseph to death he simply put him in his prison, where he was shortly elevated to the

Joseph found favor in his eyes and became his attendant. Potiphar put him in charge of his household, and he entrusted to his care everything he owned. [Gen. 39:4]

post of assistant warden (Gen. 39; see esp. 39:1 and 40:3–4). Faithful service meant two things for Joseph. First, it meant understanding and keeping God's laws; second, it meant careful and responsible obedience to the desires of the earthly authorities over him. But that faithful service had landed Joseph in slavery and then in prison. God, however, sees everything. God arranged for two of Pharaoh's servants to spend time in prison, where they discovered that Joseph was a man of excellent character and intimate acquaintance with God's Word. It took a while, but eventually this encounter led Joseph to stand before Pharaoh and to become viceroy of all Egypt (Gen. 40–41).

Coram Deo

Joseph trusted that the invisible, good hand of God's providence would reward his life of modeled integrity. Eventually he was honored by the God he honored, but it didn't happen until he endured great difficulty and pain. The faithfulness of Joseph was a patient faithfulness that trusted God before he could see ahead to the victory. Model Joseph's patience, trust, and integrity in a world that scorns such virtues.

For further study: Psalms 18:1–29; Matthew 25:14–30; Hebrews 12:1–3; James 1:2–4

60 The Suffering Servant

oseph was both a faithful and a suffering servant. As a matter of record, it was his faithfulness that brought about his suffering. His brothers hated him because he reported their sins. They hated the symbol of his responsibility, the robe his father had lavished upon him. They hated and rejected his dreams, which showed God's plan for them. Infuriated, they captured him and sought to kill him. Reuben, however, persuaded them to delay their plans, and after they had cooled down a bit, Judah came up with the idea of selling him into slavery.

As we have seen, Joseph's faithfulness in serving and his expertise in interpreting the Word of God (which came to him in dreams) brought him to the attention of Pharaoh. Joseph was exalted to viceroy of Egypt. In the providence of God there came a great famine over their entire world, and Jacob sent his remaining sons to Egypt to buy grain.

The brothers of Joseph came to Egypt and met with a strange and severe man who was in charge of all the grain. He accused them of being spies and interrogated them. They told him about their family and that they had a little brother at home. This was news to Joseph, because he had been sold into slavery before the birth of Benjamin.

> "Come now, let's kill him and throw him into one of these cisterns and say that a ferocious animal devoured him. Then we'll see what comes of his dreams." [Gen. 37:20]

The strange man told them that he would sell them grain, but only if one of them would stay behind under guard, and that they would have to bring their youngest brother along next time. Looking at one another, the guilty brothers said to themselves, "God is punishing us because we ignored Joseph's cries" (Gen. 42:21).

When the brothers returned with Benjamin, Joseph gave extra favors to him to see if the brothers would abuse him the way they had abused Joseph. Seeing that they had changed their ways, Joseph revealed himself and invited all of them to come to Egypt and live there (Gen. 43–45). Joseph had suffered much, but out of his suffering and faithfulness had come salvation for his people.

Coram Deo

When we find ourselves in trouble it is easy to conclude that we are suffering for the sake of righteousness. Sometimes, however, we suffer because we deserve to suffer. Ask God to help you discern the difference and to act in such a way that you suffer only for him, not because of sin.

For further study: Isaiah 52:13–53:12; Philippians 2:1–11; 1 Peter 2:18–25

61 The Providence of God

After the death of Jacob, Joseph's brothers feared Joseph would now wreak vengeance for what they had done to him years before. Joseph reassured them that all had been forgiven, and pointed out that in the providence of God, their evil acts had been turned to a good purpose.

Genesis shows that sin does not thwart God's purposes. God created this world with a positive destiny and fully intends to bring that destiny to pass. God is able to redeem humanity and work in such a way that positive results come even from evil actions. The fall of Adam did not change his purpose, nor was he thwarted by the universal wickedness of humanity before the flood.

The doctrine of divine providence comes from the Latin *provideo,* and means that God literally oversees everything. This means more than that God foresees and knows everything before it happens. It means God sees in order to superintend everything. Everything in space and time is fully before the view and administration of God.

That God sees everything we do is an uncomfortable truth. We want God to notice us when we are in distress, but we do not want him watching when we sin. In the Bible, however, providence focuses on the fact that God

"You intended to harm me, but God intended it for good to accomplish what is now being done, the saving of many lives." [Gen. 50:20]

sees for the purpose of working all things for our good. God's governing of history cannot be resisted or overthrown. People may rebel against God, but as Psalm 2 points out, God simply laughs at their efforts. No matter how much evil they plan, the rulers of the sons of Adam cannot bring them to pass to overthrow the King God has established. What is intended for evil God simply works so that it brings good in the end. When Joseph's brothers sought to eliminate him they advanced God's plan of redemption. Satan thought he had defeated God when Jesus was crucified, but he that sits in the heavens laughed: Satan had merely sealed his own doom.

Coram Deo

The same is true when Satan attacks the kingdom and its citizens today. Providence is more easily discerned in "hindsight." Think back on one or more times when life seemed totally out-of-control. Did God use those events in a special way? Offer prayer of praise for God's faithful providential care as you reflect upon his ordering of your life's affairs.

For further study: Genesis 45:1–11; Romans 8:28–39

137

62 Reuben's Terrible Sin

B efore he died, Jacob called his sons to pass on to them the blessings—and judgments—of the covenant God had instituted with Abraham and passed on to Isaac. It was customary in the old covenant, and formally legal in the Sinaitic law, for the firstborn son to receive a double portion of the inheritance, and to be the captain of his brethren (Deut. 21:15–17). Jacob calls attention to this as he speaks to his firstborn: "Reuben, you are my firstborn, my might, the first sign of my strength, excelling in honor, excelling in power" (Gen. 49:3).

What a statement this is. Reuben as firstborn excels in everything. How horrible, then, for this excellent son to fall into monstrous sin and pervert these great gifts. In Genesis this happens almost every time: the firstborn is set aside because of his sin, and a later son inherits because of his faithfulness. Ishmael is set aside in favor of Isaac. Esau is set aside in favor of Jacob. Cain is set aside in favor of Abel and then Seth. Adam, the most excellent of all men, possessing in his genes every strength of the human race, is set aside in favor of a second Adam.

Reuben's great sin, recounted briefly in Genesis 35:22, was incest. Before Sinai brother-sister incest was not forbidden, and Abraham in fact married his sister (as did

> "Turbulent as the waters, you will no longer excel, for you
> went up onto your father's bed, onto my couch and defiled it."
> [Gen. 49:4]

Adam's sons). By implication of Genesis 2:24, however, crossgenerational incest was forbidden from the beginning (see Gen. 19:30–38). Thus, under the Sinaitic covenant, crossgenerational incest carried the death penalty, while brother-sister incest did not (Leviticus 20:11–12, 17).

Reuben's sin of incest was a sin of seizing his father's role. In the ancient world, sleeping with your predecessor's concubines, or taking responsibility for them, signified that you had taken over his kingdom (see 2 Sam. 3:7–8; 16:22; 1 Kings 2:21–22). To do this while the father lived attacked his authority (Deut. 22:30; 27:20). Reuben would have inherited Jacob's realm, but because he was impatient and tried to seize it prematurely, he lost it altogether.

Coram Deo

The story of Reuben illustrates how easy it is for one sin to lead to another. At the root was Reuben's coveting of his father's authority and his concubines. Pray that the Spirit of God would give you an abiding sense of contentment that you would not be led into one sin followed by another.

For further study: Genesis 4:1–7; Hebrews 2:14–18; James 1:12–18

63 **Men of Violence**

R euben was disqualified to receive the blessing of
the firstborn. The next son in line was Simeon
and the third was Levi. Jacob in his oracle puts
them together with the word *brothers*. They were not simply siblings, but were two of a kind. Genesis 34 tells why
he disqualified them both. The sons of Jacob by Leah (including Simeon and Levi) had a sister named Dinah. It
was the particular duty of elder brothers to watch over
younger sisters. On one occasion Dinah's brothers failed.
She went to visit some local girls, and Shechem, a prince
of the area, seduced her. This was a forcible seduction, because the young man was so infatuated with her that he
lost control.

Shechem was honorable and wanted to marry her (contrast 2 Sam. 13:14–15). As was customary, Shechem and
his father negotiated with Dinah's brothers Simeon and
Levi for her hand, offering as a marriage gift anything
the brothers wanted. They asked Jacob and his family to
live with them and enjoy their land. And when Simeon
and Levi asked them to circumcise themselves and join
the covenant of the Lord, they gladly did so. Considering
the pain involved, these men were serious about making
things right and perhaps serious about converting to the
true religion.

Simeon and Levi were not honest in their negotiations,

> "Simeon and Levi are brothers—their swords are weapons of violence." [Gen. 49:5]

however. After Shechem's family had been circumcised and were still incapacitated in pain, they attacked and slaughtered every one of them. This scandal made Jacob (and God) stink in the nostrils of all the people around them. God's witness was destroyed, and Jacob had to move away.

In the ancient world justice often was administered by and through patriarchal families. Modern equivalents of police, regulations, and judicial systems were not yet fully in place, especially in remote desert areas. The concept of justice was not absent even there, however, and it behooved people to act more honorably than did Simeon and Levi.

Coram Deo

While the worst sin of Simeon and Levi was the blasphemy of misusing the covenant sign, Jacob particularly curses them for their violence. Modern movies all too often glorify violence and vengeance. Read Romans 12:17–13:7. What do these verses say about this trend? Make a list of three principles outlining when violence is justified and when it is not. Seek to abide by those principles in both your actions and your thoughts.

For further study: Isaiah 60:15–22; Romans 12:17–13:7; 1 Timothy 3:1–3

64 The Blessing of Judah

L ike Reuben, Simeon, and Levi, Judah committed a horrible sin that could have disqualified
him from inheriting the blessing of the firstborn.
The events recorded in Genesis 38 show him to be unsta-
ble and untrustworthy. Also, Judah came up with the plan
to sell Joseph into slavery (Gen. 37:26–27). We find, however, that Jacob passes the rights of the firstborn to Judah.
Judah will be like a lion, the king of beasts, and thus will
rule his brothers. He will receive rich blessings, washing
his garments in the best of wine.

What accounts for this? In Genesis 43:9 we see Judah's
repentance. Unlike the older brothers, Judah changed his
ways. He had abused Joseph, but he offers his own life as
a ransom for Benjamin. He leads his brothers in repentance. Because of this change of heart he shows that he is
ready to be the ruler in the family.

Jacob tells Judah that the scepter of rule will not depart
from him until *Shiloh* comes (Gen. 49:10). This expression
is also translated "until he comes to whom it belongs" and
"until he comes to whom tribute belongs." We are not exactly sure of the precise meaning of the Hebrew term found
here. We can be sure, however, to whom it refers. The ruler's
staff will remain with Judah until someone comes, and
after that there will be no more successors in the tribe of

> "Judah your brothers will praise you; your hand will be on the neck of your enemies; your father's sons will bow down to you."
> [Gen. 49:8]

Judah to bear the crown. In time a son of Judah and of Judah's descendant David, will come to the throne, but this son will have no successors. The Greater Judah will reign forever over all the nations.

The blessing is not only rulership but also prosperity (v. 11). As the sign of Melchizedek's reign was bread and wine, so the sign of Judah's blessing is wine. So huge will be Judah's vines that it will be possible to tether a donkey to them, and the donkey will not be able to pull away. So plentiful will be the harvest that the price of wine will fall to the point where wine will be used for washing clothes. As the reign of the son of Judah will extend to all nations, so will his wine.

Coram Deo

Christ *before his death* (in the upper room), *in his death* (with the repentant thief and believing centurion), and *by his death* (for his brothers and sisters of faith) lavished blessings upon his people. As you observe Christ's death, consider specific ways it has blessed you. Pray that this blessing will pass through the generations of your house.

For further study: Hosea 5:8–15; Revelation 5:1–10

The historical narratives of the Old Testament often seem dark pictures of human history hung before a brilliantly back-lit window—a view sundrenched by God's plan of redemption. Nowhere is this more true than when considering the exodus and Moses as an Old Testament type of the Messiah.

Moses, God's mediator extraordinaire, perfectly prepared and inserted into history in the fullness of God's time to save the enslaved . . . Israel, the weakest of all people, saved from the death angel . . . by blood spread upon the doorpost, top and sides in the sign of a cross . . . the baptism through the Red Sea . . . the voice of ethical holiness from the mountain . . . the brass serpent set upon a cross before the eyes of the dying that they might live . . . the water pouring from the rock. . . . It is impossible to avoid the atonement and resurrection in Exodus. Its symbols and shadows are ubiquitous.

Exodus and
the Plan of Redemption

So we approach these meditations with awe and excitement, the major events associated with God's plan of redemption that eventually culminated at the cross. In our study of Exodus we will look at some of the most important elements in the history of Israel. As you study, especially note God's intervention in time/space history as he begins to set his creation back on track. We will also examine God's call of Moses, God's revelation of his name and his characteristic holiness, and his intervening work to bring his people out of bondage. A series of studies on the Ten Commandments will be taken from John Gerstner's teaching cassette tape series "Handout Theology."

A life lived *coram Deo* seeks to recognize that all of life is lived in the sight of God. As you study this month, prayerfully ask God to show you more of himself in his Word.

R.C. Sproul

65 Moses the Mediator

he Book of Exodus begins with the enslavement of the Israelites by a new Pharaoh, probably after the overthrow of the dynasty of rulers who had accepted Israel into Egypt. This new dynasty did not regard the covenantal relationship that Joseph's Pharaoh had established with God's priestly nation. The Hebrew people were fulfilling God's command to be fruitful and multiply (Gen. 1:28), and their large numbers in the land of Goshen threatened Egyptian cultural stability. Thus, Pharaoh ordered the slaughter of all male Hebrew infants.

Moses' parents, however, quietly disobeyed the tyrant's command. They placed him in an ark (the same word used for Noah's ark) and hid him along the river from Pharaoh's killers. God saw to it that Moses was found by Pharaoh's daughter, who adopted him as her son. In this way, Moses was reared in the Egyptian court as an adopted member of the royal household.

When he was about forty years old, Moses saw an Egyptian taskmaster mercilessly beating a Hebrew slave. Moses intervened to save the oppressed man and slew the Egyptian. To Moses' surprise other Hebrews reacted against him and asked, "Who made you a ruler over us?" As a member of the royal household Moses might have had a right to do what he had done, but realizing that Pharaoh would

> When the child grew older, she took him to Pharaoh's daughter
> and he became her son. She named him Moses, saying, "I drew
> him out of the water." [Exod. 2:10]

be angry, he fled in fear. Arriving in the land of Midian, he came upon young women who were being abused by a gang of thugs. He fought off the oppressors, allowing the women to water their flocks.

We can see in these incidents two early pictures of Moses' ministry as a mediator. He would be used by God to destroy the Egyptian oppressors. Drawn from water, he would give water to God's people. He would defend the bride of God against her enemies and often would be rejected by his own people. In these ways Moses revealed to the people of the old covenant the nature of the messianic work that Jesus would accomplish for his people some 1500 years later.

Coram Deo

At Easter we celebrate the redemption wrought by Christ with the cross and his resurrection. Reflecting on that redemption, realize that the process of redemption that began with the promise in Gen. 3:15 took a great step forward with the work of Moses. As you study Exodus compare the mediatorial work of Moses with that of Jesus.

For further study: Deuteronomy 34:10–12; 1 Timothy 2:1–6;
Hebrews 3:1–6; 8:1–6; 9:15; 12:22–24

66 Moses the Meek

M oses meek? This man who attacked an Egyptian overseer and later took on a band of bullies? Certainly. Only a strong man can be meek because only a strong man can temper his strength and use it in a controlled way.

What does it mean to be meek in the Bible? It does not mean to be a Casper Milquetoast. Rather, it means to be *humble before God.* Moses was not weak because he was meek before God. He believed and obeyed God, even when it hurt. Hence, he became strong with God and strong with God's people.

Moses was forty when he fled Egypt. He lived a peaceful life for another forty years in Midian with one of Abraham's godly descendants (Gen. 25:2; Exod. 18:9–12). At eighty Moses was called out of leadership retirement by God to deliver the Hebrews from bondage. On that occasion Moses told God, "Lord, I'm not the man you want. I'm retired. Forty years ago I was ready to lead; but now I'm happy just being a shepherd. Please call somebody else" (Exod. 4:10–13).

God replied, "I will be with you." "God with us" is the literal meaning of *Immanuel,* and this was God's *Immanuel promise* to Moses. This should have been enough, but God gave Moses miraculous signs to perform before Pharaoh

> Now Moses was a very humble [meek] man, more humble than anyone else on the face of the earth [Num. 12:3]

(Exod. 4:1–8). Yet Moses remained reluctant. "I've lost my rhetorical skills," he said. "Surely there is someone more qualified to be your preacher" (Exod. 4:10). Then God said, "I made your mouth, and I will give you My words to say. I've no need for human oratory" (Exod. 4:11–12).

Though Moses was fearful and reluctant, he obeyed God. He became meek before the One who made him. He believed what God said, spoke what God told him to say, and did what God told him to do. That is what it meant for Moses to be meek and to function as a mediator for Israel. It is also what God requires of each of us today as we minister his Word and his ways to a lost and rebellious generation.

Coram Deo

God has empowered us with a greater tool than that he gave to Moses: the presence of Holy Spirit. If you are reluctant to say and do what God requires, take a closer, prayerful look at Exodus 3 and 4. What is the Word that God has given us and what continuing miraculous testimony has he placed at the heart of our worship? Where do we find God's marching orders for the new covenant?

For further study: Philippians 2:1–11; 1 Peter 5:1–7

67 Moses at the Burning Bush

One day while pasturing Jethro's flocks, Moses saw a bush burning on the side of a mountain. Amazed that the bush was not consumed, Moses investigated. There he heard the very voice of God command him to take off his shoes, because he was standing on holy ground.

What is holy ground? In the ultimate sense, holy ground is ground where God is. In a lesser sense, we have an awareness of "sacred space" in our feelings about our church buildings. Older people who grew up in a particular church may have strong feelings about the building because it houses their memories. Perhaps they were married there, a loved one's funeral service was held there, their children were baptized there, or they were converted there.

In a greater sense, "sacred space" is the environment around God. When we remember that the first human was made of soil we can understand why "holy ground" is seen ultimately as the company of human beings around God's throne. The church, considered as people, is holy ground in this higher sense. The great memorial in the church that we are called to remember is the Lord's Supper: *"Do this as my memorial."*

Before God called Moses to deliver the Hebrews he called him to holy ground, to the *Mountain of God* (Exod. 3:12). God said he had heard the cry of the Israelites and had seen

> "Do not come any closer," God said, "Take off your sandals, for the place where you are standing is holy ground." [Exod. 3:5]

the oppression inflicted on them by the Egyptians (3:9). God always sees both the sufferer and the oppressor, and when he redeems his people he also destroys their oppressors. Moses' first question to God was, "Who am I?" (3:11). In a sense, Moses did not know who he was until God told him. God named those who are to come on his holy ground, who are to join his holy multitude. God also named himself *Yahweh*, a contraction of "I AM WHO I AM."

God has given a new name to members of the new covenant: *Christians*. He has revealed for himself a new name as well: *Jesus*. We are now God's holy ground, and like Moses we must treat the holy ground of the church with care.

Coram Deo

The place we meet to worship is not inherently more holy than any other place—until it has been a transcendent threshold over which one stepped into God's presence. Once that has happened this space ought to be a place of anticipation, because here God has met with his people. With what sense of expectation and memory do you approach the presence of God as you enter into a place of corporate worship?

For further study: Isaiah 6:1–8; Jeremiah 1:4–10; 1 Peter 4:12–19

68 The Holiness of God

At the burning bush, Moses encountered God in his holiness and majesty. Here God announced his intention to redeem Israel from Egypt. The first purpose of their deliverance was not to provide the Hebrews with a nicer place to live, or even to set up a God honoring nation. First and foremost it was to worship God (Exod. 3:12, 18). Worship is our required response to the holiness of God and worship is our first act of obedience. Worship is where the kingdom of God starts, before it flows out into transformed families, businesses, and societies. Over the next several meditations we shall consider the holiness of God and our response of worship.

In Isaiah 6 we find the call of Isaiah to be God's prophet. The call came in the year King Uzziah died after a reign of over fifty years. The land was in consternation and God gave to Isaiah a vision of himself enthroned as the true, deathless, permanent King of Israel. Around God's throne were flaming angels, called "seraphim," who ceaselessly sang the words "holy, holy, holy."

In modern English, if we want to emphasize an idea we *italicize* or <u>underline</u> it. In ancient Hebrew the way to give emphasis was through repetition. When Jesus wanted to stress something, for instance, he would say "truly, truly," which in Hebrew was "*amēn, amēn*." The strongest form of repetition for emphasis was the threefold or triple repeti-

> "Holy, holy, holy is the L ᴏ ʀ ᴅ Almighty; the whole earth is full of his glory." [Isa. 6:3b]

tion. Only one of God's attributes is ever emphasized by such a triple repetition: his holiness (compare with Rev. 4:8). The angels do not sing "loving, loving, loving," or "sweet, sweet, sweet," or even "wrathful, wrathful, wrathful." The supreme attribute of God they celebrate is his holiness. How sad it is that so much of our modern worship is oriented toward good feelings and superficial gaiety, with little attention given to the awesome holiness of God. So overwhelming was the angelic confession of God's holiness that the very "doorposts and thresholds shook" (Isa. 6:4). If we are to see the kind of reformation in our day that shakes our foundations we must recover a sense of the holiness of God.

Coram Deo

While seraphs shield their eyes from the holiness of God, the Bible says we shall behold him as he really is. Read 1 John 2:28–3:3 and contemplate beholding God's holiness in heaven. If this were the moment of beholding what John describes, would you be confident and unashamed? What does the world not know about God that you do?

For further study: Exodus 15:1–19; Leviticus 19:1–2; 20:7, 26; 1 Peter 1:14–16; Revelation 4:1–11

153

69 Reacting to God's Holiness

I t was after Isaiah felt the presence of the glory of God filling the temple that he became a prophet. But that ordination to God's great work came through an experience of unimaginable pain, for when Isaiah experienced the holiness of God he likewise experienced the unholiness of Isaiah.

It is an interesting contrast that the children of Israel heard God's voice and cowered, pushing the mediator Moses ahead of them to deal with the Law-giver. Israel feared and ran from God's audience with them. Isaiah feared, and he worshiped and called down judgment upon himself.

The unrighteous person doesn't want the presence of holiness and desires to strip God of power and authority. The person refuses to acknowledge a holy God or to submit to his lordship.

The unrighteous cannot abide God; the righteous cannot abide himself or herself in God's presence. The righteous person finds God's holiness no less uncomfortable than does the unrighteous. It is traumatic for unholiness to encounter true divine holiness. But the trauma comes from a true appraisal of God and self.

After God spoke to Habakkuk (chap. 2) the prophet's response was, "I heard and my heart pounded, my lips quivered at the sound; decay crept into my bones, and my

> "Woe to me!" I cried. "I am ruined! For I am a man of unclean lips, and I live among a people of unclean lips, and my eyes have seen the King, the Lord Almighty." [Isa. 6:5]

legs trembled" (Hab. 3:16a). After Job heard God's voice, he said, "I despise myself and repent in dust and ashes" (Job 42:6).

Isaiah was as righteous a man as could be found in the year of King Uzziah's death. Yet he was molded as a prophet by three reactions to God's holiness. First, he cried out in terror: "Woe is me, for I am ruined." God can do something with those who know their need for cleansing. Second, he cried out of his need for forgiveness, realizing that it wasn't just outward sins but inner corruption that stained his lips. Third, he accepted the forgiveness and dedicated his cleansed life to whatever God called him to do.

Coram Deo

It is an awe inspiring thing to live *coram Deo*. One immediately knows when entering the presence of holiness that the status quo of life is gone forever. When you go before God's face in prayer, do you perceive his holiness? As your inflated view of self is diminished in his presence, be moved as was Isaiah, first to repentance, and then to self-sacrificing praise.

For further study: Exodus 33:12–23; Ezekiel 1:25–2:2; Habakkuk 2; Romans 11:33–12:2

70 A Just and Holy God

God moved into the tabernacle after it had been set up by Moses and Aaron in the wilderness (Exod. 40). God lit the altar fire in front of the tabernacle as a sign of his presence and of his holiness. The judgments rendered on the altar were God's judgments, so the fire was his fire (Lev. 9:24). Those set aside to be priests had to be especially careful, because God's holiness is a "consuming fire" (Heb. 12:29).

What belongs to God is not a toy for anyone's amusement. It seems harsh that God consumed the sons of Aaron, Nadab and Abihu, when they brought "strange fire" before God in Leviticus 10. God also struck down Uzzah the Kohathite when he reached out to help God by steadying the Ark of God in 2 Samuel 6 (see pp. 68–69; Book 1, pp. 62–63).

We don't know what kind of fire so offended God that he immediately required the lives of his priests. We do know, however, that God's holiness cannot be trifled with. These priests evidently didn't think it mattered how they approached God in worship, despite warnings that it mattered a great deal. They paid the penalty that we might learn something about God. He is holy. He justly acts to honor his justice.

The death of Uzzah teaches us more. It was centuries since the law had been given. One of the rules that had been drilled into Uzzah was that he must never, ever, touch

> "Among those who approach me I will show myself holy; in the sight of all the people I will be honored." [Lev. 10:3b]

the throne of God. God had said, "If you touch it, you die" (Num. 4:15). Uzzah gave lip-service to those rules, but surely they were for another time and place. He knew it would be wrong to touch the Ark, but he thought it would not be as bad as letting the Ark fall to the ground.

As noted in our meditation in Book 1 God would not have been offended by the Ark touching the ground, for it was not defiled. The hand of a sinful human being was. Beyond that, God's feeling about what is and is not holy had not change between Sinai and the reign of David. Since God changes not, his concern for justice and holiness has not changed in the time since Uzzah. We still stand before a consuming fire.

Coram Deo

As Protestants we celebrate the "priesthood of all believers." We also know that Christ has taken the death penalty due us for abusing God's holiness through our rebellion. But if you are a "priest" before God, does today's lesson give you a sober view of what your calling means? Do you live carefully as a priest within the sphere of God's awesome holiness all the time?

For further study: Romans 12:1–2; Colossians 3:1–17; 1 Thessalonians 4:1–8

157

71 The Father We Fear

God *is* holy. Nothing can change that fact. When we use the word *holy* we tend to think of moral righteousness or purity. This is not wrong, but it can be misleading. God's holiness extends beyond being pure. He is set-apart and "other than" or "different from" everything else. When the Bible speaks of God's holiness, it refers preeminently to his transcendence. God is superior to anything in the created realm.

If that is so, then why does the first petition of the prayer Jesus taught his disciples ask that God's name be hallowed? Jesus, it seems, is not praying for God to become holy, but rather asking that his name be hallowed in the human heart. Jesus wanted God's honor among people to reflect the truth of his transcendence. In fact, the first thing that we should realize when we pray this petition is that we are praying for our own heart. We are asking for the grace to see God as he truly is, to be able to approach him as did Isaiah, with wondrous apprehension of our sinfulness.

But there is something wondrously incomprehensible about Jesus' first petition. This totally transcendent God is near. He is knowable and immanent as well. Jesus doesn't tell us that our prayer is futile because we cannot approach the living God. Nor does he advise focusing on some representation of the transcendent God made of stone or metal. He simply tells us to toddle up to God in infant trust and call him "father."

"Our Father in heaven, hallowed be your name." [Matt. 6:9]

This first petition should establish a grand tension in our hearts. Here is a God that must be worshiped in utter awe-filled brokenness and is, at the same moment, *Abba*— "Daddy." Edmund P. Clowney describes the uniqueness of such a God in his essay on "A Biblical Theology of Prayer":

"What immense brevity! Jesus had rebuked the lengthy eloquence of the Pharisees and the endless chanting of the heathen. Repeating 'OM' a thousand times may induce a change of consciousness, but it does not address the God of heaven. Neither may we convert the prayer Jesus taught into a mantra and mumble a hundred 'paternosters' as steps on a ladder to heaven. It is enough to pray as Jesus taught us" (D. A. Carson, ed., *Teach Us to Pray: Prayer in the Bible and the World*, 1990).

In biblical religion something is holy if it has the touch of God upon it. When God touches us, we become holy.

Coram Deo

When we see even a small glimpse of God's holiness we must bow in worship. The first petition of the Lord's Prayer brings us face to face with the need to learn the holiness of God's name. Ask God today to make you more aware of his holiness, so that you may understand how to both love and fear him more than ever before.

For further study: 1 Samuel 2:1–10; Isaiah 40:12–31; Revelation 15:1–4

72 Approachable Holiness

The attribute of holiness is not limited to God the Father, but also is seen in the *Holy* Spirit and the Lord Jesus Christ. When we wrote in meditation 71 (p. 158) that we are holy because God has touched us, that touch is nothing less than the person of the Holy Spirit. The holiness of God has become intimately part of the believer's life. Paul reminds us in 1 Corinthians 6:18–19 that one reason we must flee sexual immorality is that the vessel of our sexuality is also the temple where God dwells.

And when we understand that Christ is fully God and so fully sharing of the attribute of separateness, it becomes almost inconceivable what Jesus did in coming among us as fully immanent—sharing in our existence. In the earthly ministry of our Lord we can see most graphically his holiness and humankind's reaction to holiness.

While most people say nice things about Jesus, even if they are not Christians, in his own day those who met him wanted to kill him. Those who loved him could not understand that their friend and confidante, he who shared their meal times and wearied himself healing their diseases, was fully capable of stilling the storm with the authority of the Creator of the winds.

Jesus had finished preaching and he and his disciples got into a boat to cross the Sea of Galilee. The furious storm that suddenly arose even overcame the courage of

> They were terrified and asked each other, "Who is this? Even the
> wind and the waves obey him!" [Mark 4:41]

seasoned fishermen who were experienced in these waters. Yet Jesus slept until the disciples shook him awake and said, "Master, do something, or we perish!" What did he do? He looked around, assessed the situation, and then commanded in a loud voice, "Peace, be still!" And instantly the cosmos obeyed.

Yet this holy God had time for them. He cared about their hurts and did not reject them when their terror of him equaled what they had felt toward the storm. As Christians we know we can be comfortable in the presence of Jesus Christ. Even though we have an innate antipathy and fear of the Holy One, and even though we recognize that we are unholy, in Christ we are welcome.

Coram Deo

Read the selections in "For further study" in the light of Isaiah 6 (see pp. 152–55). Some parts of the modern church continually intend to remove all holiness from Jesus Christ. But did the response of the disciples differ markedly from that of Isaiah? Should they have seen Jesus only as "one of the guys"? Surely the Christian's response is found in Psalm 139:23–24. Make that psalm your prayer today.

For further study: Matthew 14:22–27; 17:1–7; Luke 5:1–11; Hebrews 10:1–22

161

73 *Yahweh*: His Personal Name

A t the burning bush Moses encountered the holiness of God and learned the importance of worshiping a holy God. And he also learned a name for the God he was to worship—the God who was about to confront Egypt's pantheon of idols. We shall look at four of the names of God to learn what it means to be delivered from bondage into the household and service of God.

In Exodus 3 God used the name "I AM," probably pronounced *Yahweh*, which in our Bibles is rendered "LORD." For Moses, who knew the God of Abraham, Isaac, and Jacob and who came from a culture that worshiped the gods of the sun and Nile and crocodile, this identification had implications. Some peoples, including Eastern religionists and many in the modern West, worship some nameless, formless force. Darkness obscures the face of this nonbeing.

By giving Moses his name, God identified himself as real and personal. God's name authorized Israel to call upon him for help. It means that God is self-existing and has life in himself. Unlike humans or parts of creation, God is not dependent upon anyone or anything for his existence.

Polls consistently show that 95 percent of Americans claim to believe in some kind of god. We would describe these people as *theists*. Often, when people are pressed as to the *nature* of the god they profess to believe in, their answers are ambiguous. They turn to such phrases as

God said to Moses, "I AM WHO I AM. This is what you are to say to the Israelites: 'I AM has sent me to you.' " [Exod. 3:14]

"supreme being" or "something greater than ourselves" or "the force" to describe the unknown and far-off god of contemporary culture.

Polls never ask the specific question, "Do you believe in the God who thundered from Sinai: 'You shall have no other gods before me'?" "Do you recognize the God who demands absolute obedience?" "Do you believe that our eternal destinies will be determined by his judgment—either eternity in heaven or in hell?" How many people profess to believe in a God like that?

A god without a name is safe. He has no character or personality to make demands or cause fear. On the other hand, only the God who is can deliver a nation out of slavery or a person out of sin.

Coram Deo

Using a Bible study resource or just keeping a notepad at hand while reading the Bible brings to light dozens of names that describe the character and attributes of the "I AM" God more fully. Use these names as you pray to engrave into your heart a description of the Father, Son, and Holy Spirit as revealed in Scripture.

For further study: Exodus 33:17–34:8; Mark 14:60–62; John 8:48–58; Acts 17

74 *Adonai*: Sovereign Lord

Yahweh focuses on God's self-existence and the fact that only God has life in himself. Often in our Bibles this word is written "Lord," or occasionally "God," with all capital letters. When we encounter the word *Lord*, typeset in upper- and lower-case letters, the Hebrew term behind it is *Adon*, which means "Master." The addition of the suffix *ai* intensifies the meaning of the word, so that *Adonai* means the supreme Lord, the Lord of all. This word stresses the sovereignty of God as All-ruler.

Sovereignty has become a divisive issue among Christians. Defining what it means and discerning whether it eliminates the possibility of free will among humans has caused many schisms. We understand that it was the first great controversy to threaten the hard-won unity of the newly freed churches of the former Soviet Bloc.

Our Adversary effectively causes dissension over sovereignty because he knows this is a point of human vulnerability. First, we hate any idea that our choices are limited. We still want to bite the fruit of being like God. Second, the church's entire concept of God stands or falls on the basis of what kind of God we serve. Sovereignty is essential to God. The moment we negotiate on this point, or dilute the concept of sovereignty, we are playing around with God's character. If God is not sovereign, God is not God.

Moses said to the LORD, "O Lord, I have never been eloquent,
neither in the past nor since you have spoken to your servant."
[Exod. 4:10a]

Third, only a sovereign LORD can give confidence to stand apart. That lack of understanding of the *Adonai* nature of God made Moses think that convincing the Israelites to leave Egypt and the Pharaoh to let them go all depended upon his silver tongue. Of course that was not the case for Moses. We who can look ahead in the story know that the exodus had very little to do with Moses and Aaron as orators. It had a great deal to do with God as *Adonai* over nature and over lives.

When the Christian stands before Almighty God he or she stands before absolute authority over life. Adonai authority empowers faith, hope, and service for a sinful human being.

Coram Deo

If you struggle to understand how sovereignty, free will, and responsibility work together, a study of the Book of Romans, possibly using Book 1 of this series should help. Ephesians 2:1–10 speaks especially clearly to God's work in our lives. Pray that Christians everywhere may joyfully embrace a richer, fuller, and more biblical understanding of this essential doctrine.

For further study: Deuteronomy 3:24; Psalm 119:129–44; Ephesians 2:1–10

75 *Elohim*: Intensely God

T he first name of God recorded in the Bible is a plural word, *Elohim*. Some see in the use of *Elohim* a similarity to the royal "we," the "imperial plural" used by kings. Little evidence supports such an explanation. Many evangelicals have thought that *Elohim* refers to the tri-unity of God. However, even that Hebrew text traditionally used in Judaism to affirm the oneness of God—the *Shema* in Deuteronomy 6:4—uses the word *Elohim:* "Hear O Israel: The LORD [*Yahweh*] our God [*Elohim*], the LORD is one." Remember that God revealed himself progressively through biblical history and the revelation of the Trinity did not come until a later time.

I think the best explanation is found in an ancient Semitic language grammatical construction called the "abstract plural." It is sometimes called "the plural of intensity." Book 1, pp. 42–43, looked at the meaning of this unity in diversity. For considering Exodus and the God revealed there, however, it is important to recognize that this abstract plural does not indicate any kind of polytheism. Nor does it imply a notion that God is a composite being. But his being and all of his attributes can be described as "intense."

All that God is lives and breathes with the intensity of completeness. When Moses asked to see God's glory he was confronted with the *Elohim* nature of God. The in-

166

> Then they said, "The God of the Hebrews has met with us. Now let us . . . offer sacrifices to the LORD our God" [Exod. 5:3a]

tensity of that glory was so great that he could not behold God and live. God had to put him in a protected place in the rock, cover him over, and then show him just one facet of his character, his intense goodness.

God as *Elohim* best shows himself in the person of Jesus Christ his Son. Only God who is so intensely and utterly transcendent and powerful could continue to be God while at the same time being intensely in our presence as a fellow human being. God has pervaded all of history with the intensity of his care and concern for insignificant creatures who rebelled against him. He fills the world now with the intensity of his presence. He fills each of his children with the love and peace and security that only *Elohim* can provide.

Coram Deo

The church is called to manifest God's unity and diversity. A collection of weak, diverse peoples has been built into far more than the sum of its parts. Only through the complete church can we intensely glorify and serve. We have many gifts and functions that uniquely fit together. Consider your place in that body. What has God given you to bring to the people of God?

For further study: Genesis 18:1–22; 1 Corinthians 12:1–6; Ephesians 4:1–16

76 *El Shaddai*: All-Powerful

l *Shaddai* has been translated as "he who is sufficient," "the thunderer," and "the overpowerer."
The Greek equivalent, found in the New Testament, is *Pantocrator,* meaning "the All-powerful One."
When God revealed himself by this name to the patriarchs
in Genesis he focused on his power, revealing himself as
the God who makes and keeps his promises. It was a name
that demanded faith in what was coming but not yet; the
God behind the promise was sufficient for now, even if the
fulfillment of the promises could not be seen.

To Moses and the men of his generation, God revealed the
name *Yahweh,* or LORD, which in redemptive history means
"the God who keeps the promises he made to the fathers."

How strong is God? Does he have any limits at all? Can
he make the rock so big that he cannot move it? Scripture
tells us that there are things God cannot do: He cannot lie.
He cannot tempt to sin. He cannot do anything that is unworthy of the Creator of the heavens and earth. One of the
best answers to the question of God's strength and suffi-
ciency comes from the *Children's Catechism*. The question
asks: "Can God do anything?" The child's answer is "Yes.
He can do all his holy will."

God can do anything he wants. If he wants to take one

> "I appeared to Abraham, to Isaac, and to Jacob as God Almighty, [*El Shaddai*], but by my name the Lᴏʀᴅ I did not make myself known to them." [Exod. 6:3]

lowly man in Ur named Abram and promise that his descendants will be as many as the stars in the sky, he can make that promise, and he can carry it out. If he wants to take a nation of slaves and wrest them from the mighty hand of the Egyptian army, if he wishes to provide for that nation for forty years as they wander through one of the most barren areas of wilderness in the world, he is more than up to the demands of the task.

God said to Moses, "You don't need to doubt that I can do what I promise, because I am *El Shaddai*. I am the One who made promises to the Fathers and you have seen me keep them. Now sit back and see if I don't do what I have said I will do."

Coram Deo

God fulfils each of his promises. Write down an example of how God has fulfilled a promise in your life. Now think of a promise made in God's Word. Thank God for the confidence you can place in him. Also thank him that he does not always give us what we *want*, when it is not what we really *need*.

For further study: Genesis 35:9–15; Numbers 11; Isaiah 41:8–16; Romans 8:28–39

77 The Plagues of Egypt

Just as God reveals his character in his names, so he also displays it in his deeds. Ten plagues fell upon Egypt before they released the Hebrews. The first nine can be arranged in three cycles of three each. In the first three plagues, the distress was upon both the Egyptians and the Israelites living in Goshen Province. These first three plagues were not so much destructive as irritating. They were warnings.

The first plague turned all the surface water in Egypt to blood. To drink, the people had to dig new springs. The second was a plague of frogs and the third a plague of gnats coming up out of the dust (compare Gen. 3:17). Pharaoh's magicians duplicated the first two plagues, but were defeated by the third, saying, "This is the finger of God" (Exod. 8:19).

During the second cycle, the land of Goshen was set apart and the Israelites no longer experienced the plagues. God had given them a taste of judgment, but then delivered them. Aaron's staff was used in the first three, but now Moses simply announced the plagues. They were more serious and debilitating, but not horribly destructive. The fourth plague was biting flies, the fifth a plague on livestock, and the sixth a plague of painful boils among the

> Then the LORD said to Moses, "Now you will see what I will do
> to Pharaoh: Because of my mighty hand he will let them go;
> because of my mighty hand he will drive them out of his country."
> [Exod. 6:1]

people. As the magicians were defeated after the third, so they were driven from Moses' face after the sixth.

The last three plagues were brought about by Moses' staff. No longer did Aaron stand as "mediator" between Pharaoh and Moses. These three plagues were horribly destructive. After each, Pharaoh promised to let Israel go, but then reneged on his word. The seventh plague was hail that destroyed the crops. Eighth came locusts that destroyed whatever survived the hail. Last came three days of total darkness. This palpable darkness infested the air, like plagues three and six. The first plague against the Nile and the ninth plague against the sun attacked the two main gods of Egypt.

Coram Deo

In Francis Thompson's poem, "The Hound of Heaven," God says to the sinner, "All things betray thee, who betrayest me." Genesis 1 provides various categories of creation. The plagues "de-create" the world of Egypt, as the Egyptians lose the gifts of Genesis 1. Do you notice correlations between the plagues and the categories of creation in Genesis 1?

For further study: Genesis 1; Joshua 24:1–7; Psalm 135:1–14; Hebrews 11:24–29

171

78 The Passover of God

W e come now to the tenth plague, the slaughter of the firstborn of Egypt. God identified it as a plague against the Egyptian gods, implying that in some sense these men had made themselves gods. More broadly, as we saw, God had defeated the Sun God and the Nile God and all the magicians of Egyptian religion. Since Pharaoh was considered a god, however, killing his son would be the ultimate judgment against the Egyptian religion. In this way the liberation of Israel from Egypt was foremost a religious, not a political event.

At midnight on the day of Passover God struck down the firstborn of all the cattle of Egypt, the firstborn of all the nobility, and the firstborn of all commoners, from the greatest to the least. Only those who had slain a lamb as a substitute and smeared the blood on the doorposts of their houses found their households spared. The salvation of the firstborn son had the effect of saving the entire household, including the livestock.

Passover took place at midnight and the next day was the first of a new period in history. God told the Israelites that the month of Passover was to be the first month of their religious year. Their entire religious calendar was to date from this event, as the western calendar dates (approximately) from the birth of the world's Redeemer.

> "On that same night I will pass through Egypt and strike down every first-born—both men and animals—and I will bring judgment on all the gods of Egypt; I am the LORD." [Exod. 12:12]

Protestants sometimes minimize the rituals of the Christian religion because the Medieval Catholic Church abused these rituals. In Exodus 12, however, we see God commanding his people to observe the ritual of Passover annually. God is interested in training his people in patterns of righteousness. He establishes rituals to help them become rehabituated to the ways of his kingdom. In the new covenant, God has replaced Passover with the Lord's Supper, but he is every bit as concerned that we honor him by observing the Lord's Supper often and in the way he prescribed. If the Medieval church erred by celebrating the sacraments without the Word, the Protestant and evangelical churches of today err by having the Word too often without the sacraments.

Coram Deo

What specific rituals has God commanded in the New Testament? Consider rituals described in 1 Corinthians 11, Matthew 23, and Ephesians 5:19. Are they neglected in the church today? What specific benefits might come to you and the church at large if these rituals were taken more seriously?

For further study: Matthew 23:23; 1 Corinthians 5:6–8; 11:20–33; Ephesians 5:19

79 The Red Sea Song

O ne of the great recurring patterns in the Bible is that after God delivers his people, they sing a new song. The "Song at the Red Sea" (Exodus 15) is one of those songs, as is the "Song of Moses" (Deuteronomy 32) composed after God preserves Israel in the wilderness. The "Song of Deborah" celebrates the defeat of Sisera (Judges 5), and David wrote psalms to commemorate God's defeat of the Philistines. In the new covenant, we find the saints singing a new song, the "Song of Moses and the Lamb" (Revelation 15).

The first verse of the "Song at the Red Sea" (15:1b) was taken up as a refrain and while Moses and the men sang the verses, Miriam and the women danced with tambourines and sang the refrain (15:20–21).

The song celebrated God's victory over his enemies, those who had dared to attack and oppress his bride. Under divine inspiration, Moses did not hesitate to call God a "warrior" (v. 3). He rejoiced that God hurled Pharaoh's finest officers and chariots into the sea (v. 4). Like the wicked at the time of Noah's flood, Pharaoh's army sank like stones into the watery depths (vv. 5, 10), while those who followed Noah remained dry (v. 8; compare with meditation 45, pp. 104–5).

We are given insight into the motives of Pharaoh's army in verse 9. They were seeking to recover the spoil the Is-

> "I will sing to the LORD, for he is highly exalted. The horse and its rider he has hurled into the sea." [Exod. 15:1b]

raelites had gained in Egypt, and they wanted to experience the perverse pleasure of slaughter. Moses made it clear that they deserved destruction, and he showed no pity toward them.

Because God had stretched forth his mighty arm to save them, the Israelites could be confident that he would finish what he had started. Moses predicted that they would indeed be led to the place of God's dwelling (v. 13) and that they would be planted like a new Garden of Eden, like a new post-flood vineyard on God's holy mountain (v. 17; compare Gen. 9:20).

Other nations trembled with fear. God's people, however, could be confident in the face of future enemies because they had seen the Supreme Warrior fight on their behalf.

Coram Deo

Does the fierce joy of the "Song at the Red Sea" seem a bit strange to you? Why does it seem to bother our sensibilities to praise God's destruction of his enemies? Perhaps you need to adjust your outlook on God's holy war against sin. This song has been set to music more than once. Why not find a musical version to use in church or family worship?

For further study: Psalms 44:3–7; 118:13–29; 1 Corinthians 15:54–57; 1 John 5:1–5

80 Saved by the Law?

fter God showed himself to be a Warrior at the Red Sea he showed himself to be a righteous, law-giving Governor at Mount Sinai. We shall camp here at the Mountain of God for a short while, viewing the subject of the law of God. We will use segments from John Gerstner's video/audio cassette series "Handout Theology" as our guide.

Jesus taught that a Christian saved by grace alone is more moral than the moralists. Jesus said our morality must exceed that of the Pharisees. If a Christian learns his morality from Judaism or any other source, he is not learning Christian morality. Bear in mind that Judaism, both in Jesus' day and ours, involves a grave distortion of the ethics God gave to ancient Israel.

Moralists are legalists. The term *legalism* is used in several ways. The word's meaning is opposite to *salvation by grace* when *legalism* infers that keeping the law achieves merit by which a person can obtain a divine reward. The Bible, however, teaches that no one ever does a good deed, for even the act that outwardly seems to be flawless is corrupted by hostility to God.

Although the Christian is saved apart from law-keeping, he or she is not saved from the duty of law-keeping. A Christian, saved by grace through faith alone, is grateful and willing to serve Christ by keeping his holy law. It is an act

176

> "For I tell you that unless your righteousness surpasses that of the Pharisees and the teachers of the law, you will certainly not enter the kingdom of heaven." [Matt. 5:20]

of love. Justification is by faith alone, but not by faith that stands alone. Justifying faith is working faith. It pours out good works, though the works do not contribute one iota to being justified.

The Christian is commanded and empowered to do a better job of law-keeping than does anyone else. The moralist who seeks salvation through works always softens demands to fit abilities. This compromises God's morality. Moreover, without the power of the Holy Spirit, the moralist cannot obey, even outwardly. Even when the moralist seems to exceed the Christian in outward works those deeds always fall infinitely short as regards inward attitude. Only the Christian is given the grace to truly understand and the power to keep the law to a significant degree.

Coram Deo

In what specific ways does Jesus in Matthew 5 tell us to exceed the righteousness of the moralists? Do any of his statements bring you under conviction? Have you so separated Christian faith from law-keeping that you have drifted from God's moral standards? If so, make it a matter of prayer and reformation.

For further study: Galatians 3:15–25; 5:1, 16–18; Ephesians 2:1–10; Titus 2:11–15

81 Holy Anxiety

P aul writes to the Philippians that we obey Christ because it is God who works in us the desire and ability to serve him faithfully (Phil. 2:13). Paul also states, however, that our obedience is to be accomplished in a spirit of fear and trembling. Fear and trembling? Ordinarily these are not thought of as Christian virtues. How many times did Jesus say, "Fear not"? What about obeying through joy and enthusiasm?

Well, joy and enthusiasm are certainly not excluded, but Paul is saying that we must also have a holy fear and respect for God's commandments. God means business, and if we find ourselves temporarily bereft of joy and enthusiasm, we had better maintain at least some fear and trembling.

Jesus spelled this out when he said, "Watch and pray, so that you will not fall into temptation" (Mark 14:38). The Christian is born of God and God is continually working, yet much sin remains. So the believer walks carefully, anxious to avoid sin and constantly asking forgiveness for failure. As long as there is sin in Christians, there is need for anxiety and trembling.

We are to have no anxiety about God. God has made promises and we are to believe him. We are to have joyous confidence in his work within us. Yet we are to feel anxiety about our sin. The more we love God, the more we

> Therefore, my dear friends, as you have always obeyed—not only in my presence but now much more in my absence—continue to work out your salvation with fear and trembling. [Phil. 2:12]

tremble and fear at the thought of displeasing him. We love him and don't want to grieve his Spirit. "Blessed are those who mourn," said Jesus (Matt. 5:4). We mourn over our sins while we are confident that Jesus forgives us. It is an amazing psychological state, because *blessed* means "happy." We are plainly told that happy are those who are sad. Only the Christian experiences this delight, that sorrow at ourselves is joined with happiness in Christ.

So, we are to be anxiously confident—confident in God and anxious about ourselves. We are not anxious and afraid that God will fail us or leave us, but we are anxious and fearful that we will fail God and depart from him.

Thankfully, such anxiety is only earthly. Once our sanctification is complete and we are glorified in heaven, we will fear sin no more.

Coram Deo

How familiar are you with this sort of fear and trembling, this holy anxiety and mourning over self? If you don't know much about it, take a closer look at yourself today and a particular sin in your life. Discern your inner motives of rebellion and bring them in shame to the feet of the Savior.

For further study: Isaiah 64:1–7; Romans 3:10–18; Jude 22–25

179

82 Loving the Law

O h, how I love Your law!" cries the psalmist from his heart. Few modern Christians would ever make such a statement. In fact, most ignore the law, taking a low, unscriptural view of its relevance for today. There are several reasons why we as Christians should desire to love God's law.

First, we love the law because when it condemns us it drives us to Jesus who saves us. The law keeps reminding us of our beloved Savior and Lord, and reminding us of how much we depend on him. It keeps forcing us back. How can we help but love such a wonderful device. The more of the law we know, the more fully we are driven to Christ.

Second, just as our remaining sin hates the law because the law condemns it, so we, in our renewed minds, love the law because it is the word of our Savior. The law describes the character of God and the image of God, seen most clearly in the perfect human being, Jesus Christ. As we love God we love to learn more about what the law reveals about him. As we want to be more Christ-like in our lives, the law shows us what Christ is like.

Third, we love the law because we are saved by it—that is, we are saved by Christ's keeping of the law. The law is holy, just, and good, and Jesus kept it fully. As he admired and obeyed it, so we also admire and seek to obey it because we are in union with him.

If we sing "My Jesus, I Love Thee," we should also sing "Oh, How Love I Thy Law."

If we sing "More Love to Thee, O Christ," we should also sing, "More Love to Thy Law."

If we hate the law, we hate Jesus, because he is the embodiment of the law. If we love the law, then we love Jesus.

You cannot love the law and hate Christ, O Jew; and you cannot love Christ and hate the law, O Christian. The Jew who says he or she loves the law, yet rejects Christ as the fulfillment of all the law points to, does not love the law at all. Such a person loves only a figment of personal imagination. Similarly, the Christian who says he or she loves Jesus, yet rejects the law, does not love Christ. You cannot be a true Jew unless you love Christ and you cannot be a true Christian unless you love the giver of the law, Moses. They stand or fall together.

Coram Deo

If we love Christ, we will study the Old Testament Law in all its details, because they reveal Christ to us. This will prove an exciting project for any believer. How about making a thorough study of the Mosaic Law through your Bible study or Sunday school?

For further study: Joshua 1:6–9; Psalm 119:41–48, 113, 120; John 14:15–21

83 No Other Gods

The first commandment forbids the worship of or service to any god apart from the true God. At the mountain God revealed himself as the One who had created the world and redeemed Israel from Egypt. He now reveals himself to the church as the God who saved the world through Jesus Christ.

Literally, the first commandment says that we are to "have" no other gods. Anything that comes between us and God is a false god. Anything we put before the service and obedience of God is a false god. Thus, if we prefer fishing or playing golf to worshiping on the Lord's Day, then fishing or golf is an idol for us on that day. We may not bow down to our golf clubs, but we definitely put golf before God and break the first commandment.

Similarly, if we love money more than God, we break the first commandment. If we refuse to tithe a full 10 percent of our income to God, we show that we love money more than the holy law of God. We trust money more than we trust God. We are afraid we won't have enough money if we tithe, so the fear of inconvenience or poverty has taken precedence over the fear of God.

Of course, idolatry in the usual sense of the word is a clear violation of the first commandment. When you carve wood into the shape of an image and bow down to it or to some created thing, you have broken the law. No fit representation for God exists in human form. However,

"You shall have no other gods before me." [Exod. 20:3]

the primary idol is not the carved image; after all, the idol is made or designated by humans. Behind idolatry is the worship of humankind as god. The ultimate form of idolatry is always the worship of oneself. We are the ones who create the idols in the first place and thus worship ourselves.

Idolatry has been a concern of the church since the earliest days. Orthodox Christianity regards the Jehovah's Witnesses and the Mormons as idolaters because they deny the deity and the worship of Christ. These groups worship a false god of their own devising. In the early days of the church there were many similar heresies, all of which involved denying the true deity of Christ. When the early church condemned these heresies she was acting in support of the first commandment.

Coram Deo

It is all too easy to center affections around some "thing." Take a close look at your life and see if there are material things or desires for comfort and luxury that you have placed at the center of your heart. If so, you have broken a vital link with God and need to go to your knees and ask that the Searcher of hearts will show you the idols to break.

For further study: Luke 9:57–62; Romans 1:16–32

84 No Images

The first commandment forbids covenantal idolatry, which means anything in our lives before God. The second commandment forbids liturgical idolatry which involves using any created thing in worship as a medium between God and us. The first commandment deals with the object of worship while the second concerns the method of worship.

In some forms of Judaism, in Islam (which uses the Old Testament selectively), and in some Christian churches, the second commandment is mistakenly interpreted as forbidding any representation of biblical scenes or any representational art (Islam). Actually, the commandment forbids pictures of anything, including Jesus, if used for the purpose of worship. It does not forbid having stained glass windows or pictures in the church, but it does forbid bowing down to them or seeking to worship God through them. After all, God decorated the Tabernacle with cherubim and other pictures, so simply having decorative or illustrative pictures in church is not the issue.

Nobody directly worships idols of wood and stone or bronze and paint. Those who bow to images maintain that they are rendering service to the invisible person represented by the image. Thus the golden calf made by Aaron was to represent the Lord (Exod. 32:4–5). In the second commandment, however, God completely forbade any such worship. He declared that he was not to be wor-

> "You shall not make for yourself an idol in the form of anything in heaven above or on the earth beneath or in the waters below."
> [Exod. 20:4]

shiped through icons, images, or any other artifact or medium.

There is only one Mediator between God and man, one true Image of God, and it is through him only that we are to worship. That one, Jesus Christ, is presently in heaven and is no longer visible.

The second commandment states that God is jealous. Like a husband, God insists that his bride be faithful to him. He is infuriated when she is faithless, when she renders to statues or icons the worship due him alone. The issue is not what god is being depicted, but that any object has become the focus of worship. This jealousy of God is not a vice but a virtue. God commands us to worship him alone, not because he needs our worship, but for our good. He is jealous because he loves us and does not want us to defile or harm ourselves through false worship.

Coram Deo

Since God is so concerned that worship be done the right way, we should share his concern regarding any expression of worship we participate in. Where do we go to find God's standards of proper worship? What aspects of worship commanded in the Bible need to be rediscovered and reinstituted in today's church?

For further study: Deuteronomy 4:15–24; John 4:19–26; Hebrews 1:1–4; 12:28–29

185

85 The Holy Name

People are closely tied to their names. If someone speaks your name in a crowded noisy room, chances are you will hear it. We are annoyed if someone mispronounces our name, angered if someone belittles it by deliberately abusing it, and infuriated if someone slanders it. We regard an attack upon our name as an attack upon our person.

Taking God's name lightly is forbidden by the third commandment. The first petition of the Lord's Prayer, "hallowed be your name," means that we must take God's name seriously.

Using God's name in cursing obviously violates this commandment as well. Consider that when people use the name of Jesus Christ in cursing they are inadvertently confessing that at some deep level they regard Jesus as God. Have you ever heard anyone say "Zeus-damn"? The reason people don't say that in our culture is that nobody regards Zeus as a god any longer.

Perhaps the core of the third commandment, however, has to do with using God's name in swearing oaths. If a person says "honest to God" and is lying, he has used God's name in order to perpetrate a sin. If a person swears on the Bible to tell the truth and then lies, he uses the Word of God to commit a falsehood. He seeks to draw God into his sin as a co-conspirator. Such a horrible abuse of his own name God will not overlook.

> "You shall not misuse the name of the LORD your God, for the LORD will not hold anyone guiltless who misuses his name." [Exod. 20:7]

Evangelical Christians do not take their vows before God seriously enough. To use one tradition as an example, a person who joins the Presbyterian church stands before the congregation and God vowing to make diligent use of the means of grace (Word and sacrament), to support the ministry of the church (tithe and participation), and to study the peace and purity of the church (supporting church discipline). How many people who have taken this vow don't attend church while vacationing or when relatives visit? How many give next to nothing to the work of the church? How many give little or nothing of leadership and participation in the education and program ministry of the church? How many cause grief to the servants of the congregation, the pastors and elders?

We can ask the same penetrating questions about vows taken before God in marriage.

Coram Deo

Unfaithfulness and law-breaking are bad enough, but they are compounded when we break an oath before God. How well are you fulfilling your vows before God, such as faithfulness in church membership and marriage, and the oaths taken before baptism?

For further study: Ecclesiastes 5:1–7; Matthew 5:33–37; Acts 5:1–11

86 The Day of the Lord

H istorically, the church has tended to oscillate between legalism and libertinism regarding the Lord's Day. On the one hand, certain groups have turned the Sabbath into a day of morbid sterility; but on the other hand, others have treated it as a day like any other. We confront the second tendency most often today.

The Sabbath day was considered both the first and the last day of the week. Humanity was made on the sixth day so that the seventh was the first day of the human race. The week began with the worship of God and with resting in God. Each person was to look forward to the next Sabbath, considered the end of the week, as a time to again rest in God and worship him. In the new covenant the day has been shifted forward, but it is still both the first day and the last day in the biblical conception.

The Sabbath is thus a promise that God will fulfil his work. We enter God's rest on the "first day," here and now in our lives every Lord's Day. We look forward to a final fulfillment on the "last day," the great future day of the Lord. God gives us rest now and commands us to give rest to ourselves and to our subordinates, including even our animals (Exod. 20:10). The Sabbath is therefore one of the most fundamental of all labor laws. What application may we draw from this commandment?

First, the Day of the Lord is to be kept holy, which means it is to be a day of worship. God requires us to present him as King of Kings and Captain of the Host on his day. We are to render obeisance and praise to him. Failure to attend worship is an affront to the God who has saved us. Second, a study of the Old Testament reveals that the Sabbath was also a day of festivity, because God is Life and joy. It is sad that the festive character of the Lord's Day has been so neglected by the secular pleasures which have crowded into our lives on that day.

Finally, the Lord's Day is to be a day of rest, a time of cessation from the cares of the world. Believers differ over what constitutes rest on the Lord's Day. Is it legitimate to watch a football game or a movie, read the newspaper or go swimming at the beach? The great theologians of the Protestant church have never agreed on the details of this. Suffice it at this time for us to focus upon the two points of faithful worship attendance and the celebration due when living in the Spirit before the face of God.

Coram Deo

Right now may be a good time to reassess how you keep the Sabbath. Have you carefully thought through the matter? What is the teaching of your pastor and denomination on the subject? Are you genuinely seeking to keep the day as God would have you?

For further study: Exodus 31:12–17; Isaiah 58:13–14; Matthew 5:17–20

Part 5 begins with the rest of John Gerstner's studies of the Ten Commandments. Gerstner brings unsurpassed theological precision to his discussion of these important primary tenets of our religious heritage.

Too many Christians believe that the law was only a stop-gap measure that lasted until the cross. God's people were under law, but that ended and now we are under grace. Through these studies I hope it is becoming clear that no such dichotomy exists. The Ten Commandments flow out of the character of God and his delivering power from bondage. The Ten Commandments flow naturally into the rest of the law as a unified whole. The law flows naturally and seamlessly through God's eternal plan of salvation.

After God gave the Ten Commandments he gave other commands to Israel through the mediation of Moses. The commandments entered into every sphere of life, showing that in every detail and at every moment God desires that his

The Cross and the Law

people live holy lives. And holiness begins with the details.

The first of these laws, found in Exodus 21–23, are collectively called the *Book of the Covenant* by scholars. We will consider the highlights of these passages and how they relate to our covenant promises. Then we will look again at the cross of Christ to see how the law and the cross are related in God's redemptive plan.

The conclusion we draw is this: Since God has written these laws and passed them down to us in the Bible, they are wisdom for the church for all times, and we must strive to properly apply their fundamental principles to our lives. To do this is to live *coram Deo*, in subjection to the God in whose presence we live and move and have our being.

R.C. Sproul

87 Chain of Command

I n the fifth commandment God has ordained a chain of command. No one can object to the idea of submitting to God's absolute authority, because we know that he cannot do wrong. Anything he tells us to do is for good. When it comes to submitting to other people, however, we readily find excuses to disobey and rebel. Other people, after all, are not God. As sinners they make mistakes, and we have learned not to fully trust them.

The Bible tells us that, while God is the source of all authority, he has delegated the exercise of that authority to certain people. Parents are appointed to exercise God's authority. We all start out as children and our first encounter with authority is that held by our parents. The pattern of obedience we are to render to other authorities throughout life is first learned in the home.

Parents do not automatically hold authority over their children because they gave birth to them. Rather, the authority possessed by parents is theirs by the delegation of God. Similarly, children are not to submit to their parents because of physical relationship, but because that is God's command. When we honor our parents we honor God; conversely, when we dishonor them we profane God.

The same is true in other areas of life. The Bible enjoins wives to submit to husbands, employees to employers, cit-

> "Honor your father and your mother, so that you may live long in the land the LORD our God is giving you." [Exod. 20:12]

izens to rulers, and church members to elders (Ephesians 5–6; Romans 13; Hebrews 13). Submission in such chains of command is the visible and practical expression of our submission to God.

Such submission is also limited by the fact that those in authority over us may not command us to sin, nor may they make demands outside their delegated spheres of authority (for instance, the civil ruler may not assume the duties of the father).

Liberal theologians often pit a "religion of the Spirit" against a "religion of authority." This is unbiblical nonsense. The true religion of the Holy Spirit *is* a religion of authority, because the Spirit wrote the absolutely authoritative Bible and the Spirit has set up the God-ordained chains of command we encounter in our daily lives.

Coram Deo

One test of our submission to God is found in our response of submission to other people. Take a few minutes now to examine your attitude toward those in authority: husband, elders, government, employer, and others. Are you submitting "in the Lord"?

For further study: Romans 13:1–7; Ephesians 5:22–6:9; 1 Peter 2:13–3:9

88 Wrongful Killing

M odern translations of the Bible, such as the New International Version quoted here, render Exodus 20:13, "You shall not murder." In the original Hebrew, however, it is not the verb for the act of murdering someone that is used, but a verb which means "to kill." This verb can refer to committing manslaughter as well as premeditated murder.

Thus, we find in the Mosaic law that accidental manslaughter carried a penalty (Numbers 35; Deuteronomy 19). Moreover, the law required that people be careful not to cause human death through negligence (Exod. 21:22–23, 28–30; Deut. 22:8). Therefore, a more literal translation of Exodus 20:13 is appropriate: "You shall not kill."

Does that mean it is always wrong to kill? No. We are forbidden to take upon *ourselves* the right to kill other people, and we are commanded to take care that our property is adequately maintained and safely operated so that we do not cause other people to die.

God, however, has the right to kill and has delegated that right to human beings in certain circumstances. The same God who said to Israel, "*You* shall not kill," ordered the Israelites to kill all the Canaanites in *his* name (Exod. 23:23; Deut. 20:16–17). God also said that his people have the right to kill in self-defense (Exod. 22:2), implying that defensive warfare is legitimate.

God commands capital punishment for murder. He commanded it originally as part of the Noahic Covenant (Gen. 9:5–6), reiterated it strongly at Mount Sinai (Exod. 21:12), and nowhere repealed it in the New Testament (indeed, see Rom. 12:17–13:5). God makes it clear that it is a sin to spare the life of a murderer (Num. 35:31).

In an age when sentimental secular humanism has deeply infected the Church, it is important for Christians to understand that it is *just as much a sin to spare a murderer as it is to be a murderer.* God has spoken, and we are to obey him, whether we like it, or whether his ways are approved by the mass media. An often used excuse for not supporting capital punishment is the opinion that it fails to deter crime. In fact, the Bible says that the death penalty is very much a deterrent (Deut. 13:11; 17:13; 21:21). As far as biblical religion is concerned, capital punishment for premeditated murder is not open for discussion.

Coram Deo

God alone has the authority to say who shall live and who shall die. The death of any image-bearer is a serious matter, so serious that Scripture gives clear guidelines concerning when a life can or must be taken. Are you ready to bow the knee intellectually to that statement? If today's lesson makes you uncomfortable, reflect on Proverbs 14:12.

For further study: Deuteronomy 4:41–43; 19:1–13; Matthew 5:21–26

Sexual Sin and Its Punishment

89

dultery—sexual intercourse between a married person and someone who is not his or her spouse—is forbidden in the seventh commandment. The rest of the Bible makes it clear that fornication (sex between unmarried people) is also sinful. Jesus said that to look at a woman with lust is to commit adultery (Matt. 5:28). This does not mean that temptation is sin, but rather that nursing the temptation and attempting to commit, or fantasizing about, adultery, is itself a form of adultery.

People of God are called to be scrupulous in sexual behavior. We should shun fornication, not even mentioning it (Eph. 5:3). It is interesting that the apologists of the second century A.D., in arguing for the power and truthfulness of the Christian religion, constantly pointed to the outstanding sexual morality of the Christian community of their day as bearing witness to the sanctifying power of God in their midst. Sadly, we cannot make that claim regarding the church today.

The Bible makes it clear that God punishes sin. There can be no doubt that infectious diseases like syphilis, gonorrhea, and the HIV virus are divine punishments for fornication. It is amazing to observe news commentators and liberal Christian spokespeople who deny this. These diseases would die out in one generation if people obeyed the Biblical command to stay pure.

It is true that some people contract these diseases without being guilty of sexual sin. They suffer because they live in a profligate society in which these diseases are rampant. AIDS appears to be a specific curse on those who break God's law and a general curse on a society that tolerates sexual immorality. Christians should not apologize for this obvious truth, but should call attention to it by calling society to repentance.

Men and women instinctively sense that these diseases are judgments from God, and because they hate God they purpose to deny that his hand is involved. God, however, confronts sin. We should join with him in bearing witness against immorality and in calling attention to the fact that the living God is a God of judgment.

Coram Deo

The fact that God judges sexual sin in our day should not make us smug, but neither should we be silent. Do you think the Christian community has done an adequate job of calling attention to the work of God in judging sin? Is there something you should be doing as a Christian citizen in a society that desperately needs reconciliation with God?

For further study: 1 Corinthians 5:1–13; 6:12–20; 2 Corinthians 2:5–11; Ephesians 5:1–3; 1 Peter 2:9–12

90 Private Property

P rivate ownership of property is a right guaranteed by the eighth commandment. Biblically speaking, our right to own property is not absolute; rather, it is a stewardship from God. Ultimately, God owns all the earth. For this reason, God allowed an Israelite to eat his neighbor's grapes while walking through his field, but not to gather a basket of them (Deut. 23:24–25).

This means that the Bible stands against communism and socialism. There is no biblical justification for using the power of the state to steal from others, whether by "nationalizing" industry under socialism and communism or by "controlling" industry under fascism. Private property and businesses are to remain free of control by the state, or free of control by those manipulating the power of the state for their own purposes. Communism, socialism, fascism, and numerous other "isms" simply cloak theft, whereby powerful people use the sword of the state to steal from others.

If God owns the land we do not have absolute rights over property entrusted to us. Society can properly regulate pollution, for instance (Exod. 22:6). The moral law prohibits various crimes, whether committed on private or public property, and thus it is legitimate for society to regulate ethics and morality in private industry.

For most of us, however, the temptation to steal takes

more mundane forms. If you cheat on an examination you have stolen honor from those who have not cheated. If you cheat on your income tax you are stealing because God commands us to pay our taxes (Rom. 13:6–7). If you fail to put in the work your employer expects you are stealing from him. If you fail to tithe 10 percent of your income to the work of the kingdom you are stealing from God (Mal. 3:8).

The Bible teaches that part of the tithe is to be used for the care of the poor (Deut. 14:28–29). This means care of the poor is the duty of the Church, not of the civil government. The Bible also teaches that individual Christians should watch out for the poor in their midst (Deut. 15:11). The Bible never teaches that the civil government should use the power of the sword to redistribute wealth from the rich to the poor.

Coram Deo

Surely one of the primary reasons we have an oppressive tax burden and welfare system is that the church has failed to care for the poor. What steps can your church take to recover the task of charity? How will the local church be funded in her endeavor? Is the failure of Christians to tithe related to the growth of oppressive taxation in our society?

For further study: Psalm 49:10–20; 50:1–15; Acts 4:32–35; 6:1–7

91 Is Lying Always Wrong

P erjury before a law court (and, by implication, gossip, talebearing, and other forms of destructive lying) are forbidden in the ninth commandment. Some theologians hold that this law forbids all lying in all circumstances. We notice, however, that the commandment does not stop with the word "testimony," but qualifies the false testimony as that which harms our neighbor.

Thus, most Christian ethicists maintain that the ninth commandment does not forbid all lying. It is important to deceive the enemy in wartime. Leaking false information to the enemy is necessary in order to protect the life of our neighbor, whom we are sworn to defend in wartime (including "cold war" time). Spying is legitimate in war, and one must be an expert liar in order to be a spy. Both Rahab and Jael used deception in wartime to protect God's people and to destroy his enemies, and both received praise (Joshua 2; Judges 4–5; James 2:25).

Sometimes it is necessary to lie in order to protect the life of our neighbor, as when the Hebrew midwives lied to Pharaoh in order to preserve the lives of the Hebrew children. God blessed them for their act (Exod. 1:15–21). Similarly, Christians lied to German soldiers in Nazi-controlled Europe to protect their Jewish neighbors.

> "You shall not give false testimony against your neighbor."
> [Exod. 20:16]

Another area of life where it is permissible to "lie" and deceive is in play. We don't expect football players to communicate their moves to the opposing side; rather, it is part of the game that they feint, in order to fool, the other team. We allow actors to "lie" on stage by saying words that are not their own and by playing roles that do not reflect their own character. Such innocent deceptions in games and theater are not "against our neighbor."

When it comes to our neighbor, however, we are never to lie. We are not to tear him or her down by gossip and talebearing, even if the gossip is true. We are always to tell both the truth of the gospel and the ordinary truths about everyday events.

Coram Deo

Except in exceptional circumstance, God requires his children to live lives of open, candid honesty. Are there any areas of your life where you have been lying or cheating? If so, confess their sinfulness and ask God to provide the wisdom and strength for you to stop and change, and to make restitution if that is appropriate.

For further study: Joshua 2; Judges 4–5; Proverbs 6:16–19; Isaiah 59:9–15

201

92 Covetousness and Desire

Adam coveted God's garden-house instead of guarding it. He followed the advice of Satan and tried to take it for himself. Each of us has a garden, a household, and we are not to covet those of other people. Covetousness is the desire to possess something that properly belongs to others. It is not wrong to seek to purchase your neighbor's ox, but if he refuses to sell it, it is wrong to continue coveting it. It is always wrong to desire your neighbor's spouse.

Covetousness has sometimes been singled out as the sinful desire that underlies all other sinful thoughts and actions. Because we covet what God or another person has, whether possessions or status, we may seek to tear down or even kill that person in envy. Covetousness lies behind adultery, theft, and gossip. As we mentioned, Adam's desire to make himself a little god over the true God's household was covetousness.

Buddhism is sometimes praised as the "light of the East" because of its fundamental renunciation of desire. In fact, however, the Buddhist rejection of desire opposes Christianity. Biblical religion teaches that we are designed to aspire and desire. We are to desire dominion over creation. We are to pursue lofty goals. We are to yearn for the Sabbath, eagerly desiring the intimacy of worship ex-

> "You shall not covet your neighbor's house. You shall not covet your neighbor's wife, or his manservant or maidservant, his ox or donkey, or anything that belongs to your neighbor." [Exod. 20:17]

perienced there. This is part of the warp and woof of human nature, and it is a good thing. By rejecting all desire, Buddhism strives to destroy human nature. In fact, the goal of Buddhism is the obliteration of the human personality in "nirvana." (Buddhism also suffers from a fatal inconsistency, because Buddhists have to desire to be without desire).

Because desire for true self-fulfillment is a deep and powerful aspect of human nature in the image of God, the perversion of that desire in covetousness is one of the gravest and most powerful evils. It warps and twists everything in human life. The only cure for covetousness is to focus on God and labor to redirect one's desire toward the things of God.

Coram Deo

Do you covet any of the things, or honors of friends or acquaintances? Do you covet honors accorded to officers in your church or business? Do you ever find yourself slighting others because of this? Make it your prayer that your desire be reoriented toward the things of God.

For further study: Proverbs 6:20–29; Romans 13:8–10; James 4:2

93 Slavery in the Bible

S lavery was not abolished in the Old Testament, and that fact has been a source of concern to many. Realize, first, that the condition of slavery came into the world because of sin. Slavery is a human fault, not God's. When we consider the fire of hell to be the just desert of sin, enslavement is, by comparison, a light punishment.

Second, biblical slavery was much milder than the chattel slavery once practiced in the United States. A better translation than "slave" might be "bond-servant." A person who stole money and owed a large restitution might be sold into service for a few years to pay off the fines (Exod. 22:3), or a person might become so poor that personal slavery or the sending of a child into service was necessary (Lev. 25:39). In the latter case, the servant went free in the seventh or sabbath year, when debts were canceled (Exod. 21:2).

Slaves were protected by law. Families might not be broken up. Even if the wife remained under the protection of the master until the freedman earned enough money to buy her, the husband still had conjugal rights and privileges (Exod. 21:3–4). If a master beat a slave to death, the master was put to death for murder (Exod. 21:20–21). If the master destroyed a slave's eye or tooth, the slave was to be freed (Exod. 21:26–27).

"If you buy a Hebrew servant, he is to serve you for six years. But in the seventh year, he shall go free, without paying anything." [Exod. 21:2]

A Hebrew bond-servant who did not want to go free because of attachment to the household of the master could be adopted into the household by a blood ritual (Exod. 21:4–5). If a master purchased a girl with the intention of marrying her to himself or one of his sons—a point that would be specified in the sale contract—he could not later change his mind and sell her to someone else. If he married her and abused her, she was set free (Exod. 21:7–11).

Virtually every law given by Moses touched on slavery. Such service involved training in responsibility and the preparing of the person to be set free (Deut. 15:12–18). As God had freed Israel from Egyptian bondage, so he gave laws for freeing slaves to his people from the start (Exodus 21–23).

Coram Deo

Many immigrants came to New England as indentured servants, working for up to six years to repay the cost of the ocean voyage. What do you think of this system of voluntary and compulsory service as a way to get out of debt or to pay for crimes? How does it compare with our supposedly more enlightened system of bankruptcy, prison, and welfare?

For further study: 1 Timothy 6:1–2; Philemon 1–25

94 The Penalty for Abortion

T he Bible teaches that the fetus in the womb is a living human being. A number of passages in the Old Testament testify that God oversees the child in the womb (Ps. 139:13–16; Isa. 49:1–5; Jer. 1:4–5). The unborn baby is already under God's law, as when Samson's mother was not to drink wine because her unborn baby was already under the Nazirite vow (Judg. 13:7).

In the New Testament, John the Baptist leaped for joy in his mother's womb when he encountered the unborn Jesus in Mary's womb (Luke 1:40–44). These verses indicate that both Jesus and John were living persons in their mothers' wombs, and that John as an unborn child manifested cognition and joy. With this information before us, it is clear that to kill an unborn child is every bit as much murder as to kill a baby in a crib.

Exodus 21:22–23 indicates that God commanded the death penalty for fetus killing in Israel. Some have said these verses speak only of the woman suffering harm, but this is a dubious reading of the Hebrew text. The scene is this: Two men are fighting and one of them either accidentally strikes a pregnant woman bystander or perhaps deliberately strikes the pregnant wife of his opponent. The result is that she gives birth prematurely. If there is no harm to either woman or child, the offending party still may be

206

> "If men who are fighting hit a pregnant woman and she gives birth prematurely but there is no serious injury, the offender must be fined whatever the woman's husband demands and the court allows. But if there is serious injury, you are to take life for life." [Exod. 21:22–23]

charged to pay a stiff penalty set by the husband and adjudicated by the courts.

If, however, either the mother or the child is harmed, then the penalty is eye for eye and tooth for tooth. The Bible indicates that a ransom might be taken in place of a literal application of the "eye for eye" law (Num. 35:31 with Exod. 21:30). But what if the mother or the child are killed? What if the child is born dead as a result of the blow? Then the text says, "life for life." This means that if the baby dies, it is a capital crime.

God taught Israel that abortion was murder and assigned the appropriate punishment. As in all forms of murder, that punishment was death.

Coram Deo

Inherent to all U.S. citizens are the fundamental rights of "life, liberty, and the pursuit of happiness." The first is a prerequisite to the second and third. Christians should continually convey to their state and federal senators and representatives the importance of upholding this basic right for all people, including the unborn. Have you expressed your convictions to those in authority?

For further study: Leviticus 24:17–20; Proverbs 24:7–12; Matthew 5:21–26

95 Laws of Compassion

E xodus 21–23, the Book of the Covenant, is not simply a law code. It is more like a sermon from God to Israel dealing with his commands for all of life. Thus, it contains both laws that might be part of a judicial code and also religious and moral commands. Moreover, it expresses arguments and exhortations.

In Exodus 22:21–27 we find God's commands regarding weak and defenseless members of society. In verse 21, Israelites were specifically told never to mistreat or oppress strangers in their midst. They were to remember that they had been strangers in Egypt, so that "you yourselves know how it feels to be aliens" (23:9). As God had shown kindness to them, they were to show kindness to others. As God had loved them when they were unlovable, so they were to love others. "Do unto others as I have done unto you" is the rule of Exodus.

In 22:22–24 God told the Israelites they must not oppress widows and orphans (literally, the fatherless). Throughout the Bible God manifests a ferocious concern for women and children who do not have husbands and fathers. The supremely jealous God (Exod. 34:14) will be a Husband for the widow and a Father for the fatherless, and his jealousy will burn with fury if those under his special protection are mistreated. God told Israel that just as he heard their cry when they were oppressed in Egypt, so he would hear the cry of the widow and fatherless. Just as he destroyed the Egyptian oppressor, so he would destroy them if they oppressed widows and orphans.

In verses 25–27 God tells Israel not to extort interest from a loan to the poor. These verses did not prohibit interest on a business loan or investment (Luke 19:23), but interest could not be charged for the use of money loaned to an impoverished brother. It was legitimate to take a pledge from a poor person in exchange for a loan, but there were certain essentials that might not be taken as a pledge (vv. 26–27; Deut. 24:10–13, 17–18). For example, a cloak might be taken from him during the day to prevent his using it to get other loans and becoming overwhelmed with debts, but it had to be returned at night so that he might sleep in it and be warmed.

Coram Deo

How do our immigration laws treat aliens and strangers? Does the welfare system oppress widows and orphans? Is your Christian community and denomination seriously appreciating its responsibility to care for the poor? Think of ways you and other members of your church might become more informed and involved in such questions.

For further study: Matthew 25:31–46; Luke 10:25–37; 14:15–24

96 Impartial Justice

R ecently several scholars have suggested that the Book of the Covenant in Exodus 21–23 can be divided into sections, each of which comments on one of the Ten Commandments. Thus, Exodus 21:1–11, having to do with the sabbath-year release of slaves, focuses on the fourth commandment, while 21:12–36, having to do with violence, focuses on the sixth.

The eighth commandment, dealing with property, is highlighted in 22:1–15, while perhaps the theme of 22:16–31 is "spiritual adultery," relating to the seventh commandment. Justice, the ninth commandment, is detailed in 23:1–9, while the last section of the Book of the Covenant (23:10–19) returns to Sabbath considerations.

Exodus 23:1–9 emphasizes the need for impartiality in dealing with others, especially before the court. Verse 1 forbids gossip and tale-bearing, and warns us not to be involved in a conspiracy to promote an evil cause. Verse 2 calls our attention to the reality of mass appeal and mob rule; we are not to follow the crowd but to have the courage to stand alone if the majority is wrong.

Verse 3 forbids us from favoring the poor man in a lawsuit just because he is poor. The Christian's heart tends to go out to the poor, so when we serve on juries it is important that we steel ourselves to be impartial. The place for mercy and charity is not in the court of civil justice. The poor man is as likely to be guilty as the rich. Verse 6 speaks

210

> "Do not follow the crowd in doing wrong. When you give testimony in a lawsuit, do not pervert justice by siding with the crowd." [Exod. 23:2]

to the other side of the issue, warning us not to let our instincts side with the attractively-dressed and presentable rich against those who make a poor physical presentation of themselves.

Neighborliness is enjoined in verses 4 and 5. If we help our enemy when he is in distress, we build bridges that reduce social conflict. Most of us have "enemies," people who have wronged us or been nasty to us. "Be not resentful, but helpful" is the bottom line. God desires that the community of his people keep tension and conflict to a minimum.

This section closes (vv. 8–9) with an exhortation to judges not to take bribes and to render equal justice to strangers and aliens.

Coram Deo

For many of us, jury duty is an unwelcome task. As Christians who know the Bible, however, we are better equipped to serve on juries than anyone else. God calls us to render impartial justice, and it is a privilege to serve in court. Don't try to get out of it, but study such passages as the Book of the Covenant to prepare to serve.

For further study: Deuteronomy 16:18–20; Proverbs 21:3; Isaiah 56:1–2; Micah 6:6–8

97 Ratifying the Covenant

I n Genesis 15, God told Abram in a dream to kill animals and separate them in halves. God walked between the pieces of the animals. We saw through our study that God was saying by this symbol, "May I be ripped in half if I fail to keep this covenant with Abram."

The same ritual occurs in Exodus 24. Moses set up an altar at the foot of Mount Sinai, the altar representing the presence of God. Across from the altar Moses set up twelve stone pillars representing Israel. Animals were sacrificed, and the blood divided into two portions. Half he sprinkled on the altar and half he sprinkled on the people (probably by sprinkling it on the pillars that represented the 2 million people).

This action had a double meaning. First, it represented a bond between God and Israel, a bond created by the sacrificed animal whose blood was put on both God and Israel. In the new covenant, the blood of Jesus the Mediator creates the bond between God and us.

Second, this action constituted an oath by Israel to keep the law. Before Moses sacrificed the animals, Israel pledged to keep all the law. They repeated their pledge after Moses put the blood on the altar but before he put it on the people (or on their pillars). Moses read the Book of the Covenant, and Israel pledged to obey it. Only then

> Then [Moses] took the Book of the Covenant and read it to the people. They responded, "We will do everything the LORD has said; we will obey." [Exod. 24:7]

did Moses sprinkle the people with blood. Through the blood that was being placed upon them they were bound in covenant with God, obliged to fulfil all they had just sworn to uphold.

The blood bound the people both to God and to the law. If they as a nation broke the law then their blood would be forfeit. They would no longer be bound to God, and the blood of the sacrifice would no longer cover their sins. Instead, they would bear their own guilt and would be chastised by God for their personal and national responsibility.

The severity of the punishment connected with breaking covenant with God was later seen in the fall of the northern kingdom and ultimately the destruction of Jerusalem and Judah. The curse in the end was as severe as if the nation had become like the severed animal sacrifices.

Coram Deo

In new covenant worship we hear the gospel proclaimed and pledge to keep it, trusting in the blood of Christ that joins us to God. When we eat the Lord's Supper, if we are not faithful, we stand under the same threat God pronounced against Israel. But if we trust in his blood we need never fear his wrath.

For further study: Romans 5:6–11; Hebrews 10:1–31; 1 Peter 2:21–25

98 The Need for Atonement

C ovenants of the Old Testament were ratified by the blood of animals because no man was worthy to die to satisfy God's wrath against sinful humanity. The old covenant sacrifices were a type that symbolized or pointed to the future work of Jesus Christ. This offers a good opportunity to investigate further the cross of Christ and its meaning in our lives.

Many people are not concerned about Christianity because they are not persuaded of their personal need for atonement, their need to be reconciled to God. We live in a self-centered culture often called the "me-generation." If I don't see how something personally applies to me, I'm not interested—that's the modern view.

In order to overcome this lack of concern about atonement, we must acknowledge the objective truth of Christianity. God really exists. He created and owns this world. He gave it to humankind to govern under his laws, and humanity rebeled against his authority. God is properly angry and must defend his own honor or cease being God. The proper punishment is eternal separation from his presence. These facts constitute the objective reality in which all human beings live.

It is also fact that God sent his son, Jesus Christ, to die under his wrath for the sins of his people. God now requires

> The wrath of God is being revealed from heaven against all the godlessness and wickedness of men who suppress the truth by their wickedness. [Rom. 1:18]

all human beings to acknowledge Jesus' work on their behalf, and to submit to him as Savior and King. These facts also constitute the objective reality in which all humans live.

Whether people feel the need for a savior or not, they desperately need one, for all are accountable to God, yet nobody measures up. God is holy. Sin is an objective offense against him personally. If modern, self-centered people could come to see these objective facts they would break down the doors of the Church begging for salvation. They, like the Philippian jailer, would cry out, "What must I do to be saved?"

Before we will see revival in our time, we must recover the objective truths of the gospel that have been discarded by a culture that caters only to their own desires.

Coram Deo

Even if you are a Christian you likely have been infected with the "me-generation" attitude. Do you complain that your preacher does not give you enough "practical" things to do, or self-help hints? How well do you respond to the preaching of the transforming, objective facts of the biblical message?

For further study: Romans 3:10–23; John 16:5–15

99 Three Dimensions of Sin

T he Bible presents sin in three dimensions: (1) as a debt we owe God; (2) as an estrangement growing from our enmity against God, and (3) as a crime against God. Each of these dimensions operates in every sin and has its own implications regarding our relationship with God.

To understand sin as a *debt* we recognize that God is the Creator and is sovereign over his universe. He has the right and authority to impose obligations on his creatures. If God imposes on us an obligation and we fail to perform it, we incur a debt. The fact is, we fail constantly to do what God has told us to do. In truth we are monumental debtors. But what can we bring to pay our debts? What do we have, as mere creatures, that he will accept?

Second, to understand sin as *enmity* we consider that our relationship with God is personal. God is a person and the only way we can relate to him is as a person, face to face, yet we have an inborn hostility to God. We are estranged from him and angry at him. Yet, objectively speaking, it is God who is the injured party because we have violated him.

The role Christ plays in our redemption is that of mediator, reconciling the broken relationship between God and humanity. Because God is the offended party, it is he who must be satisfied in the relationship between him and us that is to be restored. Motivated by his love for us, and

> For all have sinned and fall short of the glory of God. [Rom. 3:23]

despite his legitimate anger, God sent his Son to mediate between him and us as creatures in estrangement. But how can Jesus Christ restore that relationship?

Finally, to understand the price that must be paid to cover our *criminal debts* and to understand how Christ can be our Mediator, we must consider that sin is a crime against God. Crime must be punished. In the atonement, God the Father takes the role of governor and judge, while Christ Jesus our Lord takes the role of priest and convicted and sentenced felon. God objectively puts on Jesus Christ the responsibility for our sins, then puts him to death for those sins. On the legal basis that the sins have been paid for, God reckons our debts paid in full and accepts us as his children once again.

This is only possible as a result of the principle of substitution: Christ in place of us.

Coram Deo

It is critical that we understand the objective facts presented about sin as debt, estrangement, and crime. Read the descriptions over carefully once more, then close the book and explain the three dimensions of sin and atonement to a friend. Keep doing this until you have mastered the facts.

For further study: Acts 13:32–41; 2 Corinthians 5:16–6:2; Hebrews 9:11–28

217

100 Christa Our Ransom

I n considering the objective facts of the gospel we now focus our attention specifically on three essential words that have lost currency in modern consideration of the plan of salvation: *ransom, propitiation*, and *expiation*.

The concept of *ransom* is built upon the idea that something has been lost and must be purchased back or someone that has been held captive now must be set free. Jesus paid the ransom to set us free. Some in the early church suggested that Jesus paid the ransom to Satan, but this is not the case. Satan did not hold us captive; he was only the jailer. The Master who had taken us captive and needed to receive the ransom payment was God. He was the offended party to whom the ransom needed to be paid. Jesus, as the volunteer suffering Servant, offered himself as payment for us.

God's wrath needed to be placated or appeased. The technical term for this appeasement is *propitiation*. Many modern theologians are offended at the idea of propitiating the wrath of God, but when we understand the objective fact that God is holy and that God's anger rightly and righteously burns against our rebellion, then we will not be offended at the idea that God must be propitiated (1 Thess. 1:10). On the cross, Jesus suffered the full fury of the pains of hell under the wrath of God and thus placated God's anger.

"For even the Son of Man did not come to be served, but to serve, and to give his life as a ransom for many." [Mark 10:45]

In the design of God, Jesus' sufferings purged our sins away. The technical term for this purging is *expiation*. Expiation has to do with the act of removing or taking away our guilt by way of paying the penalty for sin to God. Our guilt was put on Jesus and was purged away under the fiery wrath of God.

Jesus took the punishment we deserve. The result is that God has been propitiated or satisfied. He is no longer angry with us. We have been ransomed from the doom that we faced. We have been let out of the prison of judgment, the prison maintained by Satan the accuser and jailer. We have been freed from judgment because God is no longer angry with us.

Christ has ransomed us by expiating our sins and thereby propitiating God's wrath.

Coram Deo

Can you rehearse the three dimensions of sin from meditation 99 (pp. 216–17)? If not, review them. Now do the same for this lesson, making sure you can explain to your friend the three things discussed today and how they are related. Understanding and committing to memory these three terms is extremely important to your understanding of the gospel.

For further study: Romans 6:15–23; 8:18–27; Ephesians 2:1–10; 4:17–28

101 Justification by Christ

"Bumper sticker theology" says "Smile, God loves you." This kind of slogan communicates to people that God will save them because he is nice and forgiving. He will overlook our sin because he is generous. Though well-meaning Christians think this way, such an indiscriminate view of salvation is implicitly pagan and radically contradicts the Bible. God is holy and cannot overlook sin. To overlook injustice he would have to sacrifice the perfect justice of his own moral character. Thus, as Exodus 23:7 and 34:7 both say, God will by no means clear the guilty. He will never let a guilty person go free and unpunished.

Think about it: If God were mushy and changeable and willing simply to dismiss sin, how much confidence could we have in him? He certainly would no longer be the Rock that never changes, the One in whom we can repose in total confidence.

Since God will not simply overlook sin, how can we be saved? If God will never clear the guilty, and we are guilty, how can we be delivered? The answer can only be that God justly removes our guilt so that we are no longer guilty and therefore no longer condemned.

God's design to remove our guilt was accomplished by the twofold work of Christ in what we call his *passive* and his *active obedience*. Jesus' passive obedience was his will-

220

> For if, when we were God's enemies, we were reconciled to him through the death of his Son, how much more, having been reconciled, shall we be saved through his life!. [Rom. 5:10]

ingness to die for our sins, while his active obedience was his day-to-day, lifelong fulfillment of the law. Sins were put upon him, and he died for his people. His righteousness is put upon us, and we live for that reason.

This transfer of sin and righteousness is called *imputation*. Our sins and sin nature were imputed to Jesus, and his righteousness is imputed to us.

Both aspects of imputation are necessary for our salvation. Transference of our sin to Jesus can make us innocent, but it cannot make us just or righteous. It is righteousness, not innocence, that gets us into the kingdom of God (Matt. 5:20). Not only is our sin transferred (*imputed*) to Christ but his righteousness is imputed to us, transferred to our credit, so that in God's sight we are righteous.

Coram Deo

There is great misunderstanding in this vital area of justification, salvation, and the lordship of Christ. Ask God to give you greater understanding of his holiness, and the reason why Jesus Christ's death was the only way in which justice could be satisfied. Pray for someone who has not received Christ's imputed righteousness and for your witness to that person.

For further study: Romans 4:1–8; 5:12–21; Galatians 2:15–21; Titus 3:3–8

102 Blessing and Curse

W hen God set up the tabernacle and the priesthood at Mount Sinai, he instructed Aaron as high
priest to bless the people. The *Aaronic benediction*, as it is called, set God's name upon the Israelites (Num.
6:27). The benediction did not simply say, "May God bless
you;" it powerfully acted to place God's blessing on the
people. Those who rejected the blessing would receive an
equally powerful curse.

The benediction consists of three statements, each of
which has two parts. The first statement says that God will
bless and keep Israel. These two parts are amplified in the
second two statements. The blessing side is expanded in
the phrases "make his face shine upon you" and "turn his
face toward you," while the guarding side is expanded as
"be gracious to you" and "give you peace." The first side
of each of the three phrases has to do with God's presence,
while the second side of each phrase has to do with his
protection.

On the cross Jesus received the wrath of God as our substitute. He experienced the curse of the covenant. We can
understand the curse as the opposite of each statement in
the Aaronic benediction. In the first sentence the equivalent curse would be: "The Lord curse you and remove all
protection from you." The cursing side of the judgment

> "The LORD bless you
> and keep you;
> the LORD make his face shine upon you
> and be gracious to you;
> the LORD turn his face toward you
> and give you peace." [Num. 6:24–26]

would be expanded to mean that God's face would not shine on Jesus, but would turn away from him. The cross on the hill of Golgotha was shrouded in darkness for three hours as Jesus cried out in desolation, "My God, My God, Why have you forsaken me?" (Matt. 27:46b). On the cross Jesus was exposed to all the torments of hell.

Similarly, the guarding side of the blessing would be inverted. God would (a) remove protection, (b) be wrathful instead of gracious, and (c) withdraw peace from Jesus and go to war against him.

Remember that the three-fold Aaronic benediction is described as putting God's name on the people. Accordingly, the three-fold curse involved stripping God's name from Jesus so that he lost God's presence and protection.

Coram Deo

Totally separated from all the blessedness of the Father, Jesus took on himself a curse for us so that someday we will be able to see the face of God. Memorize the Aaronic benediction, appreciating the two sides of each statement. Ask your pastor what it means for him to say it as a benediction.

For further study: Deuteronomy 28:1–68; Psalm 46; 1 John 2:28–3:3

103 Design of the Atonement

e now come to the last in our series on the objective facts of the gospel and the atonement. Before we can reach a dying world with the gospel we must have a clear understanding of who God is and what our Lord Jesus Christ accomplished in his atoning work. Our attention now is focused on the design of the atonement.

In a broad sense, all humankind benefits from the atoning work of Jesus Christ. But did Jesus specifically die for all? Did Jesus die for people who ultimately will not be saved? Historical Christian faith, especially in its Reformation expression, responds: No, Jesus did not die for those who will not be saved. He only died for his own sheep.

The classic Reformation doctrine of the atonement is called *limited* or *particular atonement*. This means that the benefit of the death of Christ is only for the elect, those who are to be saved. It means Christ had certain people *particularly* in mind; he suffered for them; he prays for them now in heaven, and, since the Father denies nothing to the Son, those people will be saved.

One heretical alternative to particular atonement teaches that Jesus died for all humankind; *thereby all will ultimately be saved*. Another alternative belief is that Jesus died for some people and prayed for them, and yet because they supposedly can reject Christ's love and salvation, they will not be saved. This doctrine results in a *Jesus who will be eternally frustrated in his desires*. This is an impossible notion not taught in the Bible. According to John 17:6 and 9, Jesus only prays for his sheep.

> "I pray for them. I am not praying for the world, but for those you have given me, for they are yours." [John 17:9]

Because Jesus took upon himself the infinite wrath of the infinite God, his suffering atonement is *sufficient* for all. It possesses enough value and merit to cover the sins of every person who ever has or ever will live. Because it is not God's ultimate design to save all people, however (a populated hell proves this), Jesus' death is not *efficient* for all people. Therefore, the atonement can be described this way: *It is sufficient for all, but efficient only for those previously elected by God.*

God commanded that the gospel of Christ's atoning work be offered freely to all, though we know as we obey that command that not all will respond. The preaching of the gospel is God's appointed means to call those for whom Christ died, and we can know without question that when the gospel is preached, God's elect will surely respond.

Coram Deo

Read John 17:6–26 as Jesus prays for the people God will give him. If you have accepted Christ as Savior and Lord, personalize this prayer by including your name where appropriate. If you are unsure of your position in Christ, know that it is God's delight to communicate assurance to his children. With all persistence in prayer, call out to the Father, asking him to make your calling and election sure.

For further study: John 10:11–18; 17:6–26; Romans 9:14–24; Ephesians 1:3–14

104 The Glorious House

After God spoke the Ten Commandments to the people they asked that Moses stand between them and God because the voice of God was so loud and terrifying (Exod. 20:18–19). God gave to Moses the laws we find in the Book of the Covenant, and Moses told them to the people (Exodus 21–23). Then Moses led the people in a ceremony of covenant ratification, and Moses and the elders had a communion meal with God on Mount Sinai (Exodus 24).

God next summoned Moses into the glory cloud and revealed plans for a tent in which he would dwell. As the people were living in tents, so God would also reside in a tent in their midst. Bear in mind that these tents were not teepees or wigwams. The tabernacle of God was a glorified version of the ordinary Israelite tent. The tents had walls made of wooden planks set in sockets on the ground and were held up by bars that ran horizontally along the boards. Curtains were hung over the boards creating a wall. Depending on how the sockets were arranged on the ground, with the boards standing in them, a tent could have several rooms.

The first thing the LORD told Moses was to receive a contribution from the people. The people had spoiled the Egyptians, and the spoil of the defeated enemy was to be used to build the house of God. The palace of God, where he

> "These are the offerings you are to receive from them: gold, silver, and bronze; blue, purple, and scarlet yarn and fine linen; goat hair; ram skins dyed red and hides of sea cows; acacia wood; olive oil for the light; spices for the anointing oil and for the fragrant incense; and onyx stones and other gems to be mounted on the ephod and breastpiece." [Exod. 25:3–7]

would sit enthroned and where he would be worshiped, was to be opulent in gold, silver, bronze, fine linen, and jewels. The boards of God's tent were overlaid with gold. The curtains were of costly dyed fabric, especially blue and purple. The incense-burner, lampstand, and dinner table in God's "living room" (the Holy Place) were made of pure gold, while the sink and fireplace in his kitchen (the laver and altar) were of pure bronze.

One of the things we learn from this is that it is not wrong to adorn the house of God, the place of worship. God dwells in the *beauty* of holiness. It would be wrong if we completely neglected the other duties of the church, such as missions and charity, and spent all that we had on a lavish sanctuary, but it is also an error to condemn beauty and costly appointments of God's house of worship.

Coram Deo

Compare John 12:1–8 with Exodus 25:6 and 40:9, and Leviticus 8:10–12. What connections do you see between these passages? As you reflect on these things, what do they tell you about God's interest in beauty?

For further study: Exodus 40:9; Leviticus 8:10–12; 2 Chronicles 2:3–10; 3:3–9; 4:19–5:1; John 12:1–8

105 Immanuel: God With Us

According to Numbers 2 and 3, God arranged the Israelite camp in a square with three tribes on each side. The central tribe on the east was Judah, on the south, Reuben, on the west, Ephraim, and on the north, Dan. This was an immense outer square, set back some distance from the tabernacle.

Forming an inner square immediately around the tabernacle were the Levites, also separated into four groups. On the east side, in front of the tabernacle gate, were the Aaronic priests. On the south side were the Kohathites, on the west, the Gershonites, and on the north, the Merarites.

This configuration had a number of meanings. Some scholars have pointed out that the symbol of Judah was a lion, that of Reuben was a man, that of Ephraim was an ox, and that of Dan was an eagle. These are the four faces of the cherubim who guard God's throne on its four sides (Ezek. 1:5–23; Rev. 4:6–9). Thus, the nation of Israel was functioning as a guard for God's holiness, just as Adam was supposed to guard the original garden of Eden.

Since the tabernacle faced the east, in order to come into the tabernacle a person had to move through the encampment of the Aaronic priests. The priests were the mediators who gave human access to God. A stranger would also have to come through the kingly tribe of Judah to approach the tabernacle.

> "The Israelites are to camp around the Tent of Meeting some distance from it, each man under his standard with the banners of his family." [Num. 2:2]

Perhaps most important, though, was the symbolic fact that God was in their midst, right in the center of the camp. The word *Immanuel* means "God with us," and that was the prophetic name Jesus bore during his incarnation. God was Immanuel to Israel in the wilderness. His throne, his palace, his tent of meeting, was central in the society he created. The tabernacle was not just one institution among many, side by side with state, school, and business. It certainly was not peripheral to society as is the case today. Rather, God's meeting house was the highest of all the tents—30 feet high—and positioned in the center.

There was a time when towns and cities were built with the church building on a hill in the center of town with a high steeple. It was located there for biblical and strategic purposes. In our day we need to recover that vision of the centrality of God's presence.

Coram Deo

How can the church become central in society once again? Read Mark 10:42–45, and consider what it means in relation to this question. What specific things can your local church do to acquire influence and spiritual dominion over the place where you live?

For further study: John 3:14; 12:32; Romans 12:1–2; 1 Corinthians 2:1–5

106 A House for God

At the center of the Israelite camp a courtyard was marked out by white linen curtains hung on posts. The curtains were seven and one-half feet high, which prevented anyone from seeing what was inside the courtyard. The court itself measured 75 by 150 feet. It was the court of God's palace-tent, the tabernacle.

Inside the courtyard stood three objects: an altar, a bronze basin, and a large tent. The altar was a hollow bronze shell that could be carried from place to place. When set into position, it was filled with uncut stones and used to burn the sacrifices. It was the layman's job to slay, skin, cut up, and gut the sacrifice (Lev. 1:2–6). Then the priest would take the pieces to a large bronze basin between the altar and tent. He would wash them and put them on the altar to be burned.

The laity were not allowed to go near the altar or the basin, on pain of death. Armed Levites were stationed in the courtyard to ensure the sanctity of this area. Similarly, only priests were allowed into the tent or tabernacle that was God's house.

The tabernacle had two rooms. The innermost room (the Holy of Holies or Most Holy Place) was a cube fifteen feet on each side. It was God's throne room. At first it contained only one object: the Ark of the Covenant, a wooden chest overlaid with gold into which was placed a copy of

> "Then have them make a sanctuary for me, and I will dwell among them." [Exod. 25:8]

the Ten Commandments. The lid of the chest was a slab of gold called the "mercy seat." It was the throne of God, where he "sat" between two golden cherubim. Later, three other memorial objects were put into the inner room: a complete copy of the books of Moses, a pot of manna, and Aaron's rod that blossomed.

The outer room or Holy Place of the tabernacle measured 15 by 30 feet. We can consider it a "living room," with a lamp, a dinner table, and an incense burner. In God's house, of course, these objects took on deeper meaning. The golden lampstand, made like a stylized almond tree with seven branches, represented God's people as lights to the world. The table of showbread, with twelve loaves, and later also vessels of wine, represented God's provision. The altar of incense spoke of access to God through prayer.

Coram Deo

The new covenant fulfils the old. As you consider the various objects God placed in his courtyard and house in the old covenant, think of the gifts God has given us that we might know his presence in our midst. As you pray today, thank God for those gifts.

For further study: Jeremiah 31:31–34; Hebrews 5:1–14; 9:1–28

107 At the Golden Calf

While Moses was on the mountain getting plans for the tabernacle, the people on the plain below invented their own ideas for worship. Before they had a chance to donate the Egyptian spoils of gold and silver to build Gods house, they gave much of it to build a golden calf. The people had not only taken Egyptian goods, which as "spoil" had been commanded by God, but they had brought along Egyptian philosophy and worship, which was entirely forbidden.

The golden calf did not represent another culture's god, but was a false way of approaching Yahweh, the God who had delivered them from Egypt (Exod. 32:4–6). Instead of worshiping God as he had directed, the people devised their own way of worship, which rapidly degenerated into carnality and riot.

God had delivered the firstborn sons of Israel, claiming them for himself. These young men became the priests of Israel (Exod. 24:5). At the golden calf, however, they betrayed their calling and were disqualified. When Moses called for men to join with God in executing the leaders of the apostasy, it was the Levites who came to his side. As a result, Moses told them they had been set apart for the Lord, and that they would replace the firstborn sons of Israel as priests (Exod. 32:29).

In Numbers 3 we read that God commanded that a census be taken of the Levites and firstborn sons of Israel. Then,

232

> So all the people took off their earrings and brought them to Aaron. [Exod. 32:3]

head by head they were exchanged. There were 273 extra firstborn sons who were redeemed at the rate of five shekels each. Thus, the firstborn sons of Israel, though in principle dedicated to the Lord, were always redeemed, and God took the tribe of Levi as his priests instead. In the same way Jesus serves as our Levite. Though in Adam we were initially assigned to be God's priests, we fell to sin and were disqualified. As Adam listened to the beguiling words of an animal, so Israel worshiped through one (Rom. 1:23). Because of our failure to live up to our calling as priests, God sent the perfect High Priest, Jesus Christ, to take our place.

If we had remained as priests we would have been destroyed because our sin had made us unworthy and unholy to stand in his presence. By taking our place, Jesus has removed us from the threat against us.

Coram Deo

God banished Adam from the garden. God removed himself from the camp of Israel. What reason did God give for this (Exod. 32:10; 33:3–7)? Assess your life. Have you built any idols, possibly not intending to replace God but simply to worship him as you desire, rather than as he demands?

For further study: Exodus 32:10; 33:3–7; 1 Corinthians 10:1–22; Galatians 1:6–10; 3:1–9; Hebrews 3

233

108 Garments of Glory

T wo chapters of the Bible describe the priestly garments worn by Aaron and his sons as they served God (Exodus 28, 39; see also Leviticus 8). God gave the design for two sets of garments. Aaron, as high priest, wore splendid and highly symbolic apparel while his sons wore less glorious clothes.

The garments of the ordinary priests included linen undergarments that reached from the waist to the thigh, specifically said to cover the "flesh," that is, the private parts (Exod. 28:42). Aaron also wore these undergarments. The ordinary priests were given tunics of fine linen, a sash of embroidered work, and a turban of fine linen. The Bible identifies white linen as a symbol of holiness.

Just as the Israelite layman had to wash and be clean ceremonially in order to enter the courtyard of the tabernacle (Lev. 11–15), so the priest had to be arrayed in white in order to draw near the altar and the tabernacle.

The high priest's garments went a step further, from white and holiness to the rainbow colors of glory. Over his white undergarments the high priest wore a robe entirely of blue cloth (blue was the most expensive dye in the ancient world). The opening at the top was woven like a coat of mail, indicating the high priest was God's paramount holy warrior. At the bottom were cloth pomegranates made of yarn alternating with golden bells that tinkled as Aaron walked.

Over the robe was the "ephod," a garment consisting of

> "Make sacred garments for your brother Aaron, to give him dignity and honor." [Exod. 28:2]

a waistband with gold chains that ran up and over the shoulders. On the shoulders were two onyx stones engraved with the names of the tribes of Israel. Attached to the ephod in the front was a breastpiece, like armor, but with twelve precious stones representing the twelve tribes. The breastpiece included a pouch for two mysterious items called *Urim* and *Thummim*, which were used as oracles of judgment. Finally, the high priest wore a turban with a golden plate in front on which were inscribed the words "Holy to the LORD."

The holiness of God had to be ascribed to Aaron and to the people whose names he bore. None could come *coram Deo*, not even a finely dressed intercessor, without an Intercessor.

Coram Deo

Read Genesis 3:19 and 2 Chronicles 16:19. When Aaron went before God's face his brow was covered with the golden plate. Why? Also, when he approached God's face Aaron bore Israel on his shoulders, symbolized by the ephod, and on his heart, symbolized by the breastpiece. How does Jesus Christ fulfil this symbolism? How can this picture give you more confidence in your prayer life?

For further study: Genesis 3:19; 2 Chronicles 26:19; Luke 9:28–31; Revelation 19:6–16

109 Our Great High Priest

A t Mount Sinai God established priests and also a high priest. By the time of David's day there were so many priests that they were divided into twenty-four sections with a chief priest over each (1 Chronicles 24). Thus, in the New Testament we read of priests, chief priests, and the high priest. The author of Hebrews speaks of someone even higher however: a "Great High Priest," Jesus, the Son of God.

Leviticus 16 describes the most important work of the high priest, which he accomplished on the annual Day of Atonement. On that day, after elaborate purification rituals, he was allowed to enter the Most Holy Place, the throne room of God. On that day blood was put on the ark and mercy seat to atone for all the sins of the nation.

There were two aspects to the atonement. Two goats were set apart as sin offerings. The first was slain and its blood was sprinkled on the mercy seat. Aaron then took the other goat and laid his hands on it. He confessed over it "all the wickedness and rebellion of the Israelites—all their sins—and put them on the goat's head" (Lev. 16:21). Then this second goat would be sent into the wilderness carrying the sins of Israel away. Before Aaron could offer these two goats for the sins of the people, however, he had to offer a bull for his own sins.

> Therefore, since we have a great high priest who has gone
> through the heavens, Jesus the Son of God, let us hold firmly to
> the faith we profess. [Heb. 4:14]

The Great High Priest, by way of contrast, did not need to offer a preliminary sacrifice for his sins (Heb. 7:27). He was sinless. Moreover, the Great High Priest was not only the priest offering sacrifices to God, but he was the sacrifice himself. He was both the slain goat whose blood atoned for sin, and the scapegoat who carried away our sins forever.

An additional contrast is most important. Leviticus 16:34 states that on the Day of Atonement sacrifices had to be performed once a year. The blood of bulls and goats were only ceremonial, incapable of permanently removing the sins of the people. The atonement of Jesus Christ, on the other hand, was not ceremonial.

This perfect sacrifice literally was made once for all time.

Coram Deo

The goat carrying the sins of Israel ran into the wilderness. Christ, however, took our sins as far as the east is from the west. Thank God for sending the perfect sacrifice. Read Romans 12:1–2. In view of God's mercy what is one thank offering you can make to glorify your Great High Priest?

For further study: Leviticus 16; Isaiah 53:1–7; Romans 12:1–2;
Hebrews 7; 1 Peter 2:4–10

Although we have skipped much of Exodus, Numbers, and Leviticus, we will review the highlights of those books within the context of the first chapters of Deuteronomy.

Deuteronomy is one of the most important books of the Bible since it sets forth in a full way the covenant God made with Israel. John Calvin preached more than 200 sermons from Deuteronomy. He contended that in this book God demonstrates to society the meaning and importance of justice and righteousness. Although God was addressing old covenant Israel (and thus not everything can be literally applied today), we gain wisdom and insight for our culture by studying God's covenant model for that society. Even where the covenant has been changed in Jesus Christ, God's principles for living *coram Deo* have not changed. Deuteronomy holds much that is valuable for our ethics and

God's Covenant Model

worldview. How should we react to some trends in our society that appear to be drawing society out of sight of its Judeo-Christian foundation? Many of these trends have appeared before, and were even predicted by Moses. We will be reminded that a nation turns from its God only at great peril to its future.

Additionally, Deuteronomy holds stirring challenges to heartfelt love for God. This book holds the ancient call to Israel in the *shema* to "Hear" and understand who their God is (Deut. 6:4), and it calls believers to faithfully trust him. As you study, may the Holy Spirit help you understand God's covenantal love for his people, and the corresponding obligation of God's people to live *coram Deo*—to love and serve him with all their heart, soul, and strength.

R.C. Sproul

110 Loving God's Law

hen we teach our children the alphabet we start with the song, "A-B-C-D-E-F-G, H-I-J-K-. . . . " When they get to school the youngsters learn that, "*A* is for 'apple'; *B* is for 'ball'. . . ." The Bible also includes an interesting alphabetical song: Psalm 119. It has 22 sections, one for each letter of the Hebrew alphabet. Each section has eight verses, and each verse beings with the same letter. There are 176 verses in all.

Every verse in this alphabetical psalm celebrates the law of God. Verses from 97–104 each begin with the Hebrew version of the letter *M* (in Hebrew, *Mem*). This could even be done in English, for instance:

> 97. My love is for Your law . . . ;
> 98. My enemies fear my wisdom . . . ;
> 99. More insight have I . . . ;
> 100. More understanding have I. . . .

Can you imagine a song about God's law becoming popular in our culture? Indeed, can you imagine such a song being a favorite in today's *church*? We have fallen far from the mindset of the Bible; we have strayed far from the biblical world-and-life view. Jesus came not to destroy the law but to fulfil it (Matt. 5:17), and so great was his regard for God's law that he never departed from it.

The Protestant Reformers distinguished three central purposes of the law of God. First, the law was given to show our need for a Savior. This is the *redemptive use* of the law. Second, the law was given to show us how to live in a way pleasing to God. This is the *moral use* of the law. Third, the law was given to guide society. This is the *civil use* of the law, the law as implemented in society to restrain crime.

Notice the incredible benefits of studying God's law, which we shall do through our study of Deuteronomy. The law will make us wiser than our enemies (Ps. 119:98). It will give us more insight than our teachers have (v. 99). It will enable us to outstrip our elders in understanding (v. 100). It will guard us from evil (vv. 101, 104). When we acquire a taste for it, the law will seem sweeter and more delightful than honey (v. 103). Finally, verse 102 says that if we study the law, God will personally teach us.

Coram Deo

Do these benefits seem wonderful? Do these aspects of the law still apply today? Think about why the study of the law is so seldom undertaken. Through prayer, take some time to prepare your heart to be open to accepting God's continuing uses of the law in this, the age of grace.

For further study: Psalm 19:7–11; Galatians 3:23–25;
1 Timothy 1:5, 8–10; 1 John 5:1–5

111 Who Wrote Deuteronomy?

I n the eighteenth year of his reign, King Josiah gave orders that the temple of the Lord be repaired. While it was being repaired, the high priest Hilkiah found a copy of the "Book of the Law." He gave it to Shaphan to read (in those days not very many people were trained in reading), and Shaphan realized what it was and brought it to Josiah's attention.

Convicted by its precepts and how far the people were living from them, Josiah promptly reformed the nation.

What was this book? Historically it has been understood to include the Books of Moses. During the eighteenth and nineteenth centuries, however, unbelieving secular critics formulated the notion that Deuteronomy had been written by Hilkiah and Shaphan, and thus the "discovery" was a hoax. Among liberal branches of the church this notion was adopted and became the standard line.

Educated Christians need to know more about this erroneous belief and why it arose. During the eighteenth and nineteenth centuries the idea of biological evolution influenced nearly all areas of thought. In religion it was held that human culture evolved from primitive animism (the worship of rocks and trees), though polytheism (many gods), then to henotheism (one god over all the rest), and finally to monotheism (only one God). There is no evidence that this development pattern has occurred anywhere, and the Bible flatly contradicts it, but evolutionists hold tenaciously to it.

242

> Hilkiah the high priest said to Shaphan the secretary, "I have found the Book of the Law in the temple of the Lord." He gave it to Shaphan, who read it. [2 Kings 22:8]

Liberals said the "Books of Moses" were actually crude compilations put together by the priests centuries after Moses. Supposedly they find a *J* document (using the word *Jahweh* for God), and *E* document (using the word *Elohim* for God), a *D* document (written by "the deuteronomist"), and a *P* document (written by priests). They contend Hilkiah and Shaphan wrote Deuteronomy in Josiah's time, making sure that the priests and Levites came out heroes, in order to bolster the Jerusalem priesthood.

Not one shred of evidence supports this, and it has repeatedly been refuted by conservative scholars. As we study the book of Deuteronomy—written by Moses—we shall look at a coherent literary structure and style.

Coram Deo

Liberal theologians may have reached their conclusions in order to vitiate the authority of the law. As evangelicals, we affirm Mosaic authorship of the Pentateuch. Yet, after fighting to uphold its authority, we often try to escape or ignore obeying it. Give the law the full commitment and study it deserves as the Word of God.

For further study: Deuteronomy 31:24–26; John 5:41–47; 7:16–19; Acts 15:1–7; Romans 10:5, 19

112 Covenant and Dynasty

euteronomy is laid out as a covenant or treaty document. In the Bible, covenants have a literary structure containing several sections (see pp. 16–19). The first is the *preamble*. In this section the Lord, who is making the covenant, identifies himself. In the Ten Commandments, the phrase "I am *Yahweh* your God" is the preamble. In Deuteronomy, the preamble is 1:1–5. These verses identify Moses as spokesman for the Lord, who is making this covenant with Israel.

The second section of a covenant, the historical prologue, describes how the Lord delivered the people from wrath to grace, from bondage to freedom, from sin to righteousness—in this case, from Egypt into his kingdom. In the Ten Commandments the phrase "who brought you out of the land of Egypt, out of the house of bondage" is the historical prologue. In Deuteronomy, the historical prologue runs from 1:6 to 4:40.

In order to understand what Moses said, we must bear in mind that Deuteronomy is a covenant *renewal*. God had instituted the covenant at Mount Sinai, and forty years later Moses led the people in renewing that same covenant. When God initially gave the covenant, he began the history with the deliverance from Egypt. Renewing it, Moses took up at the point where the first covenant had been made at Mount Sinai (1:6).

A covenant renewal never reverts to the previous

covenant, but fits the older covenant to new circumstances. The fundamental principles remain, but the specific applications change. God made the covenant with Israel during their wilderness travels and the law in Exodus and Leviticus is phrased to fit life in the encampment. Deuteronomy rephrases the law to apply it to the situation of living in the land.

Ancient covenants also covered dynastic succession in a section found at the end of the document. Moses died, turning the nation over to Joshua (Deut. 31:1–8; 32:44–47; 34:9). This aspect of the covenant was mentioned in 1:38. We should notice a parallel in the New Testament. Just before he died Jesus renewed the covenant with his disciples, giving them a new law (John 13:34) and turning them over to his successor, the Holy Spirit (John 14–17).

Coram Deo

Moses went to great pains to confirm Joshua as his successor, lest the people refuse to follow him. Jesus made it clear that the Holy Spirit is his successor as authority among his people while they are on earth. How faithful are you to him? Seek to know and understand the "other Comforter" Jesus sent us.

For further study: Joshua 1:1–9; Psalm 1; John 13:34; 14–17

245

113 Problems With Giants

After God created Adam and entered into a covenant
with him, Adam fell into sin and rebelled. In this
and each subsequent instance, we see God renewing his covenant to a redeemed people. Each time those
people again fell into sin. We read about the Noahic Covenant
in Genesis 9, and the next event described is the sin of Ham.
God made a covenant with Abraham, promising him a son,
and immediately Abraham fell into sin by lying with Hagar.
No sooner had God made a covenant with Israel at Mount
Sinai than they fell into sin at the golden calf. The very day
God instituted the priestly covenant with Aaron his sons
sinned and were destroyed (Lev. 9–10). God made a covenant
with David that David's house would be his home, and the
next thing seen was David defiling his house (and thus God's
house) by committing adultery and murder (2 Samuel 7, 11).

A new covenant and then a new fall into sin—that is the
sorry pattern human depravity shows in history. In
Deuteronomy 1–4, Moses rehearses the history of Israel
from Mount Sinai forward, and he shows that they fell into
sin and lost the kingdom because they did not fear the
Lord. As a result, they were not permitted to enter the
Promised Land.

Moses recounted the events recorded in the Book of
Numbers. After the people sinned by worshiping the golden

> They were a people strong and numerous, and as tall as the Anakites. The LORD destroyed them from before the Ammonites, who drove them out and settled in their place. [Deut. 2:21]

calf, God reinstituted his covenant with them. He led them to the borders of Canaan, and then the people refused to conquer the land. There were giants in the land which they feared more than God (Deut. 1:26–46).

Moses contrasted Israel with her cousins. The Moabites, descendants of Lot, took land from the Emites, who were giants like the Anakites and the Rephaites (2:9–11). The Edomites, descendants of Esau, did similarly (2:12). The Ammonites, also descendants of Lot, took their land from the giant Zamzummites (2:20–23).

At the end of the wilderness wanderings God brought Israel face to face with Og of Bashan, whose bed was 13 feet long (3:1–11). The defeat of such giants gave Israel her first piece of the Promised Land (3:12–20).

Coram Deo

How did King Saul fare against the giant? How did David (1 Samuel 17)? Here we see again the pattern of covenant and sin. Who was the "giant" that Jesus had to conquer first (Matt. 4:1–11)? What giants do you face in your life? Don't fear and flee from them, but face them in the fear of God.

For further study: Judges 3; 11:24; Habakkuk 1:5–11

114 The Sin of Moses

e have seen that each time God renewed the
covenant with his people, the first thing they did
was to sin against him. Yet God remained faithful
each time, renewing the covenant despite the sin. In the case
of Israel, God initially removed himself from the camp when
the people sinned at the golden calf, but after the tabernacle was built he moved back into their midst (Exodus 32–33,
40). The people sinned numerous times after this, but God
forgave them again and again. Finally, when they refused to
fight the giants and take the promised land, God cut them
off. He declared that they had rebelled ten times (Num.
14:22–23) and that all of them would die in the wilderness.
Their children would inherit the kingdom they had lost.

Moses renewed the covenant with the children, telling
them that he too would die in the wilderness.

To understand why Moses was excluded from entering
Canaan, we look at two incidents. In Exodus 17 it is told
that Israel ran out of water soon after they came out of
Egypt. They grumbled against Moses and put God on a
kind of trial. God told Moses to take his rod of judgment
and strike a rock in the presence of the law court of elders,
and water would come forth. God put his glory cloud on
the rock, and Moses brought the rod of judgment down
on God and the rock, and water came out (Exod. 17:5–6).
God was taking on the judgment the people deserved, and
on that basis they were given water.

A symbol is here shown to the people of an event they

> The LORD was angry with me because of you, and he solemnly swore that I would not cross the Jordan and enter the good land the LORD your God is giving you as your inheritance. [Deut. 4:21]

then could not understand, for it would be far in the future. One day the Messiah would be smitten on the cross, and water mixed with blood would pour from his side (John 19:34). A refreshing miracle for them has became a picture for us.

Years later the congregation again needed water and God told Moses to take Aaron's rod (the rod of prayer, not judgment) and speak to a rock, and water would come forth. The sins of the people angered Moses, however, and he lost his temper and struck the rock twice. God graciously gave water anyway, but he told Moses that, because he had failed to treat God as holy, Moses would not enter the land of promise (Num. 20:2–13).

Coram Deo

Read and meditate on Numbers 20:12. To Moses much had been given. The biblical principle seems to be operating here that from Moses much was required. God let the people off nine times, but Moses only did one thing wrong, and he received the same punishment. Was this a "fair" punishment? What does Moses know about God's holiness? What do you know about God? Read James 3 to get more insight into the principle involved.

For further study: Numbers 20:12; Psalms 95:1–11; 105:26–45; 106:32–33; James 3

115 The Just Society

A s Moses brought to a close the historical prologue section of the covenant renewal (see p. 17),
he reminded the people how they had heard the
law of God on Mount Sinai. This provided a transition into
the next section of the covenant, the actual law itself (Deut.
4:44–26:19).

Moses told the people that, if they obeyed the law, they
would be esteemed wise among all the nations. Righteous
living would have an evangelistic effect, because, as the
nations admired the law and sought to find out more about
it, they would be led to the God who gave the law (Deut.
4:6–8).

Surely the most valuable study of jurisprudence that
could be undertaken today would be a close examination
of the Old Testament law. We should study it diligently to
gain societal wisdom. Unfortunately, we often have a false
view of the Old Testament law. Too many people believe it
too severe. A study of God's law however, reveals quite the
opposite, for just as God is love, so his law is the expression of his love.

Something is wrong with the church in our culture today.
How do you think the average church member would react
to learn that a study of Old Testament law was being undertaken to gain wisdom for modern life and society? Most
Christians would shrink in horror at the idea. People say
the law is cruel and bloodthirsty (implying that the God

> And what other nation is so great as to have such righteous decrees and laws as this body of laws I am setting before you today? [Deut. 4:8]

who gave it also must be cruel and bloodthirsty), but the Bible says the national laws God gave Israel were wise, righteous, and just.

Part of the reason people react against Old Testament law is because they are misinformed. They have never read and studied the social laws in Exodus 21–23, Leviticus 19, and Deuteronomy 5–26. But another reason people react against the law is that they are estranged from God. They want a God of "love," as *they* define love. They don't want the biblical God of love, whose love is inseparable from justice, holiness, and righteousness.

As Bible-believing Christians, however, we need only ask ourselves one question: Has ever any government had a law as just and righteous as the law God gave to Israel?

Coram Deo

The answer to that last question is obvious, and its implications are clear: If we want to have a just society we need to learn the wisdom and principles of the law of God in its social and national dimensions. We may have to change our thinking about some things. Consider state or federal laws that might need to change to conform to the principles of God's law and character.

For further study: Psalm 147:19–20; Romans 7:12–14; 2 Timothy 3:16–17

116 The Greatest Commandment

oses' first sermon ends at Deuteronomy 4:40. A few verses later (from v. 44) we have the introduction to Moses' second sermon, an exposition of the law of God, applying it to the new circumstances Israel would face in the land of Canaan. Moses began by reminding the people how God gave the Ten Commandments at Mount Sinai, rehearsing them with several slight changes that add a different slant to the fundamental law of God (5:1–31).

Chapters 6–11 offer a general exhortation to obey God, focusing on the first commandment: "You shall have no other gods before me." Moses began by calling on Israel to *hear* (vv. 3–4). They were to hear God and to hearken to him alone.

Verse 4 is one of the most famous phrases in the Old Testament. It is so compact that it cannot be rendered into English by one simple phrase, as it is in Hebrew. The New International Version provides four overlapping translations:

1. The LORD our God, the LORD is one;
2. The LORD our God is one LORD;
3. The LORD is our God, the LORD is one;
4. The LORD is our God, the LORD alone.

Meditating on this verse, called the *shema* for the Hebrew word meaning "hear," the devout Israelite would become

> Hear, O Israel: The LORD our God, the LORD is one. Love the LORD
> your God with all your heart and with all your soul and with all
> your strength. [Deut. 6:4–5]

grounded in the fact that there is only one God and that this God is his God.

Since this God, the only God there is, has made himself my God, the only possible response I can have is to love him with all my being (v. 5). Jesus called this the first and greatest commandment (Matt. 22:36–38). Not only does it rephrase the first commandment but it summarizes all the commandments.

If we love God with all our being, which as fallen sinners we will never do in this life, we will never disbelieve or disobey him. For this reason, Jesus could say that all the law hangs on this commandment and the command to love our neighbors as ourselves (Matt. 22:40).

Coram Deo

If we really love God, we will burn to see his holy law realized in our own hearts and in the lives of our children. We will put them on our hands (labor) and foreheads (thoughts), and on our door frames (homes) and gates (civil government). Analyze whether you have made a thorough application of the commandments to your life as prescribed by God through Moses.

For further study: Deuteronomy 6:4–9; Mark 12:28–34; John 14:19–24;
2 Corinthians 5:11–15

117 Godliness and Blessedness

A s Moses exhorted Israel to obey God's law, he told them that, if they did so, God would bless them spiritually and with prosperity and wealth. In our day materialism has run amok; too much value is placed on material things. But the response to materialism in some circles has been to resurrect an old pagan antimaterialism, suggesting that wealth and prosperity are intrinsically evil. We are told that God is always on the side of the poor, as if poverty by itself, apart from righteousness, has his blessing.

Prosperity often is the blessing of God. God forbid that we should envy and rebuke someone who is enjoying prosperity as if it were automatically a sign of sinfulness. Perhaps the wealth was earned wrongfully or through exploitation, but it may be that their wealth, by the blessing of God, was earned through faithful service to others.

We must beware of attacking those whom God has blessed. Abraham, after all, was a very wealthy man, and we are told that Job was one of the richest men in the world (Job 1:3). Job lost his riches, but not because of any sin, and God gave him back double what he had lost (42:12).

Moreover, God promised to remove all sickness from Israel (Deut. 7:15). Does this mean that anyone who suffers sickness or poverty has sinned and is being judged by God? Of course not. The Book of Job and many other passages

> If you pay attention to these laws and are careful to follow them,
> then the LORD your God . . . will bless the fruit of your womb, the
> crops of your land—your grain, new wine, and oil—the calves of
> your herds and the lambs of your flocks in the land that he swore
> to your forefathers to give you. [Deut. 7:12–13]

in the Bible teach that a righteous individual may be called to suffer for the glory of God. God sometimes gives strength and wealth to the wicked in order to raise them up to chastise his wayward people.

What Deuteronomy 7:12–15 does mean, however, is that, culturally and nationally, some physical blessings do come to those who honor God. The more righteousness present in a nation, the more health and prosperity it will enjoy. There is a general cultural correlation between sin and suffering, and between obedience and prosperity. Nothing in the New Testament indicates that God has changed this promise.

Coram Deo

In *Democracy in America,* Alexis de Tocqueville wrote, "America is great because America is good; if America ever ceases to be good, America will cease to be great." He also wrote that the foundation of America's greatness was in churches where pulpits were aflame with righteousness. What can you do as an earthly citizen and a citizen in Christ's kingdom to restore the nation?

For further study: Deuteronomy 7:12–15; Job 42:10–17;
Psalm 144:9–15; Luke 12:22–34

118 The Danger of Presumption

oses told the people that the land God gave them was filled with riches. They were to inherit fields, cities, vineyards, and other benefits of the developed culture of the Canaanites. The one thing they were not to inherit, however, was the religion of the Canaanites; they were to destroy every religious artifact they found (Deut. 7:17–8:9).

Moses warned them not to forget the source of all their blessings. He told them that the time would come when, as a result of their obedience, they would enjoy much prosperity, and their silver and gold would multiply. He warned that when this happened they would be tempted to forget they owed it all to God. They would think their power, strength, wisdom, and sound economics had brought them their blessings (Deut. 8:10–18).

Moses said that God would judge them if they ever started taking credit for these benefits. Those who started believing in themselves, he said, would end up worshiping idols of stone and metal. An angry God would destroy them the same way he was about to destroy the Canaanites (Deut. 8:19–20).

Moses' message in Deuteronomy 8 conveys a solemn warning to each of us and to our society. What nations have enjoyed as much prosperity as have the United States and Canada? Their prosperity came about because, in spite of many failings, their forefathers were faithful to God. In recent years, however, North Americans have overthrown their faith and have come to believe that their blessings are simply the result of hard work and the free enterprise system. The society is turning back to the idolatry and witchcraft of New Age beliefs and practices. According to the Bible, God will not stand for this.

Moses said the only cure for this disastrous trend is to remember two things: First, remember who God is; second, remember who you are. You are a sinner who deserves nothing. God is the only source of life, strength, and wealth, and all you have you owe to him alone. Unless each nation turns back and remembers these things, each shall surely be judged.

Coram Deo

Independence is a treasured virtue that sometimes interferes with spiritual values and needs. Far from being a weakness, dependence upon God is a sign of spiritual maturity. Identify where you need to become more dependent upon God.

For further study: 2 Chronicles 26:9–16; Psalm 106:1–23

119 The Covenant Renewed

I f a nation forsakes the Lord and begins to trust itself, committing idolatry, God promises to bring judgment (Deut. 8:19–20). Is there any hope? Indeed there is, and Moses leads the people toward that hope by pointing them back to their own history. At Mount Sinai the people accepted the covenant God offered and promised to obey it. Then Moses ascended the mountain to receive further instruction from God (Exod. 24). While Moses was gone the people forsook the Lord and began to worship at the golden calf. This brought the judgment of God upon them (Deut. 9:7–17).

God told Moses that he would blot our Israel. As a sign that God, the High King of Israel, was dissolving his treaty of peace with them, Moses broke the tablets on which God had written the Ten Commandments. The official document of the covenant arrangement between God and Israel was officially broken; there was nothing to stop God from annihilating every Israelite.

God offered Moses the opportunity to become a new Abraham, the father of a new race of people who would become a replacement for Israel. Amazingly, Moses refused this great offer. Instead, Moses stood between God and Israel, pleading for Israel. He fasted and prayed for 40 days and nights, and he argued with God until God relented and renewed his covenant (Deut. 9:18–29).

> The LORD wrote on these tablets what he had written before, the Ten Commandments he had proclaimed to you on the mountain, out of the fire, on the day of the assembly. And the LORD gave them to me. [Deut. 10:4]

God, who is not a man and need not repent of anything, nonetheless graciously allowed Moses to interact with him in this matter. God accepted Moses' intercession, making a new covenant because the first had been destroyed by sin. God told Moses to chisel new stone tablets and to make a chest (ark) in which to put them. God rewrote the Ten Commandments with his finger and Moses put them in the ark. Thus, the ark of the covenant resembled a veil that protected Israel from the wrath and judgment of God (Deut. 10:1–5).

Moses rehearsed this history for Israel to teach them that if they fell into sin they could still repent. God was ready to receive them and to restore the covenant if, through repentance, they turned back to him. If, however, they would not repent they would be destroyed.

Coram Deo

We see how big the heart of Moses was and how he was willing to sacrifice personal advantage for the sake of God's people. Meditate on the fact that it is now Jesus who stands between you and God, pleading with God to forgive your many sins. Thank God for Jesus' intercession on your behalf.

For further study: Acts 3:11–23; Hebrews 9:11–28

120 Forbidden Food

O ur survey of particular laws Moses gave to the people of Israel in Deuteronomy starts with the dietary laws. The laws of clean and unclean animals were given by God in Leviticus 11 and repeated by Moses in Deuteronomy 14.

It has often been noted that there was a hygienic benefit in keeping these dietary laws. Some of the animals, if eaten, could be harmful. Most people are aware, for instance, that unless pork is cooked thoroughly it can carry a variety of diseases. But while it is true that some of these foods present medical problems, not all do. Hygiene considerations, or at least hygiene alone, cannot account for this list of acceptable and prohibited flesh. As a result, there has been discussion and debate over the rationale for calling one animal clean and another unclean.

One of the most important aspects of the dietary laws was that they set the people apart as a peculiar and priestly nation to God. They became "unclean" if they ate the forbidden flesh. Becoming "unclean" did not mean becoming sick (hygienically), but becoming unfit to draw near to offer sacrifice until after ceremonial "cleansing" by water. Thus, avoiding unclean meat symbolized clinging to the holiness and cleanliness of each individual's calling as a member of the special people of God.

Do not eat any detestable thing. [Deut. 14:3]

We can see this aspect of the dietary laws dramatically highlighted in Daniel 1. Nebuchadnezzar had brought back to Babylon the best of Jerusalem's young nobility. His goal was to educate them into Babylonian culture. He wanted to convert them to Babylonian ways and use them in his court. Daniel and his friends, however, refused to eat the unclean food put before them and courteously asked to be given vegetables instead. God blessed Daniel, and as a result, he and his friends were allowed to remain undefiled. The rest of the Book of Daniel shows how the tables were turned on Nebuchadnezzar and how eventually it was he who was converted.

In the new covenant, these laws have been "repealed" because their symbolism has been fulfilled in Christ (Acts 10).

Coram Deo

Food was but one way of showing separateness in the Old Testament. What were other ways? How can we, in the context of the new covenant, demonstrate our separateness from the world? Consider where you have been negligent in acting as a member of a holy people.

For further study: Isaiah 65:1–7; Romans 14:1–18; Titus 3:3–8

121 The Year of Jubilee

I n Deuteronomy 15 Moses told the people to keep the sabbath years God had established. Leviticus 25 develops the sabbath year laws and their meaning. Every seventh year the land was to lie fallow. Everybody's land was to rest at the same time. This required a great deal of faith: "What shall we eat?" "What if the following year we suffer crop failure? We shall have no reserve." Yet God promised that in the sixth year he would send a *triple* harvest to carry the nation through (Lev. 25:20–22). This promise of abundance was significant. The land itself would join in an act of obedience and worship; people and nature would share a first step toward the reversal of the effects of the curse.

In the sabbath year certain debts were canceled, specifically charity loans. God warned the people not to harden their hearts against the poor as they saw the year of release drawing near. Those who lent to the poor without interest, and whose loan wound up being canceled in the sabbath year, could count on God to make up the difference. The sabbath year was for Old Testament Israel only, but the obligation to be openhearted toward the poor is for us as well.

After 49 years (seven sabbath year cycles) there was an extra sabbath called the *jubilee*. This fiftieth year was a super-sabbath for the land. In the jubilee, all of the land of Israel temporarily reverted to its true owner, the Lord. To understand the jubilee, remember that God, as owner, had taken the land of Canaan from the Canaanites. They had

> At the end of every seven years you must cancel debts. [Deut. 15:1]

forfeited the right to dwell there through their sinfulness. As Israel conquered Canaan, God parceled out *his* land to the tribes. Each family received a permanent plot of good land. If it became necessary to sell the plot to raise money, the land only temporarily changed hands. In effect what was sold was not the land itself but the crops the land would produce until the jubilee. At the jubilee, God took his land back and returned it to the original steward families.

Immigrants might lease land, but they would lose it in the jubilee; thus, they settled in cities, for land in the cities was not covered under the jubilee law.

In the new covenant, the spiritual and moral teaching of the jubilee continues to be relevant. In Luke 4:19 Jesus proclaimed that the great jubilee had come. God was taking the earth back from Satan and would give it, little by little, generation by generation, to his faithful stewards.

Coram Deo

The jubilee year meant release from debt and bondage. It was a type of the jubilee that Jesus inaugurated. Salvation in Christ is God's jubilee to his people. From what has God released you? How can you act as a faithful steward by showing love to someone who seems oppressed in spiritual and emotional captivity?

For further study: Leviticus 25:8–55; 27:16–25; Luke 4:14–21

263

122 Righteous Judges

L iterally, Deuteronomy 16:18 commands that judges be set up in every "gate." The gate controlled access to the city, allowing some people in and banishing others. It was at the gates where the elders sat to render judgment. Thus, when we read references to "gates" in the Bible, very frequently the term refers to the law-court.

God, through Moses, told the people that judges were to judge impartially. Specifically they were not to accept a bribe, or as some translations render the word, a "gift" (Deut. 16:19). The purpose of a bribe or gift was to influence the judge. No one was immune from the influence of gifts; Moses said that even a wise man would be affected.

In verse 21 Moses forbade building altars and worship sites to false gods. Why was this commandment put here, in a section on the judicial system? This mystery has been solved by archeological study of the nations of that time. Judges in pagan nations settled legal matters by consulting witches, reading entrails, and examining the stars. In Israel, judgment was to be according to the Word of God alone. The use of the occult was forbidden.

In 17:2–7 Moses set up an exemplary system of justice. Under the Mosaic law, the Israelite who broke the national vow to worship God alone and openly worshiped other gods, was to be put to death. But no one was to be brought

> Appoint judges and officials to each of your tribes in every town the LORD your God is giving you, and they shall judge the people fairly. [Deut. 16:18]

to trial merely on rumor. The charge would be thoroughly investigated and corroborating evidence presented by at least two, and preferably three, witnesses. Anyone bringing a false charge was to be punished with exactly the punishment the accused would have faced. To charge someone falsely with a capital crime was itself a capital offense (Deut. 19:16–21). By these stipulations God guarded the innocent from slander and from false charges.

Finally, Moses said that if a case was too hard it could be appealed. But if, after all appeals were exhausted, the person refused to hear the court and showed contempt for God's legal system, that person could be put to death (Deut. 17:8–13). The sinner was given many chances to repent, but if he went too far, evil was "purged" from the land.

Coram Deo

These laws in Deuteronomy show us what kinds of things should bring about church discipline today. Does your denomination have a "book of order" that prescribes the conduct of trials? Are you familiar with its procedures? What does God say our attitude should be toward the elders (spiritual leaders) of the church when they are forced to render painful judgments?

For further study: Psalm 82:1–8; Romans 13:1–6

123 Rules for Rulers

At some point in the future, Moses told the people of Israel, they would seek to establish a human king. While God was to remain the ultimate ruler of his covenant people, a human king would be permitted. However, he warned, they should not run ahead of God in setting a king over themselves; they should wait until God was ready to choose the king and set up the dynasty (Deut. 17:14–15).

When that day came, three laws would particularly govern the king. First, the king was forbidden to multiply horses. Horses signaled a military power's strength and glory. The king was to glory in and depend on God alone. Also, horses were used exclusively in aggressive warfare, while Israel was to be a peace-loving nation with strong fortresses for defense. Moses warned the king not to reduce the people to the kind of bondage they had known in Egypt, in order to make them work for his glory.

Second, Moses commanded that the king have only one wife. Marriages were not to be used for international alliances, and if the king began to make such alliances his heart would be led away from God. Third, Moses commanded that the king not raise huge personal wealth by taxing the people.

Solomon, in his "fall," broke all three of these laws. He took in 666 talents of gold each year—worth untold sums

266

> The king, moreover, must not acquire great numbers of horses for himself or make the people return to Egypt to get more of them, for the Lᴏʀᴅ has told you, "You are not to go back that way again." [Deut. 17:16]

of money (1 Kings 10:14–23). He multiplied horses (1 Kings 10:26–29) and forced his people into slave labor, which caused a revolt when his son came to the throne (1 Kings 12:4–16). His wives and concubines turned his heart from the Lord (1 Kings 11:1–10).

Solomon forgot what Moses said in Deuteronomy 17:18–20, that the king was to personally write for himself a complete copy of God's law. He was to refer to it day and night, and to turn neither to the right nor to the left. Solomon also forgot what his father David taught him in Psalm 1: "His delight is in the law of the Lᴏʀᴅ, and on his law he meditates day and night."

As a result, the kingdom divided in half as soon as Solomon died, and the gold of his palace was removed (1 Kings 14:25–27). The kingdom and its glory crumbled because one man set himself above God's rules.

Coram Deo

Our nations are governed by the rule of law. While Israel was a theocracy and today's national governments are not, rulers still must abide by rules. Where do you see your civil and/or spiritual rulers flaunting the law? What tempts you to flaunt the law? Does the love of "mammon" distort your priorities?

For further study: 2 Kings 18–19; Psalm 20:1–9; Proverbs 3:1–6

124 Witchcraft and Prophecy

H aving given rules for magistrates and the king, Moses turned his attention to the priests and Levites (Deut. 18:1–8) and prophets (18:9–22). In ancient Israel the priests served God in connection with the sacrifices, and the people were to support this ministry with firstfruit offerings. In the Mosaic period, some Levites assisted the priests, but others lived in the towns as pastors of local worship assemblies (vv. 6–7). They too were to be supported by tithes and offerings. While Christ has become our only Priest, some priestly sacramental duties and the Levitical teaching ministries remain. These rest in the pastoral office, supported by tithes and gifts.

Rules governing the prophets began with certain condemnation of witchcraft in all its forms and manifestations. The purpose of witchcraft was to acquire knowledge, especially about the future. Believers in the true God were to look to the available Scriptures (for Moses' hearers the Pentateuch) alone as a source of information about the present and future.

I once visited a church where the people held seances to talk with departed relatives. When I pointed out that the Bible forbids this, they replied, "Oh, that was just for the Old Testament." Not so. God destroyed other nations for doing such things. The law against witchcraft was not peculiar to Israel. Moreover, the New Testament condemns any attempt to add to the Word of God (Gal. 1:8; Rev. 22:18). Anything God "detested" in the Old Testament (Deut. 18:12) and punished with death (Exod. 22:18) surely remains an evil in all times and places.

God promised to provide prophets for Israel. The prophet would speak God's word and would be a reliable source of information. There were two tests to determine if a someone were a true prophet. First, a true prophet would never contradict the written Word of God as it had been delivered. Second, God would give the prophet the ability to predict specific things that would come to pass, and these events would confirm his ministry. If even one prediction failed to happen the people knew that the prophet was false and was to be executed.

Coram Deo

As we approach the year 2000, false prophets are especially numerous. Some claim messages from the Virgin Mary. Others predict the specific time of the second coming of Christ. Others prophesy specific events. Is it possible that Christians are far too tolerant of this kind of activity? Pray that your church may be discerning and reject ungodly practices that masquerade as new prophecy from God.

For further study: Deuteronomy 13; 1 Samuel 28; 2 Chronicles 33:1–9

125 Cities of Refuge

C ities of refuge had been established by God long before Israel had any cities at all (Num. 35). Now Moses reminded the people to establish within the land six such cities, three on either side of the Jordan River. Highways connecting the cities to the towns of Israel were to be carefully maintained. The cities were to provide a place where people could flee when in trouble (Deuteronomy 19).

God's land was holy, and any time blood was shed on it the whole land became defiled. Consequently it would not yield its blessings. When blood was shed, deliberately or accidentally, atonement had to be made. If someone were slain, an avenger of blood was called to track down the killer and exact justice. The avenger appointed was the dead person's nearest male relative. It was this man's duty, whether he liked it or not, to ensure that atonement took place. This was not a matter of personal vengeance; the avenger was God's appointed agent to gain atonement for bloodshed.

Suppose two friends were in the woods chopping wood and the ax-head flew off one man's ax and killed his neighbor. It was the duty of the neighbor's brother to prosecute the man-killer, even though it was an accident. The killer would run to the city of refuge. There the Levites who maintained the city would be defense attorneys. The avenger was the court-appointed prosecutor, and the elders of the gate would hear the trial. Our modern system of justice has roots in the city-of-refuge judicial process.

The defendant judged to be guilty of premeditated murder would be turned out of the city of refuge, and the avenger would see to it that the sentence of death was carried out. If found innocent, the person was required to remain in the city of refuge until the death of the high priest. The death of the high priest atoned for the blood accidentally shed in the land. At that time the man-killer was free to leave the city of refuge and the avenger could no longer pursue.

In the New Testament, the magistrate was God's appointed avenger (Rom. 13:4). He was to investigate and prosecute all suspected crimes, protect the accused, provide a means of defense, and render justice.

Coram Deo

The death of our Great High Priest cleansed the land once and for all. Accidental manslaughter is no longer to be avenged. Historically, the church building has been honored as a sanctuary for people being pursued by mobs. Magistrates were not allowed to bring weapons into the church. Can the church function in this manner in any sense today?

For further study: Joshua 20:1–9; Hebrews 10:1–14

126 Corporate Responsibility

A ll blood shed in the holy land of Israel defiled the land and had to be atoned for by the shedding of the blood of the criminal. In the case of premeditated murder the land was cleansed by the execution of the murderer. With accidental manslaughter the land was cleansed by the death of the high priest. But what if the corpse was found of a person who clearly had been murdered, but by person or persons unknown? The land was indeed defiled, and someone had to pay for it or the whole land would be under a curse.

Since judgment was the duty of the elders of the "gate," it was the responsibility of the elders of the city nearest to the corpse to take care of matters. They were to kill a heifer next to a flowing stream in the presence of the priest, swearing before God that they were innocent of the crime. Just as the ashes of a heifer cleansed humans from defilement (Numbers 19), so the blood of the heifer cleansed the land of defilement as the waters symbolically carried the blood downstream and out of the holy land.

Old Testament blood rituals no longer apply in the new covenant, nor do we live in a land under special rules of symbolic holiness. God does not hold nations responsible for murders that cannot be solved, since the blood of Jesus Christ has cleansed all the land of the earth permanently. Nor is it necessary for an accidental man-slayer to hide in

> "Accept this atonement for our people Israel, whom you have redeemed, O LORD, and do not hold your people guilty of the blood of an innocent man." And the bloodshed will be atoned for. [Deut. 21:8]

a city of refuge until the death of a high priest, for the death of the Great High Priest has already occurred.

Yet we must not overlook the important implications in this passage that still hold true for us today. God held the entire Hebrew nation accountable for any act of murder. Today, premeditated murder still carries the death sentence. The only way a nation can remain clean in God's sight and receive his blessing, is by diligently investigating every crime of bloodshed and doing everything possible to bring criminals to justice.

If a nation takes a lax view of crime, God will hold that nation accountable, judging them for their low disregard for the sanctity of life.

Coram Deo

What applies to a nation applies more forcefully to the holiness of the body of Christ. Many church leaders, fearing lawsuits, are reluctant to hold accountable the people under their authority. Pray for your pastor and those with spiritual responsibility, that God will give them wisdom and courage to keep your church clean of gross sin, and that God will enable them to maintain sound discipline.

For further study: 2 Chronicles 7:12–16; Matthew 5:21–26; 1 Thessalonians 2:15–16

127 The Curse of the Tree

E ven the body of a criminal who had been put to death for a capital crime required special treatment in a land set apart as holy to God. If the executed person's body were hung on a tree, they were not to leave the body exposed overnight. The corpse must be buried on the day of the execution so that the land would not be defiled by it (Deut. 21:22–23).

When we read this law we think of crucifixions or hangings. In Israel, however, people were not put to death this way; rather, they were stoned to death. For some kinds of crimes the law specified that the dead body was to be burned with fire, probably fire from God's altar. No one was burned alive (Lev. 20:14; 21:9). In rare cases with special circumstances, the body of the stoned criminal was hung up for public display, but this provision of the Mosaic law mandated that it be taken down and buried on the same day.

If the crime was extremely heinous, the body was to be left out for the birds and wild animals to devour. Moses told Israel that if they rejected God such a curse would be theirs: "Your carcasses will be food for all the birds of the air and the beasts of the earth, and there will be no one to frighten them away" (Deut. 28:26). Abraham had frightened away the birds who came to devour his sacrifice (Gen. 15:11), but if Israel rejected the Lord, they would lose the protection that came from being sons of Abraham.

> You must not leave [the criminal's] body on the tree overnight. Be sure to bury him that same day, because anyone who is hung on a tree is under God's curse. [Deut. 21:23]

During David's reign a famine came from God, and the Lord said it was because Saul had slain many Gibeonites who were consecrated to the Lord's service. By attacking God, Saul and his house departed from Israel. To atone for Saul's crime, David was required to put seven of Saul's sons to death. Afterward they were hung on a tree for the birds to eat, but Rizpah their mother guarded them and drove the birds away until David took pity on her and buried the corpses. Only after the corpses were buried did God lift the plague (2 Sam. 21:1–14).

Jesus was actually slain on a tree where he hung for a time after his death, taking the curse for us. God saw to it through the kindness of Joseph of Arimathea that the law of Deuteronomy 21:23 was fulfilled, in that Jesus was buried on the day he died.

Coram Deo

Even in death the human body is to be given respect. The Bible does not forbid cremation, and in times of plague it may be necessary, but the normal method of showing respect for the body is through proper burial. Are their reasons why the body, even the body of a criminal, should be accorded such respect?

For further study: Joshua 8:28–29; 10:16–27; Galatians 3:1–14

128 Curses and Blessings

After Moses finished giving the law in its new form—now appropriate to the circumstances of a people settled in a holy land that truly belonged to God—he commanded the people to affirm with their own mouths the rule of God over them. When they entered the land they were to assemble for a service of ratification of certain laws. For this ceremony they would divide into two immense congregations: Half of the nation was to gather on Mount Gerizim and the other half on Mount Ebal. The Levites were to shout out a series of curses, and the entire nation was to shout back the Hebrew word *"Amen!"* (*"Let it be so!"*) after each.

Deuteronomy 27:14–26 presents the list of curses to be sounded forth and agreed to on that day. These had to do with *secret* sins. Sins committed openly were crimes, and so were punishable by the law courts Moses had established. Secret sins, however, would be punished by God alone. Those who committed idolatry in secret, who abused their parents, who craftily moved the border markers between their property and their neighbor's, who committed secret sexual sins, who oppressed the poor and the defenseless—all would be cursed by God and he would deal with them.

Then in Deuteronomy 28 Moses told the people of the blessings they would receive as a nation if they were faithful to God. They would be blessed with wealth and prosperity; they would defeat their enemies in battle; they would

> "Cursed is the man who moves his neighbor's boundary stone."
> Then all the people shall say, "Amen!" [Deut. 27:17]

have evangelistic influence over other nations; and, in general, they would enjoy regional economic, political, and cultural dominance over their neighbors. Sometimes Christians are bothered by this, but we cannot avoid the fact that the God who created this material world offers material blessings.

He also threatened material curses. The promise of blessings occupies twelve verses in Deuteronomy 28 (vv. 3–14), while the warning of curses occupies fifty-four verses (vv. 15–68). Because of our sinfulness and waywardness, we are a people who need threats more often than we need promises. Deuteronomy 28:15–68 is a nightmarish catalog of horrors—horrors that God wants us to avoid by clinging to him. Those who reject the Creator-God will find themselves estranged from the creation and the Creator, and will be dispossessed.

Coram Deo

Are you guilty of any of the secret sins listed in Deuteronomy 27:15–26? If so, you might consider meeting with your pastor and finding a way to make things right. Also read Deuteronomy 28 and consider the state of your nation. Do you think these curses may yet come to pass for your society? What can you personally do as a citizen?

For further study: Psalm 119:9–16, 105–112; Jeremiah 17:5–11; Revelation 22:1–5

277

The Death of Moses

After renewing the covenant between God and Israel, Moses prepared to die. He would not be permitted to enter the Promised Land. Therefore Moses called Joshua, and in a public ceremony before all the nation, commissioned him as his successor (Deut. 31:1–8). God then told Moses to write down all of the law and put it into the Holy of Holies next to the ark of the covenant (Deut. 31:14–29). This was his last act as the nation's leader.

On this occasion Moses recited the words of a song he had written (Deuteronomy 32). The purpose of the song was to provide an artistic form of the covenant for Israel to sing, because singing enabled them—as it enables us—to memorize things. Moses blessed each of the tribes of Israel, describing how each was to relate to the others in the nation (Deuteronomy 33; compare with Genesis 49).

Then Moses said farewell to his friends, climbed to the top of Mount Nebo, and surveyed the land God had given to Israel. The Lord's presence stood with him and said, "This is the land I swore to give to your fathers. I have let you see it, but you will not cross over into it" (Deut. 34:4). Then Moses died and went to an even better land.

The writer of Deuteronomy 34 offered an epitaph for Moses in verse 5: "Moses the servant of the LORD died . . . as the LORD had said." Of all the people in the Old Testament, none exemplified more fully what it meant to be the

And Moses the servant of the Lord died there in Moab, as the Lord had said. [Deut. 34:5]

servant of the Lord. For forty years Moses led a wayward, complaining, vicious people through the desert, putting up with one rebellion after another, enduring lies, rumors, and heartaches, and watching his old friends die without reaching the land they longed to see. Moses served God as have few other men, and he did it all according to the word of the Lord.

No one in the Old Testament was more closely associated with God's word. He feared and loved the Lord his God, and kept his word. He did the hard things God required, and because he loved God's people, he bade them to do those difficult things as well. For Moses there was no conflict between grace and law, because for him, to know God was to delight in serving him.

Coram Deo

Moses yearned to see God's kingdom manifested on earth, and as we read in Deuteronomy, he repeatedly expressed regret at not being able to enter the promised land. How about you? Do you burn to dwell in the promised land? Are you as confident as Moses was that at the time of death God will be present with you to ensure that you enter into the promised land of heaven?

For further study: 2 Corinthians 3:1–18; Hebrews 3:1–19

Broadly speaking, Joshua, Judges, Ruth, and 1 Samuel all focus on the period of the judges. Moses was the first judge (Exodus 18), followed by Joshua. Samuel may be considered the last true judge since Saul eventually became the first king of Israel. Some of these meditations were contributed by members of the Ligonier Ministries teaching staff, to whom I am grateful for special insights about an era in the history of God's people that was eventful.

The era of the judges in Israel was marked by constant struggle with neighboring peoples. Far from being obscure biblical stories, these accounts contain historical foundation stones underlying much of today's continuing Middle East conflict.

Here we are confronted by the "holy war" God declared upon the Canaanites, Hittites, Jebusites, and other inhabitants of the land that Israel was to evict. This action seems so uncharacteristic of our favorite concepts of God. Can this be the same God who loved all of the world so much he sent his only Son to redeem the lost? In the era of the judges God expresses his supreme ho-

The Period of the Judges

liness in the presence of utter evil. He not only hates evil, but he cannot tolerate it in the land of his inheritance.

God told Joshua to be strong and courageous, not only because the people of Israel would be outnumbered or out-weaponed in battle, but because they would have to carry out a difficult task as the avengers of God's holiness. If they did not deal a death blow to idolatry at once, they would themselves fall prey to idolatry later. The young nation stood at the critical point of its life. Would the people be strong enough to clean up their world and remain pure to God?

As you read and think through these passages of Scripture, look for the big picture of God's work through some of the most sinful people we meet in all of the Bible. At a dark time in Israel's history God was working to bring glory to himself. Consider how a life lived *coram Deo*—before God and unto his glory—can make a difference in the providence of God.

R.C. Sproul

130 Dynastic Succession

One of the principles of the covenant was dynastic succession. The covenant included provisions for the leader to pass the torch to a successor. In Deuteronomy Moses presented Joshua to the people as his successor, and the people laid hands on him before God. This event is a picture of the New Testament reality of the Holy Spirit as it is laid on God's people by Jesus.

In the upper room, when Jesus renewed the covenant with his disciples, he explained to them that he was going away. He told them that they were going to receive a new leader, the Holy Spirit, who would lead them in the task of taking the gospel to the world (John 14–16). The Holy Spirit would make Jesus present with them always, even unto the end of the world.

When Moses died, Joshua took over. Just as the Spirit follows the "orders" of Christ, so Joshua followed the orders of the pre-incarnate Christ, the Captain of the Lord's host. The Spirit represents Jesus to us today, as Joshua represented the pre-incarnate Christ to Israel.

Events recorded in the early chapters of Acts mirror the flow of the Book of Joshua, carrying forward the parallels between Joshua and the Holy Spirit:

- In Joshua 1, God told the people to prepare for the conquest; in Acts 1 Jesus told the disciples to wait for the Spirit and to get ready for their greater conquest.

After the death of Moses the servant of the LORD, the LORD said to Joshua son of Nun, Moses' aide: "Moses my servant is dead. Now then, you and all these people, get ready to cross the Jordan River into the land." [Josh. 1:1–2a]

- In Joshua 3–5, Israel crossed the Jordan and circumcised themselves; in Acts 2 the Spirit fell and baptized the church.
- In Joshua 6, Jericho was conquered; in Acts 3–4 the conquest of Jerusalem was begun and many were saved.
- In Joshua 7, Achan stole from God, lied about it, and was destroyed; in Acts 5:1–10, Ananias lied to God and was destroyed.
- In Joshua 8, Ai was conquered; in Acts 5:11–42, vast numbers in Jerusalem were converted.
- In Joshua 9, the gentile Gibeonites joined with Israel; in Acts 6 the Hellenistic Jews were joined to the church on an equal basis.
- In Joshua 10–12, the rest of the land was conquered; in Acts 8:4, the believers left Jerusalem to make disciples of the world.

Coram Deo

Once we see the parallels between Joshua and Acts, we also see significant contrasts: conquest by sword versus conquest by conversion; Gentiles sneaking in versus Gentiles openly invited; God working through a theocracy versus working through a church scattered among the nations. What personal advantage is it to you that you live under the new covenant of God's grace?

For further study: Romans 11:11–36; Hebrews 11:32–12:3

131 The Call to Courage

I n Joshua 1, the Lord exhorted Joshua four times to be strong and courageous. This was not a new exhortation that was given to him: Before he died Moses twice told Joshua the same thing (Deut. 31:7–8). Then Moses led Joshua before God and God said it to him (Deut. 31:23). After Moses died the Lord said three times to Joshua, "Be strong and courageous." Then the leaders of the people repeated it.

Maybe Joshua got a little perplexed after being told seven times to be strong and courageous. Did everyone think he was a coward? Clearly not, for Joshua had led the army for forty years (Exod. 17:8–13). His character was marked by great courage in the face of both the enemy and his own nation's public pressure when his stand was unpopular. Why, then, were Moses, God, and the people so concerned to give him this exhortation? Joshua knew full well that it was because of the magnitude of his task.

In Joshua 1:6 God tells Joshua to be strong and courageous as he would lead Israel to inherit the land. This would involve military leadership and prowess and also moral courage. Joshua had seen Moses lead the people for forty years while they complained, griped, rebelled, and gossiped. Now Joshua would lead the sons and daughters of these complainers. They were, by and large, a much more disciplined and God-honoring people, but it was still a fearful task. It takes similar courage today to be the spiritual leader over a congregation.

> "Be strong and courageous, because you will lead these people to inherit the land I swore to their forefathers to give them." [Josh. 1:6]

Verse 7 says that God told Joshua to be *very* strong and courageous because he would have to obey God's law. It takes courage to obey God when everyone else is going astray. It takes even more courage to obey God and command the death penalty for a criminal, especially when many in society think the criminal should go free. Today it takes courage as a pastor or spiritual leader who exercises church discipline as God commanded.

Finally (v. 9), the Lord told Joshua that he *could be* strong and courageous because God would support him. God promised that obedience would be blessed with success. It would set in motion a virtuous cycle, enabling more strength and courage to be even more obedient.

Coram Deo

Joshua was only called to conquer Canaan; we are called to conquer the world. Do you fear to share your faith? Are you an elder of a church who fears to bring down the rod of discipline upon those who disrupt the household of God through their words or actions? Leadership must be encouraged, even as we have seen with Joshua. Actively seek out those who exercise spiritual leadership over you and encourage them to graciously fulfil their responsibilities before God and the congregation.

For further study: Esther 4:9–16; Psalm 27:1–14

132 The Key to Leadership

After Israel crossed the Jordan into the Promised Land, God commanded that the entire army be circumcised because they had not practiced circumcision in the wilderness. This event put the army in a vulnerable position for several days, right under the noses of the opposing army at Jericho (compare Gen. 34:25). It took enormous faith to obey God on this occasion.

Immediately after crossing into the kingdom, both literally and ritually, Israel celebrated the Passover in the new land (5:10–12). During the Passover they ate the food of the Promised Land for the first time, and on that day the manna stopped.

Joshua went out to look at Jericho and encountered a "man" girded for war with a drawn sword in his hand. Being strong and courageous, Joshua went to him and asked him whose side he was on. The man replied that this was the wrong question. In fact he had come as commander of the Lord's army. Joshua instantly recognized that this was no man and no created angel. This was the angel of the Lord who had promised to lead Israel to victory (Exod. 23:20–23).

Joshua fell down and worshiped him and asked for his orders. The Lord told him to take off his sandals because he stood on holy ground. Moses removed his shoes at the burning bush (Exod. 3:5). The priests went barefoot in the tabernacle, because Exodus 28 and 39 describe the holy

> The commander of the LORD's army replied, "Take off your sandals, for the place where you are standing is holy." And Joshua did so. [Josh. 5:15]

garments of the priests, and there were no holy sandals. Likewise, Joshua now removed his sandals in the presence of God.

Here is the key to victory: Joshua recognized that being commander of the army did not give him the right to do as he pleased. He was merely the lieutenant of the Greater Commander, and he readily submitted his plans to those of the Lord. Moreover, Joshua recognized that the key to victory is worship. He welcomed the opportunity to come onto holy ground and worship the Lord, who was his source of strength and wisdom.

God's army had been "baptized" (through crossing the Jordan River and circumcision) and they had been fed at the Lord's table (Passover). Now they were ready to go forth and conquer.

Coram Deo

In worship we confess our sins and enter the kingdom. We hear God's marching orders, and we have communion with him. Then at the end of worship we are sent on our mission of proclaiming the gospel to a hostile, dying world. Follow the captain of the Lord's host. What ministry plans have you made that you should consciously and submissively present to him?

For further study: Matthew 28:16–20; Acts 7:27–36

133 The Holy Ban

G od told Israel that Jericho was to be destroyed as a burnt sacrifice to him. Nothing was to be taken from it because, as the first city conquered, it was a firstfruits offering to him. In the confusion of the actual battle, though, Achan, took a valuable Babylonian robe and a large amount of gold and silver. With his family he hid them. By so doing, Achan symbolically transferred his allegiance from Israel to Jericho, his love from Israel to Canaan, and his trust from God to gold.

God's anger burned against all Israel, and when they attacked a small village called Ai they were defeated. Joshua, knowing something was wrong, sought the Lord. God told him that a man in the camp had committed a sacrilege, stealing from God. Tribe by tribe, clan by clan, and finally family by family, the Israelites came before the Lord, until eventually Achan was isolated. Under Joshua's exhortation, Achan confessed his sin, and both he and his family were stoned to death and burned, just as Jericho had been.

Holy war is characterized by the holy ban, called *herem* in Hebrew. The *ban* means the opposite of sacrifice. Those who refused to accept the burnt offering of the sacrifice were themselves made burnt offerings to God. This parallel has suggested to scholars that the fire used to torch Jericho and burn up Achan would have been the same altar

> But the Israelites acted unfaithfully in regard to the devoted things; Achan son of Carmi, . . . of the tribe of Judah, took some of them. So the LORD's anger burned against Israel. [Josh. 7:1]

fire used to burn up God's sacrifices. It was a prophetic picture of the fires of hell.

In the Old Testament, this fire was used in holy war, the war of conquest. All men deserve to spend eternity in this fire, but God offers Jesus Christ as their substitute, for "he descended into hell" in our place. We should not be amazed when we see God destroying the wicked in this way. What should amaze us is that God withholds his just wrath so long and saves anyone at all.

Fire fell from God as tongues at Pentecost in Acts 2. The disciples preached the gospel through the nations, spreading the fire of God's new holy war and turning men into *living* sacrifices. This holy war remains our task today.

Coram Deo

Violations of God's expressed law often brought severe penalties, including death. Even in the New Testament, Ananias and Sapphira died as public examples of God's disciplining love. Consider his mercy that we have not been subjected to the same deserved discipline. What specific sins have you refrained from confessing? As you ask forgiveness, thank God that Christ went under the ban for you.

For further study: 1 Corinthians 5:1–11; 10:1–13; Ephesians 6:10–20

134 Misinterpreted Actions

J oshua 13–21 offers a description of the boundaries of each tribe of Israel. Although this portion of the Bible seems rather tedious, it provides information useful for understanding later events. One definite thing is communicated from the beginning: God is a God of order. In his kingdom, each person and group has a proper place.

Three tribes settled on the far side of the Jordan, called the Trans-Jordanian. They were Reuben, Gad, and half of the tribe of Manasseh (sometimes called Machir). As Joshua sent the three tribes back to their land, he exhorted them to be careful to follow the commandments and ordinances of the Lord (Josh. 22:5). Perhaps this exhortation was particularly significant for them because of their geographical separation from the rest of Israel.

Before they left the land west of the Jordan River the three tribes built a large altar at Geliloth near the Jordan River. When the rest of Israel heard about it they assumed the three tribes were defiling the Lord. After all, the Lord had made it abundantly plain there was to be only one place of sacrifice and sacramental worship in the land—the tabernacle and its altar (Deut. 12:11–14). Clearly the three tribes were setting up another place of worship. By doing so, they put themselves under the ban, and Israel prepared to go against them with the full rigors of holy war.

Before they went to war, however, they sent Phinehas

290

> And the Reubenites and the Gadites gave the altar this name: A Witness Between Us that the LORD is God. [Josh. 22:34]

the high priest with a delegation to inquire why the three tribes had done this. The leaders of the three tribes replied that this altar was not for sacrifice, but rather was a memorial. They had erected it as a gateway monument memorializing the tabernacle altar. No sacrifices would be offered on it.

Far from intending to divide the nation, they said, this altar was erected to ensure that it stayed united. "Suppose your children decide that our children are really unworthy to be part of Israel? This altar is to remind you and your children that we too are of Israel."

When Phinehas heard this he blessed them, and the war was called off.

Coram Deo

This story offers an important practical lesson for us in church life. Too often we hear a rumor, believe the worst possible scenario, and condemn the people who supposedly are involved. Wise Phinehas took steps to make sure he had *all* the facts before he passed judgment. When you are tempted to make a quick judgment, be sure you have all the facts. Especially when dealing with members of the faith, remember to exercise the judgment of charity.

For further study: 1 Corinthians 13; Ephesians 4:25–5:2; 1 Peter 4:7–11

135 Covenant Renewal at Shechem

Several times we have mentioned the structure of the covenant as presented in the Bible. In Joshua 24 a covenant renewal ceremony confirmed all the basic elements of this agreement once again. First comes the call and the identification of the king who was making the covenant (see pp. 16–17). The national leaders assembled and presented themselves before the Lord (v. 1). The Lord called them through Joshua, and it was the Lord who renewed his covenant with them.

Second, the historical record is recited of how the king had dealt with them, had delivered them, and had established his kingship over them. Joshua rehearsed how God had brought Israel out of bondage and into liberty and thereby made them his possession (vv. 2–13). The focus of Joshua's address was not on their political deliverance but on their spiritual deliverance from idolatry into the worship of the true God.

Third, the stipulations, laws, and ordinances levied by the king upon his people as their part in the covenant are reviewed. Joshua showed the people (vv. 14–15) that the law of God boils down ultimately to only one commandment: *Love the Lord your God with all your heart, soul, mind, and strength, and forsake all idolatry.* If Israel kept this commandment the nation would keep the rest as well, and would be secure.

Fourth we look at the promise of blessings and the threat

> On that day Joshua made a covenant for the people, and there at Shechem he drew up for them decrees and laws. [Josh. 24:25]

of judgment, which describes how the king would react if the people were obedient or disobedient. In verses 19–20, Joshua told them that if they worshiped foreign gods the Lord would deliver them into the hands of the nations that invented those gods, a threat amply made good in the Book of Judges.

Finally, we learn of provisions for the future, as the king documented the covenant, established visible memorials, and appointed mediating ambassadors between himself and the nation. A large stone was set up as a memorial of the covenant (v. 26), a stone that had heard all their promises and would bear witness for or against them. Joshua also wrote down the covenant, making a permanent record of it. Then he sent the people out to possess the land God had given them.

Coram Deo

Make the covenant renewal process personal. Recognizing Jesus as Lord, review the history of what God has done for you and follow the other covenant renewing steps. Recommit yourself to loving God and obeying the Lord. What do your vows mean in your life today? What does the covenant mean in your plans for the future?

For further study: Psalms 32; 51; Acts 3:17–23; Hebrews 4:1–11

136 Syncretism and Pluralism

No one is conceived in the womb as a Christian. All of us start out with our old Adamic nature under the judgment of God. It is necessary for salvation that each person be born again at some point in life. Some people are born again by the action of the Holy Spirit so early in life that they cannot remember it—John the Baptist was born again before he exited the womb (Luke 1:41, 44). But whenever it happens, new birth must happen to each person individually. What this fact means for the history of a culture is that each generation must decide for itself to follow or to reject Christ.

The generation Moses raised up in the wilderness was faithful to God and they continued faithful all the days of Joshua. The next generation, however, chose not to follow in their parents' footsteps but departed from the ways of the Lord. They committed the fundamental sin that underlies all other sins—idolatry.

Idolatry means treating as God something that is not. It means orienting your life around an ultimate concern that is not the true Maker of heaven and earth. Idolatry can take the visible form of bowing down to images made with hands. It also can take the invisible form of addiction to the things of this world, or of loyalty to a set of false ideological concepts.

The Israelites did not completely abandon outward worship of the Lord. Rather, they kept giving lip service to the central sanctuary while they paid homage to the baals and asherah poles in the groves and high places. This mixture of true religion with false is called *syncretism*. Syncretism is smorgasbord religion, combining a little of this with a little of that while calling itself orthodox.

Pluralism is modern syncretism. Pluralism rejects the idea that our culture should be based exclusively on fundamental Christian principles, while tolerating other religions. Pluralism is an ideology that says there is no such thing as absolute truth. Society becomes based upon the "plural"—the inclusion of all ideas and beliefs without any discrimination as to whether each is true or false. Pluralism denies monotheism, rejecting the claims of one true God. The greatest offense to our idolatrous society's values has come to be any insistance that there is only one truth.

Coram Deo

At what point does toleration of other religions within the culture become an open embrace of their philosophical teachings? Evaluate your own personal belief system to determine if you have crossed this line. In what ways might you or your local church and national denomination be participating in practices that stress relevance to culture over obedience to God?

For further study: Acts 15:12–21; 1 Corinthians 5:9–13; 2 Corinthians 6:14–7:1

137 The Forbearance of God

ach generation must affirm its faith in God anew; the nation of Israel, when confronted with the demands of living by faith, quickly cast off its devotion to the Lord. Shortly after Joshua and his generation died, the new generation drifted into syncretistic religion. The human heart is desperately wicked (Jer. 17:9) and runs swiftly into idolatry unless deliberately and self-consciously restrained. We see this phenomenon in the New Testament, as Paul wrote to the Galatians, "I am astonished that you are so quickly deserting the one who called you by the grace of Christ and are turning to a different gospel" (1:6).

God is faithful, even when his children try to cast him off. It was the grace of God that raised up raiders and foreign nations to plunder Israel in order to wake them up and drive them back to him. The principle God used was simple: "If you like the gods of the heathen, then you can live under the culture produced by those gods. You like the gods of Ammon? Well then, have fun living in the culture of Ammon."

Of course, the cultures produced by these idols were cruel, and Israel suffered under their domination. Soon they cried out to the Lord and promised never to commit idolatry again.

The Lord was more than ready to hear their cry. When the Israelites broke their idols, God broke the yoke of the idol-culture that enslaved them. When they returned to him,

> Then the LORD raised up judges, who saved them out of the hands of these raiders. [Judg. 2:16]

he gave them gracious liberty under the fair and equitable rule of his holy law. God did this work of deliverance by raising up judges in Israel who would, with his help, summon the army and drive the invader out of the land.

Judges 3:1–4 provides another perspective regarding why God raised up these enemies. It was so that each generation should learn how to "make war." The spiritual application is that we are to live in a state of perpetual war against sin and idolatry. We are to prosecute holy war against our own sin and in our communities against depravity and corruption. If we don't prosecute holy war against our own sin, God will raise up external scourges, using them to teach us the difference between right and wrong and the importance of making war on evil.

One way or the other, God trains his host to war against sin.

Coram Deo

List besetting sins in your life, against which you need to make holy war. Now make a list of the most flagrant specimens of corruption in your community, against which your church needs to make a determined, prophetic stand. As you pray, consider how to fight on these two fronts of your holy war.

For further study: 1 Timothy 4:7–16; Hebrews 3:12–14

138 Deborah the Judge

T
he first two judges God raised up to deliver Israel were Othniel and Ehud (Judg. 3). Ehud defeated a Moabite coalition, and the land enjoyed rest for eighty years (3:30). After Ehud's death, however, the people gradually fell into idolatry until the Lord sold them to a Canaanite king, Jabin. The commander of Jabin's army was named Sisera, and in his army he had 900 iron chariots, 900 more than Israel possessed. These Canaanite resurgents brought Israel low until they cried to the Lord. He was most pleased to hear them.

During the time Jabin dominated Israel, a woman named Deborah was judging the tribes. She held court at a place that came to be known as the "Palm Tree of Deborah," in the hills where the chariot-army of Sisera did not have as much influence (Judg. 4:5). God told her that the time was right to deliver Israel, so she called Barak ben-Abinoam, a Levite from Kedesh-Naphtali and told him to head up the holy war that would drive out the Canaanites.

Barak said he would be glad to lead the army, but only if Deborah went along. Was this cowardice? No, rather Barak knew that the Lord was with Deborah, and he wanted to be sure that the Lord would go with him. By asking Deborah to go, Barak was seeking the Lord's presence in the fight. This showed true faith, but it was also weak faith, since Deborah's command should have been enough. Deb-

298

> Deborah, a prophetess, the wife of Lappidoth, was leading Israel at that time. [Judg. 4:4]

orah honored Barak's request but told him that, because of his weakness, the honor of the victory would go to a woman rather than to him.

How could they defeat iron chariots when all they had were wooden spears and arrows? The Lord caused a great rainstorm, turning the plain around Mount Tabor to mud. The chariots foundered, and Sisera's men had to fight man to man. Sisera himself fled.

Heber the Kenite was sinfully allied with Jabin and Sisera, but his wife Jael was righteous and chose to be on the Lord's side. Taking advantage of the alliance, she lured Sisera to her tent. She gave him yogurt, put him to sleep, and drove a tent-peg through his head. Thus, a woman received the honor of the victory.

Coram Deo

God brings victory through unlikely ways and means. Military defeat at the hands of a woman was, and is, unusual. But because God is not constrained by convention, he has resources that continually surprise his people and his enemies. Do you remember a time when the Lord brought victory from an unexpected direction in your life?

For further study: Psalm 98:1–9; Romans 8:26–39; 1 John 5:1–5

139 The Song of Deborah

A s Israel sang a great song after the victory of God over Pharaoh (Exod. 15), so here in Judges 5 we find an amazing song celebrating the victory of God over the Canaanites. Let's consider two aspects of this song. First, the song celebrated God's triumph in terms of the prophecy of Genesis 3:15. That prophecy predicted a war between the woman and the serpent, and between her seed and his seed. The war of the mothers was in sharp focus in the "Song of Deborah." Deborah said that she was the mother for Israel (Judg. 5:7). She had raised up a godly generation willing to break the idols and fight the holy war. Barak and his army were her spiritual sons, the true seed of the woman.

Deborah ridiculed the mother of Sisera, a savage woman who had raised a savage son. She imagined Sisera's mother thinking about all the fun her son was having raping Israelite women (v. 30). Sisera's mother looked forward to receiving beautiful red-dyed garments from the spoil. She would not be disappointed, for her son's garments were dyed red with his own blood.

Second, the song provided a roll call of the tribes, those who showed up to fight and those who did not (vv. 13–18). Deborah praised those who came to fight. Their names are recorded for all time: Ephraim, Benjamin, Machir, Zebulun, Issachar, and Naphtali. Deborah ridiculed those who

Village life in Israel ceased, ceased until I, Deborah, arose, arose a mother in Israel. [Judg. 5:7]

did not come to fight: Reuben, Gilead, and Dan. The tribes of Judah and Simeon, far to the south, had not been expected to fight, so they were not mentioned.

As the song was sung at the watering places in Israel (v. 11), those who fought would receive a good reward of praise, and those who did not would turn red with shame.

This was the battle of the Plain of Megiddo (v. 5:19). The greater battle is Armageddon, which is fought by the church (the new Deborah) and her Greater Son throughout history against Satan and his seed. At the end of that conflict will come a new song, a song of judgment. Each of us will find our name on the list of the courageous victors or the other list of shameful cowardice. Which list will you be on?

Coram Deo

While some who failed to make the trip to battle were only ridiculed, those who were near the battle and refused to fight were cursed (v. 23). Spiritual conflict is prevalent in the lives of all believers. Many, however, shirk their call to wage war, making excuses that fall short of convincing the church, far less God. How would you fare if Deborah was writing her song today?

For further study: 1 Corinthians 9:24–27; 2 Timothy 4:1–8

301

140 God's Gracious Initiative

fter the death of Deborah, the sons of Israel again forsook the Lord and fell into idolatry. This time God did not "sell" them into the hands of other nations; he "gave" them away (Judg. 3:8; 4:2; 6:1). It wasn't long until the people were greatly oppressed and cried out to God for help.

God first sent them a prophet. Part of the prophet's duty was to prosecute God's "covenant lawsuit" against the people. The people had sworn to keep God's covenant at Mount Sinai and again on the plains of Moab (in Deuteronomy). Now God charged them with disobedience. The prophet told Israel that God had saved them from Egypt and other oppressors, but still they had not obeyed him. Thus, he implied, they deserved all their punishment (Judg. 6:7–10).

There is mercy in this judgment. If God had decided to cut the nation off completely he would not have sent a prophet. The lawsuit is a judgment but also an opportunity to repent. That God sends prophets to call his people back is evidence of his long-suffering love.

After this the angel of the Lord, who is the captain of the Lord's host (see p. 286), appeared to Gideon. Perhaps it is significant that Gideon was threshing wheat in a winepress because bread and wine are tokens of God's love and the presence of these symbols signified that Gideon would restore Israel. God took the initiative and called Gideon a mighty warrior. The Lord's angel told Gideon that God was with him.

> The angel of the LORD came and sat down under the oak in Ophrah that belonged to Joash the Abiezrite, where his son Gideon was threshing wheat in a winepress to keep it from the Midianites. [Judg. 6:11]

Gideon's faith was a bit immature. When he looked at God's judgments on Israel he thought it was a sign that God had abandoned his people. Instead, such loving judgments were signs that God was still working with them (Judg. 6:12–13). Like Moses, Gideon initially felt inadequate for the commission of God. He had to be reassured (6:14–18; compare Exod. 4:1–17).

Gideon prepared a meal to give to this "man," but the man told him to put it on a rock. Then the man put out his staff and burned up the food as a sacrifice and ascended in the flame. God would restore Israel, not because of any righteousness of theirs, but on the basis of the sacrifice. God would press the victory, and he alone would be credited with the salvation of his people. Even so, God invited Israel's participation. Even Gideon's pitifully weak faith was honored as righteousness.

Coram Deo

Judgment can be viewed as an opportunity to repent, because judgment shows that God is still working with us. What judgment has God brought into your life? Did you see it for what it was? How did you respond? Could you see his long-suffering love in the midst of the judgment?

For further study: Psalm 86:11–17; 2 Peter 3:1–10

141 Our Required Response

N ational reformation does not start with political action, though eventually it has to include political change. When God took the initiative to restore Israel he first required that idolatry be rooted out and true worship be restored. Those with whom he worked would have to separate themselves from the world's way of religion and conform their spiritual lives to him. Worship, saying "amen" to God and to his Word, is always our first duty.

Immediately after Gideon's sacrifice to turn away God's anger (see pp. 302–3), God told Gideon to tear down the altar to Baal that was in his father's yard. Apparently Gideon's father was an important man in the city, and the idolatrous shrine was kept on his property. Aware that he would be stopped if he tried to do this in the daytime, Gideon tore down the altar at night, built a proper altar to the Lord, and sacrificed a bull on it as a burnt offering. The burnt offering signified consecration and meant that the nation was to consecrate itself to the Lord anew.

In the morning the men of the city were furious, but Gideon's father stood up for his son. "If Baal is concerned about this, let Baal deal with Gideon," he said. Gideon must have been surprised to see his father willing to follow his lead.

Soon the Midianites swept into the land to plunder it. Gideon blew the trumpet and a large army came to him. Again, he must have been amazed that so many were will-

> That same night the LORD said to him, "Take the second bull from your father's herd, the one seven years old. Tear down your father's altar to Baal and cut down the Asherah pole beside it."
> [Judg. 6:25]

ing to respond to his leadership. Still unsure of himself, Gideon asked God to give him a sign. He would put out a fleece of wool on the threshing floor and if there was dew on the fleece while the ground was dry it would be a sign for him to proceed. God did so, but Gideon was still uncertain. Would God do it again in reverse, with the ground wet and the fleece dry? He did. Finally, Gideon was convinced (vv. 36–40).

Many people have wrongly inferred from this incident that it is legitimate for us to test God through the means of "fleeces." The Bible does not support that idea. Just because God did it for Gideon does not mean he will do it for us. Notice also that Gideon asked this sign with fear and trembling. He knew it was a risky request.

Coram Deo

Gideon desired that faith become sight. One confirmation after another was necessary to overcome his spiritual inertia. Hebrews teaches us that faith is the essence of things *not seen*. Perhaps your own hesitancy to initiate spiritual leadership stems from a parallel problem. Determine whether God has already given you a clear agenda and, if appropriate, boldly exert your influence.

For further study: Psalm 103:6–18; Galatians 5:1–17

142 Samson and the Philistines

F rom the womb Samson was set apart as a Nazirite. A Nazirite was under a vow to serve God with a peculiar singleness of mind. According to Numbers 6, the Nazirite was not to eat grapes or raisins and was not to shave the hair of his head until his vow was fulfilled. In the Book of Judges, men took Nazirite vows as they went into holy war (Judg. 5:2, literally: "That locks of hair hung long in Israel"). Thus, one aspect of the Nazirite was that he was a special holy warrior.

At this time, the southern part of Israel was under the domination of the Philistines. Unlike previous invaders, the Philistines were cultured and not terribly oppressive; thus, Israel relaxed under their domination and did not cry out to the Lord. Samson's job was to stir things up, to make it uncomfortable for Israel, and to heat up the desire for holy war.

The first thing Samson did when he came of age was to offer marriage to a Philistine girl. His parents thought this was wrong, but the Bible says that the Holy Spirit led him to it (14:4). Samson planned to use this offer of marriage to set up a challenge to Philistia. The marriage feast was hosted by the Philistines and one of their customs was to have a contest of riddles.

When no one was watching, Samson had killed a lion. Later, he found honey in it and took some home to eat. He had kept this a secret. So Samson's riddle said, "Out of the eater, something to eat; out of the strong, something sweet" (14:14). When the other men could not solve the riddle it appeared that Samson would emerge as the riddle master, scoring a victory over Philistine wisdom. But they threatened the bride, saying they would kill her and her family if she did not tell them the answer. She wept before Samson, so he told her the secret.

This was all according to Samson's plan. Now the girl had a choice: Would she put her trust in him, who was powerful enough to kill a lion and wise enough to defeat Philistine riddles? Sadly, she made the wrong choice and told the Philistines Samson's secret. Later, having rejected Samson's protection, she died (15:6).

Coram Deo

This story shows us that an offer of salvation is part of holy war. If the girl had put her trust in the power and wisdom of the Lord's anointed Nazirite, she and her house would have been spared. Before you engage in holy war against our fallen society, make sure you are secure in your own salvation. Do not be so concerned with others that you neglect the destiny of your own soul.

For further study: 2 Corinthians 13:1–10; 1 John 5:1–13

307

143 Samson and the Philistines

For twenty years Samson judged Israel righteously and warred against the Philistines (15:20). Then, as Judges 16 records, he fell into sin. We read first that he visited a prostitute in the Philistine city of Gaza. On his way out of town, he took the gates of the city and carried them away—but no Israelite army invaded the open city. Samson was playing games with his gift and failing to give leadership to the nation.

Then he got involved with Delilah. Perhaps she was Philistine or an apostate Israelitess. The Philistines knew her and offered her a tremendous amount of money to betray Samson. She cajoled him into telling her the secret of his strength. At first, Samson played games with her, too. He told her that if he were bound with seven fresh thongs he would be helpless. She bound him and then brought in Philistine warriors, but Samson arose and drove them away.

Samson was playing a deadly game with the gift God had given him. Next he told her that if she bound him with new ropes he would be helpless. She did so, but Samson again easily broke the bonds. Rather than seeing through Delilah's scheme, Samson regarded it as a game. He thought himself invincible.

The third time he told her to weave the seven locks of his hair into a loom. This time he drew himself closer to the fire because his dedicated head of hair was indeed con-

He awoke from his sleep and thought, "I'll go out as before and shake myself free." But he did not know that the LORD had left him. [Judg. 16:20b]

nected to his special power as a Nazirite holy warrior. Again she did what he said, but it did not work.

Finally, in answer to her fussing he told her the truth. Sure enough, she had his head shaved. God removed Samson's strength. The Philistines blinded him and made him labor for them in the humiliating role of a beast of burden. In his darkness we can be sure Samson repented before God. Slowly his hair grew back, and with it came his sense of calling as a holy warrior.

One day the Philistines had a great religious celebration. All their nobility, their priesthood, and the five kings were present, as was Samson, whom they planned to ridicule. In a final act fulfilling his Nazirite vow, Samson pulled down the temple, killing himself and all the heads of the Philistine culture.

Coram Deo

Samson drifted into sin one inch at a time, but finally there was a point when God withdrew his favor and denied him access to the gift of strength. Pride, presumption, and neglecting your spiritual gifts may result in the same end. What task has God set before you at this point in life? Are you aware of your privilege and, as Paul encouraged Timothy (2 Tim. 1:6), are you stirring up your gift into a righteous flame?

For further study: Colossians 2:1–15; Hebrews 2:1–4

144 Ordinary Faithfulness

T he story of Ruth opens with the historical narrative of how the head of an Israelite family, Elimelech, led his wife and two sons to the land of Moab, a journey of some fifty miles to the west and south of the Dead Sea. Elimelech, whose name means "God is my King," fails to honor his name and King, for he leaves the generally fruitful region of Bethlehem ("the house of bread") for a foreign land whose people dishonor God and afflict Israel.

Moab was a land under God's curse and surely the last place a faithful Israelite should have gone with his family, even when they were escaping from famine.

This outright rejection of his homeland, where God had promised his blessing, becomes the background of faithlessness against which the major themes of the book develop. The irony of this migration in search of food becomes a key to understanding the series of providential actions of God. In bringing redemption to this one family, God paints the biblical portrait of the salvation he has sovereignly decided to bring to all of his people. The work of Christ is carefully prefigured in this wonderful love story.

The Book of Ruth tells of ordinary people leading quiet lives during the time of the judges, a period otherwise dominated by war, strife, and chaos. It deals with unimportant people and unimportant events, but in a manner as to show that God is supremely active in the sovereign administra-

> At this, she bowed down with her face to the ground. She exclaimed, "Why have I found such favor in your eyes that you notice me—a foreigner?" [Ruth 2:10]

tion of all the details of the affairs of men and women. It is in that theme of ordinariness that even the simplest right decisions (or wrong decision, as with the case of Elimelech) becomes determinative.

The resulting story of right decisions and ordinary faithfulness in everyday life is used by God to produce extraordinary results. The entire story is a striking illustration of how God raises the humble and uses the weak things of this world for his glory. By obedience to the counsel of Naomi, Ruth finds favor and redemption from her redeemer-kinsman, Boaz. Ruth, the childless Moabite widow, a Gentile normally considered outside the pale of God's love and mercy, an alien to the covenant of grace, became in God's providence the progenitor of the Davidic and messianic line.

Coram Deo

The story of Ruth is one of commitments—Ruth to Naomi in chapter 1; Ruth to Naomi's people and Naomi's God in chapter 2; Ruth to the providence and sovereignty of God in chapter 3; and Boaz to Ruth and the levirate law in chapter 4. Consider a time that through your ordinary commitments, and even faithless mistakes, God has been pleased to produce extraordinary results.

For further study: Matthew 1:1–6; 1 Peter 2:4–12

311

145 Redemption in Ruth

As we in the late twentieth century read the last half of the Book of Ruth, we are made acutely aware of the immense cultural and temporal gap that separates us from that day and its practices. Although what is happening may seem strange, this passage actually gives us a glimpse of the practical application of certain divine mandates buried in the Book of Leviticus that we easily miss—mandates that mercifully provide for societal protection of the weak and unfortunate.

In Leviticus 25, under the more general discussion of the year of jubilee, we are also confronted with the idea of redemption. When we hear the word *redemption,* our tendency is to think of God's supernatural work in saving his people. But the primary emphasis in Leviticus 25 is on redemption in the here-and-now. Through the law of jubilee the land and homes are redeemed and returned to their original owners and people are redeemed to personal liberty out of slavery or servitude. It is redemption on a human scale that in Leviticus recognizes Yahweh's sovereign ownership of all things (25:23, for example).

The theory of Leviticus 25 is played out in Ruth 3–4 as Naomi determines to sell the land belonging to her dead husband in order to gain capital to survive.

What is potentially confusing in chapter 4 is that two different Israelite regulations come together in one episode. First, when Boaz makes up his mind to marry Ruth he first

> So the kinsman-redeemer said to Boaz, "Buy it yourself." And he
> removed his sandal. [Ruth 4:8).

must go to a relative, the unnamed kinsman-redeemer (Ruth 4:1, 3), for the responsibility belongs to him. Initially this relative is willing to redeem the land from Naomi. However, Boaz then reveals that, along with the land, comes the obligation to fulfil the levirate regulation. This meant that whoever redeemed the land also had to marry the dead man's relative so as to maintain that family line of descent (Deut. 25:5–6).

For one reason or another (perhaps his own family situation), the unnamed kinsman-redeemer could not do that, so he deferred to the next in line for redemption. This was Boaz. In a modification of the negative stipulation of Deuteronomy 25:7–10 (where a man unjustly refuses the levirate obligation), this positive transaction was finalized by exchanging a sandal.

Coram Deo

In Ruth we see God's providential hand guiding events, and providing for redemption. But we also see faithful people who are willing to follow God's commands to show mercy to his people. Consider how God wants you to show mercy to his people who are in need near you. Are you willing, like Boaz, to "redeem" situations on behalf of others?

For further study: Leviticus 25; Isaiah 43:1–7; Amos 2:6; 8:6; Galatians 6:7–10

146 Dark Days in Israel

T he two books of Samuel were written originally as one book. It opens at the temporary temple in Shiloh and closes with God's selection for the site of the permanent temple of Solomon (2 Sam. 24:16; see 2 Chron. 3:1). At the beginning of Samuel the nation of Israel had sunk deep into corruption. They were dominated by the Philistines and for the most part didn't care. The tabernacle at Shiloh, called a temple because permanent buildings had grown around it, was largely ignored.

Old Eli was high priest and Israel's judge. He was not an unrighteous man, but he refused to deal with his sons, who were very unrighteous. They had made it a practice to steal the best part of the sacrifices from God, ruining the acts of worship performed by the faithful remnant in Israel. They also had sexual relations with the deaconesses who assisted women at the tabernacle.

Still, some people made a point to attend the annual feasts of Passover, Pentecost, and Tabernacles. Some came to worship the Lord, others for less noble reasons.

Hannah came with her husband to one of the feasts. She went near the tabernacle to pray. Her lips moved as she prayed silently, and old Eli assumed she was just one more drunkard abusing worship. He rebuked her for being drunk in God's house, but she told him she was in misery: She was barren and the other wife of her husband constantly

314

> Now Eli, who was very old, heard about everything his sons were doing to all Israel and how they slept with the women who served at the entrance to the Tent of Meeting. [1 Sam. 2:22]

ridiculed her. Eli blessed Hannah and asked God to grant her a son.

In due course a son was born, and Hannah named him Samuel. She had made a vow to dedicate her son to the Lord, and when Samuel was weaned she brought him to Eli. Each year she visited him and brought a new handmade robe.

A comparison of Judges 13:1 and 15:20 with 1 Samuel 7:2 and 7–13 reveals that Samuel may have been born about the same time as Samson. Both men were dedicated to the Lord before birth and both were Nazirites (1 Sam. 1:11). The battle of Mizpah, in which Samuel defeated the Philistine army, probably happened right after Samson had killed the Philistine leadership. In the births of Samson and Samuel God was raising up salvation for his people.

Coram Deo

Even before the spiritual leadership in Israel cried out for God's help, God had taken the initiative to redeem his people. Samuel is but one of many examples. The divine initiative always precedes our human response. Recount times and places you have experienced God's unrequested but necessary intervention.

For further study: Romans 5:1–11; 1 John 4:7–19

147 The Capture of the Ark

E li named his sons Hophni ("Strong") and Phinehas ("Oracle"). Doubtless when they were born he hoped they would grow up to stand for the Lord and help turn the tide of wickedness in Israel. A former Phinehas (Num. 25:6–8), had turned away God's wrath by slaying a couple for the sin of fornication. Sadly, Phinehas ben Eli preferred to indulge in fornication himself (1 Sam. 2:22). Eli failed to discipline his sons, which was not only a failure of family discipline but, more importantly, a failure of church discipline.

God determined to bring judgment upon Israel for her sins and particularly upon the house of Eli. In preparation, he moved Samuel into position as Eli's adopted son (1 Sam. 3:6). When Samuel was old enough to take over (about age 20), God led Israel into war with the Philistines. Israel was defeated in battle. Determining they had lost a battle because the ark of the covenant was not with them, the superstitious leaders brought the ark out of the tabernacle and took it to the battle. The two apprentice priests, Hophni and Phinehas, went with it.

The Philistines feared the ark. They knew it was Yahweh's throne and that Yahweh had destroyed Egypt centuries earlier. Surprisingly, this made the Philistines fight harder than ever, and they won the battle (1 Samuel 4).

A messenger told Eli the bad news. When he mentioned

that Israel had been defeated again, Eli grieved. When he
said that Eli's sons had been killed, Eli mourned. But when
he told Eli that the ark of God had been captured, this
added blow was too much. Despite his failings, Eli loved
the Lord and his people. When he heard the news he fell
over backward in his chair, broke his neck, and died.

There was now no high priest in Israel. Eli and both his
sons were dead. Moreover, with the ark gone from the tabernacle, it was no longer possible to conduct the regular sacrifices. Into this ecclesiastical vacuum God sent Samuel,
who acted as a lay-priest and reorganized the religious system of Israel around his discipled prophets. Samuel's interim arrangements continued for a century, until the ark
was once again housed in a temple, built by Solomon.

Coram Deo

The story of Eli illustrates a fundamental principle
of the Bible: Church discipline is essential for social
order. Too often the leaders in the church wring their
hands over sin instead of dealing with it through exhortation and appropriate discipline. Should discipline be necessary, support the difficult stand your
church leaders must take.

For further study: 1 Corinthians 10:1–13; 2 Thessalonians 3:6–15

317

148 A New Exodus

By allowing the ark to be captured and all the adult high priestly family to be killed, God was judging Israel. At the same time, God was going into captivity symbolically with the ark. He was taking the place of his people, bearing upon himself their punishment (exile). This is one of many Old Testament pictures of the doctrine of substitutionary atonement, that God would take upon himself the punishment we deserve.

There is a third dimension to the fact that the ark went into Philistia: God was going into Philistia to make war upon it. When reading 1 Samuel it is helpful to remember that the Philistines had historical connections with Egypt, and thus the Philistine enslavement of Israel was a second Egyptian captivity (Gen. 10:13-14). In Exodus we read how God defeated Pharaoh and Egypt, and scholars have pointed out that 1 Samuel 5–6 offers a variation on the same theme.

The Philistines took the ark to the house of their god Dagon. They displayed it next to Dagon, in an inferior position, symbolizing their belief that Dagon was more powerful than Yahweh. When they came to their temple the next morning, they found the statue of Dagon fallen on its face, prostrate before the ark. They set Dagon back up, but the next day they found it on the ground again, this time with his head and hands broken off (1 Sam. 5:1–5; compare with Gen. 3:15). In the same way, God had defeated all the gods of Egypt in Moses' day (Exod. 12:12).

> The LORD's hand was heavy upon the people of Ashdod and its vicinity; he brought devastation upon them and afflicted them with tumors. [1 Sam. 5:6]

Next, God sent plagues against the Philistines: a plague of rodents and another of tumors (1 Sam. 5:6–12; 6:5). In the same way, God had sent plagues of animals (frogs, lice, locusts) and diseases (boils) against Egypt in Moses' day.

Finally, the five lords of the five Philistine cities had had enough and suspected that their keeping of the ark was responsible for their ill fortunes. They sent the ark away, just as Pharaoh drove Israel out of Egypt. Even as the Israelites spoiled the Egyptians, who pressed gold and silver upon them in order to make them leave (Exod. 11:3), so the Philistines filled a chest with five golden mice and five golden tumors, and sent it back to Israel with the ark (1 Sam. 6:1–12).

Coram Deo

Christ went into "exile" on the cross. His exodus was his resurrection, his promised land, heaven. Realize that you are also an alien and stranger in this world and thank God that Jesus is returning to lead us in an exodus to his promised land, the eternal rest. Take comfort that our God has thus conquered the god of this world. Live, then, as a people who serve a risen Savior, full of the power of the Spirit that was given to us in his great victory.

For further study: John 14:1–14; Hebrews 11:13–16

149 A New Mount Sinai

When Israel came out of Egypt, God led them to Mount Sinai and appeared to them. He told them not to try to gaze at him nor touch the mountain (Exod. 19:20–24). He told them never to look at the ark; it was always covered (Num. 4:4–6). When the ark went into battle, and when the Philistines sent it back to Israel, it was covered with a leather shield and over that a cloth of pure blue.

When the ark came back to Beth Shemesh, the cart carrying it stopped by a large rock. The Levites of the local synagogues in the area put the ark on this rock and led the people in making burnt offerings to the Lord. Later, however, some of the people lifted up the ark's covering and gazed at it, only to be struck dead. In 1 Sam. 6:19; the number 50,070 literally means "seventy men, fifty thousands." That probably means "70 men, of which 50 were chilarchs (elders over thousands)" (see Exod. 18:21).

The men of Beth Shemesh (those who survived) were struck with Sinaitic fear and asked that the men of Kiriath Jearim take the ark to their city. The ark was not taken back to the tabernacle. Apparently Samuel, who led Israel at the time, understood that the tabernacle had been permanently profaned in some sense. God was not going to restore the old system; instead God was moving Israel forward the beginning of a new and better system—the temple at Jerusalem.

> So the men of Kiriath Jearim came and took up the ark of the LORD. They took it to Abinadab's house on the hill and consecrated Eleazar his son to guard the ark of the LORD. [1 Sam. 7:1]

At Kiriath Jearim the ark was put into its own house on top of a hill and Eleazar was consecrated as a priest to guard it. We can compare this with God's enthronement on Mount Sinai. As Israel stayed in the wilderness for forty years before taking the Promised Land, so the ark remained on this hill for twenty years under Philistine rule, while Samson and Samuel judged the nation.

At the end of this period, Samuel acted as a new Moses, leading the people in a covenant renewal (1 Sam. 7:2–6). The people broke their idols and gathered at Mizpah. After they had renewed the covenant, the Philistines attacked them, but this time Israel was victorious. Samuel, as a new Joshua, led them from the "wilderness," and they reconquered the Promised Land (1 Sam. 7:10–17).

Coram Deo

We renew our covenant each time we partake of the Lord's Supper. The next time you gather with believers to celebrate that symbol of renewal, make a commitment to destroy the "idols" in your life. Commit to keep God's Law. Ask God to renew in you a reverent, holy fear of him.

For further study: Galatians 4:21–31; Hebrews 12:18–29

150 A King for Israel

After the victory over Philistia at Mizpah, Samuel judged Israel for a number of years. Eventually Nahash, king of Ammon, began to move against Israel. The people used this occasion to demand a human king (1 Sam. 12:12). They used as their excuse the fact that Samuel's sons, who judged at Beersheba, were taking bribes (1 Sam. 8:1–5). This was only a pretext because Beersheba was far out on the fringes of the nation, and all that was needed was for the two men to be deposed as judges. There was no need for a king.

God had told Israel through Moses that eventually he would give them a king—*when he was ready* (Deut. 17:14–15). Until then the nation was to regard Yahweh as king. Gideon had rejected the crown offered him, saying, "Yahweh will rule over you" (Judg. 8:23). Gideon's son Abimelech took the crown for a short time, becoming Israel's first king (in name a' least), but after three years his kingdom was demolished (Judges 9).

The last five chapters of Judges show that anarchy reigned in Israel, "when there was no king," meaning when the people refused to honor Yahweh's authority over their lives as King.

Once they had rejected Yahweh they soon demanded a human king. God told Samuel to give them one, accompanied with the warning that, because they had not properly honored Yahweh as High King, their national king would be

> And the LORD told him [Samuel]: Listen to all that the people are saying to you; it is not you they have rejected, but they have rejected me as their king." [1 Sam. 8:7]

no more righteous than they had been (1 Sam. 8:9–18). First, the king would draft their sons into his army, an army whose function was not only national defense but also personal service to the king. The army would be a corps of slaves.

Second, the king would take their daughters to be bakers. Third, the king would use his military power to steal the best of their land to give it to his favorite bureaucrats. Fourth, the king would take a tithe of their grain and wine. This was a pregnant prophecy, for it meant that the king would put himself in the place of God, receiving the tithe. Finally, the king would reduce the nation to slavery, and the people would find themselves in a new Egypt—one of their own choosing. On that day they would cry out to Yahweh, the true High King, but he would not hear them.

Coram Deo

God's plan requires God's timing. Israel was not ready for a king. Perhaps there are similar circumstances in your life. Spend the time today considering where your plans might be in conflict with God's: job advancement, marriage, prosperity, or some other area in which you have declined to trust him fully. If necessary, ask God's Spirit to slow down your personal agenda.

For further study: Proverbs 16:1–9; Ecclesiastes 3:1–8

151 Israel's First King

J udges 9 says the first king in Israel was Abimelech, but he reigned over a small area. Saul was the first human king over all Israel, and when the people asked for a king God gave them a good man for the job (1 Sam. 10:24).

But was he the "best"? We who know how Saul's life moved inexorably toward disaster might question God's choice. Saul *was* God's appointed, yet his heart never *became* wholly God's.

Saul was God's last judge of Israel. Several of those who judged Israel failed to live in keeping with their high honor. However, each became the tool of deliverance Israel needed at that moment. God demonstrated that he was the deliverer, not these demonstrably unworthy men and women. Their sins, in fact judged the ethical mediocrity out of which they had risen.

Samuel, who was a godly judge, knew this well, and his voice may have dripped with sarcasm as he introduced young Saul to his subjects with the words, "There is no one like him." The people liked what they could see: A tall, well-endowed man with the physical strength of a warrior. Saul had a charming shyness when brought from his hiding place into the limelight (1 Sam. 10:22–23). He possessed superficial godliness (vv. 11–12). He was the archetype of what Israel thought their king should be.

Samuel said to all the people, "Do you see the man the LORD has chosen? There is no one like him among all the people." Then the people shouted, "Long live the king!" [1 Sam. 10:24]

So Saul was selected by God, anointed by Samuel, and elected by the nation (1 Samuel 9–10). He proved himself first as a judge of the nation by fighting Nahash the Ammonite (1 Samuel 11). As the Spirit had empowered the judges, so the Spirit enabled Saul to defeat Ammon (Judg. 3:10; 6:34; 11:29; 14:6; 1 Sam. 10:6; 11:6).

Successful as a judge, Saul was then crowned king (1 Samuel 12). He passed all the tests, except one essential condition of kingship—submission to the High King. God gave to Saul the grace of a new, courageous heart befitting a leader, but not regeneration, for he failed to show the fruit of true repentance and never recognized the lordship of the King of kings.

Coram Deo

Grace extends to kings and presidents. Often God raises up military and civil leaders who model admirable qualities, but not godliness. Saul was such a leader. He was God's well-chosen and Spirit-gifted tool, but he was not God's "best." To have the best a people must look at themselves and their leaders with God's perspective. Pray for leaders, that some may be both tools and true vessels of the Spirit. Pray that you are a tool and vessel, whatever your role in the kingdom.

For further study: 2 Samuel 12:1–15; 1 Timothy 6:11–16

152 The Falls of King Saul

We have a tendency to look at Bible characters statically, as if they never change. We think of Saul as the wicked man he turned out to be and assume he was only marginally a good man in his early years. The Bible, however, presents Saul as a new Adam, a man of humility, grace, and gifts, anointed by the Spirit and made anew, fully fitted for this task. Given these facts, his three episodes of unfaithfulness became all the worse.

Saul's first fall occurred in 1 Samuel 13. Like Adam Saul had been given a kingdom. Like Adam he had been given a bride to protect (the nation). Like Adam he had been given a test: He was never to offer sacrifice but was to leave that task to the prophets. When the Philistines assembled to fight Israel, Saul and his army gathered at Gilgal. Saul waited for Samuel, but for seven days Samuel did not come. The people were fleeing across the Jordan, so Saul took matters into his own hands and offered the sacrifice.

Just as God accosted Adam shortly after he ate the forbidden fruit, so Samuel showed up the minute after Saul finished his sacrifice. Just as Adam blamed God and Eve, so Saul blamed Samuel and the people. Even as Adam lost his kingdom, so Saul lost his. Most people scattered; only 600 were left. But, there was still time to repent.

Saul's second failure involved his son Jonathan. Jonathan is presented as a perfect judge in 1 Samuel 14, but tragically he would never live to be king, because of his father's

> For rebellion is like the sin of divination, and arrogance like the evil of idolatry. Because you have rejected the word of the LORD, he has rejected you as king. [1 Sam. 15:23]

sins. Jonathan started a battle designed to purge the satanic Philistines from the land. Once it began, Saul started to consult the oracle of God but decided not to bother (14:18–19). Instead, he pronounced a foolish vow, forbidding the army to eat anything until the battle was over. This cut God's people off from the provisions of his land. Unaware of his father's command, Jonathan found a flow of honey and ate it. The army began to starve, left off fighting, and the battle was inconclusive.

The third, final, and decisive fall of Saul is described in 1 Samuel 15. He was commanded to destroy Amalek completely, but he spared many sheep and King Agag. When Samuel confronted him, Saul blamed the people instead of admitting his own greed, and God rejected him (16:14).

Coram Deo

Like Saul, who forbade his army to eat when God had made no such command, religious leaders sometimes ignore God's rules for behavior and start to impose human-made rules on God's people. Have you been guilty of setting your ideas of what is right and wrong above God's, perhaps in your family or church? Seek to command only what God has commanded and be silent where God has been silent.

For further study: Romans 14:1–13; Colossians 2:11–23

David and Solomon led the nation of Israel out of the anarchy and evils of the period of the judges and the beginning monarchy under Saul. They became the greatest biblical kings of Israel. They also show the victory that comes with living before the face of God and the disaster of neglecting to acknowledge his presence.

When God gave a king to his people, the focus of the kingdom was on the human king in submission to the High King. The pattern for Israel was not to be the absolutism of other monarchs. Saul, David, and Solomon were confirmed in their rule through the direct action of God's representative, or, in the case of Solomon, God himself. In Israel the king was to hearken to the word of the High King, a word mediated through the Lord's prophets. He was to be a ministering servant, drawing the attention of the people away from the surrounding pagan cultures and onto Israel's ultimate King.

When a king disobeyed, God responded, bringing discipline into his life or removing him from the throne altogether. To whom much was given,

The Lives of David and Solomon

much was required. In the end neither Saul nor Solomon stood firm in this unique office of regent for God's household, ruling before his face. In David we see a king with the soul of a singer, yet more important, with the heart of a worshiper. He was able to lead a country to greatness as he had led sheep, because he realized that he was a sheep himself, guided by a capable, loving Shepherd.

Ironically, David succeeded as a king *coram Deo*, yet he also committed the best-known example of a king's fall into sin with Bathsheba. Therefore, in addition to studying the lives of David and Solomon, we will examine the doctrine of sin.

We can learn much from David and Solomon in their successes and failures. They show us what it means to be a true leader while following God and obeying his commands. Striving to please God, to live each moment aware of his presence, is living *coram Deo*, for prince and peasant.

R.C. Sproul

153 David the Model Man

K ing David is one of the most remarkable characters in the Bible. Because we are so familiar with
him, we often fail to realize how remarkable he
was. David's potential developed in many areas. In fact, he
showed what every one of us would be like if God gave us
the grace to overcome more of the effects of Adam's sin.

First Samuel 16:12 says David was handsome and physically unblemished. He was a shepherd, which was a difficult task that required more skill than we twentieth century city-dwellers can imagine. Not only did David possess
this skill; he showed commitment and bravery in facing
both a lion and a bear in order to defend his flock.

David was also a musician. He played so skillfully that
of every musician in the land, he was summoned to play
for King Saul. The Bible tells us that, in addition to playing well, David made or invented musical instruments
(1 Chron. 23:5). He was the greatest poet Israel ever produced, writing more of the Book of Psalms than any other
author.

If that was not enough, David commands our admiration as politician and military genius. When Saul wanted
to kill him, David fled into exile with a band of fugitives.
Others who were hated by the king joined his band. Such
men are usually difficult to deal with, but from them David
molded the most effective fighting force in Israel. And, lest

He was ruddy, with a fine appearance and handsome features. Then the LORD said, "Rise and anoint him; he is the one." [1 Sam. 16:12b]

we forget, David was a great one-on-one fighter, taking down the older, more experienced, and decidedly larger Goliath.

Warriors seldom make effective diplomats, but David became the greatest statesman Israel ever knew. He succeeded in uniting the tribes of Israel into a nation, a process rendered all the more difficult by the great cultural differences that already had separated the allegiances of northern and southern tribes.

In David we see a kind of new Adam. He had much of the potential and grace of the first Adam. One wonders what he could have accomplished had he not succumbed to the temptation to adultery and murder.

Coram Deo

Do you resent people who are physically more perfect, or who display an array of amazing abilities? All of us have multiple gifts. We are unaware of, and fail to develop, many of them. Since God gives nothing by chance or to no purpose, think what interests and abilities you may have all eternity to unwrap and use. Thank God for your abilities and seek his aid in developing them more fully.

For further study: Romans 12:3–8; 1 Corinthians 4:6–7; Philippians 4:13; 1 John 3:1–3

154 The Insanity of Saul

After Saul's third rebellion against the Lord, God told Samuel to anoint someone else to be king. Leading him to the house of Jesse, the LORD commanded Samuel to anoint David as the future king of Israel. "From that day on the Spirit of the LORD came upon David in power" (1 Sam. 16:13). This is the same spiritual empowering that the judges of Israel had received (for example, Judg. 3:10; 6:34; 14:6) and that Saul earlier had received (1 Sam. 10:10).

The Spirit came upon David and left Saul. Without the guiding work of the Holy Spirit, Saul's rule over Israel deteriorated swiftly. He had neither the Spirit to direct him, nor Samuel to speak God's will to him. Saul was left alone to guide the state he ruled. The people of Israel then, indeed, had a king "like all the other nations." As in the other nations, Israel lacked mercy and no justice. Israel would not be a nation truly set apart until the coming of the promised righteous Ruler.

The text in 1 Samuel 16:14 makes the significant statement that an evil spirit *from the Lord* tormented Saul. Even the demonic world is under God's supreme authority. If God turns someone over to demons it is fit punishment for his or her sins. The church is commanded to turn impenitent sinners over to Satan for the destruction of their flesh, that their souls may be saved (1 Cor. 5:5). God never cre-

> Now the Spirit of the Lord had departed from Saul, and an evil spirit from the Lord tormented him. [1 Sam. 16:14]

ates fresh sin in people, but he can and does turn people over to the sins they have foolishly and rebelliously placed in their own lives to serve.

Once again the context of this passage has more to do with Saul's official position than it does with his personal salvation. Saul's insanity made him unfit to rule the nation. Lack of leadership provoked a national crisis. At this point, Saul's counselors suggested that he find a musical therapist whose playing would soothe the king's spirit. In the providence of God David was brought in to be Saul's therapist. When David played, the evil spirit left Saul. Thus, we see that the stability and government of the nation was in a subtle way already in the hands of David.

Coram Deo

David knew he was destined to become king, but he did not undermine Saul. Instead he applied all his skills toward helping Saul rule well. How do we respond to rulers in whom we have lost confidence and respect—in government, in church, and at work? Can you serve with the grace of David, even though you do not believe the person deserves the position of authority and honor?

For further study: Acts 4:13–23; 5:17–42; Romans 13:1–7; Hebrews 13:7; 1 Peter 2:13

155 David's Adoption into Royalty

I n 1 Samuel 17, the Philistines assembled for battle and sent out their giant champion Goliath to represent them. Day after day he taunted Israel, demanding that they send someone to battle him one-on-one. Nobody, including King Saul, volunteered—until David volunteered and succeeded. The army immediately routed the demoralized Philistines. Saul sought out David after the battle, apparently not realizing that he was the sometime court musician.

This seems puzzling until one recalls that the musician came at times of the king's distress and likely stayed in the background. Saul's insanity would hardly focus on the harpist. And how could that musician be this brash young warrior? Saul and his son Jonathan interviewed David, and Saul decided to bring David to the palace to live (1 Sam. 17:55–58; 18:1–2).

Jonathan came to love David as himself (1 Sam. 18:3) and, in token of his affection, gave David his royal robe, tunic, sword, bow, and belt. This act virtually adopted David into the family as a younger brother of Jonathan; in fact, this action was called a covenant (v. 3). It made David a potential heir to the throne. Later, Jonathan made it clear that he was ready to step aside so David might rule (1 Sam. 20:13–16, 31; 23:17).

In 1 Samuel 18 we see David hailed by the people as a warrior greater than Saul. Obviously, this did not sit well with Saul (vv. 6–16). He offered his daughter Merab to David,

> Jonathan took off the robe he was wearing and gave it to David, along with his tunic, and even his sword, his bow, and his belt.
> [1 Sam. 18:4]

if he would continue to be successful in war. Saul hoped that David, by aggressively pursuing war to show himself worthy of the hand of Merab, would be killed in battle. As David's victories mounted, Saul quickly married off Merab to another man (vv. 17–19), because he soon realized he did not want David officially tied to the throne of Israel.

Saul's younger daughter Michal loved David. The affections of Saul's household were shifting to David. Saul decided to exploit this romance by asking David to kill 100 Philistines as a dowry—something only a Samson could do. But David showed himself a champion superior to Samson by killing 200 men. In the end, Saul could do little but permit the marriage (1 Sam. 18:20–29).

Coram Deo

God did not put David on Saul's throne through revolution. It was Saul who brought David into the palace; it was the crown prince who adopted him as a brother; it was a crown princess who loved and married him. When Jonathan died, David was the most logical heir apparent to the throne. Trace how God has guided you and others so that you might have your current job, home, community, family, church, and other blessings.

For further study: Romans 8:26–39; Ephesians 1:3–14

156 The Death of Saul

When Saul tried to kill David, David fled with some loyal men. On their way into the wilderness they stopped at Nob where the tabernacle was maintained by priests. David told Ahimelech the high priest that he was on a mission from Saul and that he and his men were hungry. (Jesus referred to this incident in Matt. 12:3–4). Ahimelech gave him bread to eat. Word of this got back to Saul, and Saul had Ahimelech and all the priests killed (1 Sam. 21–22).

Over several years Saul repeatedly tried to kill David. During this period David's band enlarged considerably. There came a time when the Philistines grew bold enough to attack Israel again. They knew Samuel was dead, and David, the great warrior, had left Saul. Preparing for war, the Philistines assembled at Shunem.

Saul was terrified (1 Samuel 28). He had no prophet to turn to. He had killed the priests. God refused to speak to him in dreams. In despair he turned to witchcraft, visiting the medium in Endor. He asked her to call forth Samuel to tell him what to do. The Bible forbids attempts to contact the dead (Deut. 18:11), and Hebrews 9:27 says judgment comes to men after death. Hence, contacting the dead is impossible. When Samuel appeared as a miracle from God, the witch was frightened (1 Sam. 28:12). Samuel told Saul that the Lord was now his enemy and that he would die the next day.

336

> Saul then said to his attendants, "Find me a woman who is a medium, so I may go and inquire of her." [1 Sam. 28:7a]

Saul had been fasting for the occasion and now fell faint from fear and hunger. The witch offered him a meal, but with a last spark of wisdom he refused to fellowship at the table of demons. His men, however, prevailed on him, and he shared a meal with the witch, a meal described in the same language used to describe the sacramental meals at God's house (slaughtered ox and unleavened bread, v. 24). Thus Saul sealed his doom.

The next day the Philistines prevailed against Saul's army. Jonathan and two of Saul's other sons were slain, and Saul was mortally wounded. He asked his armor-bearer to kill him, but the man refused, so Saul fell on his own sword and died.

Coram Deo

Read 1 Samuel 15:23. What is the end product of a rebellious lifestyle? How does the life of Saul illustrate this? Because sin is self-destructive behavior, the greater our sin the more likely our life will end in tragedy and failure. Only God's intervening grace can break this vicious cycle that leads to disaster. Who among your friends needs God's gracious intervention and your active friendship? Intercede on someone's behalf today.

For further study: Romans 1:18–32; 1 Timothy 4:16; 2 Timothy 4:3

157 David Becomes King

D avid had a legal claim to be Saul's successor. Saul had repeatedly called him "my son" (1 Sam. 18:2; 24:11, 16; 26:17). Jonathan had adopted him by covenant as a brother equal to himself, and Jonathan was crown prince (18:3–4). Jonathan had yielded the throne to David by covenant (23:17–18). In addition, David was Saul's son-in-law (18:27). Yet David was only thirty years old (2 Sam. 5:4), and there still lived an older son of Saul, Ishbosheth, who was about forty years old (2 Sam. 2:10).

While there was no precedent, inheritance to the throne was not automatic in Israel. The people elected their king, though the first candidate put forward would likely be the son of the previous king. In this case the southern tribes of Judah and Simeon (which was semi-incorporated into Judah) elected David as their king, and he began to rule in Hebron. David was from Judah and had defended the Judahites and Simeonites from the Philistines for many years, so the people naturally wanted him to be king.

Because of the cultural division between northern and southern Israel, the independent-minded northern tribes were not inclined to follow the south (compare Judg. 8:1, 12:1). The Philistines had not been a problem for them, so they felt no particular loyalty to David. The commander of Saul's army, Abner, was held in great esteem by all the

> When all the elders of Israel had come to King David at Hebron, the king made a compact with them at Hebron before the Lord, and they anointed David king over Israel. [2 Sam. 5:3]

people, and he set up Ishbosheth as king over the other tribes (2 Sam. 2:9–11).

In the initial conflict David's side clearly was stronger (2 Samuel 3). David, however, wisely refused to prosecute a war. Ishbosheth's kingdom was perfectly legitimate, and he had no reason to attack it. In time, however, Ishbosheth's rule fell apart and he was killed by courtiers who hoped to curry favor with David. David had the murderous courtiers put to death, showing that he had nothing to do with revolution (2 Samuel 4).

By David's actions the northern tribes saw him to be trustworthy. Therefore they came to Hebron to crown him king. Now king of all Israel, David wisely set his capital in a newly conquered city positioned between the two halves of the nation: Jerusalem (2 Samuel 5).

Coram Deo

In our "instant" society we want things *now*. As you study David's life, notice his patience as God gradually brought him to prominence and then consolidated his influence and power. Think on a time when you asked for something, and now you know that it was not in God's good timing. How can you keep from trying to out-run God's plan?

For further study: Luke 14:7–11; Hebrews 6:9–15; James 4:1–10

158 David's Great Sin

G od made David king and placed him as guardian of the kingdom, just as he made Adam guardian of a garden. Similarly, just as Adam fell by seizing forbidden fruit, so David fell from his high estate. Just as Israel sinned at the golden calf after the Mosaic covenant was set up, so David sinned with Bathsheba after the Davidic covenant was established (2 Samuel 7, 11).

David's adultery with Bathsheba, and his murder of her husband to cover it up, were serious enough. But David was king, and the head of the new Davidic covenant; his sin was far worse than that of an ordinary layperson.

Earlier, in 2 Samuel 7, David wanted to build a house for God. God had sent the prophet Nathan to tell David that he would not build such a house; rather, God would build a house for him, and he would dwell in it with his sons. This was the unique gift of the Davidic covenant. When David later sinned with Bathsheba he defiled his house, and God withdrew. David's sin threatened the covenant God had made.

David knew the three laws of kingship (Deut. 17:16–17): (1) no large war machine; (2) one wife, and (3) low taxes. David had known since his youth that he would be king, for Samuel had anointed him. The king, above all, was required to be monogamous.

Yet David collected numerous wives. His first and proper wife was Michal, Saul's daughter. Soon, however,

> The woman [Bathsheba] conceived and sent word to David, saying, "I am pregnant." [2 Sam. 11:5]

he added Ahinoam and then Abigail to his harem (1 Sam. 25:42–43). Other wives followed (2 Sam. 3:2–5). Wise as he was in other areas, David was foolish and disobedient in the area of sex and family leadership, and he set a pattern of competing loyalties in his life that almost destroyed the kingdom.

David had gotten away with disobeying God's law for some time. Second Samuel 11:1 and 11 show that David had grown bold in his sin. Callousness had gradually caused his heart to lose its sensitivity to the things of God. Despite these blatant acts of willful sin over many years, God did not cast David off. But a day did come when the Lord would permit it no longer. When judgment came, it was meted out in sufficient strength to break both his sinful cycle and his hardened heart.

Coram Deo

Two factors in David's crime were (1) a history of sinful habits, and (2) a failure to work diligently at what he was called to do. These are things that can sneak up on any of us. Examine your heart to see if repeated sin has caused it to become callused. If you struggle with such a sin, ask God to break its hold on your life before it is too late.

For further study: Genesis 39:1–23; Ephesians 4:17–32; Hebrews 12:1–13

159 Treason Against God

T he history of David's fall provides an ideal place to stop and take a longer look at the biblical doctrine of sin. We shall examine man's sinfulness in several dimensions, using material from the lecture series on audio tape "The Doctrine of Sin" as our guide.

One of the best definitions of sin comes from the *Westminster Shorter Catechism* (answer 14): *"Sin is any want of conformity unto, or transgression of, the law of God"* (The word *want* means "lack."). First, this description of sin refers us to the law of God, which describes God's own personal character. Thus, it measures sin by a standard and provides us with a very practical way to understand any deviation from it.

Second, we see sin as a *lack* of something. Sin is a negative. It involves a rejection of God's holy character. The words we use for sin clearly bring this out. Notice how each of the following words is formed by negating another word: *un*lawful conduct, law*less*ness, *un*righteousness, *ir*reverence, *un*holiness, *dis*obedience, *un*godliness, *un*cleanness, *anti*christ spirit. In Greek, the root meaning of the word for sin means *"missing* the mark." Romans 3:23 speaks of *falling short* of God's glory.

In Genesis 1, God announced that everything he created was, like himself, good. Sin has no independent existence; it perverts something that was originally made to be good.

If we go too far with the idea that sin is a lack of good-

For all have sinned and fall short of the glory of God. [Rom. 3:23]

ness, we might wind up saying that sin does not exist at all, so there is nothing to worry about. The Christian Science cult maintains that sin is merely an illusion. In contrast, we say sin is real cosmic treason and *actively transgresses* God's law.

People are real, and their sins are also real. Created to bear the very image of God, the human's sin is a powerful perversion. Sin's rebellion is primarily oriented against the goodness of God, and only secondarily against his creation. Sin in the abstract does not have an existence as some kind of substance, but sinful people definitely have existence. Sin is real in the sense that sinful people are real.

Sin is so disastrous because it is nothing less than the image of God rebelliously committing cosmic treason.

Coram Deo

Reflect on the greatness of humanity as vice-regent of creation in Psalm 8. Consider what it means that this greatness is perverted by humanity's willful rebellion against God. Are you willing to apply the full weight of the Scripture's description of sin to your rebellion? Before you understand his grace and mercy, do you know yourself as a desperate lawbreaker, unholy, disobedient, and unrighteous in all your ways?

For further study: Psalm 8; 39; Isaiah 53

343

160 The Doctrine of Original Sin

We have all heard people say that "Everybody makes mistakes." They mean every person is a sinner—but it is easier to excuse sin by calling it a mere "mistake." Secular people believe that human beings are basically good, but that every now and then they slip up and make a mistake. Christianity, however, teaches that all human beings are fundamentally evil and that everybody sins continually.

In Book 1 (pp. 120–21) we said that it is necessary to distinguish between *sin* and *Sin*. We mean that *sins* (with a small "s") are acts of disobedience, whether in thought, word, or deed. *Sin* (with a capital "S") refers to the basic sin-nature that provokes us to the acts. To put it another way: *We are not sinners because we sin; rather we sin because we are sinners.*

There is more to original sin, however, than these acts. They come from a heart attitude that holds a basic hatred of God. This animosity naturally exists in the heart of every person ever conceived since Adam and Eve.

Theologians call this sin-nature *original sin*. Don't confuse the nature of original sin that prevails throughout humanity with the first act of sin committed by Adam and Eve. That act broke the covenant of life God had established with humanity through its representative—Adam. God chose a completely sinless person to be our perfect representative. He acted on our behalf, in the same way that representatives elected to government represent us. Our representative rebelled against God. Would we have done any less? Would we have chosen a better representative than did God (see Book 2, pp. 410–11)?

Original sin that infects the soul today is the *result* of that first actual act of sin. Human sins since have been the result of original sin. Without a new covenantal relationship with God we could not do other than rebel—we were born slaves to sin and dead to righteousness. Because of Adam's sin, all of his descendants are born into the world with a fundamentally evil orientation, an impulse to rebel.

Therefore, the first act of sin broke our relationship with God. That is why we have all received punishment for Adam's sin.

Coram Deo

The fact that God punishes sin by giving us over to more sin is clearly stated in Romans 1:21–32. Read this passage carefully, noticing particularly what verse 32 says is the ultimate end of the outworking of sin. Does this teaching frighten you? It should. Ask God for help in breaking off any evil habits that cling to you.

For further study: Galatians 5:1, 16–17; Colossians 3:1–11

345

161 Are There Degrees of Sin?

A few years ago a psychologist attacked Jesus Christ for teaching that all sins are equally bad. According to this man, when Jesus said that a lustful look was equivalent to adultery of the heart (Matt. 5:28), he was saying that lustful thought is as bad as adultery. Wrote this man, this is a crazy idea. Lust may be wrong, but it is not as wrong as defiling a marriage by the act of adultery.

Had this gentleman looked more carefully at Matthew 5 he would have seen that Jesus taught that inner lust is a *form* of adultery and inner hatred is a *form* of murder. He did not *equate* lust with action in either case.

The apostle James made another point that is often taken out of context when he wrote, "Whoever keeps the whole law and yet stumbles at just one point is guilty of breaking all of it" (James 2:10). James is not saying all sins are equally heinous, but rather that God's law is, like himself, a unity. To break any particular law, small or great, is to break the unity of the whole law. To oppose God in little ways is still opposition. Sin is sin.

Are all sins equally bad? Clearly they are not, for Jesus warned the Pharisees, "You have neglected the more important matters of the law" (Matt. 23:23). When Jesus was asked to state the greatest commandment, he did not respond that all laws carry equal weight. His words of comparison clearly taught that some are more weighty.

> That servant who knows his master's will and does not get ready
> or does not do what his master wants will be beaten with many
> blows. But the one who does not know and does things deserving
> punishment will be beaten with few blows." [Luke 12:47–48a]

As Christians we need to know why some sins are worse than others because the hierarchy of sins held by society is not the same as that in the Bible. On network television it is permissible to take God's name in vain, but certain sexual swear words are censored. This hierarchy of sin does not reflect biblical principles. The first of the Ten Commandments and the opening petitions of the Lord's Prayer make this abundantly clear.

Sins which are directly intended to shake one's fist at God are worse than sins that were not intended primarily against him personally. Sins that hurt our neighbor are usually worse than sins that cause self-inflicted pain. Sins typically are aggravated when committed against authorities or the weak and helpless.

Coram Deo

Sin is aggravated by actions that cause others to sin, that are premeditated, that are committed after warnings from the church, or that break a vow made before God. What are other factors? As you come to understand the insidious nature of sin, deal first with your rebellion against God. That is where you are most guilty, and where you should immediately focus your repentance.

For further study: Proverbs 4:1–19; 2 Peter 2:10–19; 1 John 3:1–10

162 Sin and God's Law

How do we know what is sinful and what pleases God? We know because God has told us. *Sin* can be defined as any lack of conformity to, or breaking of, the law of God. An authority tells a subordinate what to do through commands and standards against which performance will be judged. We know what God wants and what he does not want, because he has given explicit commands. We find these commands in his law.

Satan wants people to sin and works overtime to pervert both the human understanding of the content of the law, and the doctrine of how the law of God applies as a whole. Because Satan knows the church is the most powerful institution on earth (Matt. 28:18–20), he works harder to pervert the church's beliefs and teachings.

Satan works to pervert the *content* of the law by persuading us that evil things are good and good things are evil. For this purpose he masquerades as an "angel [messenger] of light" (2 Cor. 11:14). For example, many Christians believe that capital punishment is wrong—though the Bible teaches exactly the opposite. This is but one of many instances where Satan has prevailed in the perversion of good and evil.

Satan also perverts the *doctrine* of the law by driving a wedge between law and gospel. Some people seek to earn salvation through the keeping of the law and seem to have

What shall we say, then? Is the law sin? Certainly not! Indeed I would not have known what sin was except through the law. For I would not have known what it was to covet if the law had not said, "Do not covet." [Rom. 7:7]

no time for the good news of salvation. If that is how you approach the law you are headed for a miserable life, because apart from the gospel, the law kills. Other Christians believe they also are freed from the condemnation of the law so they are freed from the need to study and obey. They want only the salvation that comes from the gospel and no requirement to keep God's holy commands. This is impossible.

You cannot grasp the gospel unless you know that Christ has come to satisfy the demands of the law. And you cannot live a life pleasing to God unless you know what he requires of his adopted children and seek to live in accordance with what you know he requires. You can only learn this by studying the written law God has revealed in both Old and New Testaments (see Book 1, pp. 238–39).

Coram Deo

"Either/or" thinking with respect to the law and the gospel is fatal. Some in evangelical thought today distort the necessary relationship between the two; they teach that one only needs Jesus as Savior (the gospel) without needing to pursue him as Lord (who makes righteous commands). Do not be guilty of this false doctrine. If you love him you will keep his commands.

For further study: Psalm 19:9–11; 119:9–11; 1 Corinthians 10:13

163 The Christian and the Law

God's law is like a mirror: it reflects things. The first thing the law of God reflects is the righteousness of God. The law is not given in abstraction, but it reflects the *character, values, and concerns* of the Lawgiver. As God himself is righteous, his righteousness is reflected in his law.

The second thing that the mirror of God's law reflects to us is *ourselves*. It shows our sinfulness. If we look into the mirror long enough we begin to see our blemishes and faults. A man usually looks in the mirror to make sure he has removed all the stubble from his face. A woman usually looks in a mirror to make sure she has covered up or highlighted everything she wants to change by means of makeup. A mirror shows our "faults."

If a person looks into the mirror of God's holy law he surely will see many faults. Only if a person makes himself the standard of judgment can he view himself as faultless. In order to evade a sense of sinfulness, people stop measuring themselves by the mirror of God's law and start measuring themselves against other people's faults. Lowering the standards is a quick solution to failure to achieve God's holy commands.

As a mirror, the law shows our need for salvation, not just once but every day. It continually drives us back to

> Anyone who listens to the word but does not do what it says is like a man who looks at his face in a mirror and, after looking at himself, goes away and immediately forgets what he looks like. [James 1:23–24]

Christ, our Savior and Guide. It humbles us and shows what we need to do to please God.

The Bible teaches that when we actually obey God's commands he will bless us and we will be happy. That point is made in James 1:22–25. If we listen to the law, but don't obey it, we are like people who forget everything they see in a mirror. The law has shown all our blemishes, but we don't do anything about them. If we obey, however, we shall find that the law "gives freedom" (v. 25). The man who looks into the mirror and then takes steps to change his ways "will be blessed in what he does" (v. 25).

In this way, the mirror transforms us "with ever-increasing glory" (2 Cor. 3:18).

Coram Deo

A mirror that projects a distorted image is discarded as useless. Likewise many Christians have discarded the Scriptures—and particularly the law—because they believe it is errant in what it teaches. They think it, rather than they, is distorted. Do you read the law in Scripture as an historic curiosity or to submit yourself to the Scriptures' authoritative reflection of truth?

For further study: John 8:31; 14:21; 15:7; 2 Timothy 3:16–17

351

164 The Great Promoter of Sin

S atan is an angel, a creature of God who led part of the angelic host in rebellion against God. In his hatred of God he has enlisted the human race. In the guise of a serpent he enticed Adam and Eve to sin and lose their fellowship with God.

Satan's goal is the destruction of everything that shows forth the presence and glory of God. Since human beings are the crown of creation, the very image of God himself, Satan is determined to destroy humanity. He uses human beings to strike at God and then destroys them.

Satan entices us to question the goodness of God. His suggestion that there is a better way than God's way undermines our confidence in what God says in his Word. Jesus called this adversary the "father of lies" (John 8:44).

Satan does not often appear directly to a person. Usually he promotes lies through the mouths of people who have taken his side, people who share his belief that God is unfair. Often such people are in the church. That is how it was in Jesus' day, when Satan's agents were active members of the most conservative, outwardly law-abiding of Jewish groups—the Pharisees.

As a creature, Satan can never act without at least the implicit permission of God. In a most profound demonstration of his sovereign control and redemption of all circumstances, God uses Satan as a rod to chastise wayward believers and to teach them important lessons about the

> Satan rose up against Israel and incited David to take a census of Israel. [1 Chron. 21:1]

kingdom. In Job 1–2 we read that Satan wanted to harm Job, but he could go no further than God allowed.

In 2 Samuel 24:1 we read that "the anger of the LORD burned against Israel, and he incited David against them, saying, 'Go and count Israel and Judah.' " Yet in 1 Chronicles 21:1 we read that it was Satan who incited David to number the people. Both are true. God was angry with the people so he permitted David to stumble and bring the nation into judgment. The means by which God scourged Israel was his permission for Satan to tempt David to sin. David, Satan, and God all acted freely, according to their desires, yet God's supremacy over all triumphed.

Coram Deo

Satan wants us to treat this world as our own. David treated Israel as his own people, and he intended to take pride in his kingdom's strength. That was the meaning of his unlawful census. When David repented he bought the site for the temple, the place where Israel, as *God's* people, would be numbered around *him* (1 Chron. 21:17–30 and chapters 22–29). Are there areas where you think God has no business interfering? Is this where Satan has deceived ?

For further study: Acts 13:10; Ephesians 4:27; 2 Timothy 2:26; James 4:7; 1 Peter 5:8

165 David's Psalm of Penitence

D avid had committed adultery with the wife of Uriah the Hittite, a Gentile convert who was serving in his army. To cover up his sin, David saw to it that Uriah was killed. Sometime later the prophet Nathan confronted David, who then poured out his heart in a prayer of repentance, recorded for all of God's people to use— Psalm 51. As we wrap up our consideration of human sinfulness and get back into the history of David, let us reflect on what David said in verse 3: "my sin is always before me." One of the things we notice about ourselves as Christians is that our sins come back to haunt us. The Scriptures themselves teach that our sins shall find us out. If only we could forget some of the deeds we have done.

Perhaps it was impossible for David to walk on top of his palace without being reminded that it was there that he took Bathsheba. Was it ever possible for him to sip a cup of wine without recalling how he got Uriah drunk and tried to persuade him to go home to his wife? How could he ever write another military order without remembering how he ordered Uriah to be placed in the front lines where he would lose his life?

Sometimes we feel it would be a blessing if only we could forget whatever it was we did; if only we could get away from it; if only we would not continually be reminded of it. Yet, perhaps it should cause us to rejoice if we cannot forget our sin. It is possible for a person to become so cal-

> For I know my transgressions, and my sin is always before me.
> [Ps. 51:3]

lous and hardened that the memories no longer bother, and there is no longer a care that God has been offended. That should not be the life of the child of God.

We know that one of the activities of the Holy Spirit is to convict us of sin. God is not willing that his children be involved in sin without some immediate awareness of the need to repent, and an ongoing awareness that the offense happened that will strengthen and humble them in the future. So gently and lovingly, yet firmly, God calls his people to an awareness of their sins. The Holy Spirit works to remind us of the evil we have committed, even after we have been cleansed from it through repentance. Such reminders are not designed to reconvict us of guilt that already has been forgiven. Rather, they keep us humble, lest we fall again.

Coram Deo

When we are reminded of our sin, we can become bitter against ourselves and feel defeated. Satan loves to stir up guilt during such times of weakness. Ask the Holy Spirit to instead "convict" you of righteousness, creating fresh desires to live openly before the face of God. Thank God that your sin has found you out, and that your memory is also of his loving forgiveness.

For further study: Leviticus 26:40–42; Nehemiah 1:6; Psalm 32:5; James 5:16; 1 John 1:9

166 The Consequence of Sin

Repentance of our sins brings forgiveness from God, but if those sins have hurt other people, consequences may continue to play themselves out over time. David had assaulted the integrity of another man's family; therefore it is easy to see how the integrity of his family would be assaulted. He had taken another man's wife, so his wives would be taken. He had murdered, so murder would invade his house. The principle God used to bring these consequences to bear fruit can be found in the maxim: "Like father, like son."

David's firstborn son, heir to the crown, was Amnon. Like his father, Amnon was smitten with the beauty of a forbidden woman, his sister Tamar. Like his father he decided to possess her. (2 Samuel 13). Compromised by his own sin, David failed to act against Amnon's rape of Tamar, so after two years Tamar's brother Absalom took matters into his own hands and slew Amnon.

Absalom fled into exile, and David alienated him further by failing to invite him home. When he was allowed to return David refused to see him. By the time David allowed Absalom back into his presence, Absalom had become his enemy (2 Samuel 14). Every day, Absalom stood near the city gate and intercepted anyone taking a petition to David. He told them the king would not hear them, but that he would help them instead. In this manner he stole the hearts of the people. Soon he proclaimed himself king

> Now, therefore, the sword will never depart from your house, because you despised me [the LORD] and took the wife of Uriah the Hittite to be your own. [2 Sam. 12:10]

and drove David out of power through a military and political coup (2 Samuel 15).

Upon the advice of Ahithophel, Bathsheba's angry grandfather, Absalom pitched a tent on the roof of the palace. There, in the place where David had decided to possess Bathsheba, Absalom lay with his father's concubines, an act calculated to seal the breach between himself and David (2 Samuel 16).

Civil war ensued. David knew that his sin and failure to act had brought this to pass and gave orders that Absalom was not to be killed. In the ensuing battle Absalom was caught in the woods, and though David's men refused to kill him, Joab slew him anyway. David wept bitterly, saying "If only I had died instead of you, O Absalom, my son, my son!" (2 Sam. 18).

Coram Deo

What does Romans 6:23 say is the wages of sin? At the beginning of this sad story David was afraid to die (2 Sam. 12:13). At its end he was wishing he had died (18:33). Are you even now enduring the pain of past sins—yours or someone else's? Is there a step you can take toward healing a relationship with someone that has been broken by sin? Examine your life with a goal of reconciliation while there is still opportunity.

For further study: Ezekiel 44:10–12; Hosea 10:12; Galatians 6:7–9

167 David's Charge to Solomon

When David was old, his son Adonijah plotted with Joab and Abiathar the high priest to become king. He made the mistake, however, of letting this become known before David died. Solomon's mother Bathsheba and Nathan the prophet told David about it. David had appointed Solomon to be his successor, and Solomon was favored by Nathan, Zadok the other high priest, and all the best people in the court. When David proclaimed Solomon king publicly it officially settled the matter (1 Kings 1).

When it became clear David was dying, he called Solomon and charged him to be faithful in his role as king. He told Solomon to be strong and to show himself a man. David encouraged Solomon to study God's law so as to "walk in his ways, and keep his decrees and commands, his laws and requirements." In order to rule by the light of God's holy law, Solomon would need moral strength not to be swayed by public pressure.

David also passed on to Solomon some unfinished business (1 Kings 2:5–9). The unruly and savage Joab had compromised the integrity of David's reign since its beginning. Because Joab had been close to David during his lean years in the wilderness, was part of David's deceit in killing Uriah, and was David's nephew (1 Chron. 2:16), the king had never brought him to justice. The time to call Joab to account was long passed, but now it had to be done, for Joab and his friends were sure to cause a revolt against Solomon.

Out of expediency Solomon must do what David should have done, ordering this murderer's execution.

Similarly, while the family of Jonathan was loyal to David, some of Saul's extended relatives were traitors who had conspired to overthrow Solomon. Their leader was Shimei, who had sided with Absalom. David told Solomon to kill him before he could tear up the kingdom with bloodshed.

By merciful contrast, David told Solomon to show kindness to Barzillai, who was likely an in-law of Saul's and thus had every reason to side with Shimei (2 Sam. 21:8). Barzillai was innocent and must not be unjustly caught in any overzealous settling of accounts.

Coram Deo

Among David's faults was a tendency to put off difficult decisions. With Joab he likely felt pained memories of his own conspiracy with Joab to kill Uriah. Yet David knew it was now necessary to secure peace and protect the innocent. Procrastinators still abound among church leaders who put off dealing with congregational sin until it erupts in a crisis of grief and turmoil. And we, like David, put off facing a sin or reconciling with a brother or sister we have hurt. Pray for a heart willing to be faithful now, rather than later.

For further study: 2 Thessalonians 1:12; 2 Timothy 2:2; Hebrews 13:7, 17

168 The Wisdom of Solomon

During the century between the time the tabernacle was destroyed and the temple erected, the people of Israel worshiped properly at various high places. David moved the ark to Jerusalem and established the rest of the tabernacle furniture at Gibeon, and after this the people were only to worship at these two places. There was a high priest in charge of each (1 Chron. 16:37–40). After the temple was built, the original Mosaic laws came back into effect (Deuteronomy 12), and high-place worship was forbidden (though the people sinfully continued to use these worship centers).

At the beginning of his reign, Solomon went to Gibeon to worship the Lord and God appeared to him. God told Solomon to ask for whatever he wanted and God would give it to him. Solomon requested the wisdom he would need to apply the law of God fairly to the people.

Yet there was another aspect to wisdom as well. Solomon was going to build the temple, and we are told that God used wisdom in making the world, and Bezalel used wisdom in making the tabernacle (Prov. 3:19; Exod. 28:3). As we shall see, the temple was a symbol of God's people gathered around his throne. Building the temple was a symbol of building the nation. Thus, it was fitting that Solomon possessed wisdom both to build the temple and to build the nation it symbolized.

> So give your servant a discerning heart to govern your people and to distinguish between right and wrong. For who is able to govern this great people of yours? [1 Kings 3:9]

Since Israel was to be a priestly nation, ministering God's grace to all the people of the world, the wisdom of Solomon was also evangelistic. His proverbs and sayings were published abroad and drew admiration from all the surrounding nations (1 Kings 4:29–34). People came to visit Israel and hear Solomon, going home with the good news that God was making salvation available through his people. Other nations reformed their laws and customs, benefiting from the wisdom of God's law as taught by Solomon (compare Deut. 4:6–8). Perhaps the most well known of Solomon's admirers was the Queen of Sheba, who traveled a thousand miles to learn wise leadership and rule from King Solomon (1 Kings 10:1–13).

Coram Deo

James 1:5 says that we all have Solomon's privilege of asking for wisdom. Wisdom is practical and enables you to do excellent work in all your tasks, whatever they are. Such wisdom will reform your life and gain praise and influence for God in the lives of other people. Stop now and ask God to pour out his wisdom upon you without measure, and then wisely make use of your wisdom.

For further study: Psalm 90:12; 111:10; Proverbs 1:7; 4:7;
1 Corinthians 1:25–30; Ephesians 1:17; Colossians 1:9; James 1:5

169 The Temple of God

When God instituted the Davidic covenant in 2 Samuel 7 he told David he would work with David's son when that son became king. The fullness of the Davidic covenant did not become visible until Solomon became king and the great symbols of the Davidic covenant were erected—the temple of God and the palace of the king.

First Kings 6 and 7 describes the building, dimensions, structure, and furniture of the temple, as well as the special God-given palace of God's viceroy, Solomon. The temple had an outer court, an inner court, an outer room (the Holy Place), and an inner room (the Holy of Holies). The Holy of Holies housed the throne of God, the ark of the covenant. The entire temple was the earthly palace of the High King of Israel. In the temple the ark, which had accompanied the people in their wanderings after they left Egypt, found a resting place at last. The building of the temple was the final climax of the exodus.

Let us consider three aspects of the temple's meaning. First, the temple signified the presence of God with the people. Particularly in terms of the kingdom covenant, it signified the presence of God with the king. The palace of the earthly sub-king was next to the temple, at the "right hand" of God, so to speak. This arrangement signified that the earthly king was to rule as God's viceroy.

Second, the temple showed God as house builder. The

362

first house God built was creation itself in Genesis 1. The house also memorialized the defeat of an enemy. The tabernacle was built from the spoils of Egypt, the temple of the spoils of the Egyptians, and the post-exilic temple of the spoils of Babylon, sent to Israel by the kings of Persia. The temple symbolized God's people as his true house, measured out and built according to the detailed specifications of his covenant law.

Finally, the temple showed God's holiness. Only ordained priests were allowed to set foot inside the outer room of the temple, on pain of death, and nobody except the high priest might enter the Holy of Holies, and then only once a year. God's greatness, and his separateness from sin, were graphically represented by the temple.

Coram Deo

God's new temple is the church. Once again he has built upon the spoils of the war with sin, namely reclaimed sinners. We are living stones, being built up into a spiritual house (1 Peter 2:5). It also means that we are to live according to his measurements. Because Peter builds upon this imagery so extensively, read 1 Peter 2 in order to discover how you can display his beautiful presence through your life.

For further study: John 1:14; 2:19; 1 Corinthians 3:16; 6:19; 2 Corinthians 6:16; Ephesians 2:21

170 The Fall of King Solomon

B efore he became King, David collected wives in violation of the laws of kingship found in Deuteronomy 17:16–17. Graciously, God did not allow these sins to disqualify David or destroy the order of the kingdom. The prophet Nathan announced the new kingdom covenant God established with David and his house. Shortly after this new covenant was set up, David fell into adultery with Bathsheba, a new fall that threatened to destroy the kingdom.

We see the same pattern in the life of Solomon. At the beginning of his reign, Solomon entered into a politically expedient marriage with the royal house of Egypt, and he worshiped carelessly on the high places (1 Kings 3:1–3). Yet God did not hold these sins against him, but instead appeared to him at Gibeon and blessed his plan to build the temple. God gave Solomon wisdom and godly influence throughout the world. Then, after the kingdom was settled, Solomon fell further into sin, a fall that disrupted the kingdom.

After the account of the visit of the Queen of Sheba, the pinnacle of Solomon's greatness and influence, we are told that Solomon broke the three laws of kingship. First, he multiplied gold and wealth for himself. Surely the number 666 in 1 Kings 10:14 has prophetic significance (see Rev. 13:18). Second, he multiplied horses and sent to Egypt for them (1 Kings 10:26–29). Third, he multiplied wives and concubines, and they turned his heart away from the

Lord (1 Kings 11:1–8). He also instituted forced labor, reducing the people to slavery, thereby "returning them to Egypt" (1 Kings 12:4). Solomon's godly wisdom so declined until he had forgotten the meaning of the temple he so lavishly constructed.

Just as David's great fall brought trouble on his house for the rest of his days, so Solomon's great fall brought war upon the land for the rest of his reign. Hadad the Edomite rose against him, as did Rezon of Zobah. Solomon's greatest threat arose in the person of Jeroboam, the son of Nebat, who was himself raised up by God through the prophet Ahijah to oppose both Solomon and his son Rehoboam (1 Kings 11:9–40).

Coram Deo

With God there is forgiveness and abundant mercy. He is long-suffering and slow to wrath. This was evident with both David and Solomon, yet God has appointed boundaries which, when crossed, provoked his anger and discipline. Think of Solomon if you are playing brinkmanship with sin, pushing it to the limit. For how can you tell when you have reached the limit God will tolerate. Repent immediately, before God chastises you in discipline.

For further study: Exodus 34:6; Nahum 1:3; Hebrews 12:5–11

171 The Kingdom of Jeroboam

T he apostasy of humanity at the Tower of Babel provoked God to scatter the people into many nations. Similarly, the apostasy of Solomon provoked God to divide the kingdom in half. The northern part of the kingdom, which had its own culture, was given to Jeroboam, while the southern part, consisting of Judah and Simeon (which had merged with Judah), was to remain under the Davidic dynasty.

When Solomon learned that Ahijah the prophet had announced that this would happen, he sought to kill Jeroboam, but the opposition leader fled to Egypt (1 Kings 11:40). After Solomon's death, the people gathered to make Rehoboam king. Notice that accession to the throne was not automatic in Israel; the people had to accept Rehoboam, otherwise another son of Solomon would be put forward. On this occasion, Jeroboam came out of Egypt and spoke for the people. As their leader, he asked that they be released from bondage (1 Kings 12:1–4).

These events fit a pattern we have seen. The man who was to be king was presented as one who delivered the people from bondage. Moses delivered them from Egypt and became their judge. David had to flee to Philistia, then worked to deliver Israel from bondage both to Saul and to Philistia. Next, Jeroboam came from Egypt and stood as the new deliverer. Jeroboam showed wisdom. He did not

> Jeroboam built shrines on high places and appointed priests from all sorts of people, even though they were not Levites. [1 Kings 12:31]

lead a revolution but appealed to Rehoboam to lighten the people's load. Only after Rehoboam refused did the northern tribes secede.

Next, another sad pattern from the reigns of David and Solomon was replayed: Jeroboam was given a kingdom; then he too suffered a "great fall." Fearful that his people would become attracted to the Davidic house if they went to Jerusalem to worship, he set up false worship at two sites in the north. He created a new clergy with himself as high priest, and sold the priestly offices to anyone willing to buy them. In short, he created a state-run church, subservient to the king, in order to shore up his nationalistic aspirations.

Coram Deo

Many faithful Christians suffered martyrdom in Nazi Germany because they refused to support the idolatrous "German church." It was easy to be caught up in nationalism, but the church is an international and transcendent institution. Are there ways we can allow nationalism to warp ministry? Pray today for the church universal, especially for those in troubled lands.

For further study: Isaiah 36:1–7; Daniel 3:28; 56:1–8; John 4:21–24

172 The Role of the Prophet

When Jeroboam set up his false religion, God immediately sent a prophet to confront him. Before we look at this confrontation it might be good to consider the nature of the prophetic role. A *prophet*, as that term is generally used in Scripture, speaks for someone else—almost always for God. We may say that a priest speaks *to God on behalf of the people*, while a prophet speaks *to the people on behalf of God*. Prophets are agents of God's revelation. In the New Testament, the role of the prophets is taken over by the apostles, who completed the written Word of God.

Another word used to denote a prophet is *seer*. It comes from the idea of a *see-er*, someone who "sees." A seer discerns God's will and tells it to the people. The prophet also is called "a man of God," "a servant of God," and "a messenger of God."

Most people think of a prophet primarily as someone who foretells the future. While they possessed this God-given ability, the prophets predicted certain future events for two reasons: First, a prophet predicted something that would take place in the near future, and when the people saw the prophet's prediction come to pass, they were forced to pay closer attention to the rest of the message. Second, predictions of judgment strengthened the prophets' warnings: "You'd *better* repent now, because destruction is coming."

By the word of the LORD a man of God came from Judah to Bethel, as Jeroboam was standing by the altar to make an offering.
[1 Kings 13:1]

The primary role of the prophets was to *forthtell* the Word of God. In this role they interpreted and applied Scripture to the needs of the people. As such, the prophets were social critics. They were not revolutionary radicals, calling for the overthrow of society. They were exactly the opposite—conservative radicals calling society back to God's law. Some Christians today are so tired of the left-wing social gospel that they ignore social problems. The correct response for biblical Christians is not to ignore social problems but to provide biblical solutions. We don't preach the liberal social gospel, but the true gospel that we preach has definite social and political implications.

Coram Deo

It is all too evident that many pastors capitulate their prophetic responsibility. The current tendency is to preach about "felt needs" and to avoid saying that sin is sin. Are you supporting your church in its prophetic function, as it speaks courageously and as the pastor preaches vigorously against the sins of our day? Remember, it is not your church that is to take a political stand, but through its preaching the people individually are to stand for social and political justice.

For further study: 1 Corinthians 1:17–25; Galatians 1:8;
Ephesians 3:7–12; 2 Timothy 4:2

173 The Methods of the Prophet

I t was bad enough that Isaiah, son of a leading family in Israel, had become a radically zealous preacher of the law of God. The "church" of his day did not want to hear all this talk about law and judgment; they wanted to hear about grace and love, and to feel "joy, joy, joy" down in their hearts. Then Isaiah started going around wearing sackcloth, as if in poverty and mourning. Finally, in the people's opinion, he went too far; roaming the streets barefoot and naked—for three years (Isa. 20:4).

The liberals of his day laughed at Isaiah; after all, they said, Isaiah was representative of all Bible-believing fanatics. Those who were the most offended by Isaiah were the respectable conservatives who felt that his weird behavior compromised their witness. But in fact, God had told Isaiah to do these things.

Isaiah's action was an example of "prophetic theater," a symbolic action designed to drive home a point. The prophets sometimes did bizarre things to dramatize the fact that God meant business. Ezekiel refused to speak for several years, except to shake his fist and yell denunciations at a picture he had drawn of Jerusalem (Ezek. 3:24–4:8). John the Baptist publicly denounced Herod and lost his head. Jesus Christ made a whip and drove thieves out of God's house.

> At that time the LORD spoke through Isaiah son of Amoz. He said to him, "Take off the sackcloth from your body and the sandals from your feet." And he did so, going around stripped and barefoot. [Isa. 20:2).

In addition to prophetic theater, the prophets communicated God's Word in three other major ways. One was the sermon, an address to the faithful designed to teach God's Word, to encourage godliness, and to reprove sin. Another was the prophetic oracle. An oracle is a prophecy of coming events, of which there are two kinds. The oracle of woe prophesies that disaster is coming because of the sins of the people, while the oracle of weal predicts that, after the disaster, God will restore and bless his people. Finally, the prophets communicated God's Word by describing visions that God gave them. Much of the books of Daniel, Ezekiel, and Zechariah feature such visions.

Coram Deo

Are you embarrassed by visible public stands against social evils, such as picketing and sitting to block access to abortion chambers? Is it possible that these people, by engaging in "prophetic theater," are helping wake up society to the holocaust around us? Legitimate activities can create long standing symbols remembered by people who might not otherwise hear prophetic words. Is it time for you to make such public stands for truth and righteousness?

For further study: Mark 8:31–38; Romans 1:14–17; Philippians 1:20; 2 Timothy 1:6–9

174 The Prophet and the King

The oracle the unnamed prophet delivered against Jeroboam's false religion was one of woe. It was an example of a "covenant lawsuit." One of the most important duties of the prophet was to stand as a prosecuting attorney for God, summoning the people to trial. When the people, and especially their king, broke the covenant, the prophet would bring God's lawsuit against them.

One reason the prophetic ministry came into prominence during the period of the kings is that the order of the kingdom was directly tied to another function of the prophet: He was the ambassador of the High King, the Lord. Regarding the reign of King Saul, we saw that the essential condition of the kingdom was that the human king must always hearken to the words of the High King, brought by his prophet (see pp. 328–29).

God gave a kingdom to Saul, who tried to make it his own. Then the prophet Samuel brought the covenant lawsuit against him. God gave a kingdom to David, who sought to exploit it for his own purpose; then the prophet Nathan brought the covenant lawsuit against David. God gave a kingdom to Solomon, who then broke the three laws of kingship, assuming that the kingdom was his to administer as he pleased. God raised up the prophet Ahijah to oppose him. Next, God had given a kingdom to Jeroboam, and the first thing Jeroboam did was reject God as High

> [The prophet] cried out against the altar by the word of the LORD: "O altar, altar! This is what the LORD says: 'A son named Josiah will be born to the house of David. On you he will sacrifice the priests of the high places who now make offerings here, and human bones will be burned on you.' " [1 Kings 13:2]

King and start doing things his own way. Hence, God sent a prophet to denounce him and later sent Ahijah to announce the coming destruction of Jeroboam's line (1 Kings 14:1–20).

This pattern continues throughout the books of Kings, which is why so many chapters are actually about the prophets Elijah and Elisha. These men and their followers reminded the people who the true King of the land was, and called out the "remnant" to follow him.

In a real sense, then, the books of Kings (one book in Hebrew) are not merely about the human kings of Judah and Israel. They are about the human kings of Israel and Judah, and the High King—the Lord.

Coram Deo

Pastors and church leaders would naturally rather fulfil only the priestly aspect of their work, comforting God's people. Yet, it is also their duty, and the duty of the church as an institution, to be the prophetic voice of the High King, calling nations to submit and reminding all of us that we are to live our lives in submission to King Jesus. Pray for your leaders today, that they will not shirk their God-ordained responsibilities to be both prophet and priest.

For further study: Psalm 81; 2 Peter 1:21; Revelation 1:3; 22

PART 9

Kings, prophets, and wise men—there are plenty of takers for the first job, but only a few who truly set themselves apart as God's forth-telling ambassadors, the modern day prophets. So little wisdom remains to be found. Our generation no longer looks to wisdom's Source.

Part 9 completes our survey of Israel's history by looking at the ministries of Elijah and Elisha. Their words and deeds were so spectacular that we tend to forget about the tremendous burden of persecution and rejection they faced. When we stand with Elisha, looking at the fallen cloak of Elijah and wondering if he should pick it up, we will just taste the life of the prophets of old. The ministry of calling to repentance is no more appreciated today.

We also will trace the histories of the northern and southern kingdoms to the destruction of Samaria and Jerusalem. At this time God showed both his disciplining hand and his most

Elijah, Elisha and the Divided Kingdom

tender expressions of love to a wayward people. Even as they trudged off toward Babylon, they carried with them God's promises of redemption, both from exile and eventually from sin. The books of Ezra and Nehemiah show us the unveiling of the first of those promises.

After a brief introduction to the wisdom genre of biblical literature, we will begin a look at the Book of Job.

We are covering a large portion of the Old Testament. You will benefit from spending extra time reading through some of these books to become more familiar with the details of this portion of God's Word. Working to understand his Word, and then aspiring to live by it—this is living *coram Deo*—under God's authority and unto his glory.

R.C. Sproul

175 Baal vs. Yahweh

W hen God set up the kingdom in Israel, he made a condition for the kings: They were always to hearken to the words of the prophets, the emissaries of the true High King of Israel. In a more general way, the prophets were also the ambassadors of God to the people. God always gave the people the kind of king they deserved. If there was to be reformation in the land, the people, as well as the king, had to repent. The unfaithfulness of the kings of Israel and Judah reflected the moral condition of the people.

The kingdom of northern Israel was separated from the south (Judah) and established by God in response to the sins of Solomon. The first king of northern Israel, Jeroboam I, immediately fell into sin by creating a syncretistic religion. As noted earlier in our studies, a syncretistic religion mixes two or more religions as a sort of hybrid. Jeroboam's new religion was a combination of Yahwism, the true faith, and Baalism. In essence, Jeroboam and his priests claimed to be worshiping the LORD with the rituals of Baal.

When Ahab came to the throne things became worse. Ahab's wife, Jezebel, was a devotee of pure, unadulterated Baalism. She established a pure Baal cult in the land and convinced Ahab to suppress all forms of Yahwism. God raised up Elijah to confront this outbreak of hardened paganism.

376

> Elijah went before the people and said, "How long will you waver between two opinions? If the Lord is God, follow him; but if Baal is God, follow him." But the people said nothing. [1 Kings 18:21]

God brought a three-year drought on Israel that bankrupted the nation. Then Elijah initiated a contest on Mount Carmel. Both he and the Baal priests set up sacrifices, and the god who sent fire down from heaven to burn up the sacrifices would be shown to be the true God.

Elijah challenged the people before performing the sacrifice. "How long will you waver between two opinions?" he asked, but the people remained silent. Only when they saw the fire fall from God did they say, "Yahweh, the LORD, he is God!" At Elijah's orders, they killed all the prophets of Baal, and purged the land of this gross form of idolatry. It seemed as if revival had come, but the people quickly forgot the miracle and lapsed into their syncretistic ways.

Coram Deo

Too much of the church today wavers between two opinions. Jesus said hard things about this in Revelation 3:15–16. Read these verses in their context. For each believer the challenge is to live purely, on God's terms, rejecting syncretistic adultery with culture. Where have you compromised with competing philosophies, religious practices, and cultural norms? To what extent has your church and denomination added defiling practices not permitted by Scripture?

For further study: Exodus 8:16–19; Philippians 2:12–18; Revelation 3

176 The Lord's Inheritance

Y ears after God's defeat of Baalism at Mount Carmel, King Ahab looked out from his palace in Jezreel and saw a vineyard that he thought would be ideal for a royal vegetable garden. He approached the owner of the vineyard, a man named Naboth, asked him to sell it, and made him an offer.

Naboth refused Ahab's offer for a significant reason. Recall in our description of property laws that when the Lord initially gave the land of Canaan to Israel it was divided into family tracts. The ownership of these family plots was inalienable, because the land truly belonged to God and was assigned to the stewardship of various families. One could not sell land permanently. One could only lease the crops produced until the year of jubilee. Every fifty years all the land reverted to God, and he gave the plots of land back to the original families (Leviticus 25; see pp. 262–63).

Naboth reminded Ahab of this. The vineyard was part of God's original gift to his family, and he did not have the right to sell it. Moreover, he did not choose to lease it to Ahab. Naboth was faithful to the original covenant God had made with Israel. His faithfulness cost him his life.

Ahab knew that Naboth was right and that this was the law, so he realized there was nothing he could do. Depressed, he returned to the palace and sulked until his pagan wife, Jezebel, took matters in hand. Back in her home country of Tyre, there was no such law as the jubilee. Rulers held absolute power over all things, including land.

But Naboth replied, "The LORD forbid that I should give you the inheritance of my fathers." [1 Kings 21:3]

Was her husband a king or a mouse? Jezebel ordered some compromising by faithless elders of Jezreel—the very ones charged with enforcing the law—to do away with Naboth. They were to hire two scoundrels to give testimony against Naboth, accusing him of the capital crime of cursing God (Lev. 24:14). This was done, and afterwards Ahab took possession of Naboth's vineyard.

Elijah the prophet confronted Ahab. He told the king that because he had done this, God would destroy him. As the dogs had eaten the stoned body of Naboth in the field, so the dogs would lick up Ahab's blood, and Ahab's royal line would not endure. Scavenger dogs would also devour Jezebel.

Coram Deo

Naboth is one example in a lineage of believers as long as history who lost their lives because they stood for righteousness in an unrighteous society. As a layperson he knew the law and was more committed to keeping it than was the king, the appointed safeguardian of the law. In Israel's theocracy there should not have been, and in this case there was not, a conflict between religious and civil law. We do encounter such conflicts today, however. How do you choose the godly ethical decision when faced with these choices?

For further study: Leviticus 25:23–34; Deuteronomy 17:14–20; 2 Corinthians 6:11–18

177 The Mantle of the Prophet

When it came time for Elijah to be taken up into heaven, he and his appointed successor, Elisha, were at Gilgal. Elijah suggested that Elisha remain, but Elisha insisted on going along to Bethel. At Bethel Elijah again suggested that Elisha remain behind, but the servant insisted on accompanying his master to Jericho. At Jericho, Elijah urged Elisha to remain in the city, but Elisha insisted on crossing the Jordan into the wilderness with him.

Elisha knew that, as successor to Elijah, it was important for the rest of the prophets to see him in the company of the master. Of course, an additional reason was his love for Elijah and his unwillingness to be parted from him.

Elijah asked his servant what last request he might grant before he left to be with God. Elisha knew if he were to follow in Elijah's footsteps he would need the strength of the Spirit of God. The task before him was huge, and he felt his own weakness intensely, so he made bold to ask for a double portion of Elijah's spirit. Elijah replied that this was a difficult request, but that Elisha would know he had been given it if he saw Elijah depart this earth.

What made the request difficult? It was not hard for God to give a double measure of strength to one of his children. Rather, Elijah saw that the burden of such a gift would be difficult for Elisha to bear, because a double measure of

380

> He [Elisha] picked up the cloak that had fallen from Elijah and
> went back and stood on the bank of the Jordan. [2 Kings 2:13]

strength would carry with it a double measure of responsibility and hardship.

After Elijah was taken up, Elisha found the prophet's mantle lying on the ground. We can imagine his thoughts as he considered whether to take up that mantle. He thought about how Elijah had been persecuted and friendless, about Elijah's lonely life in the wilderness. He knew that picking up that mantle would mean inviting scorn and hostility from his own people. We aren't told how long Elisha looked at the mantle, but we are told that in the end he picked it up.

In the same way, we are called to take up our crosses and follow Jesus, knowing that it will bring us distress. There can be no crown for us unless first we bear the cross of rejection by the world.

Coram Deo

There are no prophetic mantles for us to pick up, but as a child of the living God we have been given a full measure of the Spirit. While this should result in a characteristic joy, it also means responsibility, hardship, and crosses to bear. Measure your heart against the challenge to live for Christ daily. What does picking up the cloak mean in your life?

For further study: Joshua 1:1–9; Matthew 10:34–39; John 15:18–25

178 The Roots of the Remnant

E lijah's departure out of the land was, in a sense, a judgment. He led Elisha, his protégé, into the wilderness. Since Elisha represented all the prophets, who in turn represented all the faithful, we can see in this a new departure from Egypt, so to speak. Ahab and his dynasty were like Pharaoh, Israel had become like Egypt, and God's people now had to make an exodus. Moses died in the wilderness without seeing the conquest of the land, and Elijah also departed in the wilderness. No one knows where God buried Moses (Deut. 34:6), and the prophets searched for Elijah's body but could not find it (2 Kings 2:16–18).

Later Elisha returned to Israel. Keep in mind that Elisha was to Elijah what Joshua was to Moses. As for Joshua, the Jordan River parted before Elisha as he entered the land. Elisha's task was to lead the godly remnant in a new conquest, and he began, as did Joshua, at Jericho. This new conquest would be unlike the first one, since there would be no transformation of the political structure of the land as a result. Instead, the conquest would result in a remnant, the church of the faithful. Elisha would train up the prophets as pastors of local assemblies.

This later conquest of Jericho was unlike the first. Joshua, under God's direction, completely destroyed that city. The people were told never to rebuild it, and it was prophesied that whoever did would lose his children as punishment

And the water has remained wholesome to this day, according to the word Elisha had spoken. [2 Kings 2:22]

(Josh. 6:26). In Ahab's day, Hiel of Bethel rebuilt the city, and received the curse (1 Kings 16:34). The city continued to labor under God's judgment, however, since its water was foul and the land unproductive.

The citizens appealed to Elisha to heal the waters. Instead of condemning them for living in Jericho, Elisha took salt (representing the covenant of God; Lev. 2:13) and put it in a new bowl (representing God's new work of grace). Elisha threw the salt into the spring, and the waters were cleansed. Jericho had been conquered by the gospel, and became a center for the remnant community (compare 2 Kings 6:1).

Coram Deo

The second Elijah, John the forerunner, also went out into the wilderness and called the people to go through the Jordan in a new baptism and enter a new kingdom. Time and time again God calls his people to new beginnings, reinvigorating them with a deeper love for Jesus and a fresh sense of the Holy Spirit. Thank God for the opportunity to start over. In his mercy he does not cast us off, but draws us back to where we can be useful again in his kingdom service.

For further study: Leviticus 19:17; 1 Kings 19:11–18; Psalm 39:11; Titus 1:13; 2:15; Revelation 3:19

179 The Threat of Judgment

I srael was called to repent by the formation of a remnant under Elijah and Elisha. To make the point clear, God brought severe judgment on the city of Bethel. *Beth-El* means "house of God," and once the city had been a center of true worship. Jeroboam, however, had put one of his golden calves there, and the city had become a center of idolatry. Hiel of Bethel defied God and rebuilt Jericho, losing his children in the process. Now the entire city of Bethel would lose some children.

Some translations say that "children" came out and jeered Elisha, saying, "Go up, baldy!" However, in the Hebrew these are clearly youths, not little children. It was a gang of teenagers, reflecting the attitudes of their parents, who mocked God's prophet.

By saying "Go up," they may have taunted Elisha to continue up to Samaria, the capital of Israel. They were ridiculing the prophet as he went to confront the king. Or perhaps they were saying to Elisha, "Why don't you follow Elijah up to heaven and leave us alone." Either way, their contempt for God and his church was manifest.

Baldness was rare in Israel, and luxuriant hair was often regarded as a sign of power and blessing (see, for example, 2 Sam. 14:26). By ridiculing Elisha's baldness, these young people were calling him and his ministry impotent.

> He [Elisha] turned around, looked at them and called down a curse on them in the name of the LORD. Then two bears came out of the woods and mauled forty-two of the youths. [2 Kings 2:24]

Under divine inspiration, Elisha cursed them, and two bears came out of the woods and slew forty-two of them. The flower of Bethel's youth was cut down. This was a mighty judgment against the city and its idolatry, visiting the sins of the father on the children because the children followed in their fathers' footsteps.

In every age the announcement of God's kingdom is one of judgment. All men and women are called to choose. In Elisha's time God was calling people to forsake idols and join the faithful remnant. It is no different today, and the cultural consequences of refusing to join with God's people are the same now as they were then: The young people and the nation will be destroyed.

Coram Deo

Just as in biblical days, children today suffer and even die for the sins of their parents. Drugs and abortion most noticeably take lives. However, lack of parental authority also contributes to rebellion among young people with disastrous effects. What more are you able to do for the young people in your community? Consider where your ministry gifts and resources can be brought to bear.

For further study: Joshua 24:15; 2 Corinthians 1:3–11; 2:12–16; 4:7–18

180 A New Start for Israel

ecause of the atrocities committed by Ahab and his house, the Lord determined to wipe out his line. On previous occasions in Israel's history, God allowed revolutionaries to kill the man on the throne and set themselves up in power. That is how Baasha, Zimri, and Omri (Ahab's father) came to the throne. Now, however, God took a more active role. He sent a prophet to anoint Jehu, the commander of the Israelite army, as king and commanded him to wipe out Ahab's entire line. Thus, Jehu's accession marks a definitive new beginning in the history of Israel, comparable to the accessions of Saul, David, and Jeroboam, who had also been expressly chosen by God before becoming kings.

As military men often are, Jehu was a cultural conservative. He felt a nationalistic loyalty to Israel and her culture, and he disliked the pagan Baalism imported into Israel by Jezebel. His men felt the same way, and they rejoiced to hear that Jehu had been anointed to take power. Immediately Jehu and his army went after King Joram of Israel and King Ahaziah of Judah, both descendants of Ahab, and killed them in battle. Then Jehu had Jezebel killed. After that, Jehu sent letters to the elders of Samaria demanding that they kill the seventy sons of Ahab living among them, which they did. Then he killed forty-two relatives of King Ahaziah of Judah, who were also part of

> Then the prophet poured the oil on Jehu's head and declared,
> "This is what the LORD, the God of Israel, says: 'I anoint you king
> over the LORD's people Israel.' " [2 Kings 9:6b]

Ahab's clan. In all of this, Jehu was supported by the faithful in Israel (2 Kings 9:11–10:17).

Finally, Jehu pretended to convert to Baalism and called for a big celebration. He lured all the priests of Baal together in Baal's temple and then had them all killed (2 Kings 10:18–28). In this way, Jehu purged the land of the foreign gods Jezebel had imported.

Sadly, Jehu was no more than a cultural conservative. Being merely a conservative, he was not interested in returning to true Yahwism. He simply wanted to turn the clock back to the syncretistic and nationalistic pseudo-Yahwism of Jeroboam. He brought no true reform, but his actions did make it possible for the remnant church to live without fear of outright persecution.

Coram Deo

Many Christians confuse authentic Christian reform with mere cultural, flag-waving conservatism, which we might call "civil religion." It is not enough to turn the public school clock back to the 1950s. It is not enough to restore the U.S. Constitution in politics and government. What are the primary differences in form and substance between a biblical culture and a merely traditional one?

For further study: Micah 6:16; Matthew 15:2–6; Mark 7:8–13; Colossians 2:8

181 Israel's Last Chance

J ehu's dynasty lasted longer than did any other in northern Israel. He reigned for 28 years, his son Jehoahaz for seventeen years, his grandson Jehoash for sixteen years, and his great-grandson Jeroboam II for forty-one years. This long period of relative stability enabled the remnant church to develop. During the reign of Jeroboam II, three great prophets emerged from the remnant: Hosea, Amos, and Jonah.

That Jehoash would name his son Jeroboam (or perhaps that Jeroboam took that as his own throne name) indicates that the official state religion of Israel continued to be the syncretistic combination of Baalism and Yahwism. This kind of semi-Baalism perpetually violated the second commandment, for it involved idols and images in the supposed worship of Yahweh. The second commandment states that those who worship through images will feel God's wrath to the third and fourth generations, and it was in the fourth generation after Jehu that his line was broken off: The son of Jeroboam II, Zechariah, reigned only six months before being overthrown in a coup.

Throughout the reign of Jeroboam II, the remnant prophets, Hosea and Amos, warned that if there were no repentance, God would destroy the nation. Jonah preached repentance to Assyria, and that nation temporarily turned to the Lord. As a result, Assyria was built up culturally and became a powerful nation, the scourge God would use against Israel.

The king of Assyria invaded the entire land, marched against Samaria and laid siege to it for three years. [2 Kings 17:5]

Because Israel did not repent, God cursed her with disastrous civil wars. Shallum slew Zechariah and reigned one month. Menahem slew Shallum and reigned for ten years. During his reign Assyria decapitalized the nation. Menahem's son Pekahiah reigned for two years. Pekah slew Pekahiah and reigned for twenty years. Assyria raided again during Pekah's reign and took several key cities. Hoshea slew Pekah, and made peace with Assyria. Then he secretly made a treaty with Egypt, and Assyria besieged Samaria, killed Hoshea in the ninth year of his reign, and destroyed the nation of northern Israel.

During these years, however, the faithful members of the remnant church moved south at the invitation of Judah's kings and were spared.

Coram Deo

God protects his church, sometimes with stability and growth and sometimes by moving her out of the way of judgment. God also gives nations opportunities to repent, but if they don't, he eventually gives them over to expressions of his judgment. God has not changed, nor have his ways. As you follow national and world news developments, can you see evidences of God's hand still at work?

For further study: 2 Chronicles 6:14–26; 7:14; Psalm 88:13; Ezekiel 18

182 The Mothers of Destiny

E ach time a new king came to the throne of Judah, Scripture records the name of his mother. This is significant, because the Bible recognizes that there is truth in the saying that "the hand that rocks the cradle rules the world." The first king of Judah was Rehoboam, son of Solomon. Rehoboam experienced shattering events in his reign. He came to the throne at age forty-one, having lived most of his life in the glories of the Solomonic united kingdom. He expected to continue in that situation, but as soon as he took the throne he lost nine-tenths of the kingdom when the northern tribes seceded. Rehoboam's instinct was to fight to regain this territory, but Shemaiah the prophet warned the people not to do so, and on this occasion they listened to the prophet (1 Kings 12).

Rehoboam's mother was Naamah the Ammonitess, a woman from a thoroughly degenerate Baalist culture. Perhaps partly because of the way he had been brought up, partly through the influence of his father, Solomon, and partly because he was angry at God, Rehoboam led the nation into radical idolatry. As a result, Rehoboam experienced another shattering judgment: Shishak of Egypt came and took away all the treasures of the palace and temple (1 Kings 14:21–28).

Rehoboam's favorite wife, Maacah, was a Jewish convert to idolatry. Their son and heir to the throne was Abijam, who followed in his parents' footsteps. It is clear that during his reign, his mother was the power behind the throne. He reigned only three years.

> [King Asa] even deposed his grandmother Maacah from her
> position as queen mother, because she had made a repulsive
> Ashram pole. [1 Kings 15:13a]

Then his son Asa came to the throne. Asa was very young, and in the early years of his reign his grandmother Maacah continued to wield power as queen mother. Asa destroyed some idols early in his reign, but not until after his fifteenth year did he have the power to depose Maacah from her position of influence (2 Chron. 15:10–16).

Asa broke with the tradition maintained by these evil mothers and brought about a renewal of the true faith in Judah. It is interesting to see that, until the evil influences are removed, even the faithful with virtuous intentions are limited in what they can do. How sad it is, and how frequent, that the evil influences are family members from whom it is most difficult to disassociate.

Coram Deo

Early in his ministry Jesus had to disassociate from his own mother and brothers because they thought he had lost his mind (Mark 3:20, 31–35). He later taught that he had brought a sword to divide faithful from unfaithful family members (Luke 12:49–53). What is "appropriate separation" from nonbelieving family members and friends? How can you continue to minister to them without being compromised by their influence?

For further study: 2 Kings 9:22; Ezekiel 16:44–48; Galatians 4:26;
1 Thessalonians 2:7

391

183 Reform and Apostasy

lthough Jehoshaphat, the son of Asa, was basically a good king, he made one foolish mistake: He made peace with Ahab, king of Israel (1 Kings 22:44). Making peace involved forming some kind of covenant, and one of the aspects of this arrangement was that Ahab's daughter Athaliah married Jehoshaphat's son Jehoram. Athaliah was the most wicked woman ever to come near the throne of Judah.

Under her influence Jehoram readily followed in the wicked ways of the kings of Israel, forsaking the righteousness of his father Jehoshaphat (2 Kings 8:18). When Jehoram died, their son Ahaziah came to the throne, and he also followed in the ways of his mother and his grandfather Ahab (2 Kings 8:26–27). It was Ahaziah who was killed by Jehu when God commanded Jehu to wipe out Ahab's house.

Jehu had strength only in the north, and it was because Ahaziah was visiting the north that he was killed. Upon learning of her son's death, Athaliah decided to take over the southern kingdom of Judah. She put to death every royal son, intending to wipe out the Davidic line completely. Unknown to her, Ahaziah's son, her grandson, was rescued. His name was Joash, and he was raised secretly by Jehoiada the high priest.

At the age of seven, Joash was publicly anointed king by Jehoiada. The people and the army, who had had enough of Athaliah's corrupt rule, rallied to him, and Athaliah was put to death (2 Kings 11).

This was a triumph for the religious conservatives in Judah. Under Jehoiada's influence, Joash repaired the temple, abolished idolatry, and broke off the evil political alliances with pagan nations. When Jehoiada died, however, Joash came under other influences. The moneyed aristocrats in Jerusalem and Judah came to him and persuaded him to break with Jehoiada's "fundamentalistic" ways and to take a more "open-minded, tolerant" approach to things. Joash abandoned the purity of God's worship and allowed idolatry back into Jerusalem. Jehoiada's son, Zechariah the high priest, a man Joash had grown up with, publicly called on Joash to repent, and Joash had him put to death (2 Chronicles 24).

Coram Deo

The tide of purity within the church seems to perpetually ebb and flow. God remains constant, but leaders present changing influences for good and evil. Because most church leaders are trained at seminaries it is incumbent for the church that these next generations of leaders be soundly taught. Where are your pastoral candidates being trained? Will they become the spiritual leaders the church will need in her continual movement toward reform unto righteousness?

For further study: Matthew 5:48; Romans 12:2; Philippians 3:17–21; Titus 2

184 Politics or Faithfulness?

A s Assyria marched throughout the ancient Near East, conquering one little country after another, King Ahaz of Judah sought to spare his country by making an alliance with Assyria. He sent gold and silver from God's temple to Assyria. His political strategy worked. Later, when Assyria destroyed northern Israel, the southern kingdom was spared.

However, Ahaz's action violated God's ways. He should have trusted solely in the Lord for Judah's defense. Instead, he subjected himself and his nation to the idolatry of Assyria, and when his son Hezekiah came to the throne, Judah was a vassal of Assyria. Hezekiah's first action as king was to restore the temple and eliminate the idolatrous worship introduced by Ahaz. He held a great Passover and invited the remnant in the northern kingdom to come to it. Many moved to Judah and were spared when Assyria destroyed northern Israel in Hezekiah's sixth year.

In the fourteenth year of Hezekiah's reign, the Philistine city of Ashdod formed an alliance to try and shake off the yoke of Assyria. Isaiah the prophet warned Hezekiah to have no part in it (Isaiah 20). He told Hezekiah that when God was ready he would deliver Judah. Hezekiah listened to Isaiah (2 Kings 18:13–16). At this time, people in Judah were willing to hearken to the prophets because they had just seen the destruction of the north, which the prophets had predicted.

Later in his reign, however, Hezekiah came under the

sway of the political aristocracy in Judah. Learning that Babylon was growing strong, Hezekiah formed an alliance with Babylon and other nations in preparation for shaking off the Assyrian yoke. Isaiah criticized him severely for this, but Hezekiah only paid slight attention (2 Kings 20). Like Saul, David, Solomon, Jeroboam, and Joash, Hezekiah fell into sin and almost lost the kingdom.

Toward the end of Hezekiah's reign, Assyria went on the march again to put down the new revolt. The Assyrians laid waste to most of Judah and besieged Jerusalem. Hezekiah turned to the Lord in repentance, and the city was spared (2 Kings 18:17–19:27).

Coram Deo

As was the case with David's adultery and murder, Hezekiah's sin exposed the nation to destruction, but also as did David, he repented, and God heard his prayer. It is usually impossible to know what motivates people to cry out to God, and whether that cry is sincere. Was the move toward God related to a change in political fortunes, or a broken and contrite heart? Be a searcher of your own heart and motivations and judge with charity the motives of others as often as possible. Ultimately, God is the judge. He will determine his response to these cries.

For further study: Proverbs 3; Isaiah 38:10–22

185 A Last Opportunity

udah's worth king was Manasseh, the son of Hezekiah. As soon as he was secure on the throne he undid all the reforms Hezekiah had initiated. He openly practiced witchcraft and, as a sorcerer-king, sponsored every form of idolatry known to the ancient world, including child sacrifice. He reigned for fifty-five years. During that time the nation became thoroughly steeped in idolatry.

Manasseh was followed by his son Amon, who was so despicable that he was killed after two years by officials of the palace. His son, Josiah, came to the throne at the age of eight. God reached into this depraved family and converted Josiah; when he was eighteen Josiah instituted the most sweeping reform in the history of Judah.

Josiah began rebuilding the temple, and shortly thereafter the priests brought to his attention a moldy book they had found in a side room. It was the book of the law, either Deuteronomy or perhaps all five of the books of Moses. Josiah read it and realized that his reformation had to be far more thorough than he had originally envisioned. Following the dictates of God's holy law, and with the prophet Jeremiah as an adviser, Josiah destroyed all the idols and the high places where the Lord was falsely worshiped. He slew all the idolatrous priests. He cleansed the temple according to the rituals of Leviticus, and led the nation in a covenant renewal.

> Neither before nor after Josiah was there a king like him who turned to the LORD as he did—with all his heart and with all his soul and with all his strength, in accordance with all the Law of Moses. [2 Kings 23:25]

This was Judah's last chance. Sadly, the nation as a whole only cooperated outwardly with Josiah; there was no wholehearted repentance. The idols were broken on the hills, but not in the hearts. Thus, "the LORD did not turn away from the heat of his fierce anger, which burned against Judah" (2 Kings 23:26).

God mercifully called Josiah home to himself before the flood of retribution poured out. The following four kings each reigned for short periods of time, and each willingly cooperated with the idolatrous hearts of the people and rejected the Lord.

Since the people wanted to live as pagans, God put them under the pagan rule of Babylon and sold them into captivity.

Coram Deo

Good leadership does not guarantee good followers. Scripture shows that when God's leaders truly led and people truly followed the nation was blessed. It was a rare blessing. While the failure of spiritual leadership is the sad legacy of Israel's kings, the other half of the story is how willingly the people followed into sin. Not even Josiah could alter that. Can you, and will you, follow effective leadership?

For further study: Psalm 119; Matthew 13:1–9, 18–23

186 The Chronicles of God

The question often arises when reading the books of Chronicles, Why are these stories told twice in Scripture? We already read about David, Solomon, and the other kings in the books of Samuel and Kings. It is helpful to know the purpose of the writer of the Chronicles. Many do not realize that these books were written long after Samuel and Kings—in fact, after the exile. They are the last two books in the Hebrew Bible, concluding the third division of literature known as "the writings."

Although telling the same stories, the writer's perspective differed radically from that found in the earlier historical books. This writer looked with the eye of a historian on the events of the reigns of Israel's and Judah's sinful kings and the godless national decline.

As the historical account unfolded, the writer knew that in the end Israel had fallen into the depths of degradation. But he also knew that wasn't the end of God's work, for even then his nation was finally regrouping after returning from a generation of exile in another land. The writer wanted his people to realize that their heritage was important. Although they no longer had a king and there was no visible reason for national pride, theirs was a wondrous national heritage. The people were still connected, both by a physical and a spiritual lineage, to everlasting promises made by Yahweh the Great King.

Further, continuing faith in Yahweh could yet make all the difference. In fact, the difference in perspective could

> Jehoshaphat stood and said, "Listen to me, Judah and people of Jerusalem! Have faith in the LORD your God and you will be upheld." [2 Chron. 20:20b]

be summarized by saying that, if the books of Kings teach that sin leads to defeat and ultimate downfall, Chronicles teaches that faith can lead to recovery and new victories.

For several reasons tradition has held that Ezra was the writer of Chronicles, not the least being the close similarity between the ending of Chronicles (2 Chron. 36:22–23) and the beginning of Ezra (1:1–3). The long genealogies he recorded were intended to show the bridge that connected the former times with the latter times. The consistent positive outlook on God's continuing promises was meant to encourage people to maintain hope for the messianic fulfillment which was finally and fully met in Jesus of Nazareth hundreds of years later.

Coram Deo

In the same way as at the writing of the Chronicles, it is important for us to look both back in time (remembering the connection we have with our spiritual forerunners) and forward (continuing to look for the ultimate messianic fulfillment promised to us by that same Jesus). Think of your own heritage, where you came from both spiritually and naturally. Thank God for his past faithfulness. What kind of legacy are you leaving for those coming after you?

For further study: Psalm 78; Hebrews 4:1–7

187 Ezra: Redemption Secured

E zra is one of four books in the Old Testament that recount the priestly history of Israel. Ezra was a scribe, a learned interpreter of the law. His wisdom was so great, in fact, that one ancient tradition held that the ancient books were lost, yet under divine inspiration, Ezra rewrote them all.

The Book of Ezra tells the story of the fulfillment of God's promise to Israel to return the people to their land after seventy years in exile. He explained to his people that they must turn from the rebellion of their forefathers and keep the covenant with God. If they were to be a covenant people, they had to be free of pagan influence and idolatry. He reiterated the promises of God and of his blessings should they prove to be faithful.

The events of Ezra's ministry, however, are not mere history. We are to learn *from*, and not just *about*, Ezra's leadership and how the remnant reestablished itself. This book tells about both the people of Israel and the faithful, sovereign, forgiving God of Israel.

The edict of Cyrus, king of Persia, allowing the return to Jerusalem and the rebuilding of the temple, opens the Book of Ezra. The prophet Jeremiah, who served from the reign of Josiah into the exile, had promised just such a return (Jeremiah 33). Yahweh is a God who is faithful to keep his promises. He can be trusted.

God's faithfulness is coupled with the power to fulfil his promises. Cyrus was, at that time, the most powerful man

> In the first year of Cyrus king of Persia, in order to fulfill the word of the LORD spoken by Jeremiah, the LORD moved the heart of Cyrus king of Persia to make a proclamation throughout his realm and to put it in writing. [Ezra 1:1]

on earth. God, however, worked in the heart of Cyrus to be kindly disposed toward the request of the people who wanted to return to their homeland. God exercises his rule over the kings of earth.

God continued to manifest his sovereignty as the former exiles met resistance in their efforts to rebuild the temple. First he acted locally, ensuring that the work would continue (5:5). God next safeguarded the work through the decree of Darius, which affirmed the decree of Cyrus before him.

Finally, God was shown to be faithful and sovereign, but also forgiving. His chosen people had turned from him time and again. Yet he heard their cries in exile and forgave them, that they might be a holy nation.

Coram Deo

Cyrus' reign was characterized by religious toleration. The peoples he ruled were encouraged to retain their respective faiths. Ours, too, is a pluralistic society. Do you seek the opportunity to live your faith before anyone with non-Christian beliefs? How can you show your acceptance of the person without crossing the line to accepting their religion as a viable alternative to the one true faith?

For further study: Proverbs 21:1–7; Lamentations 3:18–27; Romans 4:16–21

188 Conflict Management

Nehemiah was a man who knew how to handle conflict. What we know of his life and ministry from the book bearing his name indicates that he mediated and led the people through one conflict after another. Nehemiah's first conflict was apparently with God himself. Israel had been defeated in war, devastated as a nation, and scattered among the peoples. Jerusalem lay in ruins. Nehemiah, cupbearer to King Artaxerxes, was burdened with what God was and was not accomplishing.

Therefore, before God Nehemiah rehearsed an entire history of Israel's sin, and through prayer, fasting, and confession, he found relief from his burden. God then restored to him a vision of what yet might be accomplished in Israel.

Nehemiah's enthusiastic spirit of "Let us arise and build" (2:18 NKJV) resulted in substantial external conflict when he returned to Jerusalem to rebuild the city wall. Sanballat, Tobiah, and Geshem, local provincial rulers who felt threatened by a defensible city wall, harassed Nehemiah in hopes of halting the work. They resorted to lies, and conspiracy, to no avail, for Nehemiah completed the staggering job of rebuilding a wall around Jerusalem in only fifty-two days.

A third source of conflict came from within the Israelite community. People began to abuse one another by charging exorbitant rates for food and goods, causing some to sell themselves into slavery to fellow Jews in order to con-

I answered them by saying, "The God of heaven will give us
success. We his servants will start rebuilding, but as for you, you
have no share in Jerusalem or any claim or historic right to it."
[Neh. 2:20]

tinue working on the rebuilding of the wall (5:1–13). Nehemiah dealt with dissension from within with corporate
prayer, confession, and restitution. Through these strug-
gles Nehemiah himself displayed the primary example of
virtue.

Personal attacks upon Nehemiah's character and work
were a fourth scene of conflict. The attempts hindered Nehemiah, but his steadfast integrity blunted attempts to discredit him. When opponents attempted to intimidate him
by threats and innuendos, Nehemiah responded with his
classic answer, "Should a man such as I flee?" (6:11 NKJV).
His clear conscience and good standing before God enabled him to stand against intimidation. As was true in
each level of conflict management, the resolution had much
to do with the personal integrity of the leader.

Coram Deo

Being a Christian only heightens the conflict we
must resolve, because we constantly wage war against
sin and competing worldviews. What are the areas of
conflict in your life right now? If resolving those conflicts is a problem, read Nehemiah for his insights. Be
encouraged through Nehemiah, whose name means
"Yahweh has comforted."

For further study: Ezra 9–10; Acts 6:1–7; 15:6–15

189 Who Will Speak

ordecai the Jew offended one of the chief counselors of the king of Persia, a man named Haman. Full of vengeance, Haman determined to punish Mordecai and his entire race. He went to the king and convinced him to issue a decree to exterminate the Jews. What Haman did not know was that the wife of the king was a Jewess; in fact, she was Mordecai's niece, Esther. Mordecai sent word to Esther about Haman's plot and urged her to go to the king and plead for her people.

Esther was reluctant to do this. She reminded Mordecai that by the king's decree no one was allowed to approach him without being asked to do so, on pain of death. She told Mordecai that, though she was the king's wife, she had not been summoned for thirty days. Possibly she was out of favor.

One of the striking things about this story is its realism. There is nothing superficially pietistic about it. Esther feels the full weight of moral anguish and fear. She does not want to risk her life. She does not want to be the one who has to speak up. She does not want to get involved. She wants someone else to do it.

Mordecai rebuked her reluctance. He informed her that God was certain to save his people, whether through her or someone else. He asked her to consider the possibility that the reason God had made her queen was to bear witness in this situation. She could not evade her responsibility, he told her. She must speak out.

> When this is done, I will go to the king, even though it is against the law. And if I perish, I perish. [Esth. 4:16b]

Esther bowed before God's will. She asked Mordecai to lead all the people in prayer for her and then, she said, she would go to the king. She would do it even though it was against the law, because there was a higher law than the law of the human king. She would do it at the risk of her own life.

Many Christians fail to realize that they, too, are subject to a law higher than the law of the land. For example, who is willing to take risks for the silent ones, for the unborn children in the United States who are being systematically slaughtered? More than 1 million unborn children are killed every year, in part because the vast majority of Christians are silent when they should be screaming.

We need to hear the rebuke of Mordecai and become a race of Esthers.

Coram Deo

Abortion is an issue on which we cannot be silent. Not to speak out is to endorse death. There are a great many options still available to Christians to register their complaint, show unity with others of like conviction, work for political reform, and show mercy through compassion and counseling. Which of these (and other) options will you risk on behalf of the unborn?

For further study: Daniel 6:10–23; Psalm 72:12–14; Acts 5:22–32

190 What Is Biblical Wisdom?

We come now to the Wisdom literature of the Bible. The five wisdom books of the Old Testament are Job, Psalms, Proverbs, Ecclesiastes, and the Song of Solomon. The New Testament wisdom book is James. One of the best ways to get a handle on biblical wisdom is to contrast it with Greek philosophy. The word *philosophy* means "love of wisdom," but the Greeks loved a more theoretical sort of wisdom than the practical life-applications of the Hebrews. Greek philosophy tended to be abstract, but Hebrew wisdom tended to be concrete. Greeks expressed philosophy through prose discussions, while Hebrew wisdom most often was expressed in a semi-poetic literature.

The most important difference, which caused these other distinctions, was that *Greek philosophers saw God as a deponent element of philosophical reflection.* They questioned the reality of God and worked to demonstrate the logical necessity of an impersonal Unmoved Mover behind everything. *Biblical wisdom starts with the self-revelation of the personal God who created all things.* By questioning the existence of God and by fashioning a god in their own intellects, the Greeks always operated in the realm of idolatry, however sophisticated their expression. Hebrew wisdom operated wholly in the realm of worship.

Why is Hebrew wisdom so practical? It is because the

> Blessed is the man who does not walk in the counsel of the wicked or stand in the way of sinners or sit in the seat of mockers. But his delight is in the law of the LORD and on his law he meditates day and night. He is like a tree planted by streams of water. [Ps. 1:1–3a]

fundamental questions have been answered in God's revelation. Why is biblical wisdom concrete and concerned with daily affairs? It is because God created all things and is interested in every aspect of life. Why is Hebrew wisdom adorned in a semi-poetic style? It is because the writers of wisdom literature were confident about their position in God's world, and thus enabled to celebrate its beauty.

Psalm 111:10 and Proverbs 1:7 and 9:10 (see also Job 28:28 and Isa. 11:2–3) says that the *beginning* of wisdom is the fear of the Lord. The Greeks never got to this beginning point, so all their wisdom—the wisdom of this world—is no more than ashes.

Coram Deo

Wisdom comes into its fullness in the Solomonic era, after Israel had meditated on the law of God for several centuries. It was from history, as recorded in the Bible, and from God's law that God's people learned wisdom. To understand biblical wisdom we must use the building blocks that gave rise to it. Ask God to give you a new love for reflection upon his Word for day-to-day life application.

For further study: Proverbs 9; 1 Corinthians 3:18–23; James 1:1–5

191 Holy Perspectives on Life

S ince almost all biblical wisdom is written in a poetic form, we should learn the essentials of Hebrew poetry. Hebrew poetry does not rhyme as does traditional English poetry. *English poetry rhymes in sounds, while Hebrew poetry rhymes in thoughts.* Instead of repeating the same sound twice, Hebrew poetry repeats the same idea twice. Similarly, though there is a kind of rhythm in Hebrew poetry, it does not have the repetitive beat of English verse. Instead, the rhythm lies in the repetition of thoughts.

We call this repetition of ideas *parallelism*. Three kinds of parallelism appear in Hebrew poetry. The first is *synonymous parallelism*, in which the same idea is expressed twice. Consider Proverbs 1:8–9. The son is told to listen to his father and then, in parallel fashion, to his mother. The father's words are called instruction; the mother's are called teaching. Such teachings will be a garland for the head, and (parallel) a chain for the neck. In synonymous parallelism, the second phrase can expand the idea of the first, or it can simply restate the idea of the first in different words, or provide an implication of the first. In each case, we get two (and sometimes more) perspectives on a truth.

The second kind of parallelism is *antithetical parallelism*, in which the second phrase states the opposite of

> Listen, my son, to your father's instruction
> and do not forsake your mother's teaching.
> They will be a garland to grace your head
> and a chain to adorn your neck. [Prov. 1:8–9]

the first, or at least provides a strong contrast. Proverbs 3:1 says, "My son, do not forget my teaching, but keep my commands in your heart." Forgetting is the opposite of keeping.

The third type is *synthetic parallelism*, in which the second phrase carries forward the thought of the first but adds a substantially new idea to it. Proverbs 3:6 is an example: "In all your ways acknowledge him, and he will make your paths straight." If this were synonymously parallel, the second phrase might read, "and bow before him every day." As it stands, however, the second phrase adds a new idea.

Both God's world and God himself are too vast to be understood from only one perspective. Parallelism provides us with a multiplicity of perspectives on reality and makes us more sensitive and wise.

Coram Deo

Yet another form of parallelism is *climactic parallelism*, an example of which is shown to us in Proverbs 30:21–31. Read a chapter in Proverbs closely, making careful note of the types of parallelism you see in the text. How do these poetic forms help drive home God's wisdom for us?

For further study: Psalm 119:1–16; Proverbs 30:21–31; Luke 23:28–31

192 The Wisdom of God

P roverbs 1–9 introduces two "women," *Folly* and *Wisdom*. Either of them has a house, and invites us in to fellowship with her. Folly is painted as a harlot and an adulteress, her house as a brothel. Wisdom is presented as both a mother and a bride, her house as a palace. Compare these images with the great harlot and the bride of Revelation in the passages of "For further study."

In Proverbs 8, however, Wisdom takes on a more mysterious dimension. The feminine imagery falls away in Proverbs 8:22, revealing that Wisdom existed with God before the creation of the world. Many theologians, though not all, believe that when John begins his Gospel, "In the beginning was the Word, and the Word was with God," he is referring in part to Proverbs 8. In 1 Corinthians 1:24, Paul calls Christ the Wisdom of God.

Proverbs 8:22–29 states that before God created the world, there was something prior to that creation, something that proceeded from the divine mind: Wisdom. First, God sent out Wisdom, and then, on the basis of that Wisdom, he created the world. Similarly, the New Testament calls Christ the "firstborn of all creation," and the Christian Church has confessed that Christ is the "only-begotten Son of God, begotten of his Father before all worlds, by whom all worlds are made" (Nicene Creed).

It probably stretches Solomon's intent in Proverbs 8 to

> Then I was the craftsman at his side. I was filled with delight day after day, rejoicing always in his presence. [Prov. 8:30]

see these words as a *direct* reference to the Second Person of the Trinity, but we can say that the poetic picture in Proverbs 8 finds its greatest fulfillment in him. Similar analogies also might be drawn between Wisdom and the Spirit. Isaiah particularly speaks of wisdom and the Spirit in metaphorical language describing the messianic Branch out of Jesse: "The Spirit of the LORD will rest on him—the Spirit of wisdom and of understanding, the Spirit of counsel and of power, the Spirit of knowledge and of the fear of the LORD."

One thing that is very clear from Proverbs 8 is that Wisdom existed before the world was made, and the world was made according to Wisdom. If we want to understand the world, we must understand Wisdom.

Coram Deo

Wisdom also existed before the law was given, and the law was given according to Wisdom. Sometimes God's law demands we do things that seem unwise, but when we understand that his law emerges from his wisdom, we realize that it is our thinking that is faulty. How does Proverbs 14:12 contrast human and divine wisdom? Consider what this teaching implies about our call to live by faith and not by sight.

For further study: Proverbs 7; John 1:1–18; Revelation 17; 19:7–8; 21:9–14

193 The Work of Satan

One significance of the Book of Job is its insight into the work of Satan in the life of the believer. Clearly from Job 1–2, Satan is an angelic being. He was created as one of God's angels, but fell with others into rebellion. It is important to understand that Satan is a creature, because there is a current fascination with Satan that ascribes far too much power to him, so that he seems God's peer, able to frustrate God's will.

When God asked where he had been, Satan replied that he had been roaming about the earth (Job 1:7). Some people have it in mind that Satan lives in hell, but hell is where Satan and all the wicked will be sent at the last judgment. Satan now dwells on the earth.

Being a creature who dwells on the earth, can Satan be in more than one place at a time? Obviously not. Job 1:7 makes it clear that Satan roams here and there. Satan cannot do more than one thing at a time, any more than can a person. Satan is not omnipresent. While many feel they have been personally afflicted by him, most likely Satan has never bothered with you or me; he has lots of subordinate demons to work on us.

What is Satan's principal activity against us? He is the accuser of human beings before God. He and his followers also tempt humanity to sin, but their primary work is to build a case on which to accuse us. The word *satan* means "slanderer, accuser." In Job 1–2 we see this aspect hard at work, as he comes before God and slanders Job.

One day the angels came to present themselves before the LORD, and Satan also came with them. [Job 1:6]

Satan also slanders us before men. He tries to make sure that any good work done by Christ's church receives a bad name. He attacks faithful pastors, active laypeople, hardworking employees, and anyone who is serving Christ in more than an invisible and minimal way. When we hear bad reports about fellow Christians of good repute, we instantly should be suspicious.

Satan and his horde also accuse us to ourselves. He wants to make us feel guilty about our failures and shortcomings. This can paralyze a Christian quicker than can anything else. Satan wants us to doubt our salvation, because to do so is to doubt the promises of God spelled out in his Word. Such doubt can drive us to despair and spiritual impotence.

Coram Deo

The Holy Spirit also comes to remind us of sin, but his purpose is to encourage us to draw close to God for cleansing. When we are cursing ourselves and becoming depressed and alienated from God, we can be sure that this is part of Satan's program. Do you feel the accusations of Satan? The reminding of the Holy Spirit? Are there ways to tell them apart? Resist self-accusation, and beseech the Spirit's encouragement.

For further study: Isaiah 14:12–21; Luke 10:1–20; 22:31–34

413

194 The Tribulations of Job

The first chapter of Job tells us that Job was the greatest man of all the people in the East. He had a large family, vast herds, and grand wealth. He was by far the most prominent man in his political community. He was also a godly man, so much so that the Bible calls him "blameless and upright" (Job 1:1).

Satan slandered Job before God, saying that the only reason Job so zealously served God was because God had blessed him physically. God allowed Satan to put Job to the test. First, Satan slew all of Job's children and destroyed all his wealth; though Job mourned, he did not blame God. Then God permitted Satan to afflict Job with painful boils all over his body, so that the only relatively comfortable place Job could find to sit was on soft ashes.

Job wanted to die, and his wife told him how he could do it. If he would curse God, then God might go ahead and kill him and put him out of his misery (2:9–10). But that was the one thing Job refused to do. Job cursed the day of his birth, wishing he had never been born, but he did not curse God.

Job asked why life continues for "those who long for death that does not come, who search for it more than for hidden treasure, who are filled with gladness and rejoice when they reach the grave?" (3:21–22).

The Danish philosopher Søren Kierkegaard spoke of this as the most severe form of grief and sorrow that any

> After this, Job opened his mouth and cursed the day of his birth.
> [Job 3:1]

human being ever experiences, what Kierkegaard called "sickness unto death." Some desire to die more strongly than they wish for anything else in the world, but they are not to be allowed that route of escape. At this point, Job had no reason to live. He had lost everything, including the support of his wife. But Job was not allowed to die. Suicide would be a sin, and he refused to curse God. It took all of his courage and integrity just to stay alive.

One thing that stands out about Job's mourning is that it was real. He did not give off any pious platitudes. He uttered no phony "Praise the Lord!" Job's piety was not artificial, and he was not too proud to grieve. He wept and groaned and cried out in his pain, but though he wrestled with God, he did not reject him.

Coram Deo

Read Job 3. An added dimension of suffering can be seen here: God did not personally come and comfort Job in his distress. Job felt abandoned by God, experiencing what the medieval Christians called "a dark night of the soul." Have you ever had such an experience? What did you learn from it? Did you handle that experience in faith?

For further study: Job 3; Psalm 23; Luke 22:39–46; Philippians 3:10–14

Job 4

195 Job's "Comforters"

ob's three friends came to sit with him in his troubles. Initially they showed great sensitivity to his plight, for they sat silently for seven days, recognizing that no words were adequate and sharing in his grief. After Job spoke up and cursed his birthday (Job 3), however, the friends began trying to help Job understand his situation.

In his first speech (Job 4–5), Eliphaz the Temanite told Job that he should remember his own pious advice to others in the past (4:1–6). He told Job that suffering is always the result of some specific sin or sinful tendency (4:7–11). He said that he had received a vision to this effect (4:12–21). He said that Job's protestations of innocence sounded like the words of a fool (5:1–7). He told Job that the solution was to repent and turn to God (5:8–16). If Job did repent, he would find that God's chastisements were but blessings in disguise, and that afterwards God would restore to him what he took away (5:17–27).

We have to be careful when reading the speeches of Job's comforters, because much of what the friends said is objectively correct but misapplied to Job. The gist of their remarks is this: God does not punish people for no reason. Job must have done something that was wrong to bring these disasters upon himself.

It is certainly true that we eventually come to reap what

we sow. It is true that God sometimes visits us with pain
and chastisement in order to discipline and drive us back
to himself. It is also true, however, that some suffering is
sent for the benefit of other people's growth, or even simply for the glory of God in mysterious ways that we won't
understand until he tells us (John 9).

Job's friends intended to be kind, but in fact they were
cruel. As Job resisted what they said, they became more
assertive and insensitive. Job's refusal to own up to some
great sin was a thorn in the side of their neatly packaged
moralistic theology.

If Job was right and God was not afflicting him for some
particular sins, then their theology and philosophy were
wrong, and they would have to change. That was something they didn't want to do, so they strove to get Job to
conform to their ideas about him.

Coram Deo

Read Job 4–5 twice. Read the first time and notice
that in the abstract what Eliphaz says is correct and
even insightful. Then re-read the chapters as if you
were Job, and notice how everything becomes wrong
and painful. Learn from this to be careful of giving
cheap, pious advice to people in pain.

For further study: Proverbs 22; John 9; Galatians 6:6–10

Have you ever felt the need to be vindicated? "Someday the truth will come out, and they will see that I am in the right," you may say to yourself. For Job that day did come in an encounter with the almighty God, only vindication was a more fearful, humbling, and learning experience than Job might have expected. He became a far wiser man as he compared his wisdom with the reality of a Creator God.

We are put into our proper place *coram Deo* whenever we are confronted with truth. In Hebrew the first letters of the titles *Job, Proverbs,* and *Psalms* spell the word for *truth.* For this reason, these three major books of the wisdom literature have been referred to as the "books of truth." These books of wisdom and truth help us to relate all areas of life to God's providential supervision and care.

After we complete our survey of Job we will move on to a brief consideration of the Psalms, based on the teaching of Art Lindsley. There are many types of Psalms, and we will look at ex-

The Books of Truth

amples of some of these types, followed by a short overview of the Proverbs by Frederic Putnam. Then we will turn to Ecclesiastes, the most directly philosophical book in Scripture.

One of the subjects of this study will be the "fear" of the Lord. "With you there is forgiveness," relates Psalm 130, "therefore you are feared." "Fear the Lord," adds Solomon in Proverbs, "and shun evil." Obviously there is more to fearing God than cowering in his presence.

It is my prayer that you will find that the more you pursue an encounter with God the more you will understand the beauty of "fearing" our Father, and you will become a wiser man or woman.

Keep in mind the strong command of a father to his son in Proverbs 4:5: "Get wisdom, get understanding." Such a vigorous pursuit characterizes a life lived *coram Deo*, striving to seek God while recognizing his presence in our pursuit.

R.C. Sproul

196 The Patience of Job

T he words of Job 8:6 were spoken by Bildad the Shuhite, one of Job's comforters. Bildad's point was that God does not punish innocent people. Job had prayed for vindication, but no vindication had come. According to Bildad, if Job was innocent God would have vindicated him immediately. The only logical conclusion was that Job must be guilty of something.

Bildad was right that God doesn't punish the innocent, but wrong in suggesting how quickly God vindicates. For his own reasons, God often allows his people to live with slander for a long time before vindicating them. Sometimes vindication does not come at all from an earthly perspective, or it does not come until after the maligned person has died.

We should not be surprised at this, because it is what our Lord Jesus Christ experienced, and we servants are no better than our Master. It is our privilege to walk in union with him and to carry our crosses as he carried his. He was reviled, but he did not answer back a word. He died without being vindicated, as the crowds assumed he was a fraud and the Romans assumed he was a criminal. It was his resurrection that vindicated him.

The same was true of the apostle Paul. We think of Paul as a hero of the faith, but during his life he was regarded as a criminal and a heretic, often by people in the church. Much of 1 Corinthians and 2 Corinthians is a defense of his apostleship. Paul's reputation was poisoned through-

> "If you are pure and upright, even now he will rouse himself on your behalf and restore you to your rightful place." [Job 8:6]

out the Roman Empire, but he only worried about it when the slanderers stood in the way of the teaching of truth. Paul did not require vindication before people, for he knew he stood vindicated before God.

God promises a future vindication for his people, but he has never promised that it will happen now. Christians must be patient in the face of slander, as was Job. And that's the hard part: waiting. As time goes along, we are tempted to despair, to give up and stop praying. We must remember the parable of the persistent widow, which Jesus told his disciples "to show them that they should always pray and not give up" (Luke 18:1–8).

When we hear of the patience of Job, we are not to think of Job stoically enduring his suffering. Job cried out to God continually, vigorously arguing his case before him. He actively maintained his personal relationship with the Lord, being also patient in prayer.

Coram Deo

Many Christians are confused about the virtue of patience. For the Greeks, patience meant silent, stoic endurance. Scriptural patience involves active prayer and trusting God, such as we find in Job and in the Psalms. Which kind of patience do you exercise in the midst of your problems?

For further study: Romans 4:15–20; 8:17–32

197 Job's Trust and Vindication

God had taken everything away from Job and had allowed Satan to send "friends" to torment him. Yet, in the midst of his agony, Job uttered one of the most profound statements of faith. *Job said that even if God killed him, he would still trust God.*

The Bible tells us that the just shall live by faith (Hab. 2:4). Living by faith does not mean blindly grasping at a proposition in the face of all evidence, even if you're not sure it's true. Rather the faith God desires means trusting him to supply every need in your life.

God promises a future for his people, and thus our joy as pilgrims in this world is that God has prepared a place for us. God has promised that a better world will be consummated through the final victory of Jesus Christ. This is not a mere wish but a sure confidence. It is a hope that cannot fail.

Trusting God means having a personal relationship with him. Job trusted God enough to argue his case before him. Job realized, however, that he was not adequate to present his own case before God. Thus, he said, "I know that my Redeemer lives, and that in the end he will stand upon the earth" (Job 19:25). Sometimes we read too much into this verse, because the word *redeemer* does not have the tightly focused meaning in Hebrew that it has in our theology. The word means "kinsman-redeemer" (as in Ruth) and "avenger." In other words, it means "vindicator." Job knew that his Advocate was alive and would come to his rescue.

422

> "Though he slay me, yet will I hope in him; I will surely defend my ways to his face." [Job 13:15]

We don't know the degree of content Job had in his mind as he made this statement, but we do know that he looked for God to vindicate him. He was certain that God would not allow his pain and suffering to be the last chapter. He groaned in the present, but he never lost his confidence in the future that God had planned for him.

In a sense, when God appeared to Job at the end of the story, he presented himself as Job's vindication. God told Job that he had created and was in complete control of all creation. That included Job's situation. While his reasons would remain inscrutable, he was going to take care of Job, as he takes care of every one of his creatures. Job was right to trust in God, because God is altogether trustworthy.

Coram Deo

When we experience pain and grief, we tend to get angry at God, blaming him for our troubles, and shutting him out of our lives. Job teaches us that even in the worst situations, there is no place to go but to God himself. Do you accept this concept, both intellectually and emotionally in times of crisis? Pray that the Holy Spirit will reveal God's presence as both your refuge and strength.

For further study: John 6:66; Philippians 1:29; 4:4–7; 1 Peter 5:7

198 The Dark Night of the Soul

J ob's greatest suffering did not come when he lost his property, when he lost his children, when he became horribly sick and suffered great physical pain, or even when his friends tried to get him to confess sins he had not committed. Job's greatest suffering came from the fact that, in the midst of all this agony, God withdrew the assurance of his presence.

Christians go through these feelings of abandonment from time to time. The medieval theologians called them "dark nights of the soul" and the Puritans called such experiences "desertions." Just as God normally visits us with his presence and we bask in the glow of his love, so also God sometimes withdraws that sense from us and leaves us feeling utterly alone.

Has God really left us? No, but God makes us feel his absence so that we pursue him and cry out more desperately to him. Such experiences give us just a taste of what our Savior experienced on the cross when he cried out: "My God, my God, why have you forsaken me?" (Matt. 27:46). In his last speech, Job accuses God of forsaking him, saying, "You turn on me ruthlessly; with the might of your hand you attack me" (Job 30:21). At this point, it seems that Job has fallen into sin. He has stopped living by faith and has begun to rely too heavily on his feelings. Job's suffering did not begin because of any sin on his part,

> "How I long for the months gone by, for the days when God watched over me, when his lamp shone upon my head and by his light I walked through darkness!" [Job 29:2–3]

but in the midst of his suffering he fell into the sin of thinking God had abandoned him.

Job 32–37 records the speech of Elihu, a young man who had been silent heretofore. Interpreters debate whether what Elihu said is right or wrong, but it seems that Elihu spoke the truth to Job, thereby leading the discussion upward toward what God next said to Job. Elihu stated that Job's friends were wrong to accuse him of sin, and that he wanted to help Job clear his name (33:32). But he also told Job that it was wrong to accuse God of being unfair. God is not obliged to answer. He pointed to the greatness and majesty of God, and told Job to reflect on these things. God's ways are mysterious, but never wrong. Job must continue to trust in him.

Coram Deo

The great "dark night psalm" is Psalm 88. Read this psalm and see if you recognize the depth of feelings that the psalmist describes. Can you identify with the psalmist when, at the end of his depressed lament, he says that darkness has become his closest friend? Reflect upon how you might have endured if God had required you to undergo all that happened to Job. How can you pursue the Father in the darkness?

For further study: Deuteronomy 4:29; Psalm 42:1–2; 88

199 Job before God

S ometimes a child gets angry with parents or others who seem to be unjust and imagines all the things that will be said to them. "They've been unfair to me," the child thinks, "and they're going to have to answer to me." The case is well-prepared in the mind and the child may present it to friends. That parent, teacher, or youth minister is going to be made to see the truth.

But when the opportunity comes to confront this person the young prosecutor chooses to remain silent. In the face of the person of father, mother, teacher, or youth minister, it seems better to drop the matter entirely, without saying anything at all. It may be partly that the offending adult is awesome in authority, but it also may be that the person is overwhelming in love. Suddenly the child's grievances seem slight and unimportant.

That's how it was when God appeared to Job. Job had been through some horrible experiences, and God was ultimately responsible. But when Job met God, somehow the experiences no longer seemed worthy of complaint. God's greatness and his infinite love overwhelmed Job, and he felt guilty that he had ever complained to his friends about God.

God's self-revelation to Job is especially significant to us because God also recorded it in a speech to Job. Since in this life we cannot expect to see God face to face, how can we come to grips with his authority and love? How can we

> "My ears had heard of you but now my eyes have seen you.
> Therefore I despise myself and repent in dust and ashes."
> [Job 42:5–6].

have the experience Job had that will put everything in perspective for us?

God's speech to Job answers that question. God points to his work of creation, a work so vast and amazing that we can only stand mute in the face of it. God points to the wonders of that great work: the stars, the order of nature, the great storms, and huge beasts. As we contemplate the revelation of God's glory and his person in nature, we can begin to sense the immensity of his plan and goodness. Meditating on these truths will help us put the difficulties of our lives into proper perspective.

God's last word for Job was not, however, the greatness of his power. At the end God blessed Job and rewarded his faithfulness.

Coram Deo

The immediate problems of our lives often cause us to spiral inward into ourselves, so that we shut ourselves off from God's revelation. Job 38–41 provides a vision of God's greatness that will restore us to a true perspective on our problems. Job 42 promises that in his time God will reward his faithful children. In your times of despair, meditate on God's authority, majesty, and concern, as displayed in all that he has made.

For further study: Psalm 8; Romans 1:18–20; Hebrews 1:1–3

200 The Psalm-Filled Life

P
salms is part of the wisdom literature of the Old Testament and is one of the few sections of Scripture that has been published separately from the rest of the Bible. This is because the psalms consist of prayers and hymns, and thus always have been used in the church's worship and devotion. The first book published in America was the *Bay Psalm Book,* a complete collection of the psalter in verse for congregational singing.

There are a few Christian churches that sing nothing but these metrical arrangements of the psalms, continuing the tradition begun by the Calvinistic churches of the Reformation. Historically the psalms have been central in worship, and churches that sang other hymns sang *mostly* psalms. Until recently the Book of Psalms has permeated and structured the worship of the church. Many hymns that are not full-fledge versified psalms are still based on psalms, as "A Mighty Fortress" is based on Psalm 46.

The spiritual vitality of the church is proportional to the congregation's use of psalms in worship and in the lives of believers. When the church was strong, actively influencing society, its worship was characterized by psalms. When psalms are absent from worship, as they recently have tended to be, the church may become weak and ineffectual, its worship contentless. It is so today.

One of the great weaknesses of the Christian community is a weakness in prayer. We aren't very familiar with

> Ascribe to the LORD the glory due his name; worship the LORD in the splendor of his holiness. [Ps. 29:2]

the vocabulary of prayer. We stammer and stutter in prayer, or fill our prayers with strange phrases like "Lord, we just want to . . . and we just . . . and we're just here to say. . . ." Would you talk to another human being like that? How can we learn ways to pray that match the dignity of the Person we are addressing? The answer lies in the psalms. Because many of the psalms are divinely-inspired prayers, they can teach us to pray.

In recent years there has been a movement towards spontaneity in worship, as a reaction against dead formalism. With this movement has often come a dangerous cheapening of worship and a casual attitude toward God. The use of the psalms will restore to us a vibrancy of worship and a proper sense of his dignity and majesty.

Coram Deo

It is amazing that God has given us this great treasury of prayer and praise, yet we don't use it. Is there a pastor or music director who would help you to revive the heritage of psalmody in your church's congregational and choral music? Purchase and read one of the traditional psalters, which are still in print. Point out some of the lovelier words and melodies to those who lead worship.

For further study: Psalm 119:81–96; John 15:1–7; 17:6–19

201 Praying the Psalms

everal broad categories of songs can be found in the Book of Psalms. First, we have already looked at psalms of distress, which cry out to God from depression and despair when he seems far away.

Second, *psalms of adoration* address God with prayer and praise. Or through the adoration psalms we address one another with an exhortation to praise God. Examples of these are 144 and 150. Third, there are *nature psalms*, celebrating the revelation of God's beauty, order, and power in creation. These call upon the entire universe to resound with his praise. Examples include 8 and 104.

Fourth, the *enthronement psalms* celebrate the king in Israel, but only as he is a representative of the enthroned King of kings. The church today views these as references to Jesus Christ. Examples include 2 and 110.

Fifth, *penitential psalms*—psalms of confession and contrition—express our sorrow over sin as we lament that we have displeased our Lord. Examples include 6 and 51.

Sixth, *imprecatory psalms* call down God's judgment and curse against his enemies. Is it right to pray this way? Clearly it is, because God wrote these psalms for our use. We must remember, though, that when we pray for God to destroy his enemies we leave it up to him *how* he will destroy them. You and I were "destroyed" by God's judgment and resurrected to new life in the Spirit. We should hope that God will destroy our enemies by bringing them through the same experience. Examples include 109 and 137.

Seventh, *redemptive historical psalms* celebrate the mighty acts of God as he delivered his people and established his covenant, and as he remained faithful to them when they were unfaithful to him. Examples include 105 and 106.

Eighth, the *wisdom psalms*, such as 1 and 15, instruct us in God's ways, and eighth, the *psalms of thanksgiving*, such as 107, focus on our gratitude to God.

Many, if not most, psalms fall into more than one of these categories.

Coram Deo

The psalms give Christians a wide range of human experience and emotion. They instruct us about God as One who delights in the adoration and prayers of his people. As you study the psalms through the next meditations, strive to see them as models for your own personal prayers.

For further study: Acts 16:25; Ephesians 5:19; Colossians 3:16

431

202 The Revelation of God

G od's self-revelation in his creation is heralded in the introduction to Psalm 19, so it may be seen as a nature psalm, but its primary theme is praise for the whole of God's revelation through creation, through his Word, and through our lives. Verses 1–6 discuss the revelation of God's glory in creation, especially in the heavens. The Hebrew words for *heaven* and *sky* in Genesis 1:1 and 1:8 are the same. Thus, the sky and the things in the sky are said to reveal the heavenly glory of God. The psalmist says that day after day the blue sky, the clouds, and the birds "pour forth speech" about God's glory, while night after night the stars and the moon "display knowledge."

In particular, the sun portrays God's glory. The heavens are like a tent for the sun, analogous to the tabernacle, God's tent in Israel. The sun bursts over the horizon. It gives light to all things. It is supreme, moving through and governing our solar system. It gives heat to all things. The sun pictures the sun of righteousness who arises with healing in his wings (Mal. 4:2).

The second part of the psalm, verses 7–11, extols *God's revelation in his Word*. The psalmist celebrates God's laws, statutes, precepts, commands, and ordinances. Notice that these refer to commandments. God does not give us mere good advice or suggestions about how to live. He

> The heavens declare the glory of God; the skies proclaim the work of his hands. Day after day they pour forth speech; night after night they display knowledge. [Ps. 19:1–2]

tells us what he demands. Mixed in with these statements about God's law is the statement that "the *fear* of the Lord is pure" (v. 9).

The greatness of God's glory leads us to meditate on the purity of God's commandments. Now, in turn, we are led to reflect on our own inadequacy. Verses 12–14 point to God's revelation of his law in our consciences. It is critical that we ask God to use his Word to reveal our hidden faults so that we may live righteously before him. Such an all encompassing desire is what it means to live life *coram Deo*.

Coram Deo

Many Christians are familiar with Psalm 19:1. We do not often take the time, however, to reflect on how the heavens, indeed all of creation, shout out the glory of God. Spend some time exploring the night sky and wondering at the God who created the stars. Meditate on the psalmist's concluding prayer (19:14), the desire that God would be pleased with the words he spoke and with his thoughts. Are these worthy concerns for your prayer life?

For further study: Psalm 29; 103:11; 139:23–24; Micah 6:8

203 Confession of Sin

A ugustine, the greatest theologian of the early church, particularly loved the penitential Psalm 32. In this psalm David addresses the congregation—you and me. He announces his theme in the first two verses: We are blessed when our sins are forgiven. Sins are forgiven when God no longer counts them against us, and the proof of this is that we walk without deceit in our lives (vv. 1–2).

Some have suggested that David wrote this psalm after he had been restored from his sin with Bathsheba. Certainly it would fit such a context. David says that for a long time he kept quiet about his sin. He tried to cover it up, hiding it from himself and from others. But God's hand was heavy on him. As time went along his remorse intensified. He became ill as his bones wasted away. He became full of tension, unable to sleep, sensing that his strength was being sapped. Finally, however, he confessed his sin to God and received forgiveness (vv. 3–5).

In verses 3–5 David addresses God within the hearing of the congregation. He continues in verse 6, asking God to hear the penitential prayers of all his children and to protect them from the waters of his wrath.

David now turns to the congregation and addresses us. He exhorts us that we not be like dumb animals having no

> Then I acknowledged my sin to you and did not cover up my iniquity. I said, "I will confess my transgressions to the LORD"—and you forgave the guilt of my sin. [Ps. 32:5]

understanding. Horses and mules must be controlled by force, but we as God's people should be controlled by willing obedience. David tells us that those who disobey God receive many woes, as he himself found out on more than one occasion. Yet, God surrounds the one who trusts in his unfailing love. Indeed, God surrounds us with songs of deliverance (vv. 7–10).

David concludes by exhorting us to sing. Despite the pain of unconfessed sin and the sorrows which God's careful chastisement has brought our way, the fact remains that we are his and he is ours. He has saved us, and his chastisements show that we are legitimately adopted children. Therefore, we are to sing and rejoice in his presence.

Coram Deo

We can learn much from the psalms as we follow the line of thought with the psalmist. Psalm 32 displays such a progression: Blessing is announced; sin is confessed; assurance is granted; instruction is heard; praise is the response. Use these steps of response to write out a model order of worship or follow these steps in your own penitential prayer.

For further study: Deuteronomy 28; Psalm 51:1–9; John 14:21; 1 John 1:9

204 Arguing with Yourself

Distress is the feeling of the troubled writer of Psalm 42. He finds himself in exile from God's people and oppressed by God's enemies. The worst of his troubles, however, is that he feels forsaken by God. One of several psalms of distress, it reflects on the dark night of the soul (see pp. 424–25). The psalmist shows us one reason God takes us through such difficult experiences.

In verse 1 the psalmist says that he pants for God's presence the way a deer pants for water after being chased. God withdraws the sense of his presence from us in order to make us long for him all the more, guaranteeing that we don't take him for granted.

God's apparent desertion of the psalmist is not merely subjective, however. While in former times this man was once among the religious leaders in Israel, he finds himself in exile, away from Jerusalem (vv. 4, 6). his enemies are triumphing over him (vv. 9–10). From all outward appearances, this man has been rejected by God, and people are taunting him, "Where is your God?"

Many of the psalms were written by David. Certainly the experience of this psalm fits what David went through when Absalom revolted against him. David was driven from the land and could no longer lead the congregation in worship. Enemies like Shimei publicly taunted him. Certainly David felt that all of God's waves and breakers

> Why are you downcast, O my soul? Why so disturbed within me?
> Put your hope in God, for I will yet praise him, my Savior and my
> God. [Ps. 42:11]

had swept over him and that he was being swept away like the wicked at the flood (v. 7).

Notice how the psalmist deals with this intense depression. He argues with himself. He grabs hold of himself and says, "What's wrong with you? Why are you upset? Sure, everything has gone wrong, but God is still God. Hope in God, because the storm will not last forever. The time will come when you will be restored, and you will praise him who is your deliverer and your God."

As a kind of second witness, Psalm 43 deals with the same problem and ends with the same refrain. When we go through similar experiences, let us remember these psalms, because they teach us how to deal with ourselves in the midst of spiritual depression.

Coram Deo

The psalmist realizes anew that God can be worshiped even in exile, that his presence is universal. Do feelings of exile call us to trust, in the depths of depression, that God still is near? Commit to memory these promises to use the next time God seems strangely absent—even if you took the wings of the dawn or made your bed in sheol, you could not escape his loving presence.

For further study: Psalm 43; 46:1–3; Lamentations 3:21–25

205 The Lord to the Rescue

P salm 107 is a psalm of deliverance. Its theme is gratitude to God for his salvation The psalm bases its imagery on the world God created. It mentions four places that are threatening—places separated from God's good land that flows with milk and honey. God has delivered his people from these threatening places and established them in his new Eden.

First, there were those who wandered in the desert. They had neither water nor food, but God fed them. Eventually God led them into his land and gave them a city (Jerusalem), a city that exalted him and was a glory to them (vv. 4–9). The psalmist clearly alludes to Israel's experience in the wilderness, but the application is to any of us who are going through a similar experience.

Second, there were some who suffered as prisoners, bound in chains and darkness away from the sun. They had rebelled against God, so he in his faithfulness chastised them. Then they repented and cried to him, and he heard them and rescued them (vv. 10–16). Perhaps the allusion here is to Joseph, though he was not imprisoned for any sin. When Joseph imprisoned his brothers for a short time, and they repented in prison, God delivered them.

Third, there were those who rebelled against God and thus rebelled against his good creation. They became sick and drew near to sheol, the place of death. Then they re-

438

> Then they cried to the LORD in their trouble, and he saved them
> from their distress. He sent forth his word and healed them; he
> rescued them from the grave. [Ps. 107:19–20]

pented and cried to God, and he granted them new life (vv. 17–22).

Fourth, there were some who labored on the sea, away from God's land. They were carrying out God's great command to traverse and subdue the earth, but a storm broke out at sea. They almost perished, but they cried to God as did the sailors in Jonah 1. He returned them safely to land (vv. 23–31).

As an epilogue the psalmist points out that when those enjoying the fruits of a godly culture forsake the Lord their good land will turn into a waste. However, if they repent, he will turn and heal their land for them (vv. 33–42).

The psalmist tells us to think on these things and to express our gratitude.

Coram Deo

Out of what great distress has God brought you? Which of the four situations is most like your own experience? Make it a point to give thanks to God and to tell others what great things he has done for you. If you are now in distress, make this psalm your comfort, remember his past interventions in your life, and start thanking him now for what he will do.

For further study: Isaiah 40:1–11; 41:10; Colossians 2:7; 1 Thessalonians 5:18

206 Prayers of Judgment

Curses against the ungodly were the substance of the imprecatory psalms, and Psalm 109 may be the toughest. The New Testament applies it to those who crucified Christ (compare v. 8 with Acts 1:20, v. 25 with Matt. 27:39, v. 27 with Acts 2:23, and v. 30 with Heb. 2:12). Not only are such psalms as 58, 109, and 137, devoted largely to cursing God's enemies, but we also find judgment called down upon God's enemies in many places in the other psalms as well.

God instructs us to pray these psalms. He wrote them and wants to hear us pray and sing them. If they scandalize us, then it is *we* who must change our attitude. So as believers we must accept the imprecatory psalms as good words from God.

We should think of the imprecatory psalms as the other half of the two-edged sword of God's truth. When we pray for God to save people, we do not order him to do so. He is free to say no to our prayers and to leave people in their sins. Similarly, when we pray for God to judge people, we are not ordering him to do so. He is free to save them, even if we have asked him to judge them.

The prayers of judgment align our thoughts with God's holiness and righteousness. We must submit ourselves to the fact that God is a God of judgment, learning to de-

> Appoint an evil man to oppose him; let an accuser stand at his right hand. When he is tried, let him be found guilty, and may his prayers condemn him. [Ps. 109:6–7]

light in his judgments, as we delight in him. In Psalm 139, after meditating on the greatness of God's glory, the psalmist is horrified that anyone would dare rebel against him. "I have nothing but hatred for them," he says. "I count them my enemies." He calls on God to kill them (Ps. 139:19–22).

Remember that when God kills a person, it is not necessarily a physical death unto spiritual destruction. It may be a spiritual death that leads to new life. You and I were judged by God and were put to death for our sins in baptism, but we were resurrected. When we pray for God to destroy his enemies we leave it up to his discretion whether to destroy them redemptively or everlastingly.

Coram Deo

All of the psalms call on God to draw near. When he does he brings both judgment and salvation. We cannot have one without the other. Indeed, the doctrine of justification means that salvation comes *through* judgment. If you want God to draw near you must be prepared to let God be God, acknowledging his freedom to come in mercy or wrath.

For further study: Psalm 83; 139:23–24; 2 Timothy 4:14–18

207 Mercy Found in the Depths

One of the most loved psalms throughout all of church history, the penitential Psalm 130, has been set to music by great composers. Preachers and theologians have written on it. As many of the psalms, Psalm 130 gives us words to use when we are in deep distress. The psalmist begins in the depths, near to death, near to sheol and the grave. He feels the weight of his sinfulness, and he calls to God: "Lord, hear my voice."

He continues his address to God in verses 3 and 4, saying that if God kept a record of our sins, none of us could stand before him. But God forgives our sins, he says, and therefore God is feared. This surprises us as modern Christians who understand so little about the true fear of God. We would understand that a God of wrath is feared. We would understand if the psalmist wrote that a forgiving God is loved. But it seems odd for the psalmist to say that God is feared precisely because he forgives sins.

The psalmist, though, is amazed and humbled by God's forgiveness. He is overwhelmed by the fact that God, who is infinite and all powerful, would stoop to forgive his sins. His response is to fear God more than ever before.

There are two ways to "fear God." Both involve true trembling at his greatness, but they run in opposite directions. One sort of fear is mixed with hatred, so that we flee from God, but certainly without love in our hearts. But there is also the fear that is mixed with love, so that we

442

> If you, O LORD, kept a record of sins, O Lord, who could stand?
> But with you there is forgiveness; therefore you are feared.
> [Ps. 130:3–4]

shyly and tremblingly seek to draw near to him despite his great majesty.

The psalmist talks to himself in verses 5–6. He tells his soul to wait on God. Things are hard right now here in the depths, he says, but God is faithful. The psalmist tells himself to trust in God's Word, for it promises that the dawn of redemption will come.

Then in closing the psalmist speaks to the congregation in verses 7–8. He tells Israel to hope in the Lord, because the Lord loves them and will redeem them. He tells them to hope in the coming Messiah, who will deliver Israel and the world from all their sins.

Just so, we can still share in the psalm writer's anticipation as we look for the Messiah's return and the fullness of our redemption in the resurrection.

Coram Deo

This psalm has been memorized by many of the church's great saints. That is a good idea, for it turns our thinking from self-pity to God-awareness in the low moments when we need to live before God's face. As you imprint these words in your heart, ask yourself, "Do I cherish the presence of the Lord the way a tired watchman would the glowing sunrise after a long wait in the dark?"

For further study: Psalm 17; 139:7–12; Isaiah 6:1–8

208 The Blessings of Unity

We don't know for certain why Psalms 120–134 are called *psalms of ascent*. Perhaps the thought is that they "ascend" to God as praise, though this is true of all the Psalms. Traditionally, it has been held that these psalms were sung as pilgrims attending the great feasts approached or ascended the mountain on which Jerusalem and the temple stood. Whatever the origin, it is possible to see these psalms as a series of steps moving upward toward "Jerusalem" where we will meet and magnify the Father.

Psalm 133 is a wisdom psalm that celebrates the oneness of God's people. This unity is not the unity of people who get together by compromising with one another. Rather, it is born as a result of people being drawn together by a greater influence. The psalm expresses this by means of two analogies.

First, unity is like the anointing oil that was poured on Aaron and flowed down his beard and onto his robes. Oil is a common symbol of God's influence on man through the Holy Spirit. Aaron, as high priest, represented the spiritual unity of Israel and pictured the Great High Priest, Jesus Christ. Thus, the picture is that God creates unity by anointing his Messiah (*messiah* means "anointed"), and the divine anointing flows from the head of the Messiah down onto his robe, which represents his people. In plain language: God gathers us into unity around Jesus

444

> How good and pleasant it is when brothers live together in unity! It is like precious oil poured on the head, running down on the beard, running down on Aaron's beard, down upon the collar of his robes. [Ps. 133:1–2]

by the Holy Spirit, who proceeds from the Father through Jesus to us.

Second, unity is like the dew of heaven falling on God's holy mountains. Water again is a common symbol of God's gift of the Holy Spirit and of new life. Dew comes down from heaven onto the top of God's mountain, where his temple is found, and then flows down the mountain. The mountain is where God's people gather and receive his blessing as they hear his Word.

In Genesis 11 God scattered the wicked at the Tower of Babel, lest in their sinful unity they became too powerful. In John 17 Jesus prays that we may all be one. Christian unity creates power in ministry. As members of one body we can lean on and support one another. The more unified the church becomes, the brighter the light of her witness.

Coram Deo

As in ancient Babel, God's desire for unity has its limits: He wants his people united around truth, not error. Sometimes believers are too zealous for Christian unity. Luther, who wanted unity, said, "Peace if possible, but purity at all costs." Can you think of some examples of times, perhaps in your own denomination, where unity has been purchased at too dear a price?

For further study: Romans 15:5; Ephesians 4:3–13; Colossians 3:14

209 Songs of Praise

Hallelujah in Hebrew means "Praise the LORD" or, literally, "Praise YAH!" There are four groups of psalms that are called *"hallel* psalms" because they include the word *Hallelujah* (Pss. 104–6, 111–18, 135–36, and 146–50). One group was sung at Passover (Pss. 111–18), and Jesus sang them with his disciples on the night he instituted the Lord's Supper (Matt. 26:30). Psalm 150, is the climax of the last group of *hallel* psalms.

Verse 1 of Psalm 150 tells us *where* to praise God. We are to praise him in his sanctuary and in his mighty heavens. "In his sanctuary" and "in his heavens" form parallel statements in the thought scheme of the poetry. The tabernacle and temple were "cosmic models" which represented the world under the blue canopy of the sky. The world itself was designed as God's temple, the place where all things would praise him.

Verse 2 tells us *for what* we are to praise God. We praise him both for his mighty deeds and for his greatness. We recount what he has done for us in the past, and we praise him for his excellent attributes.

Verses 3–5 tell us *how* to praise God. The psalm commands that we praise him with musical instruments and lists eight of them in two groups of four. Between the two groups he tells us to praise God with dancing. A wide range of worship experiences can be covered under these instruments. He mentions both quiet and loud instruments, both melodic and percussive.

> Let everything that has breath praise the Lord. Praise the Lord.
> [Ps. 150:6]

It is clearly implied that these instruments accompany singing, particularly the singing of the psalms. Thus, the proper way to praise God is with many varied instruments and great enthusiasm.

Finally, verse 6 tells us *who* is to praise God. Everything that has breath is to praise him. Human beings, as the captains of creation, are to lead in this praise, but they are not the only things that praise. Anything that "has breath," which may mean in this context anything that gives off vibrations (sounds), is to be brought into the service of God's praise by his human priests.

Worship as defined by the psalms denotes exuberant praise. There is to be nothing lackluster regarding the participation of the congregation and its people, individually or corporately.

Coram Deo

Those who lead worship should invite robust participation while providing excellence in choral and instrumental artistry. Worship styles may vary, but one element remains constant: God alone is our audience, and we are to direct our heartfelt expressions of praise toward him for his pleasure. Whatever the sound of your instruments, do your weekly worship experiences rise to the praise of Psalm 150 worship?

For further study: Nehemiah 9:5; Romans 15:11; Ephesians 1:1–14

210 Mental and Moral Purposes

D o you actually read prologues or prefaces? Authors usually use them to thank family or friends for their patience, or secretaries and editors for their help. Because of this, readers frequently jump right to the "real content" of a book. But an author often uses the prologue to explain a book's purpose or origin, or to tell readers what to expect from it—often giving exactly what we need to know in order to understand or properly use what we will read.

A few of the biblical authors explain why they wrote, though not necessarily at the beginning of the book (for example, Deut. 30:15–20; Luke 1:1–4; John 20:30–31; 1 Pet. 5:12; 1 John 5:13; Jude 3; Rev. 1:1).

Solomon also helps us understand why he wrote by telling the book's two main purposes in Proverbs 1:2–6. The first is an *intellectual* or *mental purpose*, that we continually grow in our understanding of the Lord, life, and even the understanding of the proverbs themselves. This growth will be demonstrated by our knowledge and insight throughout life. The second is a *moral purpose,* that we become increasingly wise and able to apply the proverbs to our lives. This wisdom and ability to apply proverbs will be exhibited in our growing prudence, discretion, and righteousness.

Neither is a short-term purpose. We need to guard against becoming discouraged when we can't make sense of a par-

448

ticular proverb, or figure out how it applies to our situation. They are, after all, called "riddles" (1:6). Nor is either purpose ever finally achieved, since even the wise will increase their learning as they continue to study this book and install its precepts in their specific circumstances (1:5).

Because there are so many brief nuggets of material, and because they are not organized logically or topically, it is often tempting to read the proverbs mechanically and without much thought ("a chapter a day keeps folly away").

But rather than skim them, looking for a particular verse, or hoping for one to strike our fancy, we must study them systematically, seeking foundational wisdom and applying its understanding.

Coram Deo

The proverbs demand *study* if we are to benefit from them as Solomon intended. We need to *think* about what a proverb says about the world and our lives, how God would have us *respond* to the situation it describes, and then *evaluate* our response when we actually face that circumstance. Use this "think, respond, and evaluate" model as the progressive steps to wisdom when you study the proverbs.

For further study: Joshua 1:8; Ezekiel 3:1–3; 2 Timothy 2:15; 3:16

211 To Fear Is to Obey

F ear of the LORD (1:7)—the theme of the proverbs —has nearly as many interpretations as interpreters. The best way to understand it is to look at another passage that addresses our attitude toward the Word of God. Proverbs 3:1–12 describes our attitude toward this book: We are to cherish it (3:1–3) and obey it (3:5–6, 11–12).

Since our ability to cope with life and its situations is invariably warped by the consequences of the fall, we often make bad decisions and fail to respond wisely to whatever faces us. We therefore need guidance in order to live wisely. Since God created the universe with Wisdom "at his side" (8:30), the wisdom of the proverbs is based on truths that were built into time and space at creation. They are woven into the design of all things and reach far deeper than we can ever discover by our own thought.

According to Proverbs 3:1–12, as we submit our own wisdom and understanding to God's (3:5–6a), our lives will increasingly conform to the laws that govern the world. Thus we will be straightened out (3:6b). This helps us understand how to acknowledge him in all our ways (3:6a).

To acknowledge God in our lives is to obey the wisdom and knowledge that he reveals in the proverbs. As we read a proverb we may be tempted to think that it does not really apply to us. Considering some of these bits of instruction, we may think things do not work out that way

> Trust in the LORD with all your heart and lean not on your own understanding; in all your ways acknowledge him, and he will make your paths straight. Do not be wise in your own eyes; fear the LORD and shun evil. [Prov. 3:5–7]

in our experience, so we do not understand how this observation could possibly be right. These verses warn us against this dangerous attitude of leaning on our own understanding, admonishing us to fear the Lord and live by his wisdom.

Proverbs 3:4, 7–10 give three examples of the blessings of this submission: favor with God and others (3:4), health and refreshment (3:7–8), and satisfaction of our needs (3:9–10). Proverbs 3:11–12 then warns us that we will be disciplined and rebuked by what we read. When the Lord uses a proverb to teach us, we are not to reject or despise that correction (contrast this attitude with that of 3:1–3); we are instead to see in its rebuke the loving discipline of our heavenly Father.

Coram Deo

When you read the Book of Proverbs, your heart should be humble—God is revealing how to order your life according to eternal truths. As you continue to read and study the proverbs, ask God for deeper understanding as to how you should fear and acknowledge him in all your ways. How does one go about seeking wisdom with the fervency of a prospector's quest for silver or gold (Prov. 8:10–11).

For further study: Matthew 13:44–46; Hebrews 4:12; 12:5–11

212 Wisdom's Moral Imperative

S cholars often contrast the authority of the Law and Prophets ("Thus says the LORD") with the "sanctified common sense" of the proverbs ("It seems to me . . ."). Some even say that proverbs are suggestions that we are free to accept or reject. Certainly we need wisdom to know when and how to apply a proverb— but don't allow that grain of truth to camouflage the lie that the proverbs are not inerrant Scripture.

Proverbs 8 includes both an emphatic statement of proverbial authority and one of the great invitations of the Bible (8:32–36). Wisdom gives four reasons for her demand that we choose life by listening to her and keeping her ways.

First, Wisdom alone teaches truth. Her words are true, noble, and right, never wicked, crooked, or perverse (8:5–9). They are absolutely trustworthy. What would we not give for advice we could trust wholeheartedly (8:10–11)? Trustworthy wisdom and advice too often lie neglected in the Word of God.

Second, *Wisdom gives better rewards* than any other possible investment of time, effort, or energy. The fruits of this investment include power, justice, riches, honor, wealth, and righteousness (8:12–21).

Third, *Wisdom alone knows the secrets of creation*, since, as the firstborn of all creation (8:22–24), she was there beside God as he worked (8:25–30a), and rejoiced in all that

> "Blessed is the man who listens to me, watching daily at my doors, waiting at my doorway. For whoever finds me [wisdom] finds life and receives favor from the Lord." [Prov. 8:34–35]

---

he made (8:30b–31). Who would not follow counsel based on perfect understanding of life?

Fourth, *Wisdom alone gives life.* Do we want to live or to die (8:35–36)? Will we mold our lives by the wisdom of the proverbs, or disregard their instruction? This appeals to our self-interest.

Martin Luther allegedly said: "The greatest thing I can do for God is to believe him." If I truly believe that the best thing for my car is to change the oil every three thousand miles, then I will change it every three thousand miles. If I truly believe that "the purposes of a man's heart are deep waters" (20:5a), then I will ask God to help me not judge by surface appearances, but to give me understanding to draw out the wisdom hidden in the heart.

Coram Deo

God has saved us from death to life. If wisdom is indeed the way of life, then we have a moral obligation to live wisely—to fear the Lord—by obeying the counsel he so freely and lovingly gives in the proverbs. Do you tend to judge by the surface look of things? How can you develop deeper discernment to apply Scripture to your life's issues?

For further study: Ephesians 4:18; Philippians 4:6–7;
Colossians 1:9; 2:2; 1 John 5:20

213 A Final Appeal

C omplex issues become "sound-bites," in which emotion or "expert opinion" often replaces facts and logic. The many dictionaries and encyclopedias in our culture encourage us to think ourselves knowledgeable, wise, and understanding. In Proverbs 30:1–6, Agur, an otherwise unknown sage, probably from northwest Arabia, raises a problem that should trouble everyone who studies Proverbs—the problem of our own foolishness, ignorance, and stupidity.

In Proverbs 30:2–3, Agur laments his stupidity (2a), characterized by his inability to understand people (2b), his failure to learn wisdom (3a), and his ignorance in knowing the holy God (3b). The more he seeks wisdom and understanding, the more he realizes the depths of his ignorance and foolishness.

Agur then raises a further complication. Where can we find wisdom? Who is mighty enough or wise enough to give true wisdom or knowledge? Who controls the wind or the sea? Who created, and thus understands, the world?

Since the answer to these questions is "God," the real burden is the first question (4a): Who can go up to heaven and bring wisdom back to us? Agur answers by saying that God has not left us to our own abilities, but has given us his tested and true words, which will give us his perfect wisdom, knowledge, and understanding (5a). As we trust

> "Every word of God is flawless; he is a shield to those who take refuge in him. Do not add to his words, or he will rebuke you and prove you a liar." [Prov. 30:5–6]

them we will take refuge in their Source (5b), because God's Word always points to God himself.

At the same time, however, we must beware of the temptation to fall back on our own wisdom (1:7; 3:5–6)—especially as we grow in wisdom—and thus try to put our words on a par with his (30:6). Even if we appear to succeed at being self-sufficient in our own understandings, we eventually will be rebuked. Our delusion that our own wisdom is as good as God's will be unmasked.

Agur thus says that we should not despair, but that we should instead persevere in our study of the proverbs, knowing that in them we have the trustworthy Word of God, which is designed to give us the wisdom we lack.

Coram Deo

Especially if we succeed in life's accomplishments, it is easy to become caught up in an inflated sense of our own understanding. Agur calls us to a realistic appraisal of our abilities, warning us against exulting in our wisdom. Reread Proverbs 30:1–6, focusing on your tendency to elevate your thoughts to the level of God's. Share in Agur's lament and thank God for his graciousness in revealing his wisdom.

For further study: Romans 11:33; 1 Corinthians 1:17–2:16; 3:19; 2 Corinthians 4:7

214 Time Line or Vicious Cycle?

I n ancient pagan thought the world was not regarded as the creation of a personal God. Instead, the world had "always existed." *God* was simply another way of saying "world" or "nature." Perhaps the world emanated out of this god and one day will be reabsorbed by "it." Since the world is eternal, it would have to emanate back out and be reabsorbed over and over for eternity. Today we call this the myth of an "oscillating universe." According to this conception, the universe goes from "big bang" to "big crunch" again and again forever.

This is an old idea in scientific dress. The pagan usually sees time and history as circular; life is a vicious cycle of insignificance. There is no escape, but if life becomes too painful, you can always commit suicide. This "myth of eternal return" was strongly promoted by Friedrich Nietzsche. He said that human life oscillates between times of Apollonian rationality, order, and purpose, and Dionysian irrationality and chaos. Taking Nietzsche seriously, such writers as Ernest Hemingway held that death ultimately wins, so the only way to cheat death is by taking dominion over it through suicide.

In *The City of God,* the great early theologian Augustine pointed out that the Christian and biblical view of time completely contradicts the pagan view of cycles. The biblical view is linear. The Bible says that time and history have a beginning at the point of creation. The world is not

> The wind blows to the south and turns to the north; round and
> round it goes, ever returning on its course. [Eccles. 1:6]

"self-creating," nor is it eternal. Rather it was created by God, who is a Being completely separate from the material. The world and human life have an orderly and purposeful starting point and are moving toward a destiny. Whatever cycles may appear to exist in history are really *spirals* moving upward toward God's planned and prophesied future.

Thus, each human being has a destiny. Each of us has a future, an *eschatology* in God's plan. Life has meaning in terms of that plan because God actively superintends it. Each of us has a part to play. Faith in God leads to hope in his plan, and such hope breaks us out of the despair caused by the myth of eternal cycles.

The battle between Christianity and secular humanism is largely the battle between the line and the circle.

Coram Deo

Jesus is the *Alpha* and the *Omega*, the Beginning and the End. Our ultimate hope as believers is that we will be raised to life eternal when God consummates his kingdom at the end of history. What is the difference in your concept of the God of history from that of the pagan world? Is your hope in the God whose plan moves purposefully onward?

For further study: Psalm 95:1–7; Jeremiah 29:11; Ephesians 1:11

215 Life under the Sun

The phrase *under the sun* is a constant refrain, occurring twenty-nine times in Ecclesiastes. To understand it we need to go back to Genesis 1. There the sky is described as a firmament over the earth and as a kind of symbolic barrier between heaven and earth. In that firmament God put the sun, moon, and stars. To live "under the sun" is to live in this world.

If a person's entire worldview is drawn from things under the sun and he does not acknowledge the heavenly world, then his life will be full of pessimism and despair. Life under the sun is indeed cyclical to some extent. The sun does rise and set. The weather does come around the same way every year. Indeed, according to Genesis 1, the sun, moon, and stars were appointed to regulate these cycles.

Genesis 1 and the remainder of Scripture show us, however, that the world under the sun is not the entirety of creation. There is also the created angelic heaven "above the sun." Outside of the creation there is God himself. In order to get a true perspective regarding what goes on under the sun, we need a vantage point beyond the sun.

The philosophy that sees things only in terms of this world that is under the sun, is called *secularism*, after the Latin word *secula*, which means "world." Looking only at the material, the world under the sun, the secularist inescapably and inevitably comes to the conclusion that life

> I have seen all the things that are done under the sun; all of them are meaningless; a chasing after the wind. [Eccles. 1:14]

is ultimately meaningless. Only the man or woman of faith can look at the world from a perspective that stands above the sun and makes some sense out of the apparent treadmill of life on earth.

The Bible gives us that heavenly perspective. We have received a message from beyond this world. From our perspective above the sun, we can see that the treadmill is really moving toward a destiny, that the cycles are really expanding spirals, and that life does have meaning, even if we do not personally see exactly where our present circumstances fit into the great plan of God. Life may appear to be meaningless and pointless. It may sometimes seem to be out of control. But we confidently affirm that it is none of these things, for Christ made a new reality when he broke through into the world under the sun.

Coram Deo

A person's worldview determines thinking and ultimately behavior. There is usually an observable consistency between worldview and lifestyle. Since this is true for the secularist *and* for the Christian, how consistently does your lifestyle correspond with what you say you believe? Are you following in the steps of Christ onward, or around in circles with the world?

For further study: Philippians 2:5–16; 4:8–9; James 3:13

216 "Chasing after the Wind"

T he "Teacher," as the philosopher-author of Ecclesiastes is known, spends most of chapters 1
and 2 discussing all the various ways in which
he personally had sought to find the meaning of life. He
tried philosophy, looking at the world under the sun, but
found that esoteric wisdom leads inevitably to sorrow and
grief (1:12–18). He tried hedonism and the pursuit of pleasure, but found it empty (2:1–3).

Then he tried power and wealth, not for their own sakes,
but in order to accomplish great works. In the end he looked
over all of his accomplishments and found them to be
empty (2:4–11). He stopped to reflect on his circumstances,
and realized that eventually he would die, and all that he
had accomplished would fall into the hands of others. His
heirs might be fools who would destroy all his achieve-
ments. This too he found to be empty and futile (2:12–23).

Then the Teacher shifts gears from the perspective under
the sun to the perspective above the sun, under heaven. A
man or woman can indeed find satisfaction in eating and
drinking, in work, and in wisdom, but only after realizing
that they are given him by God for God's purposes
(2:24–26).

The Teacher critiques three philosophical outlooks on
life that were common in the ancient world. In fact, they
are prevalent today. The ancient stoics, faced with the mean-

> I thought in my heart, "Come now, I will test you with pleasure to find out what is good." But that also proved to be meaningless. [Eccles. 2:1]

inglessness of life under the sun, said that the key to happiness was through seeking control of one's emotions and being imperturbable. But where does this lead? Nowhere, says the Teacher. Philosophy leads only to more despair.

The ancient Epicureans sought to achieve happiness through the maximization of pleasure and the avoidance of pain. They found, though, that when one has "enough" pleasure, life becomes boring. Thus, they decided to seek the *optimum* rather than the *maximum* pleasure.

However, changing words does not remove the problem: Pleasure for its own sake becomes empty soon enough.

The ancient political philosophers sought to achieve happiness through the development of a balanced state or through great empires and mighty works. But such human works do not endure, as the Teacher had personally discovered.

Coram Deo

To deny that pleasure, wisdom, and work are not ultimately worthy of our pursuit does not disqualify them from worth entirely. Have any of God's good gifts to you become out of balance and out of proper perspective in your motivations for living?

For further study: Philippians 3:1–16; Colossians 1:24–29; 1 John 2:15–17

A Time for Everything

As we have seen, the Bible teaches that time is linear and that history is moving toward a goal that has been determined by the wise plan of God. The fact that history is real for God, since he made it, was scandalous to the ancient Greeks and other pagans. For the ancient pagans an eternal god could have nothing to do with a world of change.

According to the pagan view, history was in flux, a place of constant change. Thus, history was the opposite of eternity, for pagans believed the nature of eternity could not involve change. For the pagan, salvation meant escaping from the world of "change and decay" into a world of timelessness. For instance, the stoics argued that people should seek to be changeless—imperturbable in the midst of the changing scenes of life. The Platonists argued that people should fix their minds on timeless *ideals*, and seek to ignore the flux of change around them.

The New Testament assaulted this mentality by saying that God Incarnate entered the flux of history. This was scandalous to the Greeks. The idea that history and change are good and under the providential control of God was monstrous to them. The notion that the eternal God would be willing to enter time was an absurdity.

Ecclesiastes 3 presents the biblical view of time, which is the opposite of the conceptions developed by the Greeks. In the Bible time is not a burden, but an opportunity. Change

> There is a time for everything, and a season for every activity under heaven. [Eccles. 3:1]

is not evil, but rather an opportunity to grow and develop. For sinners time means the opportunity to repent. Since we cannot do everything at once, the Bible says that there are appropriate times for everything in life (Eccles. 3:1–8).

How can we as finite creatures with limited mental capacities understand and illustrate the infinity and eternity of God? One way we can is by being diverse. The fact that time involves flux means that we have the opportunity to be images of God in different ways at different times: planting and uprooting, killing and healing, weeping and laughing. For the Christian, history is not the opposite of eternity, but rather the way God's eternal realities become manifest in the creation.

Coram Deo

Many Christians are under the impression that they should feel the same way all the time. This is not biblical thinking. The psalms show people experiencing great diversity of emotion in response to the changing scenes of life. Each presents a new and fresh opportunity to model the love of Christ. With what emotional response are you now approaching your changing circumstances? Can you honor Christ in the midst of these feelings?

For further study: Romans 14:10–12; Colossians 3:1–4;
1 Peter 5:8–11; 1 John 3:1–3

463

218 Everything Has a Purpose

I n the ancient world the primary concern of philosophers was the nature of reality and the essence of things. We call this *metaphysics*. Since the ancient pagans rejected the truth that God created the world out of nothing, they sought to understand the world in terms of itself. Eventually this investigation broke down, since no one could explain how the presumed oneness of all things could be reconciled with the evident diversity in the world.

When pagan thought revived in the modern world, it shifted its attention to the problem of knowledge, a concern we call *epistemology*. How is it possible to know anything?—That was the question. The biblical answer is that God designed the human mind so that people could understand the essential things about him and the world. Then, the Spirit of God works with human minds to give knowledge. Rejecting this answer, early humanists tried to imagine ways in which data from the world "enter" the mind. Eventually this investigation also broke down, since there seemed no way to explain how any human knows anything, and in fact it may be that all our knowledge is mere illusion and insanity.

Nineteenth-century philosophers shifted their attention to the *philosophy of history*. Under the influence of Christianity they accepted the notion of linear time and destiny, but they rejected the idea that history was an unfolding plan of God. So, eventually the investigation broke down

464

> I thought in my heart, "God will bring to judgment both the righteous and the wicked, for there will be a time for every activity, a time for every deed." [Eccles. 3:17]

once again, because they had no reason to assume the truth of linear time and destiny.

Twentieth-century philosophy returned to the concerns expressed in the Book of Ecclesiastes: What is a human being, and what is the meaning of human life? Martin Heidegger, in his book *Sein und Zeit* (*Being and Time*), said that each person experiences a sense of having been thrown into life, not knowing where he or she came from or where he or she is going. Such life exists in a meaningless and terrifying here and now. Jean-Paul Sartre carried forward this notion in his book *Being and Nothingness*.

By way of contrast, the biblical view is that time is moving toward a final judgment when God will evaluate every single thing that has ever happened. In the final analysis God will give everything in history its meaning.

Coram Deo

We have already seen (pp. 456–57) that each person has a destiny. Not only is our end significant, but all experiences of life leading to that end are similarly significant. Nothing in your life lacks meaning. Share this profound truth with someone today who could use encouragement in the faith.

For further study: John 4:35; Romans 12:15;
1 Corinthians 9:19–27; 2 Timothy 4:2–5

In Part 11 we finish our survey of the wisdom literature, completing our philosophical study of Ecclesiastes and looking briefly at the Song of Songs, the greatest story of romantic love ever written. We then will move on to the prophets.

In the Hebrew Bible, the "former" prophets were the historical books of Judges, Samuel, and Kings. These books give a prophetic understanding of how God works through history. We will spend more time with the "latter" prophets—Isaiah, Jeremiah, Ezekiel, and Daniel.

During the reign of the wicked King Ahab in northern Israel, God instituted a new prophetic movement. These men called the nation to repentance and gave solemn warning of the dire coming judgments. They also summoned a remnant to remain faithful, as Israel and Judah lapsed further into sin.

What difficult, heart-breaking ministries these men undertook. God's call to Isaiah promised

Wisdom Literature
and the Latter Prophets

him that no one would listen to his message, but at least he offered more words of encouragement than did Jeremiah, who was subject to character assassination, physical brutality, the sight of the ruined city and temple, and finally death in forced exile. Ezekiel's prophecies were directed toward the people in Babylonian exile and Daniel's to the Babylonians themselves, as well as to all people of all times.

In your personal study of the lovers of Song of Songs and the words of the prophets, measure the level of your faithfulness in an increasingly sinful world. We shall see that the prophetic Word of God still convicts, afflicts, and comforts, even as it calls us to live justly and to maintain purity in God's house. Such continuing self-inspection helps the believer to live *coram Deo,* under the gaze of and in the presence of the all-knowing God.

R.C. Sproul

219 The Inscrutability of History

ecause we human beings exist in time, the meaning of our lives relates intimately to historical events and realities. In Ecclesiastes the Teacher looked at life from the secular perspective and saw only a meaningless treadmill of futility. He shifts perspective, however in Ecclesiastes 3:1, which says that there is an appointed time for everything, "a season for every activity under heaven."

God has appointed a diversity of experiences, each of which has its proper perspective and place in our lives—a *time* God has chosen. The New Testament provides two different words for the concept of time that recognize this diversity. *Chronos,* refers to the mere passage of time. *Kairos,* refers to time as events or *special* times. Ecclesiastes 3 infers the latter concept, God's appointed times for us. There is, says the Teacher, a time to be born and a time to die, a time to embrace and a time to refrain from embracing. Christians know, if they understand Scripture at all, that every event in life comes from the loving, providential hand of God. As Ecclesiastes 3:11 puts it, God has made everything beautiful in its time.

Made in God's image, we have a built-in desire to understand the world and history. We want the "big picture." As we mature throughout all eternity in heaven we will increasingly understand that big picture. In this world we

are still mere babes in understanding, and we only know
a few things. Ecclesiastes 3:11 recognizes the limits of our
knowledge. God has put eternity into our hearts, so that
we desire to know all things, though we cannot fathom
what God has done from beginning to end. We must be
satisfied to know in part (1 Cor. 13:9), confident that God
will gradually reveal all things—at the proper time.

Those who claim to *know* all things right now are sinful and arrogant; they have inevitably reduced the world
to the dimensions of their own minds. This is the origin
of secular ideology and the wellspring of much cruelty,
as people seek to impose their distorted worldviews on
others.

Coram Deo

The world of knowledge multiplies at an alarming
rate, causing us to despair of ever really knowing much
at all. God encourages us to explore his world, and
when Adam classified the animal kingdom he became
the first scientist. God delights in our exploration of
creation and history, but mandates that we pursue
knowledge "according to truth." Outside of your vocation, how are you pursuing knowledge?

For further study: Romans 11:33–36; Hebrews 5:12–6:3

220 The House of Mourning

E
cclesiastes chapters 1–3 lays out the foundational perspectives of the book: *meaningless life perceived under the sun versus purposeful life perceived under heaven*. The rest of Ecclesiastes illustrates and amplifies these two perspectives.

Suffering is one of the most pervasive characteristics of human life. Virtually all pagan religions and philosophies try to reject or ignore the fact of suffering. Hinduism and Buddhism treat it as unimportant or even an illusion. Stoicism tries to ignore suffering (see p. 462). Epicureanism tries to bury it in pleasure (see p. 461). Political philosophies try to alleviate it. Modern existentialism tells us to embrace death in a form of psychological suicide (see p. 465). Only biblical religion faces pain and suffering honestly.

The Teacher tells us that it is better to spend time in the house of mourning than in the house of mirth. This is because death comes to all men, and it comes in many forms. Not only will we all eventually die physically, but we experience a form of death when we lose loved ones, when our dreams die, when we fall into horrible diseases, when we lose our job, and when we experience social disruptions and church splits. As noted when we looked at Leviticus (pp. 260–61), the Old Testament symbolized this pervasive experience of death by making aspects of life ceremonially "unclean," which meant symbolically dead.

> It is better to go to a house of mourning than to go to a house of feasting, for death is the destiny of every man; the living should take this to heart. [Eccles. 7:2]

Romans 5:14 tells us that death reigns under the sun. Jesus himself was known as a "man of sorrows," and while the Bible tells us that Jesus wept at Lazarus' tomb and wept over Jerusalem, it never tells us that he laughed (though doubtless he did). As a full participant in human life, Jesus fully understood human sorrows and was touched by human grief.

Too much of modern Christianity partakes of the world's attempt to deny death. We often hear a kind of "prosperity gospel" preached over radio and television. Disagreeable subjects like sickness, suffering, and death should be avoided if we want church growth. We don't sing the psalms, but instead sing songs full of superficial happiness. The Teacher invites us to take the reality of life more seriously.

Coram Deo

Certainly the Bible teaches that we are to be joyful; we are not to cultivate a long-faced outlook on life. But our joy is to be realistic, not artificial. The perspective of life "under heaven" enables us to face death squarely. Think through the last funeral you attended. Was death treated in a realistic, biblical fashion? Did you see some ways in which the reality of death was covered up, ignored, or rejected?

For further study: Psalm 116:7–19; Proverbs 13:14; 1 Corinthians 15:20–28

221 The Bottom Line on Life

As the Teacher concludes he provides us with the foundations of a biblical philosophy of life. First, he tells us that death does indeed pervade our existence. Not only so, but death is the destiny of each of us. Second, in God's goodness, death is not the whole story. God provides times of joy as well as times of sorrow. We can and should enjoy the good things God gives us, as well as mourn the hard things he finds necessary to send our way. "Enjoy life," says the Teacher, "because nothing is better for a man under the sun than to eat, drink and be glad" (Eccles. 8:15).

Third, death is not the last word, because after death comes the judgment. Therefore, says the Teacher, in the midst of enjoying life, we must not break God's law, because God will bring everything into judgment. The young person should rejoice in his or her strength and vigor. Youth should be enjoyed, because the older person no longer has the ability to do as much. The body decays, and our vitality fades (12:1–8). The young man should bear this fact in mind, and live accordingly.

Fourth, the wise man should expose himself to the words of sages, because they are like goads that drive him to think seriously about life. The goad is a long, pointed stick, by which livestock can be prodded, guided, and turned when headed in the wrong direction. The words of sages are also

> Now all has been heard; here is the conclusion of the matter: Fear God and keep his commandments, for this is the whole [duty] of man. [Eccles. 12:13]

like nails that firmly fix the realities of life in place. These two benefits of godly wisdom arise from the fact that such wisdom comes from the Great Shepherd (12:11).

Finally, as the Teacher has told us repeatedly, true wisdom shows us the limits of human knowledge and understanding. This should cause us to live by faith, confident that, even if we don't understand all of life, there is One who does, One who is firmly in control.

The bottom line is this: We are to fear God and obey him, knowing that he will evaluate everything in our lives. God sovereignly disposes our lives here below, "under the sun," and he sovereignly judges our lives when we stand before him.

Coram Deo

On the Lord's Day we take a break from the treadmill of our work, and we eat and drink and rejoice before God, as the Teacher commends. In what other ways should the weekly experience of worship reinforce the fundamental wisdom and insight of Ecclesiastes? The activities of the wise each day are conducted with eternity in view. Does this perspective change the priorities with which you approach today's events?

For further study: Nehemiah 8:8–12; Isaiah 58:13–14; James 3:13–17

222 The Song of Songs

The Song of Songs, also called "Canticles" or the "Song of Solomon," has a history of controversy. It is clearly a song about love between a man and a woman, including the physical dimension. Indeed, it celebrates the joys of the marital relationship. Some have questioned whether it belongs in the Bible. It does not seem to be spiritual enough to be included in the canon of Scripture; indeed, some of its intimate language seems downright embarrassing.

Early Jewish expositors decided that the Song was really applying romantic love to the relationship between Yahweh and Israel. According to them, the marriage of the Lord and his people was set forth in the book as an allegory. Early Christian expositors continued to look at the book allegorically, seeing in it a symbolic description of Christ's love for his church, and hers for him. But, while certainly the Song can be *applied* in a general way to the relationship of Christ to his bride, there is no reason to believe that such a symbolic application is the book's primary focus.

One of the worst influences of pagan philosophy on the early church was the idea that sexual love is always tainted with evil. Perpetual virginity came to be prized more than marriage. This departs from the Bible, where virginity is a gift to be given to the beloved on the wedding night. Many in the church came to believe that sexual expression, even

> Solomon's Song of Songs. Let him kiss me with the kisses of his mouth—for your love is more delightful than wine. [Song of Songs 1:1–2]

in marriage, is sinful and should be endured only for the sake of having children. Naturally, the Song of Songs, which celebrates the joy of physical love, had to be reinterpreted by those whose view of sexuality was so narrow.

According to the Bible, however, the marital relationship in all of its aspects, including the physical, is a great gift of God. It is not to be despised, but enjoyed. Genesis 2 explicitly says that it was "not good" for the man to be without a wife. From the biblical perspective, marriage is good, including sexual union within marriage.

Therefore, we should not be surprised to find a book in the Bible that celebrates this benefit of God's grace to his children.

Coram Deo

The Song of Songs can help us have a healthy view of the goodness of romance in courtship and marriage. If you are married, consider doing a study of the book with your spouse. If you are single, read it with the view of preparing to commit yourself totally to the one God might give to you in marriage. Has Western culture's abuse of human sexuality affected your perception of the good relationship between a man and a woman?

For further study: Ephesians 5:21–30; 1 Peter 3:1–9

223 The Beauty of Compliments

L ow self-esteem is regularly stated to be one of the most pervasive emotional conditions among women. Men, however, also suffer from bad self-images. As a "manual of love" the Song of Songs shows us the importance of compliments, and surely true praise and valid compliments will do wonders to restore a sense of real self-worth to the partners in a marriage.

For the most part, the Song of Songs is simply an exchange of mutually-upbuilding compliments between two lovers, back and forth, one compliment after another. The Song is a celebration of the good points of the other person.

How many marriages begin on a basis of compliments and end in an exchange of insults? Your spouse has the greatest power in this world either to affirm you or to destroy you. The comments of people we love weigh heavily upon us, either for good or for bad. Studies have shown that the compliments and criticisms we receive as children from those we respect have a great deal to do with shaping our later lives.

The Song of Songs also shows us that we should openly receive true compliments. We should believe the good things our spouse and friends say about us. In 1:5 the bride frankly says, "Dark am I, yet lovely." She goes on to say that her darkened skin has come from working in the sun, but in spite of this, she recognizes her own value, her true beauty.

"How beautiful you are, my darling! Oh, how beautiful! Your eyes behind your veil are doves." [Song of Songs 4:1a]

We pointed out (pp. 474–75) that the Song is not to be regarded as a simple allegory of Christ and the church, but since the church is married to Christ we can gain useful insights into our celestial marriage relationship with him. In our praise we compliment him; but notice in the Bible that he also compliments us. We were made as the very images of God, and we must not despise that image as a factor in assessing our worth, in spite of the problems sin has introduced.

Notice how Paul, the Groom's spokesman, addresses the trouble-torn bride in 1 Corinthians 1:1–9. The bride is sanctified, holy, enriched in every way, lacking in no spiritual gift, preserved to the end, and destined for blamelessness. Only after affirming believers in this way does Paul go on to point out some areas in which improvement is needed.

Coram Deo

Are you the kind of husband or wife who compliments your spouse, or are you mostly critical? How about those you associate with on the job, in the classroom, or in the church? The other-affirming principles of the Song apply both in marriage and to every other covenantal relationship. Encourage one another.

For further study: 2 Samuel 19:5–14; Psalm 10:17; 1 Corinthians 1:1–9; 1 Thessalonians 5:8–11, 15; Hebrews 3:13

224 Delighting in Beauty

The Song of Songs progresses from Solomon's courtship of his bride through the early days of their marriage. In chapters 1–2 Solomon woos the Shulamite maiden, and she affectionately responds to his advances. In 2:4 and 3:6 we find Solomon taking her to the palace to present her to the court. Then in chapter 4 Solomon praises her beauty as she stands fully dressed and veiled. He mentions her beautiful eyes, her raven hair, and what he can see of her body as it moves beneath her garments (4:1–5). He even says that she smells good to him (4:10–15—a locked garden is one that captures good scents).

Chapter 5:1 says that the marriage has been consummated. The new wife yearns to be with her husband, but he is about his business (5:2–6:3). Later in the day Solomon remembers her beauty and longs to be with her also (6:1–9). Next we find her public presentation before the people as their queen. They fall in love with her and want to see her more often (6:10–13). In chapter 7 the newly married couple is alone, and Solomon admires her physical beauty in privacy. The language in chapter 7 is naturally more intimate.

What we see throughout the Song is the delight that both the husband and the wife take in each other and in each others' bodies. There is no hint of comparison here, as if the husband compares his wife's body to the beauty of other women he has known. His eyes are for her alone. Happy is the man who has never known another woman

Your navel is a rounded goblet that never lacks blended wine.
Your waist is a mound of wheat encircled by lilies. [Song of
Songs 7:2]

with physical intimacy and the woman who has known only her husband. A benefit of fidelity is that they have no basis for unwanted comparisons.

The negation and depreciation of the human body, which is still present among some Christians, is characteristic of pagan culture, not of the Bible. The Bible teaches us that God made human beings in his own image, as the crown of his creation. While God is a Spirit without a physical body, in *some* ways our physical bodies do reflect his beauty and glory. We should delight in this and in one another *within the strict confines of marital privacy.*

Both clothed and unclothed, adorned and unadorned, scented and unscented, married couples should regard the loveliness of one another.

Coram Deo

The abundance of exposed flesh in our public marketplace today makes it more difficult for husbands or wives to believe their spouses only have eyes for them. As Job, covenant with your eyes (Job 31:1) that you will not gaze or long for someone besides your marriage partner. If you are married, are there ways you can strengthen your fidelity to the person with whom you are one flesh?

For further study: Job 31:1; Matthew 5:27–30; Luke 11:33–36

225 The Message of the Prophets

Very often the New Testament speaks of "the Law and the Prophets," which leads some people to think that the precepts in these two parts of Scripture stood against one another. Indeed, much of liberal theology is based on a supposed dichotomy between these two sets of books, the notion that the prophets were at war with the law and with the priests who maintained the law. Nothing could be further from the truth.

The biblical perspective states that God is sovereign, and every word he speaks has the force of law. Thus, whether God speaks through Moses or Isaiah, his Word is law. Preeminently, the law, the five books of Moses, is the foundation for God's revelation. The prophets God raised up throughout the Old Testament had, as their fundamental mission, the task of calling the people back to the revealed law of God. We see this most fully in Jesus Christ, the greatest Prophet, when he says that he has no intention of abolishing either Moses or the prophets, but rather that he is going to fulfil them. Immediately after saying this, Jesus began calling the wayward people back to the true meaning of the Mosaic law in his Sermon on the Mount.

The prophets denounced Israel when the nation departed from the social aspects of God's laws. They spent more energy, however, denouncing Israel's religious sins, for worship stands at the heart of society. The prophets decried such ecclesiastical abuses as ritualism, externalism, and

480

> "Do not think that I have come to abolish the Law or the Prophets; I have not come to abolish them but to fulfill them." [Matt. 5:17]

formalism, proclaiming that God hates religious practices that merely go through the motions of worship. They told the people that true worship expresses fearful love and love-filled fear for God.

But the prophets never attacked the law, either in its social or in its ecclesiastical dimensions. God had set up the rituals, externals, and formalities in the first place. Too often today we throw the baby out with the bath water. We don't want any forms or any liturgy. However, we cannot worship without some kind of form. The prophets knew that it is possible to have externals without the internal, but it is never possible to have the internal without the external.

If our heart-attitude does not issue in external obedience to God's laws, including his rules for worship, we have nothing.

Coram Deo

The Protestant Reformers sought to reform the church, not to reject everything from the past. This was true of their approach to worship as well. How well do you know the great forms and structures of worship that God has given the church through the ages? How does your worship properly honor the biblical forms for the church?

For further study: Psalm 40; Romans 14:19; 1 Corinthians 10:31; 14:40

226 The Message of Isaiah

Isaiah began his message with some heavy words. He brought God's indictment against the people. He said that Israel was like a bunch of rebellious sons, like wild animals that could not be tamed. He accused the people of being sinful, loaded with guilt, evildoers, and corruption. The people Isaiah addressed saw themselves as loyal Israelites, people bound in covenant with God (as they chose to understand him). They believed their religiosity far exceeded that of other nations. It must have come as a shock that Isaiah identified them as filthy sinners.

What if a preacher today talked like this in a congregation of Christians? "Hellfire and brimstone" preaching has just about disappeared. Yet Isaiah was one of the most educated men of his time. He was a member of the nobility, traveling in the highest circles of Israel. There is some evidence that he was of the royal house, though this inference is contested by some scholars. When Isaiah spoke his fiery words he was not a crazy preacher standing on a street corner with a sign. His words carried weight. We can learn from Isaiah that there is indeed a time and a place for wise, educated preachers to talk straight to their congregations about sin.

Isaiah called them "Sodom and Gomorrah (1:10)." He told them that God was sick and tired of their religious activities, their sacrifices and festivals, because they were ig-

> "Ah, sinful nation, a people loaded with guilt, a brood of evildo-
> ers, children given to corruption! They have forsaken the LORD;
> they have spurned the Holy One of Israel and turned their backs
> on him." [Isa. 1:4]

noring true social justice (1:11–15). He advised them to
start defending the good, seeking justice, reproving the
ruthless, defending the orphan, and pleading for the widow.
He did not tell them to take the easy way, to set up a political bureaucracy to do these things. Rather, he told them
that each of them needed to stand up publicly and be
counted on the side of justice for the oppressed.

God's invitation is issued in 1:18, "Come now, let us reason together." God told the people who had been indicted
that, if they would repent, their sins would be washed away,
and they would eat the best of the land. He also told them
that, if they continued to rebel, it was they who would be
eaten—by the sword. With such options, what was clearly
reasonable was heartfelt repentance.

Coram Deo

What Isaiah delivered was part of the "whole counsel of God," the rest of the story we often prefer not
to hear. There are times when pastors must speak
the whole counsel. Does your church stifle or intimidate your pastor, perhaps unintentionally, so that
some subjects about sin are off-limits from the pulpit? Give him the freedom to speak all of God's Word
to you.

For further study: Joel 2:11–32; Matthew 28:16–20; Acts 20:20, 24, 31

227 The Messiah's Reign

In the days of the judges the northern tribes of Zebulun and Naphtali were oppressed by Sisera the Canaanite, until God raised up Deborah and Barak to deliver his people (Judges 4–5). *Barak* means "lightning bolt." In Isaiah 9 the prophet drew from the history of Barak a prophetic analogy concerning the coming Messiah. Isaiah said that in the land of Zebulun and Naphtali a "great light" would be seen, a greater Barak who would deliver the nation from sin and enslavement, the consequence of sin.

Then Isaiah moved forward in the history of Judges to the story of Gideon, who delivered Israel from Midianite oppression (Judges 6–8). Isaiah said that the future Messiah would save Israel "as in the day of Midian's defeat" (Isa. 9:4).

What would bring this about? "For to us a child is born," said Isaiah. The coming Messiah would be a greater Barak, a greater Gideon, and he would deliver the people once and for all. Gideon refused the crown saying, "I will not rule over you, nor will my son rule over you. The LORD will rule over you" (Judg. 8:23). The greater Gideon, however, is God Incarnate, and "the government will be upon his shoulders" (Isa. 9:6).

The Bible speaks of rule as a heavy weight. Rebels think that it is nothing to rule over people. They seize the robe of office, never realizing that the robe is extremely heavy.

> The people walking in darkness have seen a great light; on those living in the land of the shadow of death a light has dawned. [Isa. 9:2]

Young people do not have the maturity and strength to hold up such a heavy garment. The Bible reserves the weight of office for elders, who, by their experience, have learned wisdom and discernment.

In a sense the fullness of government is too heavy for any person to shoulder. In order to bear such government, one would have to be like Atlas, holding the entire world on one's shoulders. Such an Atlas was the coming Messiah. He would have the strength and the wisdom to bear the governmental weight of the whole world.

Some liberal expositors have maintained that Isaiah 9 only predicts the coming of Hezekiah, the good king who would restore Israel in the near future. But the language of Isaiah 9 cannot possibly be intended for any mere human king: Wonderful, Counselor, Mighty God, Everlasting Father, Prince of Peace (9:6). Only the Incarnate Son of God merits such ascriptions.

Coram Deo

Knowing Christ as we do, and walking in more light of revelation, should cause us to long all the more for his second coming. Do you think about his coming? With what emotions do you anticipate his full and complete reign when his kingdom comes in power?

For further study: Matthew 13:13–33, 38–43; Revelation 22:7–21

228 The Great Good News

T he greatest of the Servant songs of the second part of Isaiah is found in Isaiah 52:13–53:12. It describes the coming sufferings and glories of the Messiah. Isaiah leads into this passage with an interesting statement of what God is going to do. Isaiah 52:7 tells the people to reflect on the excitement of the runner who brings good news of victory. After a battle, a trained runner would carry the message of either victory or defeat to the nation. As the runner came over the hills and became visible to the people, they could tell by how he ran whether the news was good or bad. Was his running heavy-footed? The battle was probably lost. Was his running dance like? The battle was doubtless won.

The runner proclaims, "Your God, the God of Israel, has been victorious, and now he reigns over a new conquest!" The conquest in this case is Israel herself, conquered anew *for* God and *by* God. Isaiah says that God has done this by baring "his holy arm in the sight of all the nations" (52:10). God has accomplished a great victory by his mighty power and has established his rule.

Isaiah tells us that God's Servant has acted with cunning and will prosper in his service of bringing in God's kingdom (52:13). From what has gone before, we might expect Isaiah to describe how the Servant shamed and smashed God's en-

486

> How beautiful on the mountains are the feet of those who bring
> good news, who proclaim peace, who bring good tidings, who
> proclaim salvation, who say to Zion, "Your God reigns!" [Isa. 52:7]

emies. After all, there are many passages in the Bible that describe God's victory in such terms. But Isaiah does exactly the opposite. Turning to God's method of achieving victory, he tells us that, though God's Servant will in time be lifted up, first he will be regarded with horror. Men will be appalled at him, and his appearance will be so ugly and marred that he will be scarcely recognizable as human (52:14).

Isaiah's point is that, before there can be any kind of cultural victory or transformation, there must first be a victory over the rule of sin. And the only way there can be victory over sin is if someone pays the penalty sin deserves and sets sinners free.

Coram Deo

The response in Zion to the Servant's work is said to be fierce joy and rejoicing (Isaiah 52 and 54). The good news of the gospel is that Christ, as our Suffering Servant, has paid the penalty for our sin, setting us free. If you have not felt very joyful recently, read Isaiah 52–54 aloud. Were these passages designed to communicate Jesus Christ? Do you know him as Suffering Servant, Savior, and King?

For further study: Isaiah 59:15b–21; Matthew 12:14–21; 1 Peter 5:1

229 The Messiah's Sufferings

Victory would come to God's Servant through his sufferings. Isaiah 53 is one of the clearest descriptions of the sufferings of Jesus found in the Bible. We will look at a few aspects of sufferings he bore as he paid the penalty for our sins. Isaiah says that he was a man of sorrow, familiar with suffering (v. 3a). He also says that Jesus did not have a beautiful face that would attract people (v. 2). The burden of our sins weighed down on him, with the result that many people regarded him as ugly—quite a contrast to the glory and beauty God originally designed for his image-bearers, humanity. Just as we tend to turn away from disfigured people to avoid looking at them, so the crowd avoided looking at Jesus as he bore our sins (v. 3b).

Like Job before him, Jesus was regarded by the crowd as smitten by God for his sins (v. 4). The crowd did not recognize that it was for *their* transgressions that he was being crushed. God placed our sins on him, and that has made possible the victory of God and transformation of the world (v. 5–6, 11–12).

One of the hardest trials we can endure is to be accused falsely. We instantly leap to defend ourselves when we are wrongly accused. We demand public vindication. But Jesus, we are told, did not open his mouth to defend himself when he was wrongly and hatefully accused (v. 7).

> He was oppressed and afflicted, yet he did not open his mouth; he was led like a lamb to the slaughter, and as a sheep before her shearers is silent, so he did not open his mouth. [Isa. 53:7]

Twice in Isaiah 53:7–8, Isaiah says that the suffering servant was oppressed. Remember that in Isaiah 1 the prophet began by condemning Israel for oppressing the poor. Now we see that Jesus is one of the oppressed poor, in order to gain the victory over the oppressors by dying for their sins.

Every Jew looked forward to children, but Jesus was cut off and had no descendants (v. 8). Yet two verses later (v. 10), Isaiah tells us that "he will see his offspring." Though Jesus had no physical children, all of redeemed humanity are given to him as his adopted sons and daughters.

God rewarded his Servant by giving him the spoil, the whole earth, that he might divide it and give it to his offspring (53:12).

Coram Deo

Psalm 22 is a chillingly accurate prophecy of the agony Christ suffered on the cross. As you read it, reflect on the high cost our Savior paid for our redemption from sin and death. Give him praise for the great love demonstrated in his atonement for your sins.

For further study: Psalm 22; 1 Corinthians 1:27–31; Colossians 1:14, 20–22

230 Jeremiah: the New Moses

J eremiah was the son of Hilkiah, one of the priests of the temple. Because there were so many priests, God instructed David to set them up in twenty-four "courses" or groups (1 Chronicles 24). Each course served for two weeks in the year under its own chief priest. During the rest of the year when they were not on duty, members of the courses resided in towns through Israel as teachers and preachers (compare Luke 1:8–9). Jeremiah grew up in the town of Anathoth in Benjamin.

God appeared to Jeremiah, saying he was predestined to be a prophet. "Before I formed you in the womb," said God, "I set you apart. I appointed you as a prophet to the nations" (Jer. 1:5). Jeremiah protested that he was both too young and a poor speaker. Nobody would listen to him. God should find someone else. This response reminds us of Moses, who also protested that he had no speaking ability, but God called him to service anyway (Exodus 3–4).

God's response to Jeremiah was similar. "Don't say you are only a child. You will go where I tell you, and you will say exactly what I tell you to say." This would have reminded the people of Jeremiah's day of what God told Moses: "You will go to Pharaoh and tell him what I say."

This is a chilling analogy. The call of Jeremiah establishes that Judah had become Egypt in God's eyes. Her worship was like the Egyptians' worship of false gods. Just as God made war on the gods of Egypt through Moses, so

> "Ah, Sovereign Lord," I said, "I do not know how to speak; I am only a child." [Jer. 1:6]

he would make war through Jeremiah on the godlessness that had grown up around the temple.

This analogy was appropriate in more than simply a spiritual sense. At that time the people of Judah were being drawn again to the power of the nation of Egypt. As Judah looked to Egypt for protection against Nebuchadnezzar, they rejected God's statement that he had given the world into Nebuchadnezzar's hands (see Jeremiah 27). So enamored were they by the Egyptians that Judah was also adopting Egyptian worship practices when they put Egyptian gods in the temple; all the while they also pretended to worship the Lord.

Just as God led his people out of Egypt, so God was going to lead the remnant out of Judah into the wilderness of Babylon. Also as in the case of the wilderness wanderings, God eventually would restore them to the land.

Coram Deo

Today many churches have allied with the Egypt of secular humanism. Secular influences are more subtle than would be the setting up of idols beside the pulpit, but friendship with world philosophy still is devastating to godly purity. We need Jeremiahs who will call God's people into faithful remnant churches. Where do you stand: In Egypt? Or in a true church?

For further study: Leviticus 11:45; Acts 7:34–43; Hebrews 8:7–12

491

231 Jeremiah's Temple Sermon

God told Jeremiah early in his sad career to go to the gate of the temple and denounce the people. Imagine the scene. The temple liturgy has begun, rich with God-ordained pageantry and music. As part of the liturgy, the people sing three times, "This is Yahweh's temple." But their worship is hollow as they look to Egyptian gods and ways. Suddenly in their midst, the young prophet Jeremiah cries out judgments against the people and the temple.

Jeremiah told them that their worship was worthless because they dealt unjustly with each other and oppressed foreigners, widows, and orphans. They sacrificed blood to strange gods, they stole, murdered, committed adultery, perjured themselves, and burned incense to Baal (Jer. 7:6–9).

They thought they could do all of this and then show up at church and say, "We are safe" (7:10). They committed these abominations right in God's face and expected him to accept them anyway. They had a new, perverse hymn:

Free from the law! Oh blessed condition.
  We can sin as we please and still have remission.

"That is not how it is going to be," said Jeremiah. "Remember Shiloh?" he asked. Surely they did. The story is found in 1 Samuel 1–4. The people lived in sin, and only

> Do not trust in deceptive words and say, "This is the temple of the
> LORD, the temple of the LORD, the temple of the LORD!" [Jer. 7:4]

a few came to the feasts. The godly high priest Eli did not restrain his sons from fornication and blasphemy. God brought in the Philistines to destroy the defiled tabernacle; it was never rebuilt. A century later the temple was built, but the tabernacle never again operated.

"This is how it is going to be," said Jeremiah. "God is going to bring in new Philistines—the Babylonians. They will destroy this defiled temple, because you have made an idol of it."

The people did not like this message. The priests and nobility knew he was attacking them. They began to conspire against Jeremiah and sought to have him put to death. Later on Jesus came with the same message, quoting Jeremiah 7:11 against the temple of his day. These priests were equally offended and carried out their desires to put him to death for it.

Coram Deo

Jeremiah's task was extremely unpleasant, and the task of calling a people to purity hasn't grown easier today. Consider that judgment must begin in the household of faith, and in particular in our own hearts. Ask the Holy Spirit to search your heart and help you confront sin to which you may be blind.

For further study: Acts 24:24–25; 2 Timothy 4:2–5; 1 John 2:12–16

232 In the Potter's Hands

G od told Jeremiah to visit a potter (Jeremiah 18). The potter was working with a wheel turned by a pedal operated by his foot. He threw clay into the center of the wheel, but perhaps he did not get the clay precisely centered, because as he tried to work with the clay it became lopsided. The potter had to smash it down and start over. Then, he shaped the clay into a pot that was pleasing to him.

God was a potter, and Israel was the clay. If God announced destruction on a nation and it repented, he would spare it. If he announced blessings to a nation and it forsook him, God would destroy it. The message was clear: Though God had not yet chosen any Gentile nation, he might well turn to the Gentiles if they repented. By the same token, though he had originally chosen Israel, he would surely destroy her if she continued down her wicked paths. Moreover, through Jeremiah God had been announcing destruction for Israel; but if Israel repented, God would relent. The clay was his, and he could shape it any way he chose.

The people responded to Jeremiah's message by mounting a campaign of defamation against him (18:18). They started spreading lies about his character and behavior to discredit him. Clearly they were rejecting God's offer of peace.

In response God told Jeremiah to return to the potter

> "O house of Israel, can I not do with you as this potter does?" declares the LORD. "Like clay in the hand of the potter, so are you in my hand, O house of Israel." [Jer. 18:6]

and buy a nice pot (Jeremiah 19). Jeremiah was to take it out to the place where broken pots were thrown and hurl it into the heap, shattering it. Under God's direction Jeremiah informed the people that this was God's intention for them.

How did the people react? Pashhur, who was "chief officer" among the priests of the temple, had friendless Jeremiah beaten and put in stocks, not only brutally wounding him, but also exposing him to public ridicule (Jeremiah 20). When Pashhur had Jeremiah released the next day, Jeremiah told him that God had given Pashhur a new name: "Terror on Every Side."

In the future, disaster would surround this man, and he would find out what it was like to have no friends, being hated by everybody.

Coram Deo

The Book of Jeremiah shows the prophet giving Israel one opportunity after another to repent, just as Moses gave Pharaoh many chances to change his mind. God still deals with us that way. While he is long-suffering, God's patience is limited. Do not presume upon his grace or ignore the warnings that are prelude to chastisement.

For further study: Exodus 34; Nehemiah 9:25–35; 2 Timothy 1:15–17

233 The Mark of a Prophet

J eremiah was no different from you and me. Made in God's image, he loved beauty and peace and enjoyed the companionship of others. He did not enjoy bringing God's message of woe to the people, and he did not like being persecuted. His soft heart never hardened under persecution, and he did not become an embittered loner, rejecting human company. Rather, he continued to suffer when he was rejected.

Jeremiah might have given up. He might have become one of the false prophets who preached only "peace and love." These preachers never upset anybody. After all, they said, Isaiah told us to comfort God's people and speak peace to Jerusalem (Isaiah 40). There are plenty of such preachers today, who say, "God loves you just as you are."

The Bible's message is, "God loves you and demands that you change your ways." Isaiah was sent to comfort the afflicted; Jeremiah was sent to afflict the comfortable. Those who groan over sin and wickedness are to be comforted. Those at ease in sin, who perpetrate evil in society, need to be afflicted.

From time to time true prophets experience affliction from angry sinners; Jeremiah experienced it often. We have heard Jeremiah tell the wicked Pashhur that in the future his name would be "Mr. Terror on Every Side." In fact, that was the name Jeremiah was being called (Jer. 20:10). The

> I hear many whispering, "Terror on every side! Report him! Let's report him!" All my friends are waiting for me to slip, saying, "Perhaps he will be deceived; then we will prevail over him and take our revenge on him." [Jer. 20:10]

leaders of the city were out to get Jeremiah, and when people saw him on the street they would say, "Here comes Mr. Bad Luck. Let's turn him in and get him in trouble."

Jeremiah's associates (the "friends" of v. 10) also conspired against him. They hoped he would commit some sin so they could discredit him. His fellow priests hated him because his faithfulness exposed their unfaithfulness. They had to condemn him in order to keep looking good in the public eye. So it is today. If you stand up for what is right, whether in the pulpit or on the job, some will attack you. Such is one mark of a true disciple of the holy God.

Coram Deo

The media delights to expose sins committed by ministers of God's Word. Gossip grapevines inside the church run rampant with exaggerated tales and lies about those in authority. As Christians we should not uncritically believe scandalous reports. Even when such tales turn out to be true, we should grieve and pray for the person involved, resisting the temptation to gloat and gossip. Better, pray now for leaders, that they will be protected from discredit.

For further study: Matthew 5:3–16; Galatians 6:1–5; James 5:16

234 Great Is Thy Faithfulness

J eremiah began prophesying during the reign of the good king Josiah. Though many of the priests and prophets refused Jeremiah's message, Josiah and others listened. After Josiah died, however, people began to turn away from Jeremiah. The prophet lived to see Jerusalem and the temple sacked and burned. He saw the people he had sought to save dragged off into captivity. Jeremiah ministered to those left behind; but they too rejected his message and finally dragged him off to Egypt, where he eventually died.

As Jeremiah sat outside the ruins of Jerusalem, he composed five poems that comprise the Book of Lamentations. Each of these five poems has 22 stanzas, for the 22 letters of the Hebrew alphabet. The first, second, and fourth poems (chaps. 1, 2 and 4) have one verse per letter, following the alphabet. The third poem has three verses for each letter. The last poem has 22 stanzas, but does not follow the alphabet.

This is an alphabet of God's work. The city deserved destruction because she had played the harlot and refused to repent. She had rejected Jeremiah, calling him "Terror on Every Side" (Lam. 2:22); thus she had rejected God.

But because of all his daily sufferings, Jeremiah had learned something about God's mercies in the midst of affliction. The people were going to be afflicted in much the same way Jeremiah had been.

> Because of the LORD's great love we are not consumed, for his compassions never fail. They are new every morning; great is your faithfulness. [Lam. 3:22–23]

Jeremiah reminded himself, and told the people in the process, that God is faithful, even to those who have been unfaithful but then turn to him. If they sought him they would find him. Jeremiah had learned that God's love means that his people will not be completely consumed. Every morning brings a new sign of God's love and compassion, for it gives a new opportunity to repent and serve him.

Thus, in the heart of his book, in the center of the third poem, Jeremiah told those left standing by their burned-out temple that those who waited on the Lord would find him faithful. Those who sought him would find him. Those who waited quietly would see his salvation. Those who accepted his judgments as just, who did not kick against them, would find his peace (Lam. 3:19–33).

Coram Deo

If God really wanted to destroy us, he would not send prophets to warn us. He would not let us live and daily give us new opportunities to change our ways. As long as we still live, God is showing us mercy. If there is some change in your life that would help you follow Christ as Lord more closely, yet you have been postponing it, set it in motion today, with the promise before your eyes that God is faithful.

For further study: Jeremiah 30; Matthew 12:39–42; Acts 5:31; 2 Timothy 2:25

235 The Departure of God

Nebuchadnezzar came up against Jerusalem at the beginning of his reign and took select young people back to Babylon to be trained at his court. Among them was Daniel. A few years later, when Jerusalem rebelled, Nebuchadnezzar took many of the nobility of the city to Babylon and resettled them in comfortable dwellings along the Chebar canal. Among them was a young priest named Ezekiel.

Five years later God appeared to Ezekiel in a vision of the holy chariot of cherubim (Ezekiel 1). God anointed Ezekiel to be a prophet to the people in exile. Ezekiel's message was that God was going to destroy Jerusalem. The exiles were not to look back to the old ways, to the old city, but were to look up to God and forward to a new day when God would restore Israel.

For several years Ezekiel preached this message, but the exiles did not listen. Jerusalem continued to rebel against Nebuchadnezzar, and finally Nebuchadnezzar destroyed her. This was the destruction Jeremiah witnessed and lamented.

The most powerful vision Ezekiel communicated to the exiles is found in Ezekiel 8–11. In this vision Ezekiel was transported to Jerusalem. As he entered the north gate of the city, he saw people committing idolatry there. As he entered the north gate of the temple, he saw more idolatry. He saw the leaders and priests worshiping the gods of Egypt.

> Then the glory of the LORD departed from over the threshold of the temple and stopped above the cherubim. [Ezek. 10:18]

All of this was taking place *"coram Deo,"* before God's face in his own holy temple. God told Ezekiel that he had been pushed to the limit. Ezekiel saw God proclaim judgment on the defiled temple and city. Those to be saved were marked out, and the rest were destroyed. Meanwhile, the glory cloud of God ascended from the golden cherubim in the Holy of Holies. God moved to the threshold of the temple and called for fire to be poured out on the city.

Then God's glory cloud mounted the chariot and flew off to the east, stopping once on the Mount of Olives as if to survey the destruction. Finally, God departed the scene, leaving the city desolate and exposed to Nebuchadnezzar, his unwitting servant.

Coram Deo

Ezekiel's vision of departing glory warns that there is a limit to what God will endure from his people. If they continue to sin, he will remove his presence. When God departs, the enemy comes in because protection has been removed. Jesus said this to the churches in Revelation 2–3. Are we experiencing such judgment in our Western nations? Pray that God will come near with revival, rather than depart in judgment.

For further study: Jonah 3:4–10; Acts 7:39–42; Hebrews 3:12–15

236 The Valley of Dry Bones

E arly in his ministry Ezekiel was told to prophesy against the mountains of Israel. On these mountains wicked people offered sacrifices at "high places," shrines to various gods. These shrines including altars erected to the Lord, where people worshiped in ways God had specifically forbidden. God told the people through Ezekiel that he would slay those who worshiped at these altars and would scatter their bones around their shrines in the mountains. This would happen when God brought judgment upon the nation.

After the destruction of Jerusalem, Ezekiel was taken by God in a vision to a valley filled with bones. These were the bones of the idolators, representing the death of Israel as God's holy nation. God asked Ezekiel, "Son of man, can these bones live?" Well, maybe some bones might live, but these? These, the bones of the most wicked nation of all, the nation that knew God and then rejected him? Can such bones as these live?

If these bones can live, then any bones can live. Ezekiel expressed his hope that it might be so. "You alone know, O LORD," he said.

Ezekiel was told to prophesy to the bones. The prophetic message that had called destruction down upon the wicked nation would now be a means of her resurrection. As Ezekiel preached in this graveyard he heard a rattling sound. Bone began to join with bone, and then sinew came upon the bones, and soon the valley was crowded with corpses.

> He asked me, "Son of man, can these bones live?" I said,
> "O Sovereign LORD, you alone know." [Ezek. 37:3]

Then God told him to prophesy to the Breath, a reference to God's Spirit. "Call on the Breath to enter these corpses," said God. As Ezekiel did so, the corpses came to life again, standing as a holy army ready to do God's will.

This picture of national resurrection draws from God's original creation of Adam, when God made Adam of dust and then breathed into him the breath of life. Resurrection, we are taught, is a new creation. This prophecy received its first fulfillment after the exile, when the Jews came back into the land and were reestablished as God's people.

Though this passage focuses on national resurrection, the imagery also tells us that God will raise our mortal bodies. Our hope for eternity is in the resurrection of our total persons.

Coram Deo

Ours is a God who turns darkness into light, the wrath of rebels into the praise of his name, and dead bones into living soldiers. He is unexpected in his mercy and surprising in his graciousness. With him the future (living bones) always surpasses the past (a graveyard). What is this glorious future, this inheritance in his Son, that is laid up for you? Do you entertain the hope of it?

For further study: 2 Chronicles 34–35; Psalm 130:1–3; Isaiah 26:19

237 Faithful Witness

ebuchadnezzar was a rather gracious conqueror. It was only after many provocations that he destroyed Jerusalem, and even then he did not kill all the people, but deported them. Before this he resettled some of the most prominent Israelites in Babylon. Babylon was a civilized nation, and it was easy for the resettled Jews to compromise with Babylonian culture. God raised up four men in the palace of Nebuchadnezzar whose lives demonstrated that God's people should never compromise.

In Daniel 3 we read that Nebuchadnezzar set up a huge idol of gold and commanded that all his servants bow down and worship it. Perhaps he got this idea from the vision God gave him in Daniel 2, where he and his reign were portrayed as a head of gold. Maybe he thought this made him worthy of worship. He was very surprised when three young Jewish men who were serving in his court refused to go along with his plan.

When God appeared to men in the Bible such great sounds as the rushing of wind, a trumpet blast, or earthquake noises usually attended his appearing. Likewise Nebuchadnezzar commanded that a whole array of instruments were to blast sounds to call the people to worship. When the sound was heard, everybody bowed down, except for Shadrach, Meshach, and Abednego.

Indignant, Nebuchadnezzar set up a fiery furnace, made it even hotter than usual and had the three men thrown

> "But even if he does not [rescue us], we want you to know, O king, that we will not serve your gods or worship the image of gold you have set up." [Dan. 3:18]

into it. To his astonishment when he looked inside the furnace, he saw the three young men walking around, and a fourth man with them. Nebuchadnezzar's comment was that the fourth looked like a "son of the gods" (Dan. 3:25).

Nebuchadnezzar at that point realized that he had overstepped his bounds in setting up an idolatrous image of himself. He welcomed the three young men back to his court and pronounced that the God of Israel was to be honored throughout his empire. His pride continued to trouble the emperor, however. Later on, God continued his work in Nebuchadnezzar by humbling him with insanity for seven years and then restoring him (Daniel 4). Then Nebuchadnezzar realized that there was only one God and worshiped him. This confession from the lips of a foreign ruler and despoiler all began with the faithful witness of three young men.

Coram Deo

We never know the impact our witness will have on other lives. Examine yourself today to see if you have been compromising in places where you should be standing firm. Ask God to give you the wisdom to know when to stand firm and the strength to visibly represent Christ wherever he calls you to live and work.

For further study: Genesis 39:1–6; Daniel 1; 1 Timothy 4:12–16

238 The Visible Hand of God

The biblical doctrine of divine providence teaches that God controls everything that comes to pass. He is the great Overseer of history, and nothing happens outside his control. He raises up one nation and puts down another, according to his plan. We sometimes speak of the "invisible hand of God" directing all human affairs.

On one occasion that invisible hand became visible. We read in Daniel 5 that, sometime after the death of Nebuchadnezzar, his son Belshazzar came to the throne. The Bible does not tell us why, but one day Belshazzar decided to host a great feast. It occurred to him to use as drinking cups the sacred vessels of the temple, which had been brought to Babylon from Jerusalem. During the feast he and the people used God's vessels to toast their pagan gods.

To get the full import of this story, think back to 1 Samuel 4–6 (see pp. 318–19). At that time the tabernacle was defiled and the ark was captured by the Philistines. While the ark was in Philistia, God used it to make war on the gods of the Philistines. When the ark was brought in close contact with the idol Dagon, it fell and broke to pieces. In fear the Philistines eventually returned the ark to Israel.

The same thing happened in Daniel's day. The opening verses of chapter 1 tell us that the sacred vessels of the temple were brought to the palace in Babylon, along with Daniel and his friends. God made "holy war" on Nebuchadnezzar through the young men, and Nebuchadnez-

> Suddenly the fingers of a human hand appeared and wrote on the plaster of the wall, near the lampstand in the royal palace. The king watched the hand as it wrote. [Dan. 5:5]

zar eventually repented. Then God made holy war on the gods of Babylon, as the sacred vessels were brought in contact with them. God's hand appeared and wrote on the wall that God was bringing an end to Belshazzar's reign, and that his kingdom would be divided.

Greek historians tell us that this party was held while Cyrus besieged Babylon. Babylon had stores to last for years and such strong walls that no one could break them down. Belshazzar's feast flaunted his invulnerability. God's hand-written message appeared on the wall, however, showing that walls are under his control. That same night Cyrus diverted the flow of the river Euphrates and walked into Babylon, right under the walls of the city, bringing down Belshazzar's reign.

Coram Deo

Belshazzar's feast was a counterfeit table of the Lord, but God prepares a table before us in the presence of our enemies. He is our wall, and his feast is the Lord's Supper. Though enemies surround us, as Gog and Magog about the Holy City, we can relax and rejoice (Rev. 20:9). God's walls, unlike those of Babylon, are secure. Remember this security the next time you celebrate the Lord's Supper.

For further study: 2 Chronicles 26; Psalm 23; 1 Corinthians 11:23–26; Revelation 20:9

239 The Son of Man Victorious

I n Daniel 2 Nebuchadnezzar had a dream from God. He saw a gigantic statue of a man with a head of gold, chest of silver, thighs of bronze, and legs of iron. This statue symbolized world empires God was setting up to rule until the coming of the Messiah: Babylon, Persia, Greece, and Rome. Then a stone cut without hands, representing the altar of true worship (Exod. 20:25), struck and smashed the statue. Then the altar grew until it became a mountain, showing that God's kingdom would eventually cover the earth. The contrast in this vision is between the humanistic political empires of men and the worship-centered empire of God.

In chapter 7 Daniel had a vision showing the same historical progression, but with other images. This time the contrast was set out differently. Daniel saw the four empires as four beasts: Babylon as a winged lion, Persia as a bear, Greece as a leopard, and Rome as a terrifying beast. Then Daniel saw God enthroned in heaven and the kingdoms of the world given to a man-like figure. The contrast is between the bestial nations, ruled by the original beast, the serpent (Genesis 3), and the true humanity of the kingdom of God, ruled by his restored images.

It is clear that the one who is "like a son of man" refers not simply to a godly kingdom to come, but also and primarily to an individual. As "man" he is human, but as "like"

> In my vision at night I looked, and there before me was one like a son of man, coming with the clouds of heaven. He approached the Ancient of Days and was led into his presence. [Dan. 7:13]

man, he is divine. What Daniel sees is nothing other than the ascension of Jesus Christ to heaven, an event described in more detail by John in Revelation 4–5. The disciples saw Jesus ascend to heaven into God's glory cloud as they stood on the Mount of Olives. Daniel and John saw Jesus enter that glory cloud, into heaven itself. He approached the Father, and was given "an everlasting dominion that will not pass away" (Dan. 7:14).

Jesus did not receive this kingdom for himself alone. As Nebuchadnezzar represented Babylon, so Jesus represents the kingdom of God. In union with Jesus we are also rulers of the world. Thus, Daniel 7:27 says that "the sovereignty, power and greatness of the kingdoms under the whole heaven will be handed over to the saints, the people of the Most High."

Coram Deo

Kingdoms have come and gone, yet the kingdom of God has not yet come in fulness. The next time you recite the Lord's prayer, take the opportunity to consider that we yet pray that "thy kingdom come." Just how much do you desire this world to end and Christ's kingdom to be fully inaugurated?

For further study: Galatians 4:1–6; Revelation 3:14–20

We complete our survey of the Old Testament by looking at the Minor Prophets, the last twelve books of the Old Testament.

The apocryphal book Ecclesiasticus, written by Yeshua ben Sirach around 190 B.C., spoke of the "twelve prophets" as a book parallel to Isaiah, Jeremiah, and Ezekiel (Ecclus. 49:10). From this we see that these twelve prophecies were regarded as a group and were probably all written together on one scroll. The Jewish historian Josephus also referred to these twelve shorter books as one work (*Against Apion* 1:8).

In his great treatise *The City of God*, Augustine called these twelve in Latin the "Minor Prophets" (*City of God* 18:25). In Latin *minor* does not mean "unimportant" but "shorter." In our tradition we continue to refer to the Hebrew "Book of the Twelve" as the Minor Prophets. Look for the major lessons you can learn from these books:

Through an adulterous wife and nation, Hosea speaks to us of God's faithful, pursuing love, and redemption.

Joel uses a locust invasion to solemnly prepare us for God's day of judgment.

The Book of the Twelve

Amos and Obadiah summoned the nations to God's dock for their injustice against the weak and powerless.

Jonah and Nahum apply mercy and judgment to the Assyrians. Jonah in particular portrays a God whose grace exceeds that of reluctant prophets.

Micah gives us a three-fold way to live *coram Deo*: (1) doing justice; (2) loving mercy, and (3) walking humbly with God.

Habakkuk confronts us with the challenge to live by faith, demonstrating trust, and practicing the real lordship of Christ

Zephaniah presents a picture of God that begins in the church and moves out into the world with the aim of salvation.

Haggai, Zechariah, and Malachi were written to the returned exiles and so offer us insights into the reconstruction that continues to be needed in the temple of God—the people of God. We are called to renewed, radical faithfulness.

Consider how their messages help you live *coram Deo*, before God and to his glory.

R.C. Sproul

240 Hosea and His Times

Although Hosea began prophesying about ten years after Amos, his prophecy is placed first among the writings in the Book of the Twelve. There is theological reason for this: Hosea's prophecy is the longest and the most complete. In a sense, he presents all the major themes found in the other books: covenant, judgment and restoration, and the Lord's personal relationship with his wayward people.

Hosea seems to be the only prophet who came from the northern kingdom of Israel rather than from the southern Judah. His familiarity with the culture and ways of Israel has persuaded most scholars that Israel was his native land. His prophecy is directed almost entirely against Israel, though he has severe warnings for Judah as well.

Despite this orientation toward Israel, Hosea 1:1 dates his prophecies by Judahite kings Uzziah, Jotham, Ahaz, and Hezekiah. Hezekiah came to the throne just before the destruction of Israel and the fall of its capital, Samaria. Uzziah's reign overlapped the last years of Jeroboam II, the last notable king of Israel and the only northern king mentioned by Hosea. It is as if the kings after Jeroboam II were deemed unworthy of mention. Jeroboam II is mentioned because his long reign set the course of the nation toward destruction. Perhaps by mentioning the kings of Judah, some of whom were godly rulers, Hosea was setting a contrast. The wicked rulers of the north were de-

> "The word of the LORD that came to Hosea, son of Beeri, during the reigns of Uzziah, Jotham, Ahaz, and Hezekiah, kings of Judah, and during the reign of Jeroboam son of Jehoash king of Israel."
> [Hosea 1:1]

stroying each other and their nation, while the true Davidic kings of the south continued on in succession, father to son, generation after generation.

Jeroboam II reigned for 41 years, long enough to establish a cultural pattern. His son, Zechariah, lasted six months before being murdered by Shallum. Shallum reigned for only one month before being overthrown by the rebel Menahem. Menahem ruled ten years, but his son Pekahiah only governed two years before being murdered by Pekah. Pekah was murdered by Hoshea, who reigned nine years until God brought the Assyrians to destroy the kingdom. All of these kings chose to ignore the warnings uttered by Hosea.

Coram Deo

People have always suffered from corrupt government. Upheavals due to unrest are still so common that we are unable to understand or appreciate each situation. Based upon news reports and recent political events, pray for a specific country and its leaders who are in a time of crisis. Specifically pray for the role of national Christians and the church in providing godly leadership and influence during turbulent times.

For further study: Amos 5; Philippians 3:20–21; Hebrews 13:15–17

241 Hosea and His Wife

G od instructed Hosea to marry a woman named Gomer. There is no reason to think that Gomer was a woman of ill repute at the time of her marriage, but God told Hosea from the start that she would be an adulterous wife, and her children would be of questionable parentage. God was calling Hosea to experience a taste of what God had experienced with Israel. God had married Israel in her youth, knowing in advance that she would prove unfaithful.

How painful this must have been for Hosea. Yet, because of his love for her and God's command, he married Gomer anyway and put up with her unfaithfulness for years while she bore three children. Finally, in language reminiscent of a legal divorce, Hosea left Gomer. True to her character she sold herself into prostitution (Hosea 2:2; 3:1–2). Hosea bought her out of her life of shame, restoring her as his wife (Hosea 3).

These tragic events were a prophetic allegory for Israel. Israel had repeatedly been unfaithful to God, and eventually would sell herself into Assyrian bondage. Yet, because of his love, God would eventually buy his people back from bondage and restore them to himself.

God told Hosea to give symbolic names to each of Gomer's children (Hosea 1:4–11). The first son was to be named *Jezreel*, meaning "God Scatters." Years before, God had raised up Jehu to destroy the wicked dynasty of Ahab,

> When the LORD began to speak through Hosea, the LORD said to
> him, "Go, take to yourself an adulterous wife and children of
> unfaithfulness, because the land is guilty of the vilest adultery in
> departing from the LORD." [Hosea 1:2]

and Jehu had properly done so at the battle of Jezreel. Unhappily, Jehu did not turn the nation back to the Lord, but reestablished Ahab's Baal cult. Because of this, Israel would receive the same judgment Ahab had received at Jezreel.

Gomer's second child, a girl, was to be named *Lo-Ruhamah*, which means "No Pity," or "Not Loved." Her name meant that God would no longer love and pity the ten northern tribes of Israel, though he would continue to love the two southern tribes of Judah. Those in Israel who wanted to be saved needed to ally with Judah.

Gomer's third child was a boy named *Lo-Ammi*, which means "Not My People." God was rejecting Israel as his people, though eventually he would return to them and join them to Judah.

Coram Deo

Other children would be named in advance of their birth by God. Think of how the birth of Christ concludes the story of Hosea. Jesus, whose Hebrew name *Yeshua* is related to *yasha*, which means "salvation," would be the One through whom and by whom God would return his people unto himself. Think of how God has replaced each of the names given to Hosea's children in his people, the church.

For further study: Luke 1:26–38; Romans 8:12–17;
2 Corinthians 5:14–21; 1 Peter 3:18

242 Hosea and His Message

The prophets were called by God to bring his covenant lawsuit against the nation of Israel. At the beginning of his series of oracles (Hosea 4–14), Hosea summoned the nation to hear God's charge against them. In Hosea 4:2, God charged them with breaking the Ten Commandments, mentioning cursing, murder, adultery, stealing, and lying. Not only were the people doing these evil deeds, but they were doing them repeatedly, so that "bloodshed followed bloodshed."

God judged the land by letting the people experience the consequences of their behavior. The land did not yield its produce, the people were wasting away, and even the animals were dying off (Hosea 4:3). The people were litigious, constantly bringing lawsuits against one another (4:4).

Why had this come to pass? Israel was not faithful to God, their true Husband. They did not love him, nor acknowledge him as their sovereign (4:1). Thus, God would reject them and bring them under judgment.

Ultimately, judgment came upon them because they had "rejected knowledge" (4:6). It is a serious thing when a nation rejects the knowledge of God. A parallel in Western culture is that, while theology once was regarded as the queen of the sciences and held a position of supremacy in the curricula of schools and universities, now theology is hardly even taught. "Comparative religions," which

516

> Hear the word of the Lord, you Israelites, because the Lord has a charge to bring against you who live in the land: "There is no faithfulness, no love, no acknowledgment of God in the land."
> [Hosea 4:1]

usurped its place, is regarded as simply a subdivision of anthropology.

But as bad as it is for a nation to reject theology, it is worse when the church does so (4:6–9). How often we hear evangelical Christians say that they don't want to wrestle with doctrinal issues. They only want a "sweeter, closer walk with Jesus." This anti-intellectualism is reflected in some preaching and teaching, and in some songs we sing in worship.

It is a great evil when "head knowledge" is pitted against "heart knowledge." If we don't know what God is like, we cannot have a real relationship with him. If we don't know what he wants, we cannot be faithful to him.

Coram Deo

Are your heart and mind prepared before you hear God's Word? Covenant fidelity is nurtured through a meditative dependence on God's self-disclosure. Christians should grasp onto his truth with a white-knuckled grip. It is of no profit to Christians if they hold a high view of Scripture and fail to do what God has said.

For further study: Deuteronomy 4:29; John 14:21; Colossians 3:2; 2 Timothy 3:16–17; 1 Peter 1:13

243 Nature in Uproar

We don't know when Joel prophesied. Because it seems Isaiah quoted Joel, many expositors believe Joel was one of the earliest prophets; but perhaps it was Joel who quoted Isaiah. While Joel referred to Judah and Jerusalem several times, we assume that his prophecy was directed primarily toward Judah, the southern kingdom.

This world is God's, and when people sin against him God summons the world to participate in his judgment against humankind. Beginning with the Garden of Eden, thorns and thistles multiplied against sinners. Joel uniquely focused on this theme by describing a horrendous locust plague. Several kinds of locusts invaded in succession. There followed a drought in which the land became so dry that great fires spread across the countryside (Joel 1).

The most pointed aspect of this devastation, said Joel, is that it prevented the people from offering sacrifices to God. The locusts ate the grain of the cereal offering and the grapes of the drink offering. Cattle and sheep died in great numbers (1:9, 13, 18). Thus the people were cut off from worshiping God in the manner he had prescribed.

Joel instructed the people to tell their children, grandchildren, and great-grandchildren about this devastating invasion because it foreshadowed another invasion to come. Joel 2 describes God's coming judgment of the land.

518

> What the locust swarm has left the great locusts have eaten; what the great locusts have left the young locusts have eaten; what the young locusts have left other locusts have eaten. [Joel 1:4]

On that occasion he would bring in another locust army to punish the people for their sins. Many commentators believe that the locust imagery of Joel 2 is a symbolic prediction of the Assyrians and Babylonians who would be brought by God to destroy northern Israel and southern Judah, respectively. Joel 2:20 hints that a human army is what the passage really predicts.

Whether the locusts in Joel 2 are literal or figurative (or both), the message of Joel is summarized by a line from Francis Thompson's famous poem "The Hound of Heaven." In that poem, the Divine Pursuer tells the fleeing sinner, "All things betray thee, who betrayest Me." If we do not obey God, even his world will rise up against us.

Coram Deo

Our culture focuses on the present. We often fail to learn from the past. A greater problem is our failure to prepare future generations for the world they will inherit. Joel knew the importance of teaching children. Make it your goal at home or with children at church to prepare the next generations for the future by reminding them of God's judgments and blessings in the past.

For further study: Deuteronomy 4:9; 11:18–21; 2 Corinthians 4:16–18; 2 Timothy 4:1–8

244 The Day of the Lord

I n Genesis 1:5, God called the light "day." Thus, *day* in the Bible means "time of light," or "light-time." Because God's glory shines around him, whenever he appears there is light. The expression "day of the Lord," therefore, refers to a time when God appears. There is a second aspect to the "day of the Lord," however. In Genesis 1 we are told repeatedly that God saw what he had made and it was good. God was judging. Judging requires sight, and seeing requires light. Thus, when God appears and shines his light, it is a time of judgment.

The day of the Lord, then, is a time when God comes to his people. He shines his light upon them, exposing their deeds, and passes judgment on them.

At various times in the history of the church and in the history of nations, God chooses to pay a visit and to bring judgment. These events are often predicted by the prophets and are called "days of the Lord." Joel 2, for instance, prophesies a coming day of the Lord when an invading army would devastate the land. Joel says that the sun, moon, and stars would be darkened. God's day outshines all other light. Sun, moon, and stars refer to the rulers of the nation, for according to Genesis 1:14 and 16, these heavenly objects were created in part to function as symbols and were set up as rulers. Thus, they are often used to symbolize rulers, as in Genesis 37:9–10.

After the day of the Lord, God would restore the people to the land and bless them. This prediction refers to the restoration of the Jews after the Babylonian exile. Then Joel said that a greater day of the Lord would come, when the Holy Spirit would be poured out and the people have a new vision of God (Joel 2:21–32). Peter announced the fulfillment of this prophecy at Pentecost (Acts 2:16–21).

The greatest day of the Lord will be when Jesus Christ returns to earth to judge the living and the dead. Before that time, however, every Sunday is the Lord's Day, or day of the Lord. On the Lord's Day, Jesus summons us to his house to be evaluated by him and to worship him. each Lord's Day is a little foretaste of the day of the Lord, as the communion meal is a foretaste of the marriage supper of the Lamb.

Coram Deo

The relationship between the day of the Lord and the Lord's Day is more than simple semantics. Because our weekly celebration of the Lord's Day is a foretaste of that final Day, we do well to prepare ourselves properly. What specific things can you do to prepare for your next worship encounter with God?

For further study: 2 Peter 3:3–15; 1 John 3:2–3

245 The Judgment of the Nations

A mos was born in Tekoa, a small town south of Bethlehem in Judah, the southern kingdom. He was a farmer by trade, but God called him to go to Israel, the northern kingdom, and prophesy against its sins. Amos preached when Uzziah was ruling Judah and Jeroboam II was ruling Israel. Thus, his ministry overlapped the beginning of Hosea's.

Amos 1–2 records a famous sermon by the prophet. He began by saying that a great day of the Lord was drawing near. God was about to judge the nations. He began with Damascus in Syria (1:3–5). Syria had piled sin upon sin—three, yea four—and God's patience was exhausted. The sin mentioned, torture of captives, is a form of oppression. In the day of the Lord God would act on behalf of the helpless.

Then Amos turned to Gaza in Philistia (1:6–8). The Philistines would also be judged for cruelty. Tyre in Phoenicia (1:9–10) was due wrath because the Tyreans had sold God's people into slavery, ignoring the covenant of brotherhood between David and Hiram of Tyre.

By now the Israelite audience was shouting "Amen." God was going to act against all their enemies. Amos had intended this reaction and now moved from Gentile nations to Israel's "cousins." The Edomites, descendants of Esau who had often oppressed Israel, were doomed

> This is what the LORD says: "For three sins of Damascus, even for four, I will not turn back [my wrath]. Because she threshed Gilead with sledges having iron teeth I will send fire upon the house of Hazael that will consume the fortresses of Ben-hadad." [Amos 1:3-4]

(1:11–12). So were the vicious Ammonites (1:13–15) and savage Moabites (2:1–3), both descended from Lot.

Amos may have shocked his audience at this point, because the next nation listed for destruction was Judah (2:4–5). The crowd may have kept cheering, because Israel had often been at war with Judah. While the nations were being judged for cruelty, Judah would be judged for idolatry.

Then, however, Amos turned to Israel. Israel was also guilty of adding sin to sin, and God was going to visit her with his wrath also. We can imagine that there were no "Amens" coming from the crowd as Amos told them that they were as cruel as the Gentiles and as idolatrous as Judah. God would treat them the same way he would treat their guilty neighbors (2:6–16).

Coram Deo

A valuable lesson is taught here. God who is just must judge righteously, whether he acts on behalf of his own people or her pagan neighbors. Israel and Judah presumed an automatic exemption from God's righteous pronouncements against sin. Let us not carelessly make the same presumption on the part of the church.

For further study: Genesis 18:20–25; Deuteronomy 4:23–27

246 The Right Social Gospel

B usinessmen sometimes say in jest, "I hire a lawyer to keep me out of jail." The humor points to a sad reality, however: Those with wealth and power often abuse it to the detriment of the weak and impoverished. Amos attacked the rich in Israel, not for being rich (Abraham and Job were, after all, enormously wealthy) but for abusing their riches. Even in a relatively free society it is possible for a rich man to bribe a judge or hire a bullying lawyer to win out over a weaker opponent. Even in a free society it is possible for those with power to run roughshod over those who have none. How much worse it is when those with power use it to manipulate society or to enact laws that favor one group over another.

American high school students often have been required to read a biography of Supreme Court Chief Justice Oliver Wendell Holmes, regarded popularly as a great American jurist. However, from a Christian standpoint, Holmes promoted the exceedingly evil philosophy of utilitarianism. His position was that law should reflect the opinions of the majority, not some "higher" law. He worked to destroy the Christian tradition of biblical and "natural" law that had made America great. As a result of Holmes's influence, many horribly immoral things, such as abortion, are legal.

Christians should never separate faith from godly social action. Christian people have been on the front lines

> You trample on the poor and force him to give you grain. . . . You oppress the righteous and take bribes and you deprive the poor of justice in the courts. [Amos 5:11–12]

of social change ever since the beginning, when Roman Christians risked their lives to rescue infants who had been left to die by their parents in the hills surrounding the city.

Sadly, many Bible-believing Christians today oppose social action. In the nineteenth century, liberal Christianity said that salvation came through social action, creating the "social" gospel. Seeking to preserve the great truths of orthodox Christianity, most conservative Christians came to feel that any expression of a social gospel was liberal and defamed Scripture. We must not fall into that trap. Salvation comes through faith, not through actions and works, but true faith always manifests itself in action, including legitimate social action.

Coram Deo

The church in America is stratified. Those in middle-class churches seldom encounter the poor and are often fairly insensitive to their plight. When social justice advocates speak out about the poor, we tend to react against their exaggerations and unbiblical philosophies. We should also hear legitimate points they raise. What social issues would Amos speak out on today as he looked at your city and the nation at large? Are you as interested in justice?

For further study: Isaiah 1:21–26; Micah 6:9–16; James 5:1–5

247 The Wicked Brother

C ain hated Abel, his younger brother, because Abel
was faithful to the Lord. As the older brother,
Cain was to be Abel's guardian (his "brother's
keeper"). Instead, he murdered Abel (Genesis 4). This introduces the brotherhood theme in the Bible. This theme
becomes prominent in the stories of Jacob and Joseph. We
recall that Joseph's older brothers did not guard him, but
instead sold him into slavery. A generation earlier Esau
persecuted Jacob. Esau, the older, despised the covenant
and virtually gave it away to Jacob. When the time came
for Jacob to collect, however, Esau decided to murder him.

The enmity of Esau (Edom) against Jacob (Israel) continued through the Old Testament and into the New Testament era. The entire book of Obadiah is directed against
Edom. We don't know exactly when Obadiah prophesied.
Certainly it was shortly after Jerusalem had been laid low
by a Gentile army. Each time Jerusalem was sacked, the
Edomites stood by and rejoiced (Obadiah 11). Then, when
the Gentiles had gone home, the Edomite vultures descended on the stricken city to pillage it (vv. 13–14).

When Esau sold his birthright to Jacob for a bowl of
lentils, he makes the oddly worded request: "Let me have
some of that red stew" (Gen. 25:30). While it is impossible to know for certain, some scholars suggest that Esau

526

> The vision of Obadiah. This is what the Sovereign LORD says about Edom—We have heard a message from the LORD: An envoy was sent to the nations to say, "Rise, and let us go against her for battle." [Obadiah 1]

thought this may have been blood soup, forbidden food under the covenant (Gen. 9:4). Because of this event, Esau received the extra name "Edom," which means "red."

Many scholars also believe that Haman the Agagite, the enemy of the Jews in Esther, was a descendant of King Agag of the Amalekites, who fought King Saul (1 Samuel 15). The Amalekites had intermarried with the Edomites (Gen. 14:7; 36:12). Certainly the conflict between Edom and Jacob was still alive in the days of Esther.

The Herods were Edomites, called in Greek "Idumeans." One Herod tried to kill the infant Jesus; another put him on trial, and yet another put Paul on trial. But eventually the Edomites disappeared, fulfilling the prophecy of Obadiah.

Coram Deo

Have you ever caught yourself jealously smiling in secret when a brother in the Lord has been laid low? This "Esau-tendency" is part of the sin-nature in all of us. If you perversely enjoy such secret passions, ask God to help you turn them into godly compassion, as you seek to live more fully the life of Christian brotherhood.

For further study: Genesis 25:23–34; 37; Psalm 137:7–9

248 The Reluctant Prophet

J onah began prophesying early in the reign of Jeroboam II of Israel. About thirty years before Jeroboam II came to the throne, God had allowed the Syrians to devastate northern Israel (2 Kings 13:7). In the years that followed, during the reigns of Jehoahaz and Jehoash, God continued to punish Israel at the hands of the Syrians and Moabites (2 Kings 13:17–20). God chose to grant relief, however, when Jeroboam II became king. In accordance with Jonah's prophecies, Jeroboam made the kingdom a mighty power once again (2 Kings 14:25–27).

It soon became apparent that Jeroboam II was not going to be any more faithful than his fathers had been. Jonah knew that God would bring more judgments upon Israel. But Jonah did not expect his next assignment from God: He was to preach judgment against Assyria.

Notice in 2 Kings 14:27 that "since the LORD had not said he would blot out the name of Israel from under heaven, he saved them by the hand of Jeroboam." But Jeroboam and Israel then turned their backs on God once again, ruining their last chance to repent. God withdrew his gracious words of warning, and left the nation to sink into destruction.

Instead, God took his prophet and his presence to the Gentiles. Moses prophesied that this would happen. If the people provoked God by worshiping idols, God would pro-

528

> But Jonah ran away from the LORD and headed for Tarshish. He went down to Joppa, where he found a ship bound for that port. After paying the fare, he went aboard and sailed for Tarshish to flee from the LORD. [Jonah 1:3]

voke them to jealousy by taking his grace to other nations (Deut. 32:21). Jonah knew this prophecy. Perhaps he sensed God was turning his back upon northern Israel. Because he loved his own people, his own congregation, Jonah was reluctant to leave them.

We know for sure one factor in Jonah's reluctance: He knew God would grant the Assyrians repentance (4:2). Jonah knew that the grace of the gospel would have a mighty impact upon Assyrian life and culture. Obedience to God's law would result in national blessings. The Assyrians would grow into a mighty power. Such a power would likely be God's instrument to punish Israel. Jonah did not want to be involved in bringing this to pass.

Coram Deo

When we look at Jonah sympathetically, we can understand why he did not want to go to Nineveh. All the same, he was disobedient to God's explicit command. What has God commanded that you have not wanted to do? Or perhaps God's Word says you must not do something that is your desire. Pray that God will give you the desire to trust his wisdom and sovereign determination over all of life.

For further study: Psalm 18; 106; Acts 13:42–49

249 Signs of Grace to the World

After Nineveh repented and converted to Yahweh, Jonah was angry at God. He went outside the city and made a booth to shade himself from the burning sun. The booth was not enough, so God caused a large plant to spring up to give him more shade. Jonah was comforted that something was finally going as he wished. Then the plant withered, and the sun blazed down on him, and Jonah became angry again.

God explained the object-lesson to Jonah this way: The plant represented Nineveh. The plant shaded and protected Jonah from the sun. Just so, the converted Ninevites would shade and protect Israel from tribulation. Just as the plant sprang up overnight, so Nineveh had converted overnight. If the plant died, Jonah would be scorched. Just so, if Nineveh fell away from the faith, Israel would suffer. Therefore, it was a blessing for Israel when the Gentiles receive the gospel.

It was true that by converting Assyria God was raising them up to be a mighty power. It was also true that God would use that mighty power to punish Israel in the future and that Israel would go into Assyrian captivity. But when the Israelites were deported to Nineveh, they would find groups of true believers there who were still clinging to Jonah's message preached a century before. These people would shelter the Israelites in their captivity.

> But the LORD said, "You have been concerned about this vine, though you did not tend it or make it grow. It sprang up overnight and died overnight." [Jonah 4:10]

God's loving provision for all and his intention to bring the good news to the Gentiles is also seen in Jonah 1. When Jonah fled from God, he boarded a ship bound for what is now Spain. God sent great storms, and the ship was almost destroyed. The sailors cried to their gods, but to no avail. Then Jonah told them it was his fault, and the true God was causing the storm. The result of this message from Jonah was that "the men greatly feared the LORD, and they offered a sacrifice to the LORD and made vows to him" (Jonah 1:16). The Bible could hardly make it any clearer: These men were converted. Notice that the sailors tried to save Jonah (1:12–15). Here again, Gentiles are acting as protectors to an Israelite. Jonah should have gotten the message.

Coram Deo

Orthodox Christianity affirms that the events in the Book of Jonah happened exactly as they are recorded. It is possible to become so caught up with defending the historicity of these events that we fail to see their meaning. Consider the meaning of the object-lesson that God saved Jonah by putting him into a fish after he had been thrown into the sea. God preserves his people even when he chastens them.

For further study: Genesis 12:1–3; Matthew 12:38–41; 13:1–9

250 The Coming Messianic King

I f any book in the Old Testament confounds the higher critics it is Micah. Micah clearly predicted concrete future events that actually came to pass, and no one can maintain that Micah lived after the events he predicted. For instance, Micah 3:12 stated that "Zion will be plowed like a field, Jerusalem will become a heap of rubble, the temple hill a mound overgrown with thickets."

When was this statement written? All the evidence supports Micah's own claim to have made these statements over a century before the destruction of Jerusalem (Micah 1:1). A liberal critic, however, might insist that Micah simply made a lucky guess. Or, perhaps a later writer inserted Micah 3:12 into the text, after Jerusalem had been destroyed.

Such pseudo-intellectual games have little credibility, and it is even more difficult to play this game with Micah 5:2–4. Those verses claim that a ruler would come out of Bethlehem, a ruler whose origins were from days of eternity. Micah claimed that Israel would suffer without a king until this King was born. He claimed that the greatness of this King would reach to the ends of the earth.

Now, a liberal critic might say, "Well, David came from Bethlehem, so Micah was expressing a hope that a new David would arise." This is true as far as it goes, but what about Micah's confident prediction in 5:3 that there would

> He will stand and shepherd his flock in the strength of the Lord, in the majesty of the name of the Lord his God. And they will live securely, for then his greatness will reach to the ends of the earth. [Micah 5:4]

be no king in Israel from the destruction of Jerusalem until this new David was born? What about his prediction that the greater David's fame would reach to all the world? Were these merely lucky guesses?

The liberal critic has no real answer, but is forced to reject the clear statement of the text anyway. To admit that Micah meant what he said would force the liberal critic to recognize the reality of predictive prophecy. This would force him to recognize that the prophets were inspired by God, and would lead him face to face with the Bible's claim to be inspired, infallible, and inerrant. Since the critic will not bow the knee to the God of the Bible, he is forced to play ridiculous games with the text of the Bible.

Coram Deo

Not all prophecies have yet come to pass. Many concerning the return of our Lord Jesus are reserved for the end times. Passages such as in Micah should reinforce our belief in the authority of Scripture and the reliability of predictive prophecy. Use this confidence to live expectantly before God, knowing that his coming again is certain and will bring history to a culmination.

For further study: Isaiah 40:9–11; 53; Matthew 2:1–6

251 God's Controversy

W hen Israel entered the land, the entire nation stood on mounts Ebal and Gerizim to swear allegiance to the law of God (Deuteronomy 27; Joshua 8). This pledge of allegiance was witnessed by these two mountains and, by implication, all the mountains of Israel. Later, as Israel and Judah corrupted their ways, God called on the mountains to judge Israel (Micah 6:1–2). The mountains had seen it all, the making and breaking of the vow. The mountains would hear the case God prosecutes against Israel and would pass judgment. If Israel was guilty the land would spew the people out into captivity.

God reminded Israel that he had redeemed the Israelites from captivity and had given to them a spacious and gracious land and wise leaders. All he required was that Israel act justly, love mercy, and walk humbly before him (Micah 6:8). These things the people had not done.

True religion, according to Micah, is not a sweet smile, a nice personality, or pious words. True religion involves, first, a total commitment to God's justice. The basis and standard of justice is the righteousness of God himself, and it is revealed in his law. True religion involves a passionate commitment to the law of God, including its social dimensions and applications. We are to love the law because it is God's law, and we are to obey it as it applies to all walks of life: business, home, politics, and the arts.

Second, true religion involves a total commitment to

> Hear, O mountains, the LORD's accusation; listen, you everlasting foundations of the earth. For the LORD has a case against his people; he is lodging a charge against Israel. [Micah 6:2]

God's mercy. It means that in our commitment to justice we are not interested in harming people or destroying them, but rather in seeing them saved. True mercy does not excuse sin, and true mercy may entail excommunicating a person from the church for a time. But these are the extremes of justice. Primarily, mercy causes us to seek ways of healing.

Finally, true religion means walking humbly with God. Walking with God means remaining in close, consistent fellowship with him. Walking humbly means submitting to him, doing what he says, simply because he says to do it. Finally, walking humbly means being grateful to him and giving continual thanks to him for all his many benefits.

Coram Deo

Who would not want to know what the Lord requires of them? Scripture provides profoundly simple answers: Love the Lord your God with all your heart, soul, strength, and mind, and your neighbor as yourself (Deut. 6:5; Lev. 19:18; Matt. 22:37, 39; Mark 12:30; Luke 10:27). Act justly, love mercy, and walk humbly with God (Micah 6:8). Use these responses to evaluate your walk before the face of God. They are of tremendous help in living *coram Deo*.

For further study: Deuteronomy 30:17–20; Psalms 89:11–18; James 1:23–27

535

252 The Destruction of Nineveh

The prophecy of Nahum needs to be taken with that of Jonah. After Jonah's ministry in Nineveh, the city was covenanted to the Lord. After a couple of generations, however, the Assyrians reverted to their old ways. When people have a knowledge of God and then rebel against him, they become worse than they were before. The Assyrians became known throughout the ancient world for great cruelty in warfare.

The Assyrian empire dominated the ancient Near East, and both Israel and Judah were forced to recognize its superpower status and pay tribute. When Hoshea, the last king of Israel, conspired with Egypt and withheld tribute, the Assyrians conquered and destroyed the nation. The larger reason Israel was destroyed was for provoking the Lord beyond the limits of his forbearance.

About a century later, God raised up Nahum to predict Nineveh's doom. Nahum reminded the Ninevites that "the Lord is good, a refuge in times of trouble. He cares for those who trust in him" (1:7). God had loved and protected the Ninevites of an earlier generation (Jonah 4:11), but the nation had rejected him and had continued in obstinacy for over a century. The Ninevites had seen God's patience with Israel run out, but they failed to learn from it. Now God's patience with Assyria had run out, and they too would experience his wrath.

536

> But with an overwhelming flood he will make an end of [Nineveh]; he will pursue his foes into darkness. [Nahum 1:8]

God was angry that Nineveh had rejected him and had become an exceptionally cruel people. From what Nahum writes, however, it seems he was most angry because the Assyrians had attacked Judah, the seat of his government and witness (1:12–15). God became furious when his church, his covenant ones, was attacked.

Although all three chapters of Nahum are about Nineveh, and his prophecy was doubtless sent to the Assyrians, the primary audience seems to be Judah. The southern kingdom, Judah, also turned its back upon God. Nahum wrote in the early days of Josiah's reign. The destruction of Nineveh was to be a sign to Judah that God's patience does run out. With his colleagues, Zephaniah and Jeremiah, Nahum was calling Judah to repentance.

Coram Deo

When your pastor preaches strongly and pointedly, do you take it to heart? Or do you critically apply the message to others? It is easier to point the finger at sin in another's walk than to admit our own stumblings. Judah missed Nahum's point—God's patience may run out. Study your own life to see where you may be provoking the Lord beyond the limits of his long-suffering.

For further study: Psalms 2:1–6; 17:13–15; Zephaniah 2:1–15

253 The Dilemma of Habakkuk

osiah was the last good king of Judah. With the help of Jeremiah and other prophets, Josiah led Judah in a national reformation, but sadly the revival was short-lived. After his death, the nation sank to new lows of violence and injustice. The prophet Habakkuk tells us that he came before God and complained. He asked God to arise and defend the righteous poor (1:1–4) who were trying to live godly lives amid the corruption of Jewish society.

God replied to Habakkuk that he was indeed going to take action. He was going to raise up the Babylonians, who would conquer and devastate Judah (1:5–11).

This provoked Habakkuk to raise a second question, which was in essence, "I admit that we are bad and deserve judgment, but the Babylonians are worse than we are. How can you, O God, allow the wicked to destroy those who are relatively more righteous?" (Hab. 1:12–17).

God replied that he would use the Babylonians to punish Judah, but that he would then punish the Babylonians for their wickedness. The Babylonians were going to devour all the nations (2:5), but they would be utterly devastated when it was their turn for judgment (2:6–19, esp. v. 16).

Meanwhile, "the righteous will live by his faith" (2:4), because in spite of appearances, "the LORD is in his holy temple" (2:20). What does it mean to live by faith? It does not mean merely believing *in* God. Rather, it means be-

538

lieving God, believing what he says, and living according to that belief. For Habakkuk and his generation, and for us, it means that in the middle of the confusing events of history we are to trust God and rely on him.

Habakkuk 2:4 implies that if a person has faith—that is, if he lives faithfully—he will find life. The New Testament quotes this sentence several times to affirm that life and salvation come through faith, not through works. Habakkuk was confronted by a looming national disaster. He looked at social, cultural, and possibly personal death. In the midst of this uncertainty he found life and salvation in God. The way to obtain that life and salvation from God is by living faithfully with him.

Coram Deo

Although obviously the Latin phrase *coram Deo* was not used by Habakkuk, this phrase suggests the same answer to life that God revealed to him. Living in faith, demonstrating trust, and practicing the real lordship of Christ is another way to define *coram Deo*. With Habakkuk we are called to live life in the presence of God, under his authority and to his glory. Have you adopted this concept as the theme for your walk with Christ?

For further study: Joel 2:27–32; 2 Corinthians 1:3–11; Jude 1:3–5

254 The Prayer of Habakkuk

G od told Habakkuk to live by faith. Modern liberal existential Christianity says that faith is a "leap in the dark." We don't know who or what is out there, but we must live a life of commitment anyway. We count on an unknown and unknowable "Other" to give our lives meaning. This, of course, is in direct opposition to the biblical view of faith. God tells us to trust him because we know what he has done. We know him personally because he has revealed himself, and we know about him because his ways are recorded in Scripture.

The prayer of Habakkuk 3 shows the biblical concept of faith. This prayer was once sung in the church as a hymn. Perhaps we should return it to worship, because it is one of the greatest songs ever written.

Habakkuk begins (v. 2) by saying that he has heard about God and what he has done. This is no "leap in the dark." Then follows the first stanza of the hymn (vv. 3–7), in which Habakkuk recalls how God's glory cloud-chariot moved from the area of Edom (Paran) to Mount Sinai to greet the people who had been delivered from Egypt. God tore down ancient empires such as Egypt in order to save his people. This is something we know about the God in whom we put our faith.

Stanza 2 (vv. 8–10) recalls how God split the Jordan River to enable the people to enter the land he was giving them. Stanza 3 (vv. 11–15) recounts God's mighty deeds

540

The Sovereign LORD is my strength; he makes my feet like the feet of a deer; he enables me to go on the heights. [Hab. 3:19]

during the conquest of the land: The sun and moon stood still (Joshua 10), and the leaders of the Canaanites were stripped of power (Joshua 11; Judg. 1:5–7). The "sea" of the enemy nations was trampled by the angelic "horses" of God (vv. 8, 15).

Stanza 4 (vv. 16–19) applies these historical facts to Habakkuk's own context. Who is the God we trust? He is the God who fights for his people and tramples their enemies. True, disaster is coming on Judah. True, crops will fail and the people will suffer. But God has not forgotten his people and he never will. This is the great "but" that reverses history and brings the gospel. He will act to save them as he always has. This confidence is based on God's firm control from his seat of authority in his heavenly temple (Hab. 2:20).

Coram Deo

The "high place" Habakkuk refers to is the place of worship, the temple on Mount Zion in Jerusalem. Habakkuk ends his song with worship. He thanks God in advance for a deliverance he does not yet see. How can Habakkuk 3 be the prayer of someone in distress today? By faith thank God for his coming deliverance in your own life crises.

For further study: Psalms 3; Matthew 6:9–21; Hebrews 12:17–26

255 The Day of the Lord

Zephaniah was a great-grandson of King Hezekiah, and he prophesied with Jeremiah and Micah in the early days of King Josiah's reign over Judah. His theme is the "day of the LORD," which he mentions about twenty times in the three chapters of his brief book. As we have seen (pp. 520–21), the "day" of God is the time when he draws near and probes men and nations with the searching light of his investigation. The particular day of the Lord prophesied by Zephaniah was the destruction of Jerusalem and the shaking of the world that would occur under Babylonian King Nebuchadnezzar.

Zephaniah provides three perspectives on the day of the Lord. First, he affirms that *judgment begins at the house of God*. The priestly nation of Judah, and her capital Jerusalem come under the most severe condemnation (1:4–2:3). The church has been given the greatest light and the greatest responsibility; therefore, she now comes under the most careful scrutiny.

Second, *judgment does not stop with God's house*. When God brings judgment on the covenant community he also judges the world. Thus, the destruction of Jerusalem and Judah will be followed by a conquest of the whole world. To the west Philistia will fall; to the east Moab and Ammon will disappear; to the south Cush will be slain, and to the north Assyria will be no more (2:4–15). Consequently, none

> The great day of the LORD is near—near and coming quickly.
> Listen! The cry on the day of the Lord will be bitter, the shouting
> of the warrior there. [Zeph. 1:14]

of these nations seems to have lasted beyond the days of Nebuchadnezzar.

Then Zephaniah returned to Jerusalem and Judah, pronouncing more woes against them (3:1–8). This led him to the third aspect of the day of the Lord, *that judgment leads to salvation.* Zephaniah retains his international vision, maintaining that after the exile, not only would daughter Zion be restored, but many Gentiles also would convert to the Lord and serve him (3:9–20).

By the days of the New Testament many God-fearing Gentiles worshiped in the synagogues. So large was this movement that Paul actually became the apostle to the Gentile nations.

Coram Deo

If, as has been noted, each Sunday is the day of the Lord, would Zephaniah be useful study for weekly worship? How should Zephaniah's three great themes empower our worship? What are some ways judgment and salvation come on the church and on the world in worship? Do you believe that Lord's Day worship really changes history and your own personal circumstances, week by week?

For further study: Exodus 20:8–11; Jeremiah 30:4–9; Revelation 6:12–17

256 The Christian's First Priority

The prophets Haggai, Zechariah, and Malachi did not foretell God's judgment on Israel and Judah; they preached after the Jews returned from their exile in Babylon. Their purpose was to stimulate the people to faithfulness as they reestablished the house of God in the midst of the nations.

When the Jews first returned from the Babylonian captivity they quickly laid the foundation for the temple and began to rebuild it. During captivity they had longed for the opportunity to be led in procession up to worship in the temple. We find out from the books of Ezra and Nehemiah, however, that they experienced great opposition from the people who had moved into the area during the time the Jews were in exile. These people, Samaritans, did not want the temple rebuilt, and they caused so many problems that finally the Jews stopped construction.

What the Jews had erected was a crude, unfinished temple, but they considered it good enough. They turned their attention to building their own homes and establishing their lands and crops. After a few years the Samaritan opposition died down. Instead of going back and finishing the temple, though, the Jews permitted it to languish in neglect. After sixteen years God called the prophets Haggai and Zechariah to admonish the people and get them working again on his "home."

> Then the word of the LORD came through the prophet Haggai: "Is it a time for you yourselves to be living in your paneled houses, while this house remains a ruin?" [Hag. 1:3]

Haggai told them that they should be ashamed to live in paneled houses while the temple remained an unsightly barn. God's house should be the most beautiful of all, and they knew it. Haggai further admonished them that God had withheld his blessing from them because their priorities were directed in the wrong places (1:7–11).

This theological principle applies to every generation of believers. Jesus said, "Seek first his kingdom and his righteousness, and all these things will be given to you as well" (Matt. 6:33). When we seek our own well-being while neglecting the house of God, God will withhold his blessing from us. The building of God's kingdom, the glory of his house, and the glory of his name must, in every generation, be the first priority of all his people.

Coram Deo

The Old Testament tabernacle and temple were both glorious, symbolizing God's people gathered around his throne. God is less concerned with physical buildings in the new covenant, and the temple we are to build today is the community of the saints. What are some of the ways to build and beautify this temple?

For further study: Psalm 132:3–5; Micah 3:1–12; Matthew 6:25–34

257 The Coming of the King

L ike Haggai, Zechariah prophesied to those who had returned from captivity. Chapters 1–6 of his book reveal that God has cleansed his people, and provides the basis for rebuilding the temple. Chapters 7 and 8 exhort the people to stop dwelling in the past and faithfully serve the Lord in the present.

Zechariah 9–14 is one of the most complicated prophetic passages in all the Bible, but one prediction is crystal clear. The prophet addresses the "Daughter of Zion," which might be better translated simply "Daughter Zion," since Zion herself is God's daughter. She has languished under oppression, but her Deliverer, her King, her Husband, is coming.

The King is coming on a donkey. Matthew 21:5 and John 12:15 quote this verse and apply it to Jesus' entrance into Jerusalem on a donkey (Traditional Christian art also depicts Mary riding a donkey, carrying the unborn Jesus in her womb, as the holy family came to Bethlehem for Jesus' birth; but while Mary probably did ride a donkey, the Bible says nothing about it.).

Zechariah says that the One riding on a donkey brings "salvation." The word *salvation* is the Hebrew *yasha*, which is seen in the names Joshua and Jesus (see p. 515). It is used throughout the Book of Judges to refer to those who

546

> Rejoice greatly, O Daughter of Zion! Shout, Daughter of Jerusalem! See, your king comes to you, righteous and having salvation, gentle and riding on a donkey, on a colt, the foal of a donkey. [Zech. 9:9]

saved Israel from sin and oppression. The judges of Israel rode donkeys, not horses, and so the picture Zechariah paints suggests that the coming King will act as judge for God's people. He will surely deliver them from their enemies and give them a good land in which to dwell.

Zechariah goes on to say that the donkey will replace the horse because peace will rule among men and war will no longer be considered important (9:10). Peace will be proclaimed to all nations and the rule of the coming King will extend over the whole earth. This prophecy began to be fulfilled when wise men from the Persian empire traveled to Bethlehem to visit the child Jesus, and laid at his feet symbols of universal rule and glory: gold, incense, and myrrh.

Coram Deo

In Western Christianity, December 25 is the day traditionally appointed for remembering the birth of the Word made flesh. Palm Sunday remembers the entry into Jerusalem of the Prince of Peace. On a day we do not know, Christ will return as reigning King of Kings and Lord of Lords.

For further study: Psalms 97:6–8; Micah 5:2; Romans 3:24–26

258 Foundation of the Temple

When the Jews returned from the exile, they began rebuilding the temple. The physical temple represented the nation gathered around the throne of God. The stones and wood used to build the temple represented the people, and these people were unclean. They, as a nation, were carrying the sins and judgments of Israel, and those sins and judgments had not been removed. God would not come back into the physical temple until the people were clean.

Haggai had started the work of rebuilding the temple. By the time of Zechariah they had worshiped around the altar, but the temple had not been finished and consecrated. It would be necessary to cleanse the temple, but how could that be done? There were many rituals of cleansing in the sacrificial system, but they all had to do with smaller offenses committed after the tabernacle or temple had been set up. There was nothing in the Law that dealt with the serious offenses that had led to the temple's complete destruction a century earlier. How could the sacrificial system be started up again if everything was unclean? How could the temple (representing the nation) be fully cleansed?

God gave the answer to Zechariah in eight visions during the night of the twenty-fourth of the month Shebat in the second year of Darius's reign (Zech. 1:7). In the fourth vision, recorded in Zechariah 3, Joshua the high priest

> The angel said to those who were standing before him, "Take off his filthy clothes." Then he said to Joshua, "See, I have taken away your sin, and I will put rich garments on you." [Zech. 3:4]

stood before God. Joshua could not minister because he was covered with uncleanness. Since the high priest represented the nation, this was a sign of the uncleanness of all the people and of their temple. Satan was standing in the court, accusing Joshua of unworthiness and thereby preventing the temple from being built.

Then Zechariah saw God pass judgment in heaven. God rebuked Satan and declared that he had chosen Joshua. He declared Joshua clean, and thereby cleansed the nation and the temple. God stated that he was able to do this because in the future the Messiah would come and remove the people's sin. In the morning, Zechariah was able to tell the people that the nation had been cleansed, and that God was willing to return to the temple.

Coram Deo

To the same extent that the Jews returning to Jerusalem could not cleanse themselves nor their temple, neither can we be clean on our own merits before God. With us, as with Israel, only God can remove guilt, alleviate the conscience, and provide forgiveness. Make time to confess to God today and trust that he will provide through Christ the righteousness you lack in yourself.

For further study: Isaiah 6:1–5; Matthew 1:18–25

259 The Need for the Messiah

One sad story recurs many times in the pages of the Bible: God gives to his chosen people a kingdom, and as soon as they receive the kingdom they sin and ruin it. It happened with Adam. It happened with Abraham (and Hagar) after God promised him a son. It happened with Israel at Sinai after God gave the law. It happened with Saul as soon as he became king. It happened with David and Bathsheba after God promised a house for David. We find from Paul's letters that it was happening in his day as well, as soon as the church was established.

Malachi fits into this pattern. Haggai and Zechariah show the glories of the rebuilt temple. God reestablished the nation and gave her a wide open door for Gentile evangelism. In Ezra and Nehemiah, however, we find that, as soon as God set up the nation, the people began marrying foreigners and lapsed into idolatry. Malachi, prophesying about this time, lists grievous crimes being committed by the priests and people, crimes that were ruining the new opportunity God had set before them.

For instance, they were offering defiled food to God (1:7–8). They were teaching false doctrines (2:8). They were intermarrying with unconverted Gentiles (2:11). They were abandoning and divorcing their wives (2:14). They were cheating the poor, oppressing widows and orphans, and

> "A son honors his father, and a servant his master. If I am a father, where is the honor due me? If I am a master, where is the respect due me?" says the LORD Almighty. [Mal. 1:6a]

persecuting strangers (3:5). They were robbing God by not tithing properly (3:9–10).

Malachi calls on them to repent. He tells them that another day of the Lord was coming (3:2). As always, this would be a day of judgment for the church and world, but also a day of blessing for God's people and for all nations. The Messiah would come to purge the people of their sins, and to render their worship acceptable once again. The recurring sins of Israel pointed out the need for one who was a true Prophet, a holy Priest, and a righteous King—God's Anointed, the Messiah.

The light of this coming day would be the fire of the Lord's presence. It would be like a furnace to the wicked, burning them up; it would be like the warmth of the sun to the righteous. In it they would confidently assert their faith and prevail, even against the wicked (4:1–3).

Coram Deo

Take time to read all of Malachi. Notice how much of the book is written to leaders. Why is this message of purging so important to those with shepherding responsibilities over the people of God? Pray that the leaders in your church might exhibit the kind of qualities that please the Lord and honor his name.

For further study: Matthew 15:1–6; Titus 2:9–15; 1 Peter 2:17–19

260 The Law and the Prophets

hen rabbis examined the final form of the Old Testament they taught that it contained three categories of books: *homologoumena* (those accepted by all), *antilegoumena* (those disputed by some), and *pseudepigrapha* (those rejected by all).

Thirty-four of the thirty-nine books found in the Old Testament used in historic Protestant churches were accepted as authoritative by the learned men of Judaism and the early church fathers of Christianity. The five disputed books (Song of Solomon, Ecclesiastes, Esther, Ezekiel, and Proverbs), after some discussion, were finally considered authoritative and therefore canonical by the rabbis and the early church. The reason for the delay was that some believed these books contained material that "spoke against" the unified witness of the homologoumena.

Song of Solomon was questioned because of its sensuality, Ecclesiastes for its apparent skepticism. Esther did not contain God's name. Ezekiel seemed to contradict certain statements of Moses. Proverbs was disputed because it too had unresolved and seemingly contradictory elements.

Scholars demonstrated that Song of Solomon was important to teach about the sanctity and purity of the marriage covenant—between man and woman and between God and his people. Ecclesiastes realistically presents human life as seen by humans in their own realm and wis-

552

> "Every word of God is flawless; he is a shield to those who take refuge in him. Do not add to his words, or he will rebuke you and prove you a liar." [Prov. 30:5–6]

dom. The conclusion is all important. "Man under the sun" is not to be the believer's sole contemplation; there is a much higher reality over and above the sun.

Esther manifests God's presence in a dynamic way through his providential guidance and grace. Direct references to God might be absent from the book but his sovereign presence is manifest in the narrative. Ezekiel was questioned by the rabbis of the school of Shammai for apparently contradicting their own interpretation of the writings of Moses. When asked to produce one hard and fast example of this contradiction, however, they could not. Therefore, these books were universally accepted and can now be depended on as authoritative revelation from God.

Coram Deo

Two kinds of errors can derail our conception of Scripture. One is to relegate to secondary authority the biblical passages we do not like, or those that confuse us. The second is to give canonical authority to noncanonical teaching, whether it be the writings of a favorite theologian, the sermons of a pastor, or the margin notes in a particular study Bible. Reserve ultimate authority only for God's revelation.

For further study: Psalm 138; 2 Timothy 2; Hebrews 2:1–3

261 The Silent Years

B etween Malachi and John the Baptist came four hundred long years of silence—without a direct word from God to his people. Bible scholars have come up with a number of explanations for this silence. Yet, the most common theme emphasizes the restoration of the kingdom to Israel. The Jews suffered under occupation during these centuries as army after conquering army made its way through the well-worn paths of the Middle East. Humanly speaking, there was little reason for hope. Rabbis reprimanded the people for God's absence from Israel.

Two distinct views evolved through meditative reflection on the messianic nature of the prophecies. The first view was that the Messiah and his kingdom would be inaugurated as the people grew in obedience to the Law. The second perspective taught that, through Jewish nationalism, all nations would be subjected to Israelite dominion under the Messiah.

These false understandings of the nature of the coming kingdom were catalysts in the demise of intertestamental Judaism. The Jews either turned inward, obsessed with the law, or they withdrew to live in "pure" communities such as Qumran, where the Dead Sea scrolls were written.

However, during these years Judaism refined two items that significantly affected early Christianity. The synagogue

554

developed while the Jews were in exile in Babylon. After the return to the land, Judaism retained the intimacy of the synagogue as the center of life. Although God never sanctioned the institution of the synagogue by special revelation, Jesus and the apostles adopted it as a primary place of ministry and evangelism.

Tragically, the majority of Jews forsook the message given them by Moses and the prophets. They replaced it with hybrid interpretations or departed after other gods. However, there was a small movement which held tightly to the true messianic hope.

Appropriately, the New Testament opens with Simeon, one who clung tightly to orthodox faith (Luke 2:25–26).

Coram Deo

As we end these Old Testament studies, reflect on how we are spiritual descendants of such believers as Simeon. Set your hope in the biblical God alone and not in a god of your own devising. Whatever occurs in the church or society, covenant with God that you will hold fast to historic Christian orthodoxy. Praise him for the full and glorious revelation of each page of his Word.

For further study: Zechariah 8:1–12; Acts 15:13–21; Romans 11:1–5

Scripture Index

556

557